Syntactic Pattern Recognition
An Introduction

APPLIED MATHEMATICS AND COMPUTATION

A Series of Graduate Textbooks, Monographs, Reference Works

Series Editor: ROBERT KALABA, University of Southern California

Syntactic Pattern Recognition

An Introduction

Rafael C. Gonzalez

Electrical Engineering Department
University of Tennessee, Knoxville

Michael G. Thomason

Computer Science Department
University of Tennessee, Knoxville

 1978

Addison-Wesley Publishing Company
Advanced Book Program
Reading, Massachusetts

London · Amsterdam · Don Mills, Ontario · Sydney · Tokyo

Library of Congress Cataloging in Publication Data

Gonzalez, Rafael C
    Syntactic pattern recognition.

    (Applied mathematics and computation series; no. 14)
    Bibliography: p.
    Includes index.
    1.   Pattern perception.   2.   Formal languages.
3.   Automata.   I.   Thomason, Michael G., joint author.
II.   Title.
Q327.G65   001.53′4   78-5612
ISBN 0-201-02930-8
ISBN 0-201-02931-6 pbk.

American Mathematical Society (MOS) Subject Classification Scheme (1970):68A25,
68A30, 68A45, 94A25, 94A30, 94A35

Manufactured in the United States of America

ABCDEFGHIJK-HA-798

ERRATA
for
SYNTACTIC PATTERN RECOGNITION: An Introduction
Rafael C. Gonzalez and Michael G. Thomason
1978

Page xviii. The third entry under the Chapter 5 heading should read: $S \overset{*}{\underset{p(x)}{\Longrightarrow}} x$

Page 9, Fig. 1.9(b). The missing symbol is R_3.

Page 11, fifth line above Fig. 1.11. Replace 1.3.3 by 1.3.2.

Page 42, Fig. 2.10. Replace \$ by X in the four corners of the figure.

Page 43, third line below Fig. 2.11. Delete the symbol X.

Page 45, Fig. 2.12. Insert a second symbol ζ at the tail of the dashed line labeled *en*.

Page 48, the first line should read: form.

Page 51, fourth line in the example. Replace R by R_0.

Page 57. Insert the following two lines at the bottom of the page:
The *input grammar* of the SDTS is $G_i = (N, \Sigma, P_i, S)$ with productions
$$P_i = \{A \to \alpha | A \to \alpha, \beta \text{ in } R\};$$

Page 65, second line from the bottom. Remove the slash symbol /.

Page 68, first line in the second example. Replace AND by and.

Page 71. The third production on top of the page should have two A's followed by two B's. Similarly, the first production in the next line should have three A's followed by three B's.

Page 71, Fig. 3.3(a). The branches should be labeled, from top to bottom, as follows: b, b, b, a, a, a. The main branch remains labeled a.

Page 71, Fig. 3.3(b). The four a's in the fourth branch from the left should be changed to four b's.

Page 93. The five production rules in the example should be numbered (for reference) as follows: 1   2
                 3   4
                 5

Page 111, Fig. 4.10. Replace the n by a 2 in the third line under the heading String Representation.

Page 125, Fig. 4.15. The arrow pointing to the Output Tape should be labeled: Write-Only Head (as in Fig. 4.11).

Page 137, line 17. Remove first opening parenthesis.

Page 170, second line above the first equation in the middle of the page. Insert a comma between f. and $f_\$$. Also, in the fourth equation in the middle of the page, replace $f_R f_C$ by just f_C.

Page 174, Table 4.1. There should be four column headings from left to right reading: Class Numbers, Population, Class Numbers, Population.

Page 179. The last word in the seventh line should be: as.

Page 188, second line. Replace $\mathbf{M}_{\hat{f}}$ by $\mathbf{M}_f$.

Page 220, fifth line from the bottom. Replace S_1 by S.

Page 221, first line. Remove: of. Also, replace S_1 by S in the sixth line.

Page 225, second line from the bottom. Replace z, a by za.

Page 226, first line. Remove the symbols $+, k)$ in the definition of F.

Page 226, seventh and eighth lines from the bottom. Replace all occurrences of q by q_1.

Page 252, Fig. 6.13. The second word in the caption should be: classes.

Page 267, seventh line from the bottom. The second term in the equation should read: $p(q_4 | b, q_1)$

Page 268, Fig. 6.17. Draw a second arc from state q_3 to state q_4 and label it b, 1.

8-78-3500 Printed in U.S.A.

02935

To
Our
Parents

CONTENTS

SERIES EDITOR'S FOREWORD

Execution times of modern digital computers are measured in nanoseconds. They can solve hundreds of simultaneous ordinary differential equations with speed and accuracy. But what does this immense capability imply with regard to solving the scientific, engineering, economic, and social problems confronting mankind? Clearly, much effort has to be expended in finding answers to that question.

In some fields, it is not yet possible to write mathematical equations which accurately describe processes of interest. Here, the computer may be used simply to simulate a process and, perhaps, to observe the efficacy of different control processes. In others, a mathematical description may be available, but the equations are frequently difficult to solve numerically. In such cases, the difficulties may be faced squarely and possibly overcome; alternatively, formulations may be sought which are more compatible with the inherent capabilities of computers. Mathematics itself nourishes and is nourished by such developments.

Each order of magnitude increase in speed and memory size of computers requires a reexamination of computational techniques and an assessment of the new problems which may be brought within the realm of solution. Volumes in this series will provide indications of current thinking regarding problem formulations, mathematical analysis, and computational treatment.

The theory of automata and formal languages is one of the principal elements in the study of digital machines and their processing capabilities. Syntactic pattern recognition employs this theory in innovative ways to develop pattern recognition approaches that are based on knowledge of the underlying structure of pattern classes. The material in this book finds applications in such diverse fields as the physical sciences; the biological and medical sciences; applied mathematics and statistics; and computer science and engineering, including image processing, scene analysis, and artificial intelligence. This volume is the first textbook written at an introductory level with emphasis on fundamentals of formal languages and automata theory as they apply to pattern recognition and machine learning.

PREFACE

This book was written to provide students, engineers, and scientists involved in pattern recognition, digital image processing, and artificial intelligence with a comprehensive introduction to the concepts and techniques of syntactic pattern recognition.

Syntactic pattern recognition is concerned with the application of formal language and automata theory to the modeling and description of structural relationships in pattern classes. This is in contrast with classical decision-theoretic methods, in which recognition is generally performed on a strictly quantitative basis without explicit use of structural information. The capability for describing structure is particularly important in pictorial pattern recognition, scene analysis, and other applications where primitive elements and their relationships are essential characteristics.

The origin of formal language theory may be traced to the middle 1950s with the development by Noam Chomsky of mathematical models of grammars related to his work in natural languages. One of the original goals of linguists working in this area was to develop computational models of grammars capable of describing natural languages such as English and French. The hope was that, if this could be done, it would be a relatively simple matter to "teach" computers to interpret natural languages for the purposes of translation and problem solving. Although it is generally agreed that these expectations have been unrealized thus far, spin-offs and extensions of the research in this area have had a significant impact on other fields, such as compiler design, programming languages, automata theory, and pattern recognition. Applications of formal languages in the latter area followed shortly after Chomsky's initial developments, with results on automated analysis of alphanumeric characters and human chromosomes appearing in the early 1960s. Since these initial applications, syntactic pattern recognition has experienced vigorous growth as a subject of interdisciplinary study and research in such fields as engineering, computer science, information science, physics, chemistry, biology, medicine, and applied mathematics.

Most of the material dealing with syntactic pattern recognition theory and applications has been widely scattered in various technical journals, conference proceedings, and advanced monographs. Consequently, it is a rather difficult and time-consuming task, particularly for a newcomer to this interdisciplinary area, to extract from the large volume of available literature the wide range of principles underlying the subject matter. The principal objectives of this book are to provide an introduction to basic concepts and techniques of syntactic pattern recognition and to lay a foundation that can be used as the basis for further study and research in this field. To achieve these objectives, we have focused attention on material which we feel is fundamental and for which the scope of applications is not limited to specialized problems. The presentation emphasizes practical rather than strictly theoretical aspects, and numerous examples are provided to illustrate the principles developed in the text. Most of the topics covered in the book have been taught by the authors in first-year graduate courses at the University of Tennessee. We have also included revised material presented in short courses and seminars. The mathematical level is well within the grasp of seniors in a technical discipline, such as engineering and computer science, which requires introductory preparation in mathematics and probability.

Syntactic Pattern Recognition is one of three related books published by Addison-Wesley, Advanced Book Program. The first of these, *Pattern Recognition Principles* (Tou and Gonzalez, 1974), describes in detail decision-theoretic approaches and introduces syntactic pattern recognition methods. The second, *Digital Image Processing* (Gonzalez and Wintz, 1977), is concerned with techniques for enhancing, restoring, coding, and describing pictorial information. The objective of these books is to provide a unified, introductory treatment of pattern recognition and image processing concepts with emphasis on fundamentals and consistency of notation.

We are indebted to a number of individuals who, directly or indirectly, assisted in the preparation of this book. In particular, we wish to extend our appreciation to J. M. Googe, R. T. Gregory, F. N. Peebles, E. L. Hall, A. Barrero, B. M. Moret, R. G. Gruber, and G. C. Guerrant. Thanks are also due to Vicki Bohanan, Ethel Wittenberg, Mary Bearden, Cathy Henn, Pat Patterson, and Dianne Barnes for their typing and editorial assistance. In addition, we express our appreciation to the National Aeronautics and Space Administration, the Office of Naval Research, the Oak Ridge National Laboratory, the United States Army Missile Command, the Space and Missile Systems Organization, and the Advanced Research Projects Agency for their sponsorship of our research activities in pattern recognition and image processing.

Rafael C. Gonzalez
Michael G. Thomason

NOTATION

The following is a list of the principal symbols used in this book. Each symbol is listed under the chapter in which it is used for the first time.

Symbol   **Explanation**

Chapter 1

$$\mathbf{x} = \begin{bmatrix} x_1 \\ x_2 \\ \cdot \\ \cdot \\ \cdot \\ x_n \end{bmatrix}$$ vector; also pattern or pattern vector.

ω_i ith pattern class.

$d_i(\mathbf{x})$ decision function of the ith pattern class.

G_i grammar for the ith pattern class.

Chapter 2

iff   if and only if.

$A_1 \times A_2 \times \cdots \times A_n$ Cartesian product of sets $A_1, \ldots, A_n$.

2^A set of all subsets of set A.

$A, B, C, \ldots$ nonterminals.

$a, b, c, \ldots$ terminals.

$u, v, w, x, \ldots$ strings composed of terminal symbols only.

$\alpha, \beta, \gamma, \ldots$ strings of mixed terminals and nonterminals.

$|x|$ length of string x.

V alphabet; a finite set of symbols.

V^+ positive closure of V.

V^* closure of V.

λ empty string.

$\varnothing$ null string; null set.

$G = (N, \Sigma, P, S)$ grammar; N is a finite set of nontermi-
                                            nals, Σ a finite set of terminals, P a
                                            finite set of productions, S the starting
                                            symbol.

$L(G)$ language generated by grammar G.

$\underset{G}{\Rightarrow}$ derivation relation for grammar G.

$\underset{G}{\overset{+}{\Rightarrow}}$ transitive closure of $\underset{G}{\Rightarrow}$; indicates use of
                                            at least one production.

$\underset{G}{\overset{*}{\Rightarrow}}$ reflexive-transitive closure of $\underset{G}{\Rightarrow}$; indi-
                                            cates use of zero or more productions.

$\mathcal{T} = (N, \Sigma, \Delta, R, S)$ syntax-directed translation schema; N is
                                            a finite set of nonterminals, Σ a finite
                                            input alphabet, Δ a finite output alpha-
                                            bet, R a finite set of rules, S the starting
                                            symbol.

$\tau(\mathcal{T})$ translation set produced by schema $\mathcal{T}$.

$\underset{\mathcal{T}}{\Rightarrow}$ translation relation for schema $\mathcal{T}$.

$\underset{\mathcal{T}}{\overset{+}{\Rightarrow}}$ transitive closure of $\underset{\mathcal{T}}{\Rightarrow}$; indicates use of
                                            at least one translation rule.

$\underset{\mathcal{T}}{\overset{*}{\Rightarrow}}$ reflexive-transitive closure of $\underset{\mathcal{T}}{\Rightarrow}$; indi-
                                            cates use of zero or more translation
                                            rules.

| Chapter 3 |

$G_t = (V, r, P, S)$ tree grammar; the alphabet V is the
                                            union of nonterminal and terminal sets
                                            N and Σ, r, is a ranking function, P a
                                            set of tree productions, and S a set of
                                            starting trees.

$L(G_t)$ language generated by tree grammar G_t.

$G_w = (N, \Sigma, P, S)$ web grammar; N is a set of nontermi-
                                            nals, Σ a set of terminals, P a set of
                                            web productions, and S the starting web
                                            symbol.

$G_p = (N, \Sigma, P, S, I, i_o)$ plex grammar; N is a set of nonterminals, Σ a set of terminals, P a set of plex productions, S the starting symbol (called the initial NAPE), I a set of identifiers, and i_o the null identifier.

$G_h = (N, \Sigma, P, I)$ shape grammar; N is a set of nonterminals, Σ a set of terminals, P a set of shape productions, and I the initial shape.

Chapter 4

$\mathcal{Q}_f = (Q, \Sigma, \delta, q_o, F)$ finite automaton; Q is a finite state set, Σ a finite input alphabet, δ a statetransition mapping, q_o the starting state, and F the set of final states.

$L(\mathcal{Q}_f)$ language recognized by automaton $\mathcal{Q}_f$.

$\mathcal{Q}_p = (Q, \Sigma, \Gamma, \delta, q_o, Z_o, F)$ pushdown automaton; Q, Σ, q_o, and P are as for $\mathcal{Q}_f$; Γ is a finite stack alphabet, δ a transition/stack mapping, Z_o the initial stack symbol.

$L(\mathcal{Q}_p)$ language recognized by automaton $\mathcal{Q}_p$ by final state.

$L_\lambda(\mathcal{Q}_p)$ language recognized by automaton $\mathcal{Q}_p$ by empty stack.

$\mathcal{Q}_{dp}$ deterministic pushdown automaton.

$\mathcal{T}_f = (Q, \Sigma, \Delta, \delta, q_o, F)$ finite transducer; Q, Σ, q_o, and F are as for $\mathcal{Q}_f$, Δ is a finite output alphabet, δ a state transition/output mapping.

$\tau(\mathcal{T}_f)$ translation set defined by transducer $\mathcal{T}_f$.

$\mathcal{T}_p = (Q, \Sigma, \Gamma, \Delta, \delta, q_o, Z_o, F)$ pushdown transducer; Q, Σ, Γ, Δ, q_o, Z_o, and F are as for $\mathcal{Q}_p$, Δ is a finite output alphabet, δ a state transition/stack/output mapping.

$\tau(\mathcal{T}_p)$ translation set defined by transducer $\mathcal{T}_p$ by final state.

$\tau_\lambda(\mathcal{T}_p)$ translation set defined by transducer $\mathcal{T}_p$ by empty stack.

CH error of changed symbol in a string.

DE	error of deleted symbol in a string.
IN	error of inserted symbol in a string.
$\mathcal{Q}_t = (Q, F, \{f_a | a \text{ in } \Sigma\})$	frontier-to-root tree automaton; Q is a finite state set, F the set of final states, f_a a state assignment relation for terminal a.

Chapter 5

$G_s = (N, \Sigma, P, D, S)$	stochastic grammar; N, Σ, P, and S are as for G, D is an assignment of probabilities to P.
$G_{sc} = (N, \Sigma, P, S)$	characteristic grammar of stochastic grammar $G_s = (N, \Sigma, P, D, S)$.
$S \underset{p(x)^x}{\overset{*}{\Rightarrow}}$	indicates existence of a leftmost derivation of string x with probability $p(x)$.
G_L	linear stochastic grammar.
G_{NL}	nonlinear stochastic grammar.
$\mathbf{M}$	transition matrix of a Markov chain.
$\mathbf{M}_f$	fundamental matrix of a Markov chain.
$\mathbf{B}$	first-moment matrix of a multitype branching process.
$\mathcal{Q}_{sf} = (Q, \Sigma, \delta, q_o, F, D)$	stochastic finite automaton; Q, Σ, δ, q_o, and F are as for $\mathcal{Q}_f$; D is an assignment of probabilities to δ.
$p(q_j | a, q_i)$	probability that a stochastic finiteautomaton will enter state q_j, given current input symbol a and current state q_i; for spontaneous action, $a = \lambda$.
$L(\mathcal{Q}_{sf})$	language stochastically recognized by automaton $\mathcal{Q}_{sf}$.
$\mathbf{f}$	final vector for stochastic grammar.
$\mathbf{n}$	normalizing vector for stochastic grammar.
$\mathcal{Q}_{sp} = (Q, \Sigma, \Gamma, \delta, q_o, Z_o, F, D)$	stochastic pushdown automaton; Q, Σ, Γ, δ, q_o, Z_o, and F are as for $\mathcal{Q}_p$, D is an assignment of probabilities to δ.

$p(j|q_i, a, Z_l)$

probability that a stochastic pushdown automaton will select (q_j, x_j), with q_j as the next state and x_j as the string to replace Z_l on the stack, given current state q_i, current input symbol a, and symbol Z_l on top of the stack; for spontaneous action, $a = \lambda$.

$L(\mathcal{Q}_{sp})$

language stochastically recognized by automaton $\mathcal{Q}_{sp}$ by final state.

$L_\lambda(\mathcal{Q}_{sp})$

language stochastically recognized by automaton $\mathcal{Q}_{sp}$ by empty stack.

$\mathcal{T}_s = (N, \Sigma, \Delta, R, S, D)$

stochastic syntax-directed translation schema; N, Σ, Δ, R, and S are as for schema T, D is an assignment of probabilities to R.

| Chapter 6 |

R^+

positive sample set.

R^-

negative sample set.

$A_i \equiv A_j$

nonterminals A_i and A_j are equivalent.

T_i

ith tree.

1

INTRODUCTION

> One of the most interesting aspects of the
> world is that it can be considered to be made
> up of *patterns*. A pattern is essentially an
> arrangement. It is characterized by the
> order of the elements of which it is
> made, rather than by the intrinsic
> nature of these elements.
> *Norbert Wiener*

1.1 BACKGROUND

Since the advent in the middle 1960s of third-generation digital computers, we have witnessed in industry, government, and the private sector a marked increase in the attention given to problems associated with handling information. The reduction in cost and increased availability of computers have created numerous areas of research and applications not known just a few years ago. One of these areas is the use of machines for performing "intelligent" tasks normally associated with human behavior.

Although we are often unaware of it, machines capable of exhibiting limited degrees of intelligence are already becoming an integral part of our lives. Examples range from automated checkout counters at supermarkets to applications in health care and national defense. The motivations for research in machine intelligence are simple: from a socioeconomic point of view, we are interested in increased productivity and services at a reduced cost; in other areas, such as defense and space exploration, interest often lies in the development of systems whose required degree of sophistication and range of operating conditions can only be achieved by the use of machines with autonomous decision-making capabilities.

Pattern recognition techniques are among the most important tools used in the field of machine intelligence. Pattern recognition can be defined as the categorization of input data into identifiable classes via the extraction of significant features or attributes of the data from a background of irrelevant detail.

ISBN 0-201-02930-8/0-201-02931-6, pbk

Recognition is regarded as a basic attribute of human beings and other living organisms. According to the nature of the patterns to be recognized, we may divide our acts of recognition into two major types: the recognition of concrete items and the recognition of abstract items. We recognize characters, pictures, music, and the objects around us. This process may be referred to as *sensory recognition*, which includes visual and aural pattern recognition. On the other hand, we can recognize an old argument or a solution to a problem without resorting to external stimuli. This process involves the recognition of abstract items and can be termed *conceptual recognition*. In this book we are concerned with the first type of pattern recognition. Examples of concrete patterns are characters, fingerprints, physical objects, pictures, speech waveforms, electrocardiograms, target signatures, and time series.

The study of pattern recognition problems may be logically divided into two major categories:

1.   The study of the pattern recognition capability of human beings and other living organisms.

2.   The development of underlying theory and practical techniques for machine implementation of a given recognition task.

The first subject area falls in the domain of such disciplines as psychology, physiology, and biology. The second area, which is addressed in the following chapters, is in the domain of engineering, computer science, and applied mathematics.

1.2   PATTERNS AND PATTERN CLASSES

As used in this book, a *pattern* is a quantitative or structural description of an object or some other entity of interest, while a *pattern class* is a set of patterns that share some common properties. The subject matter of pattern recognition by machine deals with techniques for assigning patterns to their respective classes, automatically and with as little human intervention as possible. Consider, for example, the problem of designing a machine to recognize alphanumeric characters for the purpose of automatic mail sorting. In this case there are 37 pattern classes, one for each of the 26 letters and 10 numerals and a rejection class for all unacceptable characters. The function of a character recognition machine is to identify each input character as being a member of one of the available pattern classes.

The particular description approach used to generate patterns in a form acceptable to a machine is strongly influenced by the intended application of the recognition system. In the character recognition problem just

ISBN 0-201-02930-8/0-201-02931-6, pbk

mentioned, a typical approach is to convert each input character into a binary representation by means of a photosensitive matrix device. This measuring scheme is illustrated in Fig. 1.1. The procedure is as follows. Suppose that the character shown in Fig. 1.1(a) is projected onto a photocell matrix, as indicated in Fig. 1.1(b). If the response of each matrix cell is a 1 when it contains a sufficiently large character area and 0 otherwise, the result would be a binary representation of the input character. Figure 1.1(c) shows a typical result, where the shaded cells correspond to 1's and the white cells correspond to 0's.

It is often convenient to arrange the sensed data in the form of a *pattern vector*:

$$\mathbf{x} = \begin{bmatrix} x_1 \\ x_2 \\ \cdot \\ \cdot \\ \cdot \\ x_n \end{bmatrix}$$

where n is the number of measurements. If, for example, the measurement grid illustrated in Fig. 1.1 is of size $m \times m$, we have that $n = m^2$, and each component x_i of the vector $\mathbf{x}$ assumes the value 1 or 0, depending on the state of the ith cell in the grid for a particular input.

Another example is shown in Fig. 1.2. In this case, the objects of interest are continuous functions (such as acoustic signals) of a variable t. If these functions are sampled at discrete points $t_1, t_2, \ldots, t_n$, a pattern vector may be formed by letting $x_1 = f(t_1), x_2 = f(t_2), \ldots, x_n = f(t_n)$. In this particular representation the components of $\mathbf{x}$ are real continuous quantities in the range of the functions, unlike the binary values obtained from the measurement scheme illustrated in Fig. 1.1.

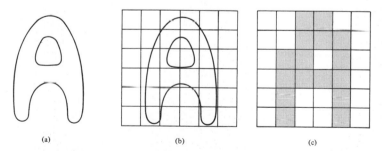

(a) (b) (c)

Figure 1.1. (a) Character. (b) Measuring grid. (c) Resulting binary pattern.

ISBN 0-201-02930-8/0-201-02931-6, pbk

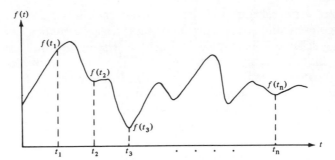

Figure 1.2. Sampling of a waveform.

Vectors of the form shown above may be interpreted as points in n-dimensional Euclidean space. Due to variabilities in the shape of most objects being measured, pattern vectors that belong to the same class will seldom be identical. This inherent variability gives rise to pattern classes that may be interpreted as "clouds" or clusters of points in n-dimensional space. Figure 1.3 is a two-dimensional illustration of this concept. The

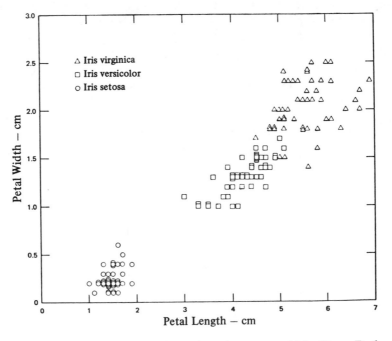

Figure 1.3. Two measurements performed on three types of iris. (From Duda and Hart [1973].)

ISBN 0-201-02930-8/0-201-02931-6, pbk

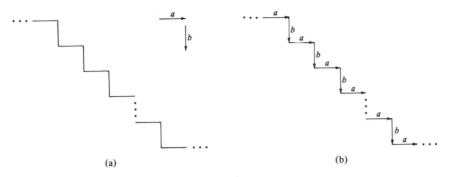

(a)   (b)

Figure 1.4. (a) Staircase structure. (b) Structure coded in terms of the primitives *a* and *b* to yield the string representation . . . *ababab* . . . .

patterns shown correspond to two measurements[‡] performed on three types of iris. The pattern vectors in this case are of the form

$$\mathbf{x} = \begin{bmatrix} x_1 \\ x_2 \end{bmatrix}$$

where x_1 corresponds to petal length and x_2 to petal width. The scatter present in each class is due primarily to variations in petal length and width within flowers of the same type. It is worth noting that these two measurements were quite adequate to separate the class of *Iris setosa* from the other two classes, but they were not as efficient in separating the *virginica* and *versicolor* types from each other.

The techniques discussed above for the generation of pattern vectors yield pattern classes that are characterized by quantitative information. In some applications, such as in machine analysis of pictorial data, the characteristics of components of interest are usually best described by resorting to structural relationships. Consider, for instance, the simple staircase structure shown in Fig. 1.4(a). This structure could easily be coded in the form of a pattern vector by using a digitization scheme such as the one illustrated in Fig. 1.1. It is noted, however, that a more efficient representation (in terms of the amount of data required) would result if we were to take advantage of the repetitive nature inherent in this particular geometrical arrangement. By defining the two *primitive elements* *a* and *b* shown, we may code Fig. 1.4(a) in the form shown in Fig. 1.4(b) and define a string of symbols *w = ababab* . . . that completely characterizes the

---

[‡]These are two of four measurements on three species of iris reported by Fisher [1936] in a classic paper dealing with discriminant analysis.

ISBN 0-201-02930-8/0-201-02931-6, pbk

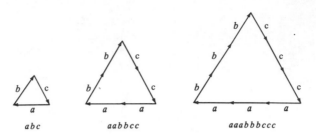

Figure 1.5. String representations of equilateral triangles.

structure under consideration.[‡] Unlike the numerical descriptions given earlier, this type of representation yields patterns composed of primitive elements whose meaning is related to the basic structure of the input data. Interconnection of these primitive elements describes a structural pattern. A pattern class is then simply a set of such patterns that are assumed to share some common properties.

Another example of a string representation is shown in Fig. 1.5. In this case, the structures are equilateral triangles of various sizes. By assuming that the lengths of the primitives a, b, and c are equal, we may represent such triangles by strings of the form $aaaa \ldots bbbb \ldots cccc \ldots$, or $a^n b^n c^n$ for short, where n is the number of primitives of each type.

It is often possible to increase the descriptional power of string representations by defining operators that allow higher-dimensional properties to be expressed in the form of a string. Four such operators are shown in Fig. 1.6. In this representation, primitives are directed line segments and the operators allow connections of these primitives only between their heads and/or tails. As an example of this approach, consider the primitives defined in Fig. 1.7(a). Figure 1.7(b) shows the primitive d and Fig. 1.7(c) is the result of using the operator $+$ with primitives c and $\sim d$ (the symbol $\sim$ indicates a reversal in direction of a primitive). Note the head and tail of the composite structure $c + (\sim d)$. Appending primitive d to this structure by means of the operator $+$ results in the structure shown in Fig. 1.7(d). A similar procedure yields the composite structure shown in Fig. 1.7(f). Finally, applying the operator $*$ to the structures in Figs. 1.7(d) and 1.7(f) yields the pattern shown in Fig. 1.7(g).

String representations are adequate for describing objects or other entities whose structure is based on relatively simple connectivity of primitives. A more powerful approach for many applications is realized through the use of tree representations. Basically, any hierarchical ordering

---

[‡]It is implicitly assumed that primitives a and b are connected in a head-to-tail manner, as shown in Fig. 1.4(b).

ISBN 0-201-02930-8/0-201-02931-6, pbk

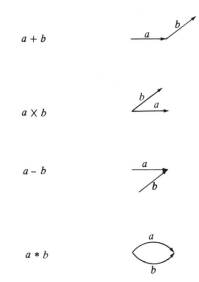

Figure 1.6. Definition of the operators +, ×, −, and * for the interconnection of pattern primitives.

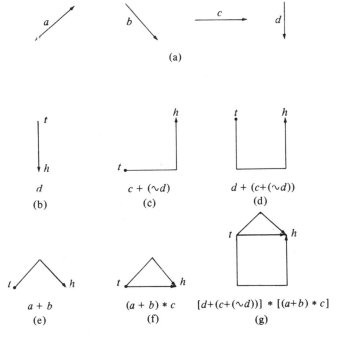

Figure 1.7. (a) Primitives. (b)–(g) Representation of some simple patterns.

ISBN 0-201-02930-8/0-201-02931-6, pbk

scheme leads to a tree structure. Consider, for example, the simplified image shown in Fig. 1.8(a). Let us define the entire image area by the symbol $. The tree representation shown in Fig. 1.8(b) was obtained by using the relationship "inside" and indicates that the first level of complexity involves regions a, b, and c inside $. Region a contains region d, which in turn contains regions e and f. Similarly, region b contains regions g and h. Finally, we see that region i is inside region c.

Figure 1.9(a) shows a simple scene composed of blocks and Fig. 1.9(b) is the tree representation obtained by using the relationship "composed of."

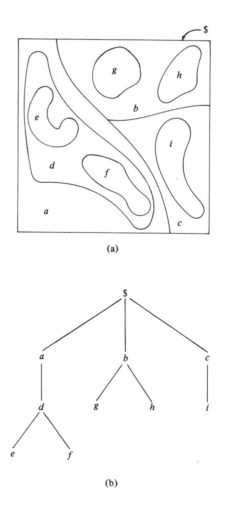

(a)

(b)

Figure 1.8. Example of tree representation.

ISBN 0-201-02930-8/0-201-02931-6, pbk

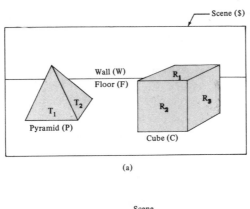

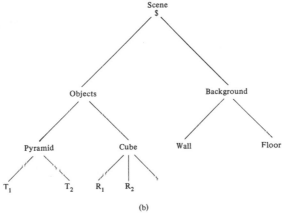

(b)

Figure 1.9. Tree representation of a simple scene.

At the first level of complexity, we see that scene $ is composed of objects and background. The latter, in turn, is composed of the floor and wall, while the objects are a pyramid and a cube. The pyramid is composed of two triangular structures, T_1 and T_2, and the cube is composed of three rectangular structures, R_1, R_2, and R_3. This representation is based on a "top-down" interpretation of the tree, starting with the overall concept of a scene, $, and breaking it down into primitive components. We would have obtained the same tree by using the relationship "part of." In this case, however, we would interpret the tree in a "bottom-up" manner. For example, the wall and floor are part of the background, T_1 and T_2 are part of the pyramid, and so forth. Similar comments hold for Fig. 1.8 if, instead of using the relationship "inside," we use the relationship "contains."

ISBN 0-201-02930-8/0-201-02931-6, pbk

As a final illustration of tree representations, consider Fig. 1.10(a), which is an aerial photograph depicting a scene composed of urban and rural land areas. Figure 1.10(b) is a tree representation using, as above, the relationship "composed of." Interpreting the tree in a top-down manner, we see that the scene can be broken down into urban and rural components. The urban area can be further subdivided into its downtown, inner city, suburb, and highway components. The downtown area is seen to be composed of recreational and commercial areas, and so forth.

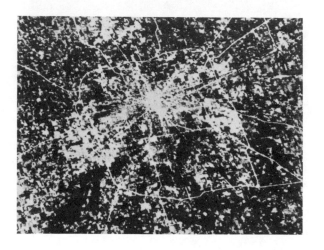

(a)

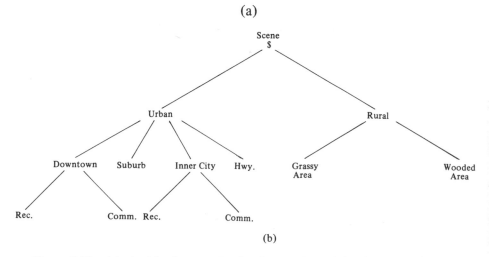

(b)

Figure 1.10.   (a) Aerial photograph of urban and rural land areas.   (b) Tree representation of aerial photograph. (From Brayer, Swain, and Fu [1977].)

ISBN 0-201-02930-8/0-201-02931-6, pbk

A string is a special case of a tree that consists of single branches and whose nodes are labeled in the same order as the symbols in the string. Similarly, trees are special cases of a class of more general representations called *webs*, which are defined as graphs whose nodes are labeled. The use of graphs for pattern recognition is illustrated in Fig. 1.11. Part (a) of this figure shows a simple object and Fig. 1.11(b) shows an approximation of this object by polygons. The interconnection of the polygons at appropriate vertices yields the graph representation shown in Fig. 1.11(c).

As a second illustration, consider Fig. 1.9 again. If in addition to the relationship "composed of" we use the relationship "connected to," we obtain the web shown in Fig. 1.12. Thus, we see that the triangular components T_1 and T_2 are joined by an arc, indicating that they are connected. The same is true for R_1, R_2, and R_3, as well as the wall and floor in the scene.

The pattern classes that result from the three representation schemes just discussed are sets of strings, trees, or webs. The properties of these "structural" classes are best exploited by the syntactic pattern recognition methods introduced in Section 1.3.3 and discussed in more detail in the remainder of the book. The reader should bear in mind that the selection of a particular representation and the techniques used for the extraction of the required pattern primitives are strongly problem oriented. Numerous examples illustrating these concepts are given in the following chapters.

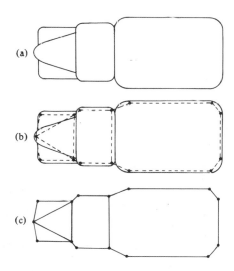

(a)

(b)

(c)

Figure 1.11. Example of graph representation.

ISBN 0-201-02930-8/0-201-02931-6, pbk

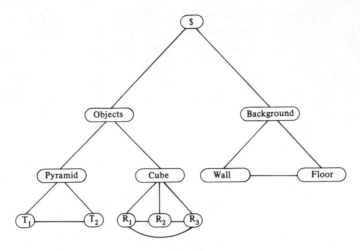

Figure 1.12. Web for the scene in Fig. 1.9a.

1.3   APPROACHES TO PATTERN RECOGNITION

Approaches to pattern recognition system design may be divided into two principal categories: (1) the decision-theoretic approach; and (2) the syntactic approach.

1.3.1   Decision-Theoretic Approach

The decision-theoretic approach is based on the utilization of decision functions for classifying pattern vectors of the form shown in Section 1.2. As an introduction to this concept, consider Fig. 1.13, which shows two pattern classes, denoted by ω_1 and ω_2. It is seen by inspection that these two classes can be separated by a straight line.

Let

$$d(\mathbf{x}) = w_1 x_1 + w_2 x_2 + w_3 = 0$$

be the equation of a separating line where the w's are parameters, x_1 and x_2 are the pattern coordinate variables (e.g., see Fig. 1.3), and $d(\mathbf{x})$ is used to denote $d(x_1, x_2)$. Any observation $\mathbf{x}$ that falls on the boundary yields $d(\mathbf{x}) = 0$ when substituted into the foregoing equation. We see from Fig. 1.13, however, that any pattern $\mathbf{x}$ from class ω_1 will yield a positive quantity when substituted into $d(\mathbf{x})$. In other words, all the patterns of this class lie on the positive side of the separating boundary. Similarly, the patterns of class ω_2 lie on the negative side of the boundary, so that $d(\mathbf{x})$

ISBN 0-201-02930-8/0-201-02931-6, pbk

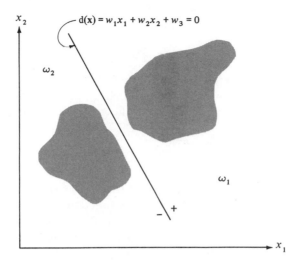

Figure 1.13.   A simple decision function for two pattern classes. (From Tou and Gonzalez [1974].)

becomes negative upon substitution of any pattern from this class. From these considerations, it is noted that $d(x)$ can be used as a *decision* (or *discriminant*) function, since, given a pattern x of unknown classification, we say that x belongs to class ω_1 if $d(x) > 0$ or to class ω_2 if $d(x) < 0$. The indeterminate condition $d(x) = 0$ indicates that the pattern lies on the boundary between the two classes.

When there are more than two classes, one approach is to establish M decision functions $d_1(x), d_2(x), \ldots, d_M(x)$ with the property that if a pattern x belongs to class ω_i, then

$$d_i(x) > d_j(x), \qquad j = 1, 2, \ldots, M, \quad j \neq i,$$

where M is the number of classes. This relationship specifies a decision rule in which each pattern to be classified is substituted into all decision functions. The pattern is then assigned to the class whose decision function yields the largest numerical value. Ties are resolved arbitrarily. It is noted that the simple example introduced above is a special case of this rule. Thus, if $M = 2$, we have that for all patterns of class ω_1, $d_1(x) > d_2(x)$ and, conversely, for all patterns of class ω_2, $d_1(x) < d_2(x)$. Defining $d(x) = d_1(x) - d_2(x)$ leads to the condition $d(x) > 0$ for x in ω_1 and $d(x) < 0$ for x in ω_2. In general, the equation of the decision boundary separating classes ω_i

ISBN 0-201-02930-8/0-201-02931-6, pbk

and ω_j is given by

$$d_i(\mathbf{x}) - d_j(\mathbf{x}) = 0.$$

The foregoing concepts need not be restricted to two-dimensional patterns and linear decision boundaries. In the n-dimensional case, the decision functions may be expressed in the general form

$$d_k(\mathbf{x}) = \sum_{l=1}^{K} w_{kl}\phi_l(\mathbf{x}), \qquad k = 1, 2, \ldots, M,$$

where the $\{\phi_l(\mathbf{x})\}$ are real, single-valued functions of the pattern $\mathbf{x}$, and $\{w_{kl}\}$ are the coefficients of the decision function corresponding to class ω_k. This equation is quite general in the sense that it can represent a variety of very complex decision functions in n-dimensional space. The usual approach is to specify first the functions $\{\phi_l(\mathbf{x})\}$. The problem then becomes one of determining the coefficients $\{w_{kl}\}$ for each class, so that the foregoing decision rule will hold for as many patterns as possible. The decision-theoretic approach to pattern recognition deals with algorithms for estimating these parameters using sample patterns in a training process. Thus, if the pattern recognition system performs well during training with a well-chosen set of representative patterns, it may be expected to perform satisfactorily when confronted with "field" data during normal operation.

There exist numerous adaptive algorithms that can be used for training a pattern recognition system. These algorithms can be divided into (1) deterministic and (2) statistical procedures. As evidenced by this breakdown, deterministic algorithms deal with the estimation of the decision function coefficients directly from the patterns without resorting to statistical considerations, while statistical algorithms are based on the statistical properties of the various pattern populations under consideration.

Although a study of these algorithms is outside the scope of this book, it is important to bear in mind that the decision-theoretic approach to pattern recognition plays a very significant role in applied as well as theoretical work in this field. The interested reader can consult, for example, the book by Tou and Gonzalez [1974] for further study on this subject.

1.3.2 Syntactic Approach

The decision-theoretic approach discussed in the previous section is ideally suited for applications where patterns can be meaningfully represented in vector form. There are applications, however, where the structure of a pattern plays an important role in the classification process. In these

ISBN 0-201-02930-8/0-201-02931-6, pbk

situations, the decision-theoretic approach has serious drawbacks because it lacks a suitable formalism for handling pattern structures and their relationships. For example, the decision-theoretic approach finds few applications to scene analysis, since in this case the structure and relationships of the various components of a scene are of fundamental importance in establishing a meaningful recognition scheme.

The syntactic[‡] approach to pattern recognition has been receiving increased attention during the past few years because it possesses the structure-handling capability lacked by the decision-theoretic approach. Syntactic pattern recognition is based on concepts from formal language theory, the origins of which may be traced to the middle 1950s with the development of mathematical models of grammars by Noam Chomsky [1956]. One of the original goals of linguists working in this area was to develop mathematical models capable of describing natural languages such as English. The hope was that, if this could be done, it would be a relatively simple matter to "teach" computers to interpret natural languages for the purposes of translation and problem solving. Although it is generally agreed that these expectations have been unrealized thus far, spin-offs and extensions of the research in this area have had a significant impact on other fields, such as compiler design, computer languages, automata theory and, more recently, pattern recognition.

Basic to the syntactic pattern recognition approach is the decomposition of patterns into subpatterns or primitives. Figure 1.14(b) shows such a decomposition of two chromosome structures in terms of the primitives defined in Fig. 1.14(a). By tracking each chromosome boundary in a clockwise direction, it is possible to detect and encode these primitives in the form of a string of qualifiers. Thus, the submedian chromosome can be represented by the string *abcbabdbabcbabdh* and the telocentric chromosome by the string *ebabcbab*.

Suppose that we interpret each primitive as being a symbol permissible in some grammar, where a *grammar* is a set of rules of syntax for the generation of *sentences* from the given symbols. These sentences certainly could consist of strings such as the ones associated with the chromosome structures described in the preceding paragraph. It is further possible to envision two grammars G_1 and G_2 whose rules allow the generation of sentences that correspond to submedian and telocentric chromosomes, respectively. Thus, the language $L(G_1)$ generated by G_1 would consist of sentences representing submedian chromosomes and the language $L(G_2)$ generated by G_2 of sentences representing telocentric chromosomes.

ISBN 0-201-02930-8/0-201-02931-6, pbk

[‡]The terms *linguistic*, *structural*, and *grammatical* pattern recognition are also often used in the literature to denote the syntactic approach.

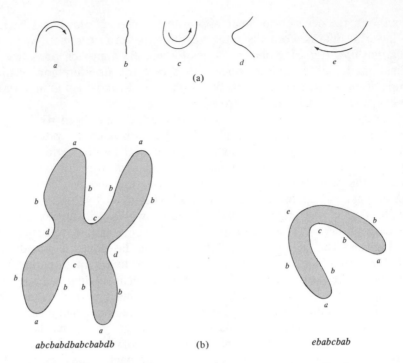

Figure 1.14.   (a) Primitives.   (b) Coded submedian and telocentric chromosomes.
(From Ledley [1964].)

Once the two grammars G_1 and G_2 have been established, the syntactic
pattern recognition process is, in principle, straightforward. Given a
sentence representing an input pattern, the problem is one of deciding in
which language the input pattern represents a valid sentence. Thus, if the
sentence belongs to $L(G_1)$, we say that the input is a submedian chromosome; if it belongs to $L(G_2)$, we say that it is a telocentric chromosome.
A unique decision cannot be made if the sentence belongs to both
languages. If the sentence is found to be invalid over both $L(G_1)$ and
$L(G_2)$, the input pattern is assigned to a rejection class consisting of all
invalid patterns. Techniques for establishing the class membership of
syntactic structures are discussed in Chapters 4 and 5.

When there are more than two pattern classes, the syntactic classification approach is the same as that just described, except that more grammars (at least one for each class) are involved in the process. In this case, a
pattern is uniquely assigned to the ith class if it is a sentence of only $L(G_i)$
and no other language. A unique decision cannot be made if the sentence

ISBN 0-201-02930-8/0-201-02931-6, pbk

belongs to more than one language, and (as earlier) if a pattern is not a sentence of any of the languages under consideration, it is assigned to a rejection class.

If the patterns are tree or web representations, the foregoing concepts are still valid, the only exception being that the recognition process is carried out by considering tree or web grammars.

1.4 ELEMENTS OF A PATTERN RECOGNITION SYSTEM

The principal function of a pattern recognition system is to arrive at decisions concerning the class membership of the patterns with which it is confronted. Several major information translation processes take place between the time a pattern is input and a decision is made by the system. These processes, which are summarized in block diagram form in Fig. 1.15, extract from the input data the discriminatory information required for classification. The functions of the blocks shown in Fig. 1.15 are described briefly as follows.

The sensor is simply the measurement device that transforms the input patterns into a form suitable for machine manipulation. Although some simple pattern recognition systems operate on the input data directly from the sensor, it is common practice to follow the sensor with a preprocessor and feature extractor. The preprocessor removes unnecessary or corrupting elements from the measured data, while the feature extractor computes from the preprocessed data the features required for classification. Finally, these features are input into the classifier, whose function is to yield a decision concerning the class membership of the pattern being processed.

The chromosome problem discussed in Section 1.3.2 is a good example of the functions performed by the various stages in Fig. 1.15. Suppose that chromosomes are digitized by a sensor that uses a grid scheme such as the one shown in Fig. 1.1. In this case, the preprocessor would consist of a set of algorithms for determining the outer boundary of the input chromosomes; the feature extractor would detect the primitive elements shown in Fig. 1.4(a) and form string representations; and the classifier would operate on each string in order to determine to which language (i.e., class) it belongs.

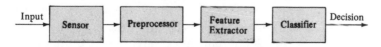

Figure 1.15. Components of a pattern recognition system.

ISBN 0-201-02930-8/0-201-02931-6, pbk

In the foregoing discussion it has been implicitly assumed that the system "knows" the information processing operations that must be performed on an input pattern in order to arrive at a decision. Although the general form of these operations is specified by the system designer, in most cases each specific operation is characterized by variable parameters that must be adapted to a given pattern recognition problem. The adjustment of these parameters is usually carried out by utilizing sample patterns in what is called a *learning* or *training* process.

Machine learning techniques may be subdivided into two principal categories: (1) *supervised* and (2) *unsupervised*. In a supervised learning situation, the system parameters are estimated by algorithms that utilize training sample patterns whose class membership is specified externally by the system designer. In this manner, the unknown parameters are adjusted to fit a situation where the pattern classes are specified and characterized by representative samples. Clearly, the ultimate success of this approach is dictated by the quality of the sample set used to train the pattern recognition system.

The unsupervised learning approach is used when there is little or no a priori knowledge about the pattern classes of a given problem. In essence, this approach attempts to extract the pattern classes present in a set of data for which the classification of the available sample patterns is not completely known.

1.5 CONCLUDING REMARKS

As indicated in Section 1.3.3, syntactic pattern recognition methods are based on concepts from formal language theory. Formal string grammars and languages are introduced in Chapter 2 in the context of pattern description and recognition, while Chapter 3 deals with higher-dimensional grammars and languages. Once a set of grammars for a given problem has been obtained, it is necessary to specify a recognition rule for assigning patterns to their respective categories. These concepts are discussed in Chapter 4, where several methods for recognizing syntactic pattern structures are considered in detail. The problems of incorporating stochastic methods in a grammatical formulation are discussed in Chapter 5. This material represents an important approach for handling pattern variability. Finally, Chapter 6 deals with the problem of learning grammars from sample patterns by means of grammatical inference algorithms.

ISBN 0-201-02930-8/0-201-02931-6, pbk

REFERENCES

The following references, which are of a general nature, are cited primarily to give the reader an overview of the principal books and journals in which syntactic pattern recognition research and applications are typically reported. References given at the end of later chapters are keyed to specific topics discussed in the text. All references are cited by the author or journal name, followed by the year of publication. The bibliography at the end of the book is organized in the same way and contains all pertinent information for each reference.

Complementary reading on syntactic pattern description and recognition may be found in the books by Fu [1974, 1977] and Tou and Gonzalez [1974]. The book by Gonzalez and Wintz [1977] deals with topics in image processing, an area of considerable interest in syntactic pattern recognition because it provides the tools for segmentation and extraction of pattern primitives.

The books by Hopcroft and Ullman [1969] and Aho and Ullman [1972] are excellent references on formal language theory; the latter covers many of the concepts used in the following chapters. Booth [1969] is primarily concerned with automata and sequential machine theory. Kain [1972] and Lewis *et al.* [1976] are examples of texts that present various aspects of language and automata theory. A number of other texts are available in this field.

Journals that often contain material related to syntactic pattern recognition include *Pattern Recognition, IEEE Transactions on Computers, IEEE Transactions on Systems, Man, and Cybernetics, Information and Control, International Journal of Computer and Information Sciences, Information Sciences, Journal of Computer and Systems Science, Communications of the ACM, Journal of the ACM, SIAM Journal on the Theory of Computing,* and *Mathematical Systems Theory.*

ISBN 0-201-02930-8/0-201-02931-6, pbk

2

ELEMENTS OF FORMAL
LANGUAGE THEORY

Observers are not led by the same physical
evidence to the same picture of the
universe unless their linguistic
backgrounds are similar or can
in some way be calibrated.
Benjamin Lee Whorf

2.1 INTRODUCTION

Formal language theory deals with mathematical models of languages
and the systems used in language generation and processing. The terminology used still reflects the early interest of researchers in natural languages
such as English and French; however, most of the contributions in language theory have been in the application and processing of languages
created for specific purposes,[‡] particularly for human–machine communications. The emphasis in language theory is on finite representations of
languages and classes of languages, based on knowledge of underlying
syntactic structure. The algebraic models of generators, recognizers, and
translators of languages invariably reflect syntax in their design, either
explicitly or implicitly.

As indicated in Chapter 1, the methods of syntactic pattern recognition
are based on mathematical systems in which the patterns of a class are
represented as elements of a language. One of the principal requirements
in designing a syntactic pattern recognition system is the development of a
grammar capable of generating a given class of patterns. Most of the
material in this chapter deals with the definition and interpretation of
several types of grammars suitable for pattern representation and recognition.

[‡]These are sometimes called *artificial* or *mechanical languages*.

ISBN 0-201-02930-8/0-201-02931-6, pbk

2.2 STRING GRAMMARS AND LANGUAGES

2.2.1 Preliminary Definitions

The following concise definitions establish some of the principal notation and concepts used in formal language theory. Familiarity with basic
set theory is assumed.

Two categories of sets of interest in formal language theory are *finite
sets*, which have a finite number of elements, and *countably infinite sets*,
whose elements can be placed in a one-to-one correspondence with the
positive integers. Given sets A and B, their *Cartesian product $A \times B$* is the
collection of all ordered pairs (a, b), a in A and b in B. For sets
$A_1, A_2, \ldots, A_n$, this may be extended to the *n-fold Cartesian product*
$A_1 \times A_2 \times \ldots \times A_n$, which is the set of all *n*-tuples $(a_1, \ldots, a_n)$ for a_1 in
$A_1, \ldots, a_n$ in A_n.

Given set A, the set of all its subsets is denoted as 2^A. The *null set* $\emptyset$ is
the set containing no elements.

A *relation* $\mathcal{R}$ from set A to set B is a subset of $A \times B$, that is,
$\mathcal{R} \subseteq A \times B$. If (a, b) is in $\mathcal{R}$, we write "*a* is $\mathcal{R}$-related to *b*" or $a\mathcal{R}b$ for
short. If for each element a of A there is exactly one element b of B such
that (a, b) is in $\mathcal{R}$, then the relation is called a *function* (or *mapping*) *from A
to B* and is sometimes written $\mathcal{R}: A \rightarrow B$. If (a, b) is in function $\mathcal{R}$, one
may write $\mathcal{R}(a) = b$.

Example: Let $A = \{u_1, a_2\}$ and $B = \{b_1, b_2, b_3\}$. Then the Cartesian
product of A with B is

$$A \times B = \{(a_1, b_1), (a_1, b_2), (a_1, b_3), (a_2, b_1), (a_2, b_2), (a_2, b_3)\}.$$

A relation $\mathcal{R}_1$ from A to B that is not a function is

$$\mathcal{R}_1 = \{(a_1, b_2), (a_1, b_3), (a_2, b_3)\},$$

and a relation $\mathcal{R}_2$ from A to B that is a function is

$$\mathcal{R}_2 = \{(a_1, b_3), (a_2, b_3)\}.$$

The collection of all subsets of set A consist of the sets $\{a_1, a_2\}$, $\{a_1\}$, $\{a_2\}$,
and $\emptyset$, the null set with no elements. The collection of all subsets of B
consists of $\{b_1, b_2, b_3\}$, $\{b_1, b_2\}$, $\{b_1, b_3\}$, $\{b_2, b_3\}$, $\{b_1\}$, $\{b_2\}$, $\{b_3\}$, and $\emptyset$.
□

Let $\mathcal{R}$ be a relation in $A \times A$. If (a, a) is in $\mathcal{R}$ for every element a in A,
the relation $\mathcal{R}$ is *reflexive*. If (a, b) in $\mathcal{R}$ implies that (b, a) is also in $\mathcal{R}$,
then $\mathcal{R}$ is *symmetric*. If (a, b) and (b, c) in $\mathcal{R}$ implies (a, c) is in $\mathcal{R}$, then

ISBN 0-201-02930-8/0-201-02931-6, pbk

$\mathcal{R}$ is *transitive*. A relation with all three of these properties is an *equivalence relation*.

For relation $\mathcal{R}$ in set A, the *transitive closure* of $\mathcal{R}$ is the relation $\mathcal{R}^+$ in which:

(i)   if $a\mathcal{R}b$, then $a\mathcal{R}^+b$; and
(ii) if $a\mathcal{R}^+b$ and $b\mathcal{R}^+c$, then $a\mathcal{R}^+c$.

The *reflexive-transitive closure* of $\mathcal{R}$ is the relation

$$\mathcal{R}^* = \mathcal{R}^+ \cup \{(a, a)|a \text{ in } A\}.$$

Example: Let $A = \{a_1, a_2, a_3\}$; then

$$A \times A = \{(a_i, a_j)|1 \leqslant i \leqslant 3, 1 \leqslant j \leqslant 3\}.$$

Let $\mathcal{R}_3 = \{(a_1, a_1), (a_1, a_2), (a_2, a_2), (a_3, a_3)\}$. $\mathcal{R}_3$ is reflexive because (a_1, a_1), (a_2, a_2), and (a_3, a_3) are in $\mathcal{R}_3$. $\mathcal{R}_3$ is not symmetric because (a_1, a_2) is in $\mathcal{R}_3$ but (a_2, a_1) is not. $\mathcal{R}_3$ is transitive.

Let $\mathcal{R}_4 = \{(a_1, a_2), (a_2, a_1)\}$, so that $\mathcal{R}_4$ is symmetric but neither reflexive nor transitive. To construct its transitive closure $\mathcal{R}_4^+$, we place elements in $\mathcal{R}_4^+$ as follows:

(i) (a_1, a_2) and (a_2, a_1) are in $\mathcal{R}_4^+$; and
(ii) (a_1, a_2), (a_2, a_1) together require (a_1, a_1) in $\mathcal{R}_4^+$,
     (a_2, a_1), (a_1, a_2) together require (a_2, a_2) in $\mathcal{R}_4^+$.

Thus,

$$\mathcal{R}_4^+ = \{(a_1, a_1), (a_1, a_2), (a_2, a_1), (a_2, a_2)\}.$$

The reflexive-transitive closure of $\mathcal{R}_4$, as a relation on A, is

$$\mathcal{R}_4^* = \mathcal{R}_4^+ \cup \{(a_1, a_1), (a_2, a_2), (a_3, a_3)\}$$

$$= \{(a_1, a_1), (a_1, a_2), (a_2, a_1), (a_2, a_2), (a_3, a_3)\}. \qquad \square$$

An *alphabet* V is a finite set of symbols, such as the binary set $\{0, 1\}$ or the set $\{A, a, B, b, \ldots, Z, z\}$ of upper- and lowercase letters.

A *sentence* x over alphabet V is a string of finite length formed with symbols from V. (The words *sentence* and *string* are used synonymously.) The *length of* x, denoted by $|x|$, is the number of symbols used in its formation. For example, with $V = \{a, b\}$, the set of length one sentences is $\{a, b\}$; length two, $\{aa, ab, ba, bb\}$; length three, $\{aaa, aab, aba, abb, baa, bab, bba, bbb\}$; and so on. Note that the symbols of a sentence

ISBN 0-201-02930-8/0-201-02931-6, pbk

are ordered from left to right with the leftmost symbol being the first in the sentence and the rightmost being the last.

Let x and y be sentences over an alphabet. The *concatenation of x with y* is the sentence xy with length

$$|xy| = |x| + |y|.$$

The *empty string*, denoted by λ, is the sentence with no symbols; it follows that $|\lambda| = 0$. This string is the identity element for concatenation in the sense that, for any sentence z over V,

$$\lambda z = z\lambda = z.$$

The empty string must be distinguished from the *null string* $\emptyset$ which nullifies when used in concatenation. For any sentence x over V,

$$\emptyset x = x\emptyset = \emptyset.$$

The symbol $\emptyset$ is also used to denote the null set.

If sentence w is written as x concatenated with y concatenated with z, say $w = xyz$, then string x is a *prefix* of w, y is a *substring* of w, and z is a *suffix* of w. Thus, prefixes of the sentence *aab* are λ, *a*, *aa*, *aab*; corresponding suffixes that complete the sentence are *aab*, *ab*, *b*, λ. Nonempty substrings are *aab*, *aa*, *a*, *b*, *ab*.

For any alphabet V, the countably infinite set of all sentences over V, including λ, is the *closure of V*, denoted by V^*. The *positive closure of V* is the set

$$V^+ = V^* - \{\lambda\}.$$

For instance, given alphabet $V = \{a, b\}$, these sets are

$$V^* = \{\lambda, a, b, aa, ab, ba, bb, aaa, \dots\}$$

and

$$V^+ = \{a, b, aa, ab, \dots\}.$$

A *language* is a set of sentences over an alphabet; that is, a language over alphabet V is a finite or countably infinite subset of V^*. For example, the set

$$L = \{x \mid x \text{ is a single } b \text{ or is a finite string of } a\text{'s followed by a single } b\}^{\ddagger}$$

[‡] We use the standard set notation in which "$L = \{x \mid P\}$" means "L is the set of all x having property P."

ISBN 0-201-02930-8/0-201-02931-6, pbk

is a language over $V = \{a, b\}$. For symbol a in V, let a^n denote the string of n concatenated a's, $n \geqslant 0$, with a^0 being interpreted as the empty string, λ; then the language above may be defined as

$$L = \{x \mid x = a^n b, n \geqslant 0\}.$$

The *concatenation* of set A with set B is denoted by AB. For languages L_1 and L_2, their concatenation $L_1 L_2$ is the set of sentences

$$L_1 L_2 = \{xy \mid x \text{ in } L_1, y \text{ in } L_2\}.$$

Letting $L_1 = \{a\}^*$ and $L_2 = \{b\}$, for example, gives

$$L_1 L_2 = \{a\}^* \{b\}$$

$$= \{\lambda, a, aa, aaa, \ldots\}\{b\}$$

$$= \{b, ab, aab, \ldots\}$$

$$= \{x \mid x = a^n b, n \geqslant 0\}.$$

A basic system studied in formal language theory is one that gives a finite set of rules for generating exactly the set of strings in a specific language.[‡] These rules of syntax are embodied in a *grammar*, defined formally as a four-tuple $G = (N, \Sigma, P, S)$ where

> N is a finite set of *nonterminals* or variables,
> Σ is a finite set of *terminals* or constants,
> P is a finite set of *productions* or rewriting rules, and
> S in N is the *starting symbol*.

It is required that N and Σ be disjoint sets; that is, $N \cap \Sigma = \varnothing$, the null set. The alphabet V of the grammar is the set $N \cup \Sigma$. The set P of productions consists of rewriting rules of the form $\alpha \rightarrow \beta$, where α is in $V^* N V^*$ and β is in V^*, with the physical interpretation that string α may be written as, or replaced by, β. α must contain at least one nonterminal.

Example: A simple grammar is $G = (N, \Sigma, P, S)$ with nonterminal set $N = \{S\}$, terminal set $\Sigma = \{a, b\}$, and productions $P = \{S \rightarrow aS, S \rightarrow b\}$. In this case, the starting symbol S is the only nonterminal, and the two productions indicate that S may be replaced by aS or by b in the course of using G and its productions to generate sentences composed of a's and b's. $\qquad\square$

[‡]There are languages that do not have such a representation; however, attention is restricted in syntactic pattern recognition to those that can be described grammatically.

ISBN 0-201-02930-8/0-201-02931-6, pbk

In the remainder of the book, nonterminals will be denoted by capital letters: $A, B, \ldots, S, \ldots$. Lowercase letters at the beginning of the alphabet will be used for terminals: $a, b, c, d, \ldots$. Strings of terminals will be denoted by lowercase letters toward the end of the alphabet: $v, w, x, y, \ldots$. Strings of mixed terminals and nonterminals will be represented by lowercase Greek letters: $\alpha, \beta, \theta, \rho, \ldots$.

Given a grammar G, let ρ and δ be strings in V^* and $\alpha \to \beta$ be a production in P. We will use the notation $\rho\alpha\delta \underset{G}{\Rightarrow} \rho\beta\delta$ to indicate that string $\rho\beta\delta$ is derivable from string $\rho\alpha\delta$ by a *single* application of a production $\alpha \to \beta$. The symbol $\underset{G}{\Rightarrow}$ represents the *derivation relation* of grammar G. We will use the symbol $\underset{G}{\overset{*}{\Rightarrow}}$ to indicate zero or more uses of the relation $\underset{G}{\Rightarrow}$, and $\underset{G}{\overset{+}{\Rightarrow}}$ to indicate one or more uses of this relation. Thus, the notation $\omega \underset{G}{\overset{*}{\Rightarrow}} \theta$ indicates that string θ can be derived from ω by applying zero or more productions from G, while $\omega \underset{G}{\overset{+}{\Rightarrow}} \theta$ indicates that it is necessary to apply one or more productions in order to derive θ from ω. Formally, $\underset{G}{\overset{+}{\Rightarrow}}$ is the transitive closure of the relation $\underset{G}{\Rightarrow}$ and $\underset{G}{\overset{*}{\Rightarrow}}$ is its reflexive-transitive closure.

Example: Consider the grammar $G = (N, \Sigma, P, S)$ with nonterminal set $N = \{S\}$, terminal set $\Sigma = \{a, b\}$, and productions $P = \{S \to aS, S \to b\}$. The terminal string $aaaab$, for example, is derived by the application of production $S \to aS$ four times and production $S \to b$ once. In terms of relation $\underset{G}{\Rightarrow}$, we write

$$S \underset{G}{\Rightarrow} aS \underset{G}{\Rightarrow} aaS \underset{G}{\Rightarrow} aaaS \underset{G}{\Rightarrow} aaaaS \underset{G}{\Rightarrow} aaaab$$

and

$$S \underset{G}{\overset{+}{\Rightarrow}} aaaab.$$

It is common practice to omit the subscript G when it is clear which grammar is involved in the process. Also, since $\underset{G}{\overset{*}{\Rightarrow}}$ includes $\underset{G}{\overset{+}{\Rightarrow}}$, the former symbol is normally used in general expressions. For example, we will use the notation $S \underset{G}{\overset{*}{\Rightarrow}} x$, or $S \overset{*}{\Rightarrow} x$ for short, to indicate that the terminal string x is derivable from starting symbol S. □

The *language generated by* G, denoted by $L(G)$, is that subset of Σ^* obtained by starting with the nonterminal S and using a finite number of

ISBN 0-201-02930-8/0-201-02931-6, pbk

productions. In set notation,

$$L(G) = \left\{ x \mid x \text{ in } \Sigma^*, S \underset{G}{\overset{*}{\Rightarrow}} x \right\}.$$

Expressing this in another way, we say that a *sentential form* of grammar G is a string over the alphabet V derivable from the starting symbol S. The language $L(G)$ is then the set of sentential forms that consist of terminals only.

Example: Consider the grammar $G_1 = (N, \Sigma, P, S)$ with nonterminal set $\{S\}$, terminal set $\{a, b\}$, and productions $\{S \to aS, S \to b\}$. Deriving strings in $L(G_1)$ in order of increasing length, we have

$S \Rightarrow b$ [using production $S \to b$]

$S \Rightarrow aS \Rightarrow ab$ [using $S \to aS$, then $S \to b$]

$S \Rightarrow aS \Rightarrow aaS \Rightarrow aab$ [using $S \to aS$ twice, then $S \to b$]

$$\vdots$$

Informal inspection of this derivation process shows that the strings in Σ^* derivable by G_1 must have a finite number of a's followed by a single b, so that the language of G_1 is the set

$$L(G_1) = \left\{ x \mid x \text{ in } \{a, b\}^*, S \underset{G_1}{\overset{*}{\Rightarrow}} x \right\}$$

$$= \{ b, ab, aab, aaab, \dots \}$$

$$= \{ x \mid x = a^n b, n \geqslant 0 \}.$$

Suppose the terminals a and b in this grammar are identified with the pattern primitives in Fig. 2.1(a), which are used to form R-L-C (resistor–inductor–capacitor) electrical networks. When concatenation of terminals in the sentences of $L(G_1)$ is interpreted as a physical connection at the junction points of the corresponding primitives, the language represents a class of networks in which any finite number of L-C sections may appear, but there is always exactly one resistor R. Several sample patterns and their representations as sentences in the language are shown in Fig. 2.1(b).   □

Example: Consider the grammar $G_2 = (\{S\}, \{a, b, +, /,(,)\}, P, S)$, which has the production set $\{S \to (S), S \to a, S \to b, S \to S + S, S \to S/S\}$. A sample derivation of a sentence in $L(G_2)$ is

$$S \Rightarrow S/S \Rightarrow a/S \Rightarrow a/(S) \Rightarrow a/(S + S) \Rightarrow a/(a + S) \Rightarrow a/(a + b).$$

ISBN 0-201-02930-8/0-201-02931-6, pbk

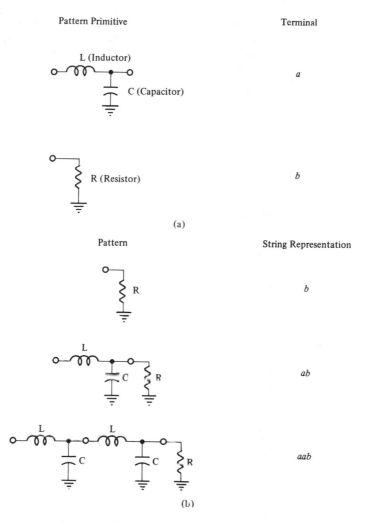

Figure 2.1. Example of pattern grammar terminals and sentences. (a) Terminals and their interpretation as pattern primitives. (b) Sample patterns and their representations as terminal strings.

The sentence $a/(a + b)$ can have any number of semantic interpretations because its "meaning" is determined by what the terminals a, b, $+$, and $/$ represent. One possible interpretation is that the grammar G_2 provides the rules for generating simple arithmetic expressions involving operands a and b, addition $+$, division $/$, and balanced parentheses. A second interpretation is that the terminals a and b represent pattern primitives and the terminals $+$ and $/$ represent ways in which primitive interconnections

ISBN 0-201-02930-8/0-201-02931-6, pbk

can occur or in which spatial relationships can exist. This is illustrated by the terminal interpretation in Fig. 2.2(a), in which a and b represent line segments, / denotes the relationship "above," and + denotes the relationship "below." With this interpretation, the sentence $a/(a + b)$ defines the pattern in Fig. 2.2(b), an uppercase letter I.   □

It is noted that in each successive step in the preceding derivation, only the single leftmost nonterminal in the existing string is rewritten; this is called a *leftmost derivation*. A *rightmost derivation* is produced by rewriting only the rightmost nonterminal in each step. We shall generally take leftmost derivations as the standard way of deriving strings. This in no way restricts the language generated by a grammar; rather, it simply forces derivations to proceed in an orderly fashion.

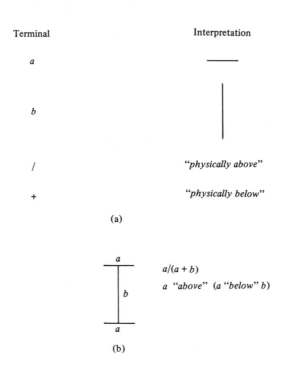

Figure 2.2. Example of pattern grammar terminals and sentences. (a) Terminals and their pattern primitive interpretation. (b) Pattern represented by string $a/(a + b)$.

ISBN 0-201-02930-8/0-201-02931-6, pbk

2.2.2 Types of Grammars

A grammar with no constraints on the form of its productions (other than the general specification of a finite set of string-rewriting rules) is *unrestricted*. Grammars, however, fall into a convenient hierarchy as restrictions on productions are imposed. This *Chomsky hierarchy* is defined as follows:

(1) A *context-sensitive grammar* has productions of the form $\theta A\delta \rightarrow \theta\rho\delta$ for θ and δ in V^*, ρ in V^+, and A in N. The term "context-sensitive" describes the fact that nonterminal A can be rewritten as ρ only when A appears in the context of substrings θ and δ. An equivalent definition is that for any production $\alpha \rightarrow \beta$ the total number of symbols (nonterminals and terminals) in β must not be less than the number in α; that is, $|\alpha| \leqslant |\beta|$.

(2) A *context-free grammar* has productions of the form $A \rightarrow \alpha$ for A in N and α in V^+. The term "context-free" arises from the fact that the nonterminal A may be rewritten as string α regardless of the context in which A appears.

(3) A *regular grammar* has productions of the forms $A \rightarrow aB$ or $A \rightarrow a$ for A and B in N and a in Σ.

These three categories of grammars are also called *types 1, 2,* and *3,* respectively; unrestricted grammars are classified as *type 0*. It is important to note that all regular grammars are context free, all context-free grammars are context sensitive, and all context-sensitive grammars are unrestricted. Of the two grammars defined at the end of the preceding section, G_1 is regular and G_2 is context free. Generally speaking, unrestricted and context-sensitive grammars provide important results in computation theory. Properties of context-free and regular grammars are important in practical applications as well as in language theory, and many grammars used in syntactic pattern analysis are type 2 or type 3.

By convention, a language is classified as the type of the most restricted grammar that generates it. Thus, for grammars G_1 and G_2 in the preceding section,

$$L(G_1) = \{x | x = a^n b, n \geqslant 0\}$$

is regular; but it can be proved that the language $L(G_2)$ cannot be generated by any regular grammar, and it must be classified as context-free.

It is noted that the definitions of context-sensitive, context-free, and regular grammars given here do not permit productions that can be used to derive the empty string λ; therefore, λ cannot be in $L(G)$. If in a specific

ISBN 0-201-02930-8/0-201-02931-6, pbk

instance it is required that λ belong to the language, then a new starting symbol $\hat{S}$ and two new productions, $\hat{S} \rightarrow S$ and $\hat{S} \rightarrow \lambda$, may be introduced, with the second production used only in the derivation of the empty sentence. However, this is rarely required in syntactic pattern processing because the sentences must provide structural descriptions of patterns, and the languages are usually subsets of Σ^+ rather than Σ^*.

Given a language L in alphabet Σ, its *complementary language* is

$$\overline{L} = \Sigma^* - L.$$

It can be shown that context-sensitive languages are *recursive*: given context-sensitive grammar G and string x in Σ^*, there is an algorithm[‡] with inputs G and x that classifies x as a member of $L(G)$ or of $\overline{L}(G)$. Basically, the idea of this algorithm is to enumerate the finite set containing each string θ in V^* such that:

(i) $S \overset{*}{\underset{G}{\Rightarrow}} \theta$ (θ is a sentential form of grammar G), and

(ii) $|\theta| \leqslant |x|$ (the length of θ does not exceed the length of x).

String x must appear in this enumeration if it belongs to $L(G)$; otherwise x belongs to $\overline{L}(G)$. This result holds for context-free and regular grammars, but it does not hold for the unrestricted case. A fundamental result of formal language and computability theory is that there exists no general algorithm that solves this *membership problem* (i.e., "Is x a *member* of $L(G)$?") for arbitrary string x and unrestricted grammar G.

It may be the case, for a given grammar G, that there is at least one sentence in $L(G)$ that has two or more distinct leftmost derivations. If this is the case, G is said to be *ambiguous* because each derivation of a string denotes a different syntactic structure and there is no way to determine which structure should be associated with a given occurrence of the string. It is not possible to develop an algorithm capable of examining an arbitrary context-free grammar and deciding whether it is ambiguous or not; however, most of the grammars used in syntactic pattern processing can be individually analyzed for ambiguity, and many are unambiguous.

There are two forms of productions for a regular grammar. A regular grammar in *right linear form* has all its productions of the types $A \rightarrow aB$ and $A \rightarrow a$ for A and B in N and a in Σ. This form corresponds to the definition of a regular grammar given earlier, but an alternative is to specify *left linear form*, in which all productions are of the types $A \rightarrow Ba$ and $A \rightarrow a$ for nonterminals A and B and terminal a. Left and right linear

---

[‡]An *effective procedure* is a finite sequence of unambiguous, executable instructions for computing a relationship between input(s) and output(s); an effective procedure that terminates in finite time with a finite number of steps having been executed for any input(s) is an *algorithm*.

ISBN 0-201-02930-8/0-201-02931-6, pbk

forms cannot be mixed in a regular grammar; if both forms appear, the grammar is context free.

All finite languages are regular because we can always develop a finite set of regular productions to derive exactly the required strings. In the case that a language generated by a regular grammar is infinite, there is finite iteration or repetition of a substring within the sentences, which gives the set a kind of regularity; for example, in the language

$$L(G_1) = \{x | x = a^n b, n \geqslant 0\},$$

the single-symbol substring a may be iterated an arbitrary number of times, and the regularity of the language is characterized as "a string of a's followed by a single b." In this text, this is called *iterative regularity*.

Every regular language is a special case of a context-free language, but there exist context-free languages that cannot be generated by regular grammars. This increased power of context-free grammars as generators arises from the property of *self-embedding*. A grammar G is self-embedding if there is in N at least one nonterminal A such that:

(i)   for some α, β in V^*, $S \overset{*}{\underset{G}{\Rightarrow}} \alpha A \beta$; and

(ii) for some θ, δ in V^+, $A \overset{*}{\underset{G}{\Rightarrow}} \theta A \delta$.

In other words, A must be able to embed itself in nonempty strings and must appear in at least one string in V^+ derivable from the starting symbol S. If the derivations include $S \overset{*}{\underset{G}{\Rightarrow}} uAy$, $A \overset{*}{\underset{G}{\Rightarrow}} vAx$, and $A \overset{*}{\underset{G}{\Rightarrow}} w$ for u, v, w, x, y in Σ^+, then the language $L(G)$ contains at a minimum all strings of the form $uv^i wx^i y$, $i \geqslant 0$, where v^i denotes i repetitions of substring v and x^i denotes the same number of occurrences of x. (This is an aspect of the so-called $uv^i wx^i y$ theorem. See, e.g., Aho and Ullman [1972].) The following example shows that self-embedding can arise even in simple pattern classes.

Example: Consider the terminals a, b, c, d defining the pattern primitives in Fig. 2.3(a). These directed line segments are the terminals in grammar $G = (\{S, A\}, \{a, b, c, d\}, P, S)$ with productions $\{S \to cA, A \to aAb, A \to d\}$. The language generated by G is

$$L(G) = \{x | x = ca^n db^n, n \geqslant 0\}.$$

$$= \{cd, cadb, caadbb, \dots \}.$$

Some sample patterns from this class are given in Fig. 2.3(b). The self-embedding nonterminal is A, for which $S \overset{*}{\Rightarrow} cA$, $A \overset{*}{\Rightarrow} a^n A b^n$, and $A \overset{*}{\Rightarrow} d$.

ISBN 0-201-02930-8/0-201-02931-6, pbk

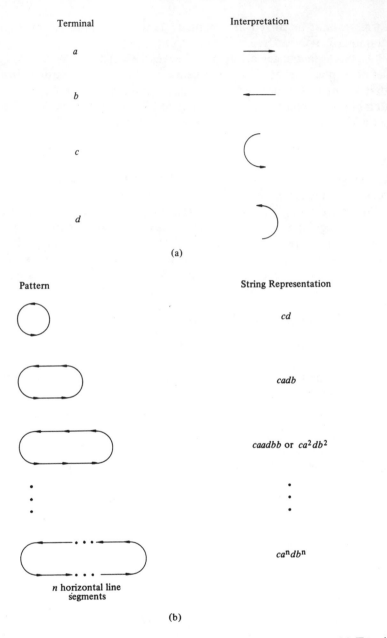

Figure 2.3. Example of terminals and sentences of a pattern grammar. (a) Terminals and their pattern primitive interpretations. (b) Sample patterns and their representations as terminal strings.

ISBN 0-201-02930-8/0-201-02931-6, pbk

Informally, the reader should see that it is impossible to have a regular grammar generating the language in this example because each application of a regular production introduces exactly one terminal into a sentential form. Regular productions are not sufficiently complex to force the number of a's always to balance the number of b's.   □

2.3 EXAMPLES OF PATTERN LANGUAGES AND GRAMMARS

The following two examples are illustrations of pattern grammars. The grammar in the first example is context free and has self-embedding nonterminals. A grammar in the second example may be either regular or context free and may be self-embedding or not, depending on the productions actually selected for a specific application.

2.3.1 Chromosome Grammar

One of the earliest uses of syntactic techniques in pattern processing was the definition by Ledley *et al.* [1965] of a context-free grammar $G = (N, \Sigma, P, S)$ for string descriptions of submedian and telocentric chromosomes. The pattern primitives shown in Fig. 2.4 are the terminals of grammar G. Note that a direction of traversal is associated with three of the segments. The idea here is to represent a chromosome as a string in $\{a, b, c, d, e\}^{+}$ corresponding to a clockwise trace of the chromosome's outline encoded as a series connection of the primitives. This string representation may be formed automatically by an outline scanner or manually. To classify the chromosome, one can try to match the string with a sentence in $L(G)$. If a match is made, the chromosome can be identified as submedian or as telocentric; if a match cannot be made, the chromosome is unidentifiable by this grammar.

The set N of nonterminals is $\{S, S_1, S_2, A, B, C, D, E, F\}$, with S being the starting symbol. The set P of productions consists of these rewriting

ISBN 0-201-02930-8/0-201-02931-6, pbk

Figure 2.4. Primitives of the chromosome grammar.

rules:

$S \rightarrow S_1$	$B \rightarrow e$	$S \rightarrow S_2$	$C \rightarrow bC$
$S_1 \rightarrow AA$	$C \rightarrow Cb$	$S_2 \rightarrow BA$	$C \rightarrow b$
$A \rightarrow CA$	$C \rightarrow d$	$A \rightarrow AC$	$D \rightarrow bD$
$A \rightarrow DE$	$D \rightarrow Db$	$A \rightarrow FD$	$D \rightarrow a$
$B \rightarrow bB$	$E \rightarrow cD$	$B \rightarrow Bb$	$F \rightarrow Dc$

If the first production used in a derivation of a sentence in $L(G)$ is $S \rightarrow S_1$, then that sentence represents a submedian chromosome; if the first production used is $S \rightarrow S_2$, then the sentence represents a telocentric chromosome. Hence, S_1 stands for the class $\langle$submedian$\rangle$ and S_2 stands for the class $\langle$telocentric$\rangle$. The six remaining nonterminals connote physical characteristics of a chromosome's outline, defined as follows:

A means $\langle$armpair$\rangle$;
B means $\langle$bottom$\rangle$;
C means $\langle$side$\rangle$;
D means $\langle$arm$\rangle$;
E means $\langle$rightpart$\rangle$;
F means $\langle$leftpart$\rangle$.

Thus, for instance, the productions $S \rightarrow S_1$ and $S \rightarrow S_2$ indicate specifically that the class of chromosomes described by G consists of two subclasses, the $\langle$submedian$\rangle$ and the $\langle$telocentric$\rangle$. The production $S_1 \rightarrow AA$ reflects the fact that a $\langle$submedian chromosome$\rangle$ is made up of two $\langle$armpair$\rangle$, and the production $S_2 \rightarrow BA$ indicates that a $\langle$telocentric chromosome$\rangle$ consists of a $\langle$bottom$\rangle$ attached to an $\langle$armpair$\rangle$. The four productions for rewriting nonterminal A define four ways in which a portion of an $\langle$armpair$\rangle$ can occur. Note that the rewriting of A reintroduces A in two of those ways; in other words, A is self-embedding and is partially defined by reference to itself. The rewriting of nonterminals B, C, D, E, and F ultimately introduces terminals into the sentential forms. For example, the production $F \rightarrow Dc$ means that a chromosome $\langle$leftpart$\rangle$ consists of an $\langle$arm$\rangle$ attached to a c-type primitive line segment.

An example of the derivation of a submedian chromosome description is the leftmost derivation

$$S \Rightarrow S_1 \Rightarrow AA \Rightarrow ACA \Rightarrow FDCA \Rightarrow DcDCA$$

$$\Rightarrow bDcDCA \Rightarrow bDbcDCA \Rightarrow babcDCA$$

$$\Rightarrow babcbDCA \Rightarrow babcbDbCA \Rightarrow babcbabCA$$

$$\Rightarrow babcbabdA \Rightarrow babcbabdAC \Rightarrow babcbabdDEC$$

$$\Rightarrow babcbabdaEC \Rightarrow babcbabdacDC$$

$$\Rightarrow babcbabdacaC \Rightarrow babcbabdacad.$$

ISBN 0-201-02930-8/0-201-02931-6, pbk

The chromosome represented by this sentence of 12 primitives is shown in Fig. 2.5. An example of a leftmost derivation of a telocentric chromosome string is

$$S \Rightarrow S_2 \Rightarrow BA \Rightarrow eA \Rightarrow eCA \Rightarrow ebA \Rightarrow ebDE$$

$$\Rightarrow ebDbE \Rightarrow ebabE \Rightarrow ebabcD \Rightarrow ebabcbD$$

$$\Rightarrow ebabcdDb \Rightarrow ebabcbab.$$

This chromosome grammar, however, is ambiguous, in part because primitives can be viewed as components of different but adjacent subsections of a chromosome outline. A second leftmost derivation of the sentence *ebabcbab*, distinct from the one just given, is the following:

$$S \Rightarrow S_2 \Rightarrow BA \Rightarrow BbA \Rightarrow ebA \Rightarrow ebDE \Rightarrow ebDbE \Rightarrow ebabE$$

$$\Rightarrow ebabcD \Rightarrow ebabcbD \Rightarrow ebabcbDb \Rightarrow ebabcbab.$$

The chromosome represented by this sentence of eight connected primitives is shown in Fig. 2.6.

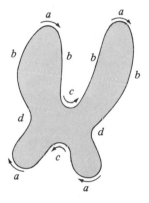

Figure 2.5. Submedian chromosome defined by sentence *babcbabdacad*.

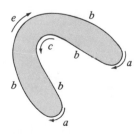

Figure 2.6. Telocentric chromosome defined by sentence *ebabcbab*.

ISBN 0-201-02930-8/0-201-02931-6, pbk

Because of its simplicity and the straightforward interpretation of its terminals, nonterminals, and productions, we shall use the chromosome grammar as an example in several sections later in the book.

2.3.2 Picture Description Languages (PDL)

The chromosome grammar is a context-free grammar whose language describes outlines of two kinds of chromosomes. Since the only operation possible between its pattern primitives is simple "joining" or connectivity at one point, no terminal symbols are needed between primitives to indicate other kinds of connections. In more general cases, however, there may be several possible operations which must be explicitly identified in the appropriate places; furthermore, balanced parentheses may also be required to establish the order in which operations are to be performed. The set of terminals for a grammar of this nature must include the left and right parentheses as well as symbols for the pattern primitives and the operations. The productions must be rules for the generation of well-formed sentences in which the parentheses are always balanced, the operators appear in appropriate locations, and the structure of the pattern class is defined.

Examples of grammars with these general characteristics that have been used successfully in a number of applications are the *picture description grammars* of Shaw [1969, 1970]. A picture description grammar is a context-free generator of a picture description language (PDL). A *picture primitive* in a PDL can be any *n*-dimensional pattern with two distinct connection points, a *head* and a *tail*, as shown in Fig. 2.7 for two-dimensional structures. The nature of the primitives abstracted as these directed line segments can be quite general since there are only two points of definition.

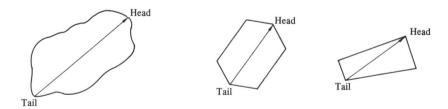

Figure 2.7. Two-dimensional PDL primitives abstracted as directed line segments.

There are four ways of joining a pair of primitives or a pair of primitive structures in PDL. These four binary operations, denoted by $+$, $-$, $\times$, $*$, are defined in Fig. 2.8. At least one of them is included in the terminal

ISBN 0-201-02930-8/0-201-02931-6, pbk

ISBN 0-201-02930-8/0-201-02931-6, pbk

alphabet of any picture description grammar. In addition, two unary operations, denoted by the symbols $\sim$ and $/$, may be applied to single primitives. The symbol $\sim$ is a head–tail reverser; for any primitive a, the primitive $\sim a$ is the same pattern but with the head and tail points reversed. The blanking or superposition operator $/$ allows multiple appearances of the same primitive in a string representation and is used together with labels to cross-reference a primitive or a primitive structure.

A primitive can be geometrically attached to other primitives only at its head or tail. *Blank* or *don't care primitives* may be used to assure connectivity in seemingly disjoint subpatterns. It is also useful at times to consider the *null point primitive*, consisting of a single head–tail point.

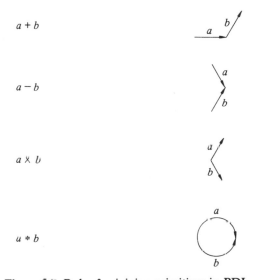

Figure 2.8. Rules for joining primitives in PDL.

Example: As an illustration of the way in which a PDL sentence represents the physical arrangement of a pattern, we will let the set $\{a \nearrow, b \searrow c \rightarrow, d \uparrow \}$ be a specific collection of primitives. The substring $(a + b)$ defines the primitive structure $\wedge$, which itself has a single head and a single tail point.

The substring $((a + b) * c)$ defines the primitive structure $\triangle$, also with well-defined head–tail points.

The substring $(((a + b) * c) + b)$ defines the primitive structure $\triangle$.

Finally, the complete sentence $(a + (((a + b) * c) + b))$ defines the pattern $\triangle$, an uppercase letter A.

There are several additional ways in which variations of the letter A can be represented with these primitives and operations; for instance, the string $(d + (((a + b) * c) + (\sim d))$ is evaluated as follows:

$$(a + b) \quad \text{defines} \quad \text{A};$$

$$((a + b) * c) \quad \text{defines} \quad \triangle;$$

$$(((a + b) * c) + (\sim d)) \quad \text{defines} \quad \triangle;$$

$$(d + (((a + b) * c) + (\sim d))) \quad \text{defines} \quad \text{A}. \qquad \square$$

Example: As an illustration of the use of label designators and the $/$ operator, we consider the primitives in Fig. 2.9. The pattern represented by the string

$$(((b^1 + a) * (((/b^1) + d) + (/b^2))) * ((a + b^2) * c))$$

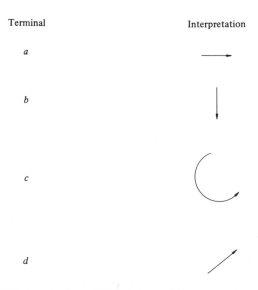

| Terminal | Interpretation |

a

b

c

d

Figure 2.9. PDL terminals and their interpretation as pattern primitives.

ISBN 0-201-02930-8/0-201-02931-6, pbk

is found as follows. Note first that b^1 is a single labeled occurrence of primitive b and b^2 is a second labeled occurrence (string b^2 cannot stand for bb because PDL requires an operator symbol between pattern primitives to establish the way in which the connection is formed). The appearance of the symbol $/$ in front of a primitive indicates that a cross-reference to the primitive will be found elsewhere in the expression; in other words, the primitive is used to construct more than one subpattern.

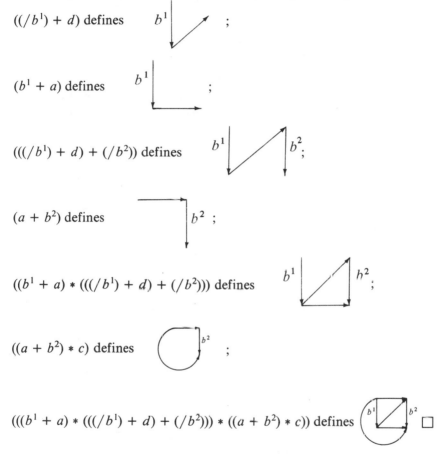

$((/b^1) + d)$ defines b^1 ;

$(b^1 + a)$ defines b^1 ;

$(((/b^1) + d) + (/b^2))$ defines b^1 b^2 ;

$(a + b^2)$ defines b^2 ;

$((b^1 + a) * (((/b^1) + d) + (/b^2)))$ defines b^1 b^2 ;

$((a + b^2) * c)$ defines b^2 ;

$(((b^1 + a) * (((/b^1) + d) + (/b^2))) * ((a + b^2) * c))$ defines b^1 b^2 □

The following rules are observed when a PDL expression is being evaluated:

(i)   Subexpressions within balanced parentheses are evaluated in order from the innermost balanced parentheses outward and from left to right for subexpressions within the same number of parentheses.

ISBN 0-201-02930-8/0-201-02931-6, pbk

(ii)   The appropriate number of connection points must be defined for primitive structures composed of joined primitives. For instance, the structure $(a + b)$ has one head and one tail; but the structure $(a \times b)$ appears to have two heads and one tail, and the structure $(a - b)$ appears to have a head and two tails. The convention is that the tail of the *first* primitive is the tail of the structure and the head of the *second* primitive is the head of the structure. Thus, in $(a \times b)$, the head of b (tail of a) is taken to be the head (tail) of the structure for any further operations.

(iii)   The / operator and label designators are used whenever the same primitive must be a component of substructures developed independently before being connected.

A grammar that generates all PDL expressions for a given set of primitives is $G = (N, \Sigma, P, S)$, for which $N = \{S, SL\}$, $\Sigma = \{+, -, \times, *, \sim, /, (,)\} \cup \{a \mid a$ is a primitive$\} \cup \{l \mid l$ is a label designator$\}$, and the productions are

$$S \rightarrow (S + S) \qquad S \rightarrow (S - S) \qquad S \rightarrow (S \times S)$$
$$S \rightarrow (S * S) \qquad S \rightarrow (\sim S) \qquad S \rightarrow SL$$
$$S \rightarrow (/ SL) \qquad SL \rightarrow (SL + SL) \qquad SL \rightarrow (SL - SL)$$
$$SL \rightarrow (SL \times SL) \qquad SL \rightarrow (SL * SL) \qquad SL \rightarrow (\sim SL)$$
$$SL \rightarrow (/ SL)$$

Also, for each primitive a there is a production $S \rightarrow a$, and for each label designator l there is a production $SL \rightarrow S^l$. For a specific application, of course, we are interested in a subset of, or variations on, these productions to define a pattern class with the appropriate structure.

Example: A PDL grammar G generating four sentences that define four representations of the capital letter A is $G = (\{S, A, B, C, D, E\}, \{a \nearrow, b \searrow, c \longrightarrow, d \uparrow, (,), +, *, \sim\}, P, S)$ with productions

$$S \rightarrow (A + (B)) \qquad A \rightarrow d \qquad A \rightarrow a$$
$$B \rightarrow (C) + D \qquad C \rightarrow E * c$$
$$D \rightarrow b \qquad D \rightarrow (\sim d)$$
$$E \rightarrow (a + b)$$

An example derivation is

$$S \Rightarrow (A + (B)) \Rightarrow (a + (B)) \Rightarrow (a + ((C) + D)) \Rightarrow (a + ((E * c) + D))$$

$$\Rightarrow (a + (((a + b) * c) + D)) \Rightarrow (a + (((a + b) * c) + (\sim d))).$$

ISBN 0-201-02930-8/0-201-02931-6, pbk

ISBN 0-201-02930-8/0-201-02931-6, pbk

This sentence defines the pattern ⟨figure⟩. It can be easily verified that the three additional elements of $L(G)$ are

$$(a + (((a + b) * c) + b)) \quad \text{defining} \quad \text{⟨figure⟩};$$

$$(d + (((a + b) * c) + b)) \quad \text{defining} \quad \text{⟨figure⟩};$$

and

$$(d + (((a + b) * c) + (\sim d))) \quad \text{defining} \quad \text{⟨figure⟩}. \qquad \square$$

A common method for studying the properties of particles in high-energy physics is by the analysis of photographs taken during an experiment conducted in a bubble or spark chamber. For example, in an electron colliding-beam experiment, two beams of electrons are caused to collide to produce electron–electron scattering across a range of angles. The scattering event is recorded on film, and aspects such as the angular distribution of the scattering are of interest. Machine processing is desirable because those photographs that provide important information must be extracted from the large number of photographs taken in a typical experiment. The following example illustrates the use of a PDL for processing pictures of this type.

Example: A negatively charged particle *TM* is injected from the left into a chamber containing a collection *PP* of positively charged particles and under the influence of a magnetic field. The particle *TM* leaves a trail and yields by-products as it interacts with the positive particles, and these are recorded on film. Each photograph contains two additional features: first, a set of registration marks on the chamber, known as "fiducials" and having precisely determined locations, allows accurate measurements of distances and locations; second, information such as the date, photograph number, or experiment number appears in a "data box" at a specific place on the film.

Described in notation similar to that used in conventional physics, the types of reactions defined are the following:

(a) *TM* interaction with *PP*:

$$TM + PP \rightarrow TM + TP$$
$$\rightarrow TM + TP + TN$$
$$\rightarrow TN;$$

(b)   Decay of negatively charged particle TM:

$$TM \rightarrow TM + TN;$$

(c)   Decay of neutral particle TN:

$$TN \rightarrow TM + TP;$$

(d)   Decay of positively charged particle TP:

$$TP \rightarrow TP + TN.$$

The by-products of a reaction can themselves undergo reactions. The number of possible reaction combinations and locations is infinite. The PDL grammar must account for these reactions as well as for the data box and fiducials.

A schematic representation of a typical photograph is shown in Fig. 2.10. The four X's in the corners are the fiducials, and the four small boxes at the top represent the data box items. The particle track primitives are given in Fig. 2.11. Exact matchings of length and curvature of photograph components with all primitives are not required; rather, the *cm*, *cp*, *dm*, and *dp* primitives are used for all negative and positive curves and negative and positive sloped lines, respectively. A dotted line, as in the *en* primitive, stands for a blank or missing line segment of known length. A jagged line, as in the *eh* primitive, denotes a blank "don't care" line segment length. The syntactic description of a photograph is ordered from left to right, beginning at the lower lefthand fiducial, *FI*, which serves as the tail for the remainder of the fiducials *FID*, for the data box *ID*, and for the particle tracks *PT*. The null point primitive, consisting of a single head–tail point, is denoted by ʓ here.

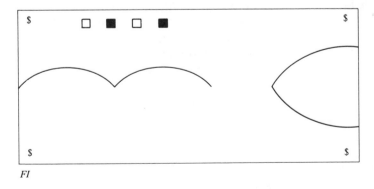

Figure 2.10. Representation of typical detection chamber photograph.

ISBN 0-201-02930-8/0-201-02931-6, pbk

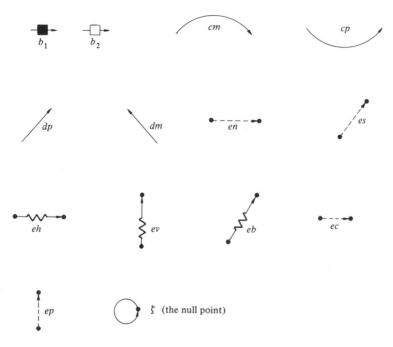

Figure 2.11. PDL primitives for detection chamber photographs. (From Shaw [1969].)

The PDL grammar $G = (N, \Sigma, P, S)$ for the class of photographs in this chamber experiment has the primitives in Fig. 2.11, together with the symbols $X, (,), +, -, \times, *, /, \sim$ as its terminals. The set of nonterminals is $\{S, FI, FID, ID, PT, X, B, TM, MP, MD, TP, TN, PD, P, N\}$, and the productions are the following:

$$S \rightarrow (es + (FI + FID \times (ID \times PT))))$$

$$FI \rightarrow (dp + (dm \times (dp \times (\zeta - dm))))$$

$$FID \rightarrow ((eh + X) + ((ev + X) - (X + eh)))$$

$$PT \rightarrow (ep + TM)$$

$$ID \rightarrow ((eb + B) + ((ec + B) + ((ec + B) + (ec + B))))$$

$$X \rightarrow ((dp \times dm) \times ((\sim dp) \times (\zeta - dm)))$$

ISBN 0-201-02930-8/0-201-02931-6, pbk

$$B \rightarrow b_2 \qquad B \rightarrow b_1$$

$$TM \rightarrow (cm + MD) \qquad TM \rightarrow (cm + MP) \qquad TM \rightarrow cm$$

$$MP \rightarrow (P + ((TM \times TP) \times TN))$$

$$MP \rightarrow (P + TN) \qquad MP \rightarrow (P + (TM \times TP))$$

$$MD \rightarrow (TM \times TN) \qquad MD \rightarrow TM$$

$$TP \rightarrow (cp + PD) \qquad TP \rightarrow cp$$

$$TN \rightarrow (en + (N \times (TM \times TP)))$$

$$PD \rightarrow TP \qquad PD \rightarrow (TP \times TN)$$

$$P \rightarrow \zeta \qquad N \rightarrow \zeta$$

The productions for rewriting nonterminals *S, FI, FID, ID, PT*, and *B* serve to define and to position the fiducials, the data box, and the entry point of the negatively charged particle. The remaining productions and nonterminals describe the reactions characterized by line segments on the photograph. For example, beginning with nonterminal *PT*, we can derive a sample particle trail representation as

$$PT \Rightarrow (ep + TM) \Rightarrow (ep + (cm + MD))$$

$$\Rightarrow (ep + (cm + TM)$$

$$\overset{+}{\Rightarrow} (ep + (cm + (cm + (\zeta + TN)))$$

$$\overset{+}{\Rightarrow} (ep + (cm + (cm + (\zeta + (en + (\zeta + (cm \times cp))))))))$$

This substring derived from nonterminal *PT* defines the primitive structure shown in Fig. 2.12. The derivations of sentences in $L(G)$, of course, must begin with nonterminal *S*. Starting with *S* and applying the productions for *S, FI, FID, B*, and *ID*, then reproducing the foregoing derivation of a substring from *PT*, gives the PDL string description of the sample photograph in Fig. 2.10.   □

ISBN 0-201-02930-8/0-201-02931-6, pbk

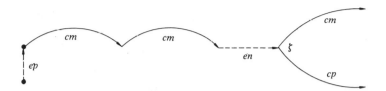

Figure 2.12. PDL structure for particle tracks in detection chamber photograph.

There are certain properties of PDL of which a user should be aware. The only commutative operator is $*$; that is, for any primitive structures S_1 and S_2,

$$S_1 * S_2 = S_2 * S_1.$$

Each of the binary operators is associative. For any structures S_1, S_2, and S_3, and for $\circ$ being one of $\times$, $*$, $-$, $+$,

$$(S_1 \circ (S_2 \circ S_3)) = ((S_1 \circ S_2) \circ S_3)$$

$$= (S_1 \circ S_2 \circ S_3).$$

The reverser operator $\sim$ has the properties that

$$(\sim(S_1 + S_2)) = ((\sim S_2) + (\sim S_1)),$$

$$(\sim(S_1 * S_2)) = ((\sim S_2) * (\sim S_1)),$$

and

$$(\sim(S_1 \times S_2)) = ((\sim S_2) - (\sim S_1)),$$

$$(\sim(S_1 - S_2)) = ((\sim S_2) \times (\sim S_1)).$$

Also, there is involution:

$$(\sim(\sim S)) = (S).$$

The operator $/$ has the properties that

$$(/(/S)) = (/S)$$

and, for $\circ$ in $\{+, -, \times, *\}$,

$$(/(S_1 \circ S_2)) = ((/S_1) \circ (/S_2)).$$

These properties establish the fact that a PDL string representation of a

ISBN 0-201-02930-8/0-201-02931-6, pbk

given pattern generally is not unique. Furthermore, complex patterns might be decomposed into primitives in more than one way, so as to yield even more descriptions as PDL sentences.

2.4 EQUIVALENT CONTEXT-FREE GRAMMARS

Two grammars G_1 and G_2 are *equivalent* if

$$L(G_1) = L(G_2).$$

It is sometimes necessary or desirable to replace a given context-free grammar G_1 by an equivalent context-free grammar G_2 that has certain specific properties. For instance, G_2 might have all its productions in some standard form, have no cycles in its derivations, or have no useless productions and nonterminals.

A number of important transformation techniques for context-free grammars are described next. In each case, one begins with G_1 and obtains an equivalent G_2 that is guaranteed to have the required characteristics. In the following discussion, it is assumed that the context-free grammar $G_1 = (N, \Sigma, P, S)$ is given.

2.4.1 Cycle-Free Grammars

A *cycle* is a derivation of the form $A \overset{+}{\Rightarrow} A$ for A in N. A grammar is *cycle free* if there exists no derivation $A \overset{+}{\Rightarrow} A$ for any nonterminal A. The existence of cycles merely wastes derivation steps and does not add any power to a grammar. A cycle can occur iff there is a set of productions, $A \to B_1, B_1 \to B_2, \ldots, B_{n-1} \to B_n, B_n \to A, n > 0$, involving single non-terminals only; thus, cycles will be eliminated if all productions of the form $A \to B$ are removed.

The transformation removing all productions in which a nonterminal is rewritten as a single nonterminal proceeds in the following way. For a specific nonterminal A, define a set $K(A)$ of nonterminals according to the recursive rules:

(i) $K_0(A) = \{A\}$.
(ii) $K_1(A) = K_0(A) \cup \{B | A \to B$ is a production in $P\}$.
(iii) $K_{i+1}(A) = K_i(A) \cup \{C | B \to C$ is a production in P for some nonterminal B in $K_i(A)\}$ for $i = 1, 2, 3, \ldots$.

When no new nonterminals are added in the construction of $K_{i+1}(A)$ from $K_i(A)$, we have

$$K(A) = K_i(A) = K_{i+1}(A).$$

ISBN 0-201-02930-8/0-201-02931-6, pbk

ISBN 0-201-02930-8/0-201-02931-6, pbk

Each set $K_j(A)$, for $0 \leqslant j$, is exactly that collection of single nonterminals derivable from A in no more than j steps. The set $K(A)$ is exactly that collection of single nonterminals derivable from A; that is, B is in $K(A)$ iff $A \overset{*}{\Rightarrow} B$.

Having determined the set $K(A)$ for each nonterminal A in N, we eliminate all productions of the form $A \rightarrow B$ (and thereby eliminate any cycles) by defining the equivalent grammar $G_2 = (N, \Sigma, \hat{P}, S)$ with productions determined according to the requirement that, for nonterminals A and B, if B is in $K(A)$ and there is a production $B \rightarrow \beta$ in P for which β is *not* a single nonterminal, then a production $A \rightarrow \beta$ is placed in $\hat{P}$.

Three important aspects of this method of constructing G_2 from G_1 are the following:

(i)   If there are n nonterminals in N, then for any nonterminal A, $K(A) = K_i(A)$ for some i, $0 \leqslant i \leqslant (n - 1)$.
(ii) There are no productions of the form $A \rightarrow B$ in $\hat{P}$.
(iii) $L(G_1) = L(G_2)$.

To establish that (i) is true, we note that in the computation of the sequence $K_0(A), K_1(A), \ldots, K_{i-1}(A), K_i(A), \ldots$, there must be at least one nonterminal in $K_i(A)$ that is not in $K_{i-1}(A)$ in order to continue. If ultimately $K(A)$ contains all n nonterminals, and if only one is added at each step, then the sequence $K_0(A), K_1(A), \ldots, K_{n-1}(A)$ must be computed and the index reaches a maximum value of $n - 1$.

It is clear from the construction that no productions of the form $A \rightarrow B$ will be placed in $\hat{P}$. The method of showing that G_2 is equivalent to G_1 is by showing language inclusion in two directions; that is, if each sentence in $L(G_1)$ is also in $L(G_2)$ *and* if each sentence in $L(G_2)$ is also in $L(G_1)$, *then* the two languages are equal. This proof is outlined informally as follows.

To show $L(G_1) \subseteq L(G_2)$, we consider a leftmost derivation of string x in $L(G_1)$. If there are no appearances of productions of the form $A \rightarrow B$ in this G_1 derivation, exactly the same set of productions may be used to derive x in G_2. But if the G_1 derivation is of the form

$$S \overset{*}{\underset{G_1}{\Rightarrow}} yA\theta \overset{+}{\underset{G_1}{\Rightarrow}} yB\theta \underset{G_1}{\Rightarrow} y\beta\theta \overset{*}{\underset{G_1}{\Rightarrow}} x,$$

in which there is a sequence

$$A \overset{+}{\underset{G_1}{\Rightarrow}} B \underset{G_1}{\Rightarrow} \beta$$

for β not in N, then nonterminal B is in $K(A)$. This means that there is a production $A \rightarrow \beta$ in $\hat{P}$ and that there is a shorter G_2 derivation of the

from

$$S \underset{G_2}{\overset{*}{\Rightarrow}} yA\theta \underset{G_2}{\Rightarrow} y\beta\theta \underset{G_2}{\overset{*}{\Rightarrow}} x.$$

Multiple sequences are handled in the same way in G_2. It is concluded that any sentence x in $L(G_1)$ is also in $L(G_2)$.

The proof that any string z from $L(G_2)$ will also be found in $L(G_1)$ is similar. If all productions used to derive z in G_2 are available in P, the sentence has an identical derivation in G_1. But if the G_2 derivation is of the form

$$S \underset{G_2}{\overset{*}{\Rightarrow}} yA\theta \underset{G_2}{\Rightarrow} y\beta\theta \underset{G_2}{\overset{*}{\Rightarrow}} z,$$

where production $A \rightarrow \beta$ is in $\hat{P}$ but not in P, then it must be the case that B is in $K(A)$ and that there is a production $B \rightarrow \beta$ in P. In G_1, therefore, there is the longer derivation

$$S \underset{G_1}{\overset{*}{\Rightarrow}} yA\theta \underset{G_1}{\overset{+}{\Rightarrow}} yB\theta \underset{G_1}{\Rightarrow} y\beta\theta \underset{G_1}{\overset{*}{\Rightarrow}} z.$$

Since this holds for all productions that are in $\hat{P}$ and not in P, we conclude that any z in $L(G_2)$ has a possibly longer derivation in G_1, and is in $L(G_1)$.

These two results taken together show that G_1 and G_2 generate the same language.

In summary, property (i) establishes an upper limit on the number of set computations required to find $K(A)$ for any nonterminal A; property (ii) means there are no cycles in derivations using G_2; and property (iii) states that G_1 and G_2 are equivalent. In the subsequent sections and chapters, we shall generally omit details of proofs of properties like these, which are available in texts devoted to the theory of formal languages.

Example: Consider the grammar $G_1 = (\{S, A, B\}, \{a, b\}, P, S)$ with productions $\{S \rightarrow aSA, S \rightarrow A, A \rightarrow BAb, A \rightarrow B, B \rightarrow aS, B \rightarrow b\}$. $K(S)$ is found as follows:

$$K_0(S) = \{S\}.$$
$$K_1(S) = \{S\} \cup \{A\} = \{S, A\}.$$
$$K_2(S) = \{S, A\} \cup \{A, B\} = \{S, A, B\}.$$
$$K(S) = \{S, A, B\}.$$

$K(A)$ is found as follows:

$$K_0(A) = \{A\}.$$
$$K_1(A) = \{A\} \cup \{B\} = \{A, B\}.$$

ISBN 0-201-02930-8/0-201-02931-6, pbk

$$K_2(A) = \{A, B\} \cup \{B\} = \{A, B\}.$$
$$K(A) = \{A, B\}.$$

$K(B)$ is found as follows:

$$K_0(B) = \{B\}.$$
$$K_1(B) = \{B\} \cup \emptyset = \{B\}.$$
$$K(B) = \{B\}.$$

To obtain the productions of G_2, it is observed first that nonterminal S appears only in $K(S)$, so the production $S \to aSA$ is placed in $\hat{P}$. Next, nonterminal A appears in both $K(S)$ and $K(A)$; therefore, productions $S \to BAb$ and $A \to BAb$ are placed in $\hat{P}$. Finally, nonterminal B is in $K(S)$, $K(A)$, and $K(B)$, so we add to $\hat{P}$ the productions $S \to aS$, $S \to b$, $A \to aS$, $A \to b$, $B \to aS$, and $B \to b$. The equivalent grammar is $G_2 = (\{S,A,B\},\{a,b\},\hat{P},S)$ with nine productions.

It is seen, for example, that the leftmost derivation

$$S \underset{G_1}{\Rightarrow} aSA \underset{G_1}{\Rightarrow} aAA \underset{G_1}{\Rightarrow} aBAbA \underset{G_1}{\Rightarrow} abAbA \underset{G_1}{\Rightarrow} abBbA$$

$$\underset{G_1}{\Rightarrow} abbbA \underset{G_1}{\Rightarrow} abbbB \underset{G_1}{\Rightarrow} abbbb$$

in G_1 can be replaced by the leftmost derivation

$$S \underset{G_2}{\Rightarrow} aSA \underset{G_2}{\Rightarrow} aBAbA \underset{G_2}{\Rightarrow} abAbA \underset{G_2}{\Rightarrow} abbbA \underset{G_2}{\Rightarrow} abbbb$$

in G_2. □

2.4.2 Grammars with No Useless Symbols or Productions

It is possible to eliminate from a given context-free grammar G_1 those nonterminals and associated productions that are useless in derivations of terminal strings. A nonterminal A is *useless* if:

(i) there is no terminal string x such that $A \underset{G_1}{\overset{*}{\Rightarrow}} x$; or

(ii) there is no sentential form $\alpha A\beta$ such that $S \underset{G_1}{\overset{*}{\Rightarrow}} \alpha A\beta$.

In the first case, A derives no terminal string; in the second case, A is not in any sentential form derived from starting symbol S. If A is useless, all productions of the forms $A \to \theta$ for any θ or $B \to \omega A\delta$ for any nonterminal B may be eliminated without affecting $L(G_1)$.

The question whether there is a terminal string derivable from A is the same question as whether $L(G_1)$ is null when A is used as the starting

ISBN 0-201-02930-8/0-201-02931-6, pbk

symbol. In other words, does $G_1 = (N, \Sigma, P, A)$ generate at least one terminal string? The answer is found by constructing a set $J(G_1)$ that contains all and only those nonterminals that do derive at least one terminal string.

Construction proceeds from $J_i(G_1)$ to $J_{i+1}(G_1)$, $0 \leqslant i$, until $J(G_1)$ itself is computed, in the following way:

  (i) $J_0(G_1) = \varnothing$.
  (ii) $J_{i+1}(G_1) = J_i(G_1) \cup \{A | \text{there is a production } A \to \alpha, \alpha \text{ in } (J_i(G_1)$
        $\cup \Sigma)^*\}$ for $i = 0, 1, 2, \ldots$.

The construction terminates when $J_{i+1}(G_1) = J_i(G_1)$, at which point $J(G_1) = J_i(G_1)$. It should be observed that nonterminal A will be placed in $J_1(G_1)$ iff there is a production $A \to x$ for x in Σ^+, so that A derives a terminal string in one step. Nonterminal B will appear in the set $(J_2(G_1) - J_1(G_1))$ iff B derives a terminal string in two steps but not in one step; and, in general, C will be in the set $(J_{i+1}(G_1) - J_i(G_1))$ iff C derives a terminal string in $i + 1$ steps but no fewer than $i + 1$ steps.

If there are n nonterminals, the algorithm will terminate after no more than $n + 1$ calculations; that is, $J(G_1) = J_i(G_1)$ for some $i \leqslant n + 1$. A nonterminal will be in $J(G_1)$ iff it derives at least one terminal string; in particular, starting symbol S is in $J(G_1)$ iff $L(G_1)$ is not null. The transformed, but still equivalent, grammar is $G_2 = (\hat{N}, \Sigma, \hat{P}, S)$, for which $\hat{N} = J(G_1)$ and $\hat{P}$ contains only those productions from P involving elements of $\hat{N}$.

Example: Consider the grammar $G_1 = (\{S, A, B\}, \{a, b\}, P, S)$ with productions $\{S \to aBA, S \to bA, A \to aA, A \to b, B \to aAB\}$. $J(G_1)$ is found as follows:

    $J_0(G_1) = \varnothing$.
    $J_1(G_1) = \{A\}$.
    $J_2(G_1) = \{A\} \cup \{S, A\} = \{S, A\}$.
    $J_3(G_1) = \{S, A\} \cup \{S, A\} = \{S, A\} = J_2(G_1)$.
    $J(G_1) = \{S, A\}$.

S and A both derive at least one terminal string, but B does not. The new grammar is $G_2 = (\{S, A\}, \{a, b\}, \hat{P}, S)$ with productions $\{S \to bA, A \to aA, A \to b\}$. $\square$

A nonterminal A is said to be *inaccessible* if there is no sentential form $\alpha A \beta$ such that $S \overset{*}{\underset{G_1}{\Rightarrow}} \alpha A \beta$. An inaccessible nonterminal is useless even if it derives a terminal string. The set of nonterminals that are *accessible* from

ISBN 0-201-02930-8/0-201-02931-6, pbk

starting symbol S is denoted $R(S)$. Construction of this set proceeds from $R_i(S)$ to $R_{i+1}(S)$, $0 \leqslant i$, until $R(S)$ is itself computed, in the following way:

$R_0(S) = \{S\}$.
$R_{i+1}(S) = R_i(S) \cup \{A | A$ in N, there is a production $B \to \delta A \gamma$ for some B in $R_i(S)\}$ for $i = 0, 1, 2, \ldots$.

The construction halts when $R_{i+1}(S) = R_i(S)$, at which point we have that $R(S) = R_i(S)$. A nonterminal will appear in $R(S)$ iff that nonterminal is in some sentential form derivable from S. No more than $n - 1$ calculations are required; that is, $R(S) = R_i(S)$ for some $i \leqslant n - 1$, where n is the number of nonterminals. The equivalent grammar is $G_2 = (\hat{N}, \Sigma, \hat{P}, S)$, for which $\hat{N} = R(S)$ and $\hat{P}$ contains those productions from P in which only elements of $\hat{N}$ appear on left-hand or right-hand sides.

Example: Consider the grammar $G_1 = (\{S, A, B, C\}, \{a, b\}, P, S)$ with productions $\{S \to aAA, A \to aAb, A \to aCA, B \to b, B \to Aa, C \to b\}$. $R(S)$ is found as follows:

$R(S) = \{S\}$.
$R_1(S) = \{S\} \cup \{A\} = \{S, A\}$.
$R_2(S) = \{S, A\} \cup \{A, C\} = \{S, A, C\}$.
$R_3(S) = \{S, A, C\} \cup \{A, C\} = R_2(S)$.
$R(S) = \{S, A, C\}$.

S, A, and C are accessible from S, but B is not. The new grammar equivalent to G_1 is $G_2 = (\{S, A, C\}, \{a, b\}, \hat{P}, S)$ with productions $\{S \to aAA, A \to aAb, A \to aCA, C \to b\}$. $\square$

In order to eliminate nonterminals that are useless by either criterion, one must first find and remove symbols not deriving a terminal string, then those that are inaccessible. The reader should verify and keep in mind that this order cannot be reversed.

It would also be desirable to reduce the size of a grammar by merging sets of nonterminals that, when used as the starting symbol, derive exactly the same set of terminal strings; that is, we would like to be able to test whether two nonterminals, A and B, are equivalent in the sense of deriving the same set of strings in Σ^+. Unfortunately, it is not possible to develop an algorithm that will perform this test for arbitrary nonterminals in context-free grammars, although it may be done by careful inspection in some specific cases. It will be seen in Chapter 4 that this test can be carried out for regular grammars.

ISBN 0-201-02930-8/0-201-02931-6, pbk

2.4.3.   Grammars with Standard Form Productions

A context-free grammar is in *Chomsky normal form* if each of its productions is either of the form $A \rightarrow BC$ for A, B, C in N or of the form $A \rightarrow a$ for A in N and a in Σ. Given grammar G_1, an equivalent grammar $G_2 = (\hat{N}, \Sigma, \hat{P}, S)$ in Chomsky normal form is obtained in the following way.

First, we examine the productions in P, and place in $\hat{P}$ all productions already of the form $A \rightarrow BC$ or $A \rightarrow a$.

The remaining productions in P must be converted to Chomsky normal form. Each of these remaining productions is of the general form $A \rightarrow \theta_1\theta_2 \ldots \theta_n$, in which each θ_i, $1 \leqslant i \leqslant n$, is either a single terminal or a single nonterminal. Each production $A \rightarrow \theta_1 \ldots \theta_n$ must be replaced by a set of productions

$$A \rightarrow Y_1 Y_{2\ldots n}$$

$$Y_{2\ldots n} \rightarrow Y_2 Y_{3\ldots n}$$

$$Y_{3\ldots n} \rightarrow Y_3 Y_{4\ldots n}$$

$$\vdots$$

$$Y_{n-1, n} \rightarrow Y_{n-1} Y_n$$

in which the subscripted Y's are nonterminals. If θ_i is a nonterminal, we make Y_i equal to θ_i; if θ_i is a terminal, we make Y_i a new nonterminal and introduce a production $Y_i \rightarrow \theta_i$.

The new nonterminals defined in this way become elements of $\hat{N}$; the new Chomsky normal form productions become elements of $\hat{P}$. The resultant grammar is G_2.

Example: Consider the grammar $G_1 = (\{S,A,B\},\{a,b\},P,S)$ with productions $\{S \rightarrow BA, A \rightarrow a, A \rightarrow abABa, B \rightarrow b\}$. In the construction of G_2, the productions $S \rightarrow BA$, $A \rightarrow a$, $B \rightarrow b$ are first placed in $\hat{P}$. The nonterminals S, A, and B are placed in $\hat{N}$.

The remaining production, $A \rightarrow abABa$, is in the form $A \rightarrow \theta_1\theta_2\theta_3\theta_4\theta_5$, in which $\theta_1 = \theta_5 = a$, $\theta_2 = b$, $\theta_3 = A$, and $\theta_4 = B$. It is replaced by the productions

$$A \rightarrow Y_1 Y_{2345}$$

$$Y_{2345} \rightarrow Y_2 Y_{345}$$

$$Y_{345} \rightarrow Y_3 Y_{45}$$

$$Y_{45} \rightarrow Y_4 Y_5$$

ISBN 0-201-02930-8/0-201-02931-6, pbk

Since θ_3 and θ_4 are nonterminals, the last two of these productions become

$$Y_{345} \to A Y_{45}$$

$$Y_{45} \to B Y_5$$

Because $\theta_1 \theta_2$, and θ_5 are terminals, we introduce new productions $Y_1 \to a$, $Y_2 \to b$, and $Y_5 \to a$. The set of new nonterminals added to $\hat{N}$ is $\{ Y_1, Y_{2345}, Y_2, Y_{345}, Y_{45}, Y_5 \}$. The Chomsky normal form productions added to $\hat{P}$ are

$$A \to Y_1 Y_{2345}$$

$$Y_1 \to a$$

$$Y_{2345} \to Y_2 Y_{345}$$

$$Y_2 \to b$$

$$Y_{345} \to A Y_{45}$$

$$Y_{45} \to B Y_5$$

$$Y_5 \to a$$

The G_1 derivation, for example,

$$S \underset{G_1}{\Rightarrow} BA \underset{G_1}{\Rightarrow} bA \underset{G_1}{\Rightarrow} babABa \underset{G_1}{\overset{+}{\Rightarrow}} bababa,$$

becomes

$$S \underset{G_2}{\Rightarrow} BA \underset{G_2}{\overset{+}{\Rightarrow}} bY_1 Y_{2345} \underset{G_2}{\Rightarrow} ba Y_{2345} \underset{G_2}{\Rightarrow} ba Y_2 Y_{345}$$

$$\underset{G_2}{\Rightarrow} bab Y_{345} \underset{G_2}{\Rightarrow} babA Y_{45} \underset{G_2}{\Rightarrow} baba Y_{45} \underset{G_2}{\Rightarrow} babaB Y_5$$

$$\underset{G_2}{\Rightarrow} babab Y_5 \underset{G_2}{\Rightarrow} bababa.$$

in G_2. $\qquad\qquad\qquad\qquad\qquad\qquad\qquad\qquad\qquad\qquad\qquad\qquad\quad\square$

A context-free grammar is in *Greibach normal form* if each of its productions is of the form $A \to a\alpha$ for nonterminal A, terminal a, and α in N^*. Note that α is a finite string of nonterminals that may be λ, the empty string. In Section 4.2.2, Greibach normal form productions will be shown to have a correspondence with a special kind of digital machine for processing the sentences in the language.

ISBN 0-201-02930-8/0-201-02931-6, pbk

To transform grammar G_1 into an equivalent grammar G_2 in Greibach normal form, we must initially describe two ways to modify G_1 that are of interest in their own right. First, let the entire set of productions for rewriting a specific nonterminal A be $\{A \to \gamma_1, A \to \gamma_2, \ldots, A \to \gamma_n\}$; then any production of the form $B \to \delta A \theta$ in G_1 may be replaced by the set of productions $\{B \to \delta\gamma_1\theta, B \to \delta\gamma_2\theta, \ldots, B \to \delta\gamma_n\theta\}$ without changing the language generated. This is true because any use of one of the new productions, say $B \to \delta\gamma_i\theta$, is equivalent to use of the two original productions $B \to \delta A\theta$, $A \to \gamma_i$, and vice versa.

A grammar is called *right-recursive* if there is at least one nonterminal A such that $A \overset{+}{\Rightarrow} \gamma A$ for γ in $(N \cup \Sigma)^*$; similarly, a grammar is *left-recursive* if there is a nonterminal A such that $A \overset{+}{\Rightarrow} A\beta$ for β in $(N \cup \Sigma)^*$. The second modification eliminates immediate left-recursion from grammar G_1.

Let the set of productions for rewriting nonterminal A be grouped into two subsets, the first subset being those productions whose right-hand sides begin with A itself, say $\{A \to A\gamma_1, A \to A\gamma_2, \ldots, A \to A\gamma_n\}$, and the second subset being those productions whose right-hand sides do not begin with A, say $\{A \to \alpha_1, A \to \alpha_2, \ldots, A \to \alpha_m\}$. Observe that the sentential forms derivable from A using these productions are in the set $\{\alpha_1, \ldots, \alpha_m\}\{\gamma_1, \ldots, \gamma_n\}^*$, that is, the sentential forms are a single α followed by a finite concatenation of γ's. Neither this set of sentential forms nor the language actually generated by the grammar is changed if the productions for rewriting A are replaced by the union of the following productions:

(i) $A \to \alpha_1, A \to \alpha_2, \ldots, A \to \alpha_m$
(ii) $A \to \alpha_1 A', A \to \alpha_2 A', \ldots, A \to \alpha_m A'$ for new nonterminal A'
(iii) $A' \to \gamma_1, A' \to \gamma_2, \ldots, A' \to \gamma_n$
(iv) $A' \to \gamma_1 A', A' \to \gamma_2 A', \ldots, A' \to \gamma_n A'$.

With these productions, the sentential forms derivable from A are still in the form of a single one of the α's followed by a finite concatenation of γ's. It is noted that left-recursion involving nonterminal A is eliminated by these new productions.

We can now describe the method for transforming grammar G_1 into an equivalent G_2 in Greibach normal form. Since each context-free grammar has an equivalent grammar in Chomsky normal form, it is assumed without loss of generality that G_1 is already in Chomsky normal form. Let the set of nonterminals be denoted by $\{A_1, A_2, \ldots, A_m\}$ with the subscripts assigned arbitrarily. It is necessary first to adjust the productions so that if $A_i \to A_j\theta$, then $j > i$. We do this adjustment in ascending order for $i = 1, 2, \ldots, m$.

ISBN 0-201-02930-8/0-201-02931-6, pbk

Suppose that this modifying of productions has reached the point that for index k, if $A_i \rightarrow A_j\theta$ is a production, then $j > i$ for all $i \leqslant k$. To extend the modification to nonterminal A_{k+1}, we must replace each production of the form $A_{k+1} \rightarrow A_j\theta$ for $j < k + 1$ by new ones. Specifically, suppose the set of productions rewriting A_j is $\{A_j \rightarrow \delta_1, A_j \rightarrow \delta_2, \ldots, A_j \rightarrow \delta_n\}$; then production $A_{k+1} \rightarrow A_j\theta$ is replaced by the set $\{A_{k+1} \rightarrow \delta_1\theta, \ldots, A_{k+1} \rightarrow \delta_n\theta\}$. These new productions are themselves modified in the same manner for as many times as necessary to obtain ultimately a collection in which each production is of the form $A_{k+1} \rightarrow a\alpha$ or the form $A_{k+1} \rightarrow A_l\alpha$ for a in Σ, α in N^*, and $l \geqslant k + 1$. We retain each production $A_{k+1} \rightarrow a\alpha$ or $A_{k+1} \rightarrow A_l\alpha$ for $l > k + 1$, and we use the procedure to eliminate left-recursion for each production $A_{k+1} \rightarrow A_{k+1}\alpha$ (this introduces the new nonterminal A'_{k+1}).

When all productions in G_1 have been modified in the manner just described, there will be three general forms of productions to consider:

(i) $A_i \rightarrow a\theta$ for a in Σ and θ in $(N \cup \{A'_1, \ldots, A'_m\})^*$;
(ii) $A_i \rightarrow A_j\theta$ for $j > i$; and
(iii) $A'_i \rightarrow \theta$.

As a result of the method used to modify the original productions, each rewriting rule for A_m will be in the first form. Each production for rewriting A_{m-1} will be in either the first form (which *is* Greibach normal form) or the form $A_{m-1} \rightarrow A_m\theta$ (which *becomes* Greibach normal form when the substitution for A_m is done). We continue substituting downward in this fashion for nonterminals A_{m-2} through A_1, then for any new variables $A'_m, \ldots, A'_1$ that were introduced. The final set of productions is in Greibach normal form.

Example: Consider the grammar $G_1 = (\{S, A, B\}, \{a, b\}, P, S)$ with productions $\{S \rightarrow BA, A \rightarrow a, A \rightarrow abABa, B \rightarrow b\}$. A Chomsky normal form equivalent grammar was found in an earlier example in which the nonterminals were $S, A, B, Y_1, Y_{2345}, Y_2, Y_{345}, Y_{45}, Y_5$. For more convenient notation here, we identify these respectively as $A_1, A_2, A_3, A_4, A_5, A_6, A_7, A_8, A_9$; the Chomsky normal form productions are

$$
\begin{array}{ll}
A_1 \rightarrow A_3A_2 & A_6 \rightarrow b \\
A_2 \rightarrow a, A_2 \rightarrow A_4A_5 & A_7 \rightarrow A_2A_8 \\
A_3 \rightarrow b & A_8 \rightarrow A_3A_9 \\
A_4 \rightarrow a & A_9 \rightarrow a \\
A_5 \rightarrow A_6A_7 &
\end{array}
$$

It is seen that the only production for rewriting A_1 is $A_1 \rightarrow A_3A_2$; this does

ISBN 0-201-02930-8/0-201-02931-6, pbk

not require modification because $3 > 1$. Similarly, the productions for nonterminals A_2, A_3, A_4, A_5, and A_6 are not modified at this time.

For the production $A_7 \to A_2A_8$, we first substitute for nonterminal A_2 to obtain the two productions $A_7 \to aA_8$ and $A_7 \to A_4A_5A_8$. The latter becomes $A_7 \to aA_5A_8$ upon substitution for nonterminal A_4.

For the production $A_8 \to A_3A_9$, we substitute for A_3 to obtain $A_8 \to bA_9$. The last of the original productions is $A_9 \to a$ and does not require modification. At this stage, we have the following productions:

$$
\begin{aligned}
&A_1 \to A_3A_2 &\qquad &A_6 \to b \\
&A_2 \to a,\, A_2 \to A_4A_5 &\qquad &A_7 \to aA_8,\, A_7 \to aA_5A_8 \\
&A_3 \to b &\qquad &A_8 \to bA_9 \\
&A_4 \to a &\qquad &A_9 \to a \\
&A_5 \to A_6A_7 &\qquad &
\end{aligned}
$$

Working downward from A_9, we find productions for A_9, A_8, A_7, and A_6 already in Greibach normal form. As the final conversions, substitution for A_6 yields $A_5 \to bA_7$; substitution for A_4 yields $A_2 \to aA_5$; and substitution for A_3 yields $A_1 \to bA_2$.

The equivalent Greibach normal form grammar is $G_2 = (\{A_1, A_2, \ldots, A_9\}, \{a, b\}, \hat{P}, A_1)$ with productions

$$
\begin{aligned}
&A_1 \to bA_2 &\qquad &A_6 \to b \\
&A_2 \to a,\, A_2 \to aA_5 &\qquad &A_7 \to aA_8,\, A_7 \to aA_5A_8 \\
&A_3 \to b &\qquad &A_8 \to bA_9 \\
&A_4 \to a &\qquad &A_9 \to a \\
&A_5 \to bA_7 &\qquad &
\end{aligned}
$$

The productions for A_3, A_4, and A_6 have become useless after this transformation, so nonterminals A_3, A_4, A_6, and their productions can be deleted from G_2 without changing the language generated.

An illustrative derivation using the Chomsky normal form productions is

$$A_1 \Rightarrow A_3A_2 \Rightarrow bA_2 \Rightarrow bA_4A_5 \Rightarrow baA_5$$

$$\Rightarrow baA_6A_7 \Rightarrow babA_7 \Rightarrow babA_2A_8$$

$$\Rightarrow babaA_8 \Rightarrow babaA_3A_9 \Rightarrow bababA_9$$

$$\Rightarrow bababa.$$

The derivation of this same sentence using the Greibach normal form productions is

$$A_1 \Rightarrow bA_2 \Rightarrow baA_5 \Rightarrow babA_7 \Rightarrow babaA_8$$

$$\Rightarrow bababA_9 \Rightarrow bababa.$$ □

ISBN 0-201-02930-8 / 0-201-02931-6, pbk

2.5 SYNTAX-DIRECTED TRANSLATIONS

A string-to-string mapping based on underlying context-free grammars is a *syntax-directed translation*. In syntactic pattern processing, this type of transformation may arise when it is necessary to map the string describing a pattern into a descriptive string in another language, or when a string defining a noisy or corrupted pattern must be replaced by an error-free string for subsequent processing.

Formally, a *translation* from language L_1 over alphabet Σ to language L_2 over alphabet Δ is a relation T in $L_1 \times L_2$. For translation pair (x, y) in T, we say that *input string x is translated to output string y*. Note that a given input may have any number of different output translations.

The formal model of a system producing syntax-directed translations is obtained by assigning a "translation element" to each production in a context-free grammar. A production in a conventional context-free grammar is an item of the form $A \to \alpha$, which indicates that nonterminal A can be replaced by α in the process of deriving a sentence in Σ^+. For the purposes of syntax-directed translation, it is necessary to think of *two* derivations occurring simultaneously. The first of these derivations yields input string x in Σ^+, and the second yields the translation of x as output string y in Δ^+. To produce the second derivation, we merge an input production of the form $A \to \alpha$ for α in $(N \cup \Sigma)^*$ with an output production of the form $A \to \beta$ for β in $(N \cup \Delta)^*$. This results in a *rewriting rule* of the form $A \to \alpha, \beta$ which indicates that nonterminal A can be replaced by α in the input string derivation and, simultaneously, by β in the output string derivation. We say that β is the translation element for α for rewriting rule $A \to \alpha, \beta$.

The mathematical system that produces translations of this nature is a *syntax-directed translation schema*, abbreviated SDTS and defined as a five-tuple $\mathcal{T} = (N, \Sigma, \Delta, R, S)$ where

> N is a finite set of *nonterminals*,
> Σ is a finite *input alphabet* (the terminals of the input strings),
> Δ is a finite *output alphabet* (the terminals of the output strings),
> R is a finite set of *rules*, and
> S in N is the *starting symbol*.

The sets N and $(\Sigma \cup \Delta)$ must be disjoint. The elements of R are rules of the form $A \to \alpha, \beta$ for A in N, α in $(N \cup \Sigma)^*$, and β in $(N \cup \Delta)^*$. In each rule, the nonterminals in α must be a permutation of those in β. Each nonterminal in α has an associated, identical one in β; and matching superscripts are used as needed to indicate which nonterminals are associated if there are repeated ones.

ISBN 0-201-02930-8/0-201-02931-6, pbk

the *output grammar* is $G_o = (N, \Delta, P_o, S)$ where

$$P_o = \{A \to \beta | A \to \alpha, \beta \text{ in } R\}.$$

A *translation form* of $\mathfrak{T}$ is defined as follows:

(i) (S, S) is a form and the S's are associated; and
(ii) if $(\gamma A \omega, \rho A \psi)$ is a form with the A's associated and $A \to \alpha, \beta$ is a rule, then $(\gamma \alpha \omega, \rho \beta \psi)$ is also a form.

We can indicate that the translation form $(\gamma A \omega, \rho A \psi)$ yields the form $(\gamma \alpha \omega, \rho \beta \psi)$ via application of a rule by writing

$$(\gamma A \omega, \rho A \psi) \underset{\mathfrak{T}}{\Rightarrow} (\gamma \alpha \omega, \rho \beta \psi).$$

If translation form (θ, ξ) yields (μ, π) by application of a finite non-zero number of rules, we write

$$(\theta, \xi) \underset{\mathfrak{T}}{\overset{+}{\Rightarrow}} (\mu, \pi).$$

This is the transitive closure of the translation relation $\underset{\mathfrak{T}}{\Rightarrow}$. The reflexive-transitive closure is denoted by $\underset{\mathfrak{T}}{\overset{*}{\Rightarrow}}$. The subscript $\mathfrak{T}$ is usually omitted when the intended SDTS is understood.

The idea of the SDTS is to use G_i for derivations over Σ^* and, simultaneously via the rules, to use G_o for derivations over Δ^*. An input string x in $L(G_i)$ is translated to an output string y in $L(G_o)$ only in the case that (x, y) is a translation form. Since each sentence in $L(G_i)$ has at least one corresponding string in $L(G_o)$, $\mathfrak{T}$ defines a *translation set*

$$\tau(\mathfrak{T}) = \{(x, y) | x \text{ in } L(G_i), y \text{ in } L(G_o), (x, y) \text{ is a translation form}\},$$

which is a relation in $L(G_i) \times L(G_o)$. In general, for a given x there may be more than one y such that (x, y) is in $\tau(\mathfrak{T})$, and the translation process is nondeterministic.

Example: Consider the grammar $G = (\{S\}, \{a, b, +, /, (,)\}, P, S)$ with productions $\{S \to (S), S \to a, S \to b, S \to S + S, S \to S/S\}$. Let this be the input grammar for the SDTS $\mathfrak{T} = (\{S\}, \{a, b, +, /, (,)\}, \{a, b, +, /\}, R, S)$, with the following rules:

$$S \to (S), S \qquad S \to S^1 + S^2, + S^1 S^2$$

$$S \to a, a \qquad S \to S^1/S^2, /S^1 S^2$$

$$S \to b, b$$

ISBN 0-201-02930-8/0-201-02931-6, pbk

Note the use of superscripts in two rules to show which nonterminals are associated. Suppose it is necessary to find a translation of string $x = a/(a + b)$ in $L(G_i)$; that is, find y such that (x, y) is in $\tau(\mathcal{T})$. By direct analogy to a leftmost derivation in G_i, we find this sequence of translation forms:

$$(S, S) \Rightarrow (S^1/S^2, /S^1S^2)$$

$$\Rightarrow (a/S^2, /aS^2)$$

$$\Rightarrow (a/(S^2), /aS^2)$$

$$\Rightarrow (a/(S^1 + S^2), /a + S^1S^2)$$

$$\Rightarrow (a/(a + S^2), /a + aS^2)$$

$$\Rightarrow (a/(a + b), /a + ab).$$

Thus, the input string $a/(a + b)$ is translated into output string $/a + ab$. This SDTS in fact has only one output string for each input string in $L(G_i)$; it translates input strings in infix notation into output strings in prefix notation. (An expression such as $a + b$ is said to be in *infix* notation because the operator $+$ appears between its operands; if the operator precedes its operands, as in $+ab$, the notation is *prefix* form, and if it follows its operands, as in $ab +$, the notation is *suffix* form.)   □

The SDTS in the preceding example is an instance of a *simple schema* in which for each rule $A \rightarrow \alpha, \beta$ the α nonterminals occur in the same order as their associates in β. In a simple schema, the superscripts are not actually needed because the nonterminals are always associated in order left-to-right.

There are two ways in which ambiguity may arise in syntax-directed translation of an input sentence to an output sentence. The first is a direct generalization of the concept of ambiguity in context-free grammars: an SDTS is said to be *ambiguous* if there is at least one translation form (x, y) in $\tau(\mathcal{T})$ such that there are two or more distinct leftmost derivations of x (using the input grammar) that result in the same output string y. Although the same translation occurs, the underlying syntax may vary between ways of producing the translation form (x, y).

The second kind of ambiguity occurs whenever input string x can yield multiple output strings. An SDTS is *ambiguous in translation* if there is at least one sentence x in $L(G_i)$ such that there are at least two translation forms $(x, y_1), (x, y_2)$ in $\tau(\mathcal{T})$ and $y_1 \neq y_2$.

ISBN 0-201-02930-8/0-201-02931-6, pbk

If there are two distinct rules of the forms $A \rightarrow \alpha$, β and $A \rightarrow \alpha$, γ in a schema, then these rules are said to reflect *semantic ambiguity*. The term "semantic" is used here to indicate that the "meaning" of using production $A \rightarrow \alpha$ in the input grammar is unclear because it offers the choice of either $A \rightarrow \beta$ or $A \rightarrow \gamma$ in the output grammar.

Example: Let the set of rules in the SDTS in the preceding example be expanded to include the rules $S \rightarrow SS$, $+ SS$ and $S \rightarrow SS$, $/SS$. Consider the input string ab. This is not a legal infix expression because an operator does not appear between the operands a and b. Two translations produced by $\mathfrak{T}$ are

$$(S, S) \Rightarrow (SS, + SS) \qquad \text{and} \qquad (S, S) \Rightarrow (SS, /SS)$$

$$\Rightarrow (aS, + aS) \qquad\qquad\qquad \Rightarrow (aS, /aS)$$

$$\Rightarrow (ab, + ab) \qquad\qquad\qquad \Rightarrow (ab, /ab)$$

These give as outputs the strings $+ ab$ and $/ab$, in which an operator has been inserted to produce an acceptable string in prefix notation. This SDTS is semantically ambiguous in translation, and it cannot be determined which of the two possible output strings should be the translation of the input sentence ab; however, this is an illustration of a translation that maps an input with an error into a correct sentence. If the output alphabet symbols have the same interpretation as in Fig. 2.2a, the prefix form sentence $+ ab$ would mean "a below b" and would describe the pattern in Fig. 2.13a whereas the sentence $/ab$ would mean "a above b" and would describe the pattern in Fig. 2.13b.   □

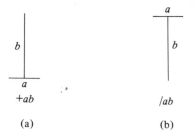

(a)   (b)

Figure 2.13. Corrected pattern grammar strings. (a) Pattern for string $+ ab$. (b) Pattern for string $/ab$.

ISBN 0-201-02930-8/0-201-02931-6, pbk

2.6 DETERMINISTIC, NONDETERMINISTIC, AND STOCHASTIC SYSTEMS

In the study of formal languages, care must be taken to understand the implications of three terms—*deterministic, stochastic*, and *nondeterministic* —that are used to describe the mathematical systems employed. These systems include the grammars and syntax-directed translation schemata already defined as well as other systems to be introduced in following chapters.

The adjective *deterministic* has the same meaning for a mathematical model in language theory as in other areas of computer and information science: at each step a unique action to be taken is indicated, so there are no alternatives to be examined and no choices to be made. As an illustration, suppose the productions in a Greibach normal form grammar G are used to derive a sentence of several symbols that has the terminal a as its first symbol. If there is only one production for rewriting the starting symbol S and introducing this terminal a (i.e., if there is only one production of the form $S \rightarrow a\alpha$), then we are certain which production must be used to begin the derivation. Similarly, if at each step in the derivation the combination of nonterminal to be replaced and terminal to be introduced serves to specify a unique production, the entire derivation proceeds deterministically. If this is true for the derivation of every sentence in $L(G)$, then G is said to be a deterministic grammar.

This kind of system must be distinguished from stochastic and nondeterministic systems; however, stochastic and nondeterministic are not synonymous terms. A *stochastic* system is one in which probabilities are assigned to alternatives in order to indicate likelihood of occurrence or to guide the process of selection. An example is a grammar in which probabilities are assigned to productions to reflect their relative frequency of use in deriving sentences. Stochastic systems are discussed in detail in Chapters 5 and 6. Stochastic considerations are an important part of syntactic pattern recognition because the pattern processing is often carried out in an environment influenced by random factors. This randomness is generally due to measurement noise in scanning a pattern and identifying the primitives or to lack of complete knowledge about the characteristics of the pattern classes.

By contrast, a *nondeterministic* system is one in which a finite number of choices may exist at any given step, yet no probabilities are assigned. This does *not* mean that all alternatives are considered equally likely; rather, it is conveniently assumed that a correct selection is always made. This concept is justified in the study of regular and context-free language theory

ISBN 0-201-02930-8/0-201-02931-6, pbk

for two reasons. First, the systems are finite, and in theory it is decidable within a finite (but possibly very long) time interval whether the selection made at a given step was appropriate; and second, a nondeterministic system associated with a specific language is often less complex than a deterministic system required to accomplish the same task.

There are cases in which construction of a deterministic system is impossible. One example of *inherent nondeterminism* is an ambiguous grammar in which probabilities are not used. Recall that the productions in an ambiguous grammar may be used to derive at least one sentence in at least two distinct ways. If given such a sentence, we have no basis upon which to select one derivation over the others, for each is syntactically correct. When working with this kind of system, language theorists are often unconcerned with probabilities and therefore simply specify that the operation is "nondeterministic."

2.7 CONCLUDING REMARKS

This chapter has introduced some basic definitions and concepts of formal grammars and syntax-directed translation schemata as generators and translators of string languages. Context-free and regular systems, which are types 2 and 3 in the Chomsky hierarchy, are emphasized in subsequent chapters, in which such topics as recognition and stochastic processing are considered.

Some illustrations of the ways in which grammars are used and strings of symbols are interpreted in syntactic pattern recognition are also presented in this chapter. For instance, the chromosome grammar is a context-free grammar developed for one specific application, whereas the PDL grammars attempt to describe syntactically a more general class of patterns.

In the following chapter, we consider several higher-order grammars capable of generating pattern structures that are more general than string representations. Thus, the material in this and the next chapter represent a comprehensive overview of the techniques available for representing syntactic patterns.

REFERENCES

Chomsky [1956] and Chomsky and Miller [1958] established many of the concepts and much of the terminology of phrase-structure string grammars. Additional references for the material in this chapter are the books

ISBN 0-201-02930-8/0-201-02931-6, pbk

by Hopcroft and Ullman [1969], Kain [1972], and Aho and Ullman [1972]. The latter is an especially thorough and careful treatment of topics such as those discussed in Sections 2.4 and 2.5, among many others. The underlying mathematics of applied modern algebra is the subject of a large number of relatively new texts oriented toward computer science and engineering, including, for example, Birkhoff and Bartee [1970] and Stone [1973].

Narasimhan [1962, 1966] is credited with the first explicit statements about formal linguistic techniques in pattern recognition. The chromosome grammar is discussed by Ledley [1965] and Ledley *et al.* [1965]. The picture description languages are introduced and applied by Shaw [1969, 1970].

Survey papers on syntactic pattern recognition include Gonzalez [1972], Fu and Swain [1970], and Miller and Shaw [1968]. Two books by Fu [1974, 1977] discuss various aspects of syntactic pattern recognition theory and applications. The book by Tou and Gonzalez [1974] contains a brief introduction to this topic and compares the syntactic approach to other classical pattern recognition techniques.

ISBN 0-201-02930-8/0-201-02931-6, pbk

HIGHER-DIMENSIONAL GRAMMARS

How long, O simple ones,
will you love being simple?
Proverbs 1:22

3.1 INTRODUCTION

The types of grammars discussed in the previous chapter are best suited for applications where the connectivity of primitives can be expressed in a head-to-tail or other stringlike manner. In this chapter we consider more general approaches to the syntactic pattern recognition problem by allowing more complex primitive description and interconnection capabilities. The grammars required to handle this added complexity are, as should be expected, more difficult to analyze on a formal basis than string grammars.

3.2 TREE GRAMMARS

Of all the grammars discussed in this chapter, tree grammars bear the closest resemblance to the concepts introduced thus far.

3.2.1 Definitions

In this section, definitions and notation useful in the study of tree systems[‡] and their grammars are established. Certain correspondences between different formulations are pointed out without proofs.

[‡]The trees considered here are *not* derivation trees used to represent the derivations of strings; rather, we are concerned with trees themselves as structures of greater complexity than strings.

ISBN 0-201-02930-8 / 0-201-02931-6, pbk

A *tree* T is a finite set of one or more nodes such that

(i)   there is a unique node, designated the *root*; and
(ii) the remaining nodes are partitioned into m disjoint sets $T_1, \ldots, T_m$, each of which in turn is a tree called a *subtree* of T.

The *tree frontier* is the set of nodes at the bottom of a tree (the *leaves*), taken in order from left to right. For example, the tree shown here has root $ and frontier xy.

Generally, two types of information in a tree are important, namely: (1) information about a node stored as a set of words describing the node, and (2) information relating a node to its neighbors stored as a set of pointers to those neighbors. As used in syntactic pattern recognition, the first type of information identifies a pattern primitive, while the second type defines the physical relationship of the primitive to other pattern substructures. The following definitions lead to a formal characterization of grammars for generating tree structures.

A *ranked alphabet* is a pair (X, r) where X is an alphabet and $r \subseteq X \times \{0, 1, 2, \ldots\}$ is a relation between X and the natural numbers $\{0, 1, 2, \ldots\}$. A common interpretation of a rank n of an element is that it denotes a function of n arguments. For example, in conventional arithmetic, the symbol $-$ has rank 2 for subtraction (a binary function of two arguments) and rank 1 for taking the additive inverse of a number (a unary function of one argument). When used in trees, the rank of a node defines the number of direct offspring of the node. It is convenient to denote the set of ranks that symbol x may exhibit by $r(x)$; thus, if x can assume ranks $r_1, \ldots, r_n$, we write $r(x) = \{r_1, \ldots, r_n\}$. Formally, this means that the ranks of the elements of alphabet X are to be specified by a function r from X to finite subsets of the natural numbers.

As an example, consider the tree shown, and let $X = \{\$, x, y, z\}$. In this case each symbol has a single rank value, $r(\$) = \{2\}, r(z) = \{1\}$, $r(x) = r(y) = \{0\}$, which equals the number of offspring of each symbol used in the tree. Note that all leaves have rank 0 and therefore define "functions of 0 arguments."

The attractiveness of tree structures in syntactic pattern recognition is their ability to describe pattern primitives with multiple/connectivity characteristics via nodes with more than one offspring. To exploit this power in

ISBN 0-201-02930-8/0-201-02931-6, pbk

a rigorous way, tree grammars are defined as generalizations of string grammars. It will also be seen that there is a correspondence between trees and strings in a context-free language.

A *tree grammar* is defined as a four-tuple $G_t = (V, r, P, S)$ where $V = N \cup \Sigma$ is the grammar alphabet (nonterminals and terminals); (V, r) a ranked alphabet; productions in P are of the form $T_i \to T_j$, where T_i and T_j are trees; and S in T_V is a finite set of "starting trees," where T_V denotes the set of trees with nodes labeled by elements in V.

By analogy with string grammars, we write

$$T_{\mathrm{I}} \overset{a}{\underset{G_t}{\Rightarrow}} T_{\mathrm{II}}$$

("T_{II} is derived from T_{I} at node a") in G_t if (1) there is a production $T_i \to T_j$; and (2) T_i is a subtree of T_{I} at node a that, when replaced by T_j, yields tree T_{II}. Similarly, we write $T_{\mathrm{I}} \underset{G_t}{\Rightarrow} T_{\mathrm{II}}$ (or $T_{\mathrm{I}} \Rightarrow T_{\mathrm{II}}$ for short) if (1) there is a sequence of trees T_{I} with node a, T_1 with node $a_1, \ldots, T_n$ with node a_n, where T_{I} is in S; and (2)

$$T_{\mathrm{I}} \overset{a}{\underset{G_t}{\Rightarrow}} T_1, \; T_1 \overset{a_1}{\underset{G_t}{\Rightarrow}} T_2, \ldots, T_n \overset{a_n}{\underset{G_t}{\Rightarrow}} T_{\mathrm{II}}.$$

Just as a conventional formal language is defined as a subset of Σ^*, so the language generated by a tree grammar is a collection of trees in which only terminals appear at the nodes. In most syntactic pattern recognition problems, S is a set of single-node trees; that is, $S \subseteq N$. Often, S is a single starting nonterminal.

The *language generated by* G_t is the set of trees

$$L(G_t) = \left\{ T \,|\, T \text{ in } T_\Sigma, \; T_i \underset{G_t}{\Rightarrow} T \text{ for some } T_i \text{ in } S \right\}$$

where T_Σ is the set of trees with nodes in Σ.

There is a correspondence between strings in a context-free language and trees generated by a tree grammar. This becomes clear when one considers strings with parentheses, as follows. Let $G = (N, \Sigma, P, S)$ be a conventional context-free grammar, and assume that the left and right parentheses are not in Σ; then its *structural description grammar* is $G' = (N, \Sigma \cup \{(,)\}, P', S)$ where there is in P' a production of the form $A \to (\alpha)$ for each production $A \to \alpha$ in P. For each derivation in G, there is a corresponding derivation in G' that inserts balanced parentheses and thereby indicates the order of productions. If symbols in Σ are interpreted as operators with an established hierarchy, there is a one-to-one correspon-

ISBN 0-201-02930-8/0-201-02931-6, pbk

dence between parenthesized expressions and expressions without parentheses, but in Polish suffix or prefix forms. These forms are identifiable directly with tree representations.

Example: As an illustration, consider the grammar $G = (\{S, A\}, \{\$, z, x, y\}, S, P)$ with productions $S \rightarrow \$AA, A \rightarrow zA, A \rightarrow x, A \rightarrow y$. There is in G a derivation

$$S \Rightarrow \$AA \Rightarrow \$zAA \Rightarrow \$zxA \Rightarrow \$zxy.$$

In the parenthesized grammar G', the corresponding derivation is

$$S \Rightarrow (\$AA) \Rightarrow (\$(zA)A) \Rightarrow (\$(z(x))A) \Rightarrow (\$(z(x))(y))$$

and this expression in prefix form, $\$zxy$, has a direct correspondence with the tree

where we used the fact that $r(\$) = \{2\}, r(z) = \{1\}, r(x) = r(y) = \{0\}$. □

3.2.2 Expansive Tree Grammars

A tree grammar is in *expansive form* if all its productions are of the form

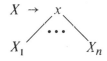

for $X, X_1, X_2, \ldots, X_n$ in N, x in Σ, and n in $r(x)$. An expansive production may be expressed in the prefix string form, $X \rightarrow xX_1 \ldots X_n$, which is seen to be in Greibach normal form. The requirement that n be in $r(x)$ means that symbol x with rank n must have exactly n offspring in a tree or, equivalently, that x stands for a function of n arguments when the prefix forms are used.

ISBN 0-201-02930-8/0-201-02931-6, pbk

Example: An expansive tree grammar for the example given in the previous section is $G_t = (\{S, A\}, r, P, S)$, with productions and rankings:

$S \rightarrow$
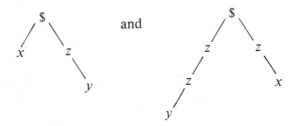
$\qquad r(\$) = \{2\}$

$A \rightarrow z$
$\qquad \qquad r(z) = \{1\}$

$\qquad A$

$A \rightarrow x \qquad\qquad\qquad r(x) = \{0\}$

$A \rightarrow y \qquad\qquad\qquad r(y) = \{0\}$

This grammar generates a denumerably infinite tree language that includes the trees

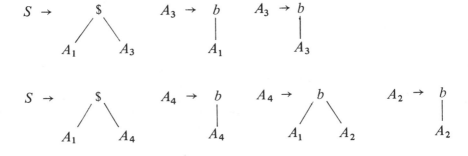

and

with prefix string forms $\$xzy$ and $\$zzyzx$, respectively. $\qquad\qquad\square$

Example: The following grammar generates the letters *C, E, AND F:*
$G_t = (V, r, P, S)$, where $N = \{S, A_1, A_2, A_3, A_4, A_5\}$ and $\Sigma = \{\$, a, b\}$. The productions are

$S \rightarrow \qquad\$ \qquad A_3 \rightarrow b \qquad A_3 \rightarrow b$

$\quad A_1 \qquad A_3 \qquad\quad A_1 \qquad\qquad A_3$

$S \rightarrow \qquad\$ \qquad A_4 \rightarrow b \qquad A_4 \rightarrow \quad b \qquad A_2 \rightarrow b$

$\quad A_1 \qquad A_4 \qquad\quad A_4 \qquad\quad A_1 \qquad A_2 \qquad\qquad A_2$

ISBN 0-201-02930-8/0-201-02931-6, pbk

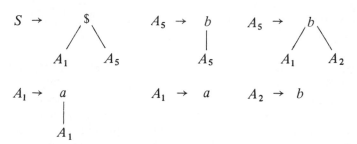

The alphabet V is the union of N and Σ, and the ranking functions in this case are $r(\$) = 2$, $r(a) = \{1, 0\}$, $r(b) = \{2, 1, 0\}$. The primitives a and b are given the following interpretation:

$$a: \rightarrow \text{(in the range of } \pm 45°)$$
$$b: \downarrow \text{(in the range from } 225° \text{ to } 315°)$$

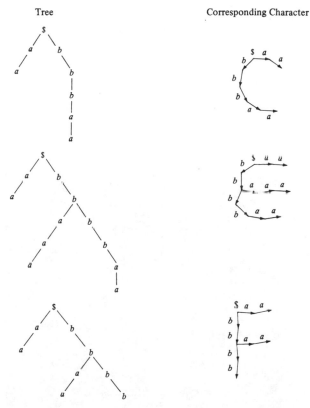

Figure 3.1. Character generation using a tree grammar.

ISBN 0-201-02930-8/0-201-02931-6, pbk

It is also assumed that the lengths of a and b are the same. Figure 3.1 shows some trees generated by G_t and their corresponding patterns.   □

Example: Another interesting application of tree grammars is found in the description of photographs from bubble chamber events. These photographs arise from experiments in high-energy physics in which a beam of particles of known properties is directed onto a target of known nuclei. A typical event consists of tracks of secondary particles emanating from the point of collision, such as the example shown in Fig. 3.2. The incoming tracks are the horizontal parallel lines. Note the natural tree structure of the event which took place toward the middle of the photograph.

Interest in pattern recognition techniques for this particular application is motivated by the fact that a typical experiment will produce hundreds of thousands of photographs, many of which do not contain events of interest. Examining and categorizing these photographs is a tedious and time-consuming task for a human interpreter, thus creating a need for automatic processing algorithms.

As an example of syntactic processing, the grammar $G_t = (V, r, P, S)$ generates trees that represent events typical of those found in a hydrogen bubble chamber as a result of incoming particle streams that are positively charged. In this case, $N = \{S, A, B\}$, $\Sigma = \{a, b\}$, and the primitives a and b are interpreted as follows:

$$a: \ \rightsquigarrow \text{convex arc}$$
$$b: \ \rightsquigarrow \text{concave arc}$$

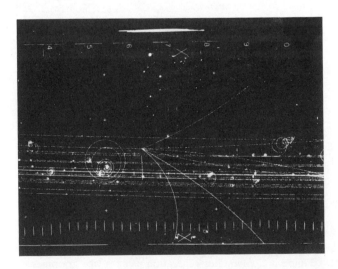

Figure 3.2. A bubble chamber photograph. (From Fu and Bhargava [1973].)

ISBN 0-201-02930-8/0-201-02931-6, pbk

The productions in P are

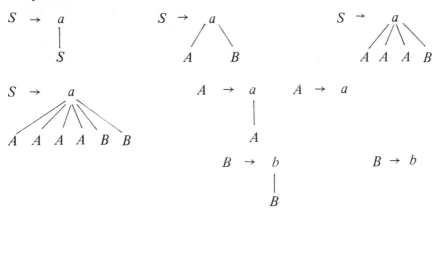

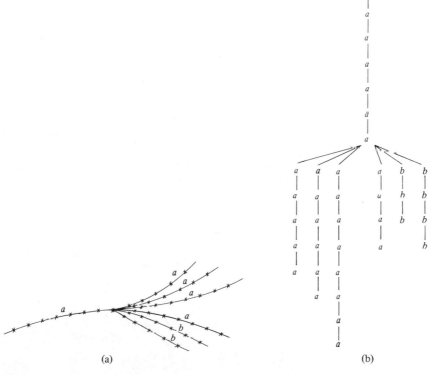

ISBN 0-201-02930-8/0-201-02931-6, pbk

Figure 3.3. (a) Coded event from Fig. 3.2. (b) Corresponding tree representation. (From Fu and Bhargava [1973].)

The rankings are $r(a) = \{0, 1, 2, 4, 6\}$ and $r(b) = \{0, 1\}$. The branching productions represent the number of tracks emanating from a collision, which occur in pairs and usually do not exceed six.

Figure 3.3(a) shows the event in Fig. 3.2 segmented into convex and concave sections, and Fig. 3.3(b) shows the corresponding tree representation. It is easily verified that this tree can be generated by G_t.   □

3.3 WEB GRAMMARS

Webs are undirected, labeled graphs. When used to represent syntactic structures, webs allow pattern descriptions at a level considerably more general than that afforded by string or tree formalisms.

3.3.1 Some Concepts from Graph Theory

A *graph* $H = (Q, W)$ is a finite nonempty set Q of *points* together with a set W of *unordered* pairs of distinct points of Q. Each pair $x = (a, b)$ of points in W is called an *edge*[‡] of H and x is said to *join* a and b. The points (a, b) are said to be *adjacent* (or *neighboring*) *points*; point a and edge x are *incident* with each other, as are b and x. If two distinct edges x and y are incident with a common point, then they are *adjacent edges*. The *degree* of a point in a graph is the number of edges incident with it. A graph with p points and q edges is called a (p, q) graph. The $(1, 0)$ graph is often called the *trivial graph*.

It is customary to represent a graph by a diagram and to refer to this diagram as a graph. An example is shown in Fig. 3.4. In this simple graph points a and b are adjacent, as are points b and c; points a and c, however, are not. Similarly, edges x and y are adjacent, but x and z are not.

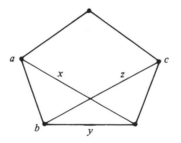

Figure 3.4. A simple graph.

[‡]In addition to (point, edge), one often finds in the literature the terms (point, line), (vertex, edge), (node, arc), (junction, branch), as well as other combinations of these terms.

ISBN 0-201-02930-8/0-201-02931-6, pbk

Figure 3.5. A graph and two of its subgraphs.

Although edges x and z intersect in the diagram, their intersection is *not* a point of the graph.

The preceding definition of a graph does not permit a *loop*, that is, an edge joining a point to itself. A graph in which no loops are allowed but more than one edge can join two points is called a *multigraph*; these edges are called *multiple edges*. If both loops and multiple edges are allowed, we have a *pseudograph*.

A *subgraph* of H is a graph with all of its points and edges in H (Fig. 3.5). If H_1 is a subgraph of H, then H is a *supergraph* of H_1. A *spanning subgraph* is a subgraph containing all the points of H. The removal of a point a of H results in the subgraph $H - a$ of H consisting of all points of H except a and all edges not incident with a. The removal of an edge x from H yields the spanning subgraph $H - x$ containing all edges of H except x.

A *walk* of a graph H is an alternating sequence of points and edges, $a_0, x_1, a_1, x_2, \ldots, a_{n-1}, x_n, a_n$, beginning and ending with points, in which each edge is incident with the two points immediately preceding and following it. This walk *joins* points a_0 and a_n. The walk is *closed* if $a_0 = a_n$ and is *open* otherwise. If a walk is closed, then it is a *cycle*, provided its n points are distinct and $n \geqslant 3$. A graph without cycles is called *acyclic*. For example, a *tree* is a connected acyclic graph.

A *directed graph* $H = (Q, R)$ is a set of Q of points together with an irreflexive relation R in $Q \times Q$. As before, the elements of R are called the *edges* of H. When shown diagrammatically, the ordering of a directed graph is represented by showing the edges as directed line segments. An example is shown in Fig. 3.6. In this case $R = \{(p, q), (q, r), (r, p), (r, s)\}$. By definition, a directed graph cannot have loops or multiple edges.

ISBN 0-201-02930-8/0-201-02931-6, pbk

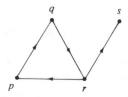

Figure 3.6. A directed graph.

Let V be a set of symbols. A graph is *point labeled* (or simply *labeled*) if all its points are assigned symbols from V. Similarly, a graph is *edge labeled* if all its edges are labeled with symbols from V. Finally, we define a *web* as an undirected, point-labeled graph. Some examples of webs are shown in Fig. 3.7.

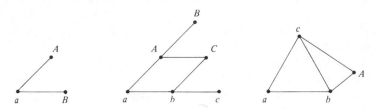

Figure 3.7. Some simple webs.

3.3.2 Web Grammars

In a conventional phrase-structure string grammar, rewriting rules of the form $\alpha \to \beta$ are used to replace one string by another. Such a rule is completely specified by specifying strings α and β; any string $\gamma\alpha\psi$ that contains α as a substring can be immediately rewritten as $\gamma\beta\psi$. Similarly, the productions of expansive tree grammars are interpreted without difficulty. The definition of rewriting rules involving webs, however, is more complicated. Thus, if we want to replace a subweb α of the web ω by another subweb β, it is necessary to specify how to *embed* β in ω in place of α. An important requirement in the definition of an embedding rule is that it must not depend on the "host web" ω because we want to be able to replace α by β in any web containing α as a subweb. A procedure for doing this is given below.

Let V be a set of labels and let N_α and N_β be the sets of nodes of webs α and β, respectively. Based on the concepts above, we define a *web rewriting rule* as a triple (α, β, f), where f is a function from $N_\beta \times N_\alpha$ into 2^V (the set of subsets of labels). This function specifies the embedding of β in place of α; that is, it specifies how to join the nodes of β to the neighbors of each node of the *removed* subweb α. Since f is a function from the set of ordered pairs $N_\beta \times N_\alpha$, its argument is of the form (n, m) for n in N_β and m in N_α. The values of $f(n, m)$ specify the allowed connections of n to the neighbors of m. For example, $f(B, A) = \{C, D\}$ means "join node B (in β) to the neighbors of node A (in α) whose labels are either C or D." We will omit the embedding specification and instead use the term "normal" to denote situations in which there is no ambiguity in a rewriting rule.

ISBN 0-201-02930-8/0-201-02931-6, pbk

A *web grammar* is defined as a four-tuple $G_w = (N, \Sigma, P, S)$ where N is the nonterminal alphabet, Σ is the terminal alphabet, P a set of web productions, and S is the starting symbol. As usual, S is in N, and $V = N \cup \Sigma$ is the alphabet of the grammar.

Example: Consider the web grammar $G_w = (N, \Sigma, P, S)$ where $N = \{S\}$, $\Sigma = \{a, b, c\}$, and P is the following set of triples:

$$\alpha \qquad\qquad \beta \qquad\qquad\qquad f$$

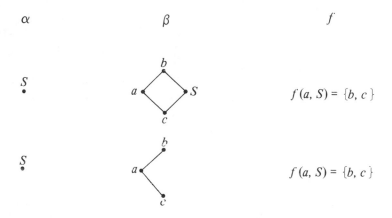

The embeddings specified by f indicate that α (i.e., $\overset{S}{\cdot}$) can be rewritten as β by connecting node a of β to the neighbors of S labeled b or c. It is noted that the embedding rules describe replacements during the course of a derivation in which the subweb to be rewritten is embedded in a host web. The only exception to the foregoing rules is in the beginning of a derivation, since the initial host web is a single point without neighbors. This trivial case, however, is completely unambiguous and thus presents no difficulties. Situations involving more complex starting webs require embedding rules that specify the allowed connections to these webs.

It is easily verified that this web grammar produces patterns of the form

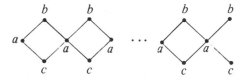

$$\square$$

The foregoing definition of a web grammar is somewhat analogous to that of an unrestricted string grammar and, as such, is too broad to be of

ISBN 0-201-02930-8/0-201-02931-6, pbk

much practical use. As in the case of string grammars, however, it is possible to define restricted types of web grammars by limiting the generality of the productions.

We shall call a web rewriting rule (α, β, f) *context sensitive* if there exists a nonterminal point A of α such that $\alpha - A$ is a subweb of β. In this case the rule rewrites only a single point of α, no matter how complex α is. If α contains a single point, we will call (α, β, f) a *context-free* rule. It is noted that this is a special case of a context-sensitive rule, since $\alpha - A$ is empty when α contains a single point. By representing strings as webs (e.g., the string $aAbc$ ... may be expressed as the web $a \rightarrow A \rightarrow b \rightarrow c$ ...) it is easily shown that these rewriting rules are analogous to context-sensitive and context-free string productions, as defined in Chapter 2.

If the terminal vocabulary of a web grammar consists of a single symbol, every point of every web generated by the grammar will have the same label. In this case we can ignore the labels and identify the webs by their underlying graphs. This special type of web grammar is sometimes referred to as a *graph grammar*.

3.3.3 Some Examples

The following examples of context-free and context-sensitive web grammars should clarify the definitions given in the previous section.

Trees

A context-free web grammar for generating trees with a single node label is $G_w = (N, \Sigma, P, S)$ where $N = \{S\}$, $\Sigma = \{a\}$, and P is the set of triples:

α	β	f
S	$S\_\_\_S$	$f(S, S) = \{S, a\}$
S	a	normal

The first embedding rule indicates that α (i.e., S) may be replaced by $(S\_\_\_S)$ by connecting a node labeled S in β to the neighbors of α labeled either S or a. Since the webs are not directed, it does not matter which end of β is connected to the host web.

ISBN 0-201-02930-8/0-201-02931-6, pbk

The trees shown next are sample generations of this grammar. Since all terminal labels are the same, they can be omitted, so that in reality we are dealing with a graph grammar.

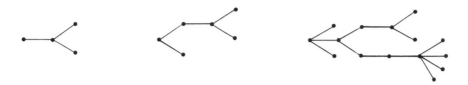

To generate the third structure, for example, we begin by applying the first production three times. This yields

where all replacements of S in the segments $\overset{.}{S}\underline{\quad\quad}\overset{.}{S}$ were carried out on the left node. Application of the second production to three of the nodes yields

The nonterminal node can be expanded by two applications of the first production, that is,

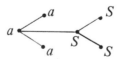

By continuing in this manner, replacing all nonterminals by terminals, and deleting the label a, we would obtain the third tree structure shown above.

□

ISBN 0-201-02930-8/0-201-02931-6, pbk

Series–parallel graphs

Consider the context-sensitive graph grammar $G_w = (N, \Sigma, P, S)$ where $N = \{A, B, C, D, E, S\}$, $\Sigma = \{a\}$, and P is the following set of triples:

	α	β	f

(1) S

$A \quad\quad B$

$f(A, S) = \{a\}$

(2) B

$A \quad\quad B$

$f(A, B) = \{A, a\}$

(3) B

$f(A, B) = \{A, a\}$

(4) C
         |
         a

$f(a, C) = \{A, a\}$
$f(a, a) = \{A, a\}$

(5) C
         |
         a

$f(a, C) = \{A, a\}$
$f(a, a) = \{A, a\}$

(6) $A|B|C$ $\qquad$ a $\qquad\qquad\qquad\qquad$ normal

This grammar generates graph structures that consist of an arbitrary number of series and parallel sections. The parallel segments are separated by at least one series element, and all structures begin and end with at least

ISBN 0-201-02930-8/0-201-02931-6, pbk

one such element. Two simple derivations are as follows:

As in the previous example, the single terminal *a* has been omitted from the final patterns.   □

Geometrical figures

The following context-sensitive web grammar generates some simple geometrical figures: $G_w = (N, \Sigma, P, S)$ where $N = \{S, A, B, C, D\}$, $\Sigma = \{a, b, c\}$, and P is the following set of triples:

	α	β	ƒ
		A	normal
(1)	S	$\begin{vmatrix} A \\ \| \\ a \end{vmatrix}$	
(2)	$\begin{matrix} A \\ \| \\ a \end{matrix}$	$\begin{matrix} b\text{——}A \\ \| \quad\ \| \\ a\text{——}a \end{matrix}$	$f(b, A) = \{b, a\}$ $f(a, a) = $ normal
(3)	$b\text{——}A$	$\begin{matrix} b\text{——}A \\ \| \quad\ \| \\ b\text{——}a \end{matrix}$	$f(a, A) = \{b, a\}$ $f(b, b) = $ normal
(4)	$\begin{matrix} A \\ \| \\ a \end{matrix}$	$\begin{matrix} b\text{——}b \\ \| \quad\ \| \\ a\text{——}B \end{matrix}$	$f(b, A) = \{b, a\}$ $f(a, a) = $ normal

ISBN 0-201-02930-8/0-201-02931-6, pbk

$$\alpha \qquad\qquad\qquad \beta \qquad\qquad\qquad f$$

(5)

$a \underline{\hspace{1cm}} B$

$f(b, B) = \{b, a\}$
$f(a, a) = \text{normal}$

(6)

b
$|$
B

$f(a, B) = \{b, a\}$
$f(b, b) = \text{normal}$

(7) A b normal

(8) B a normal

As an example, consider the following derivation:

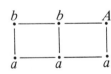

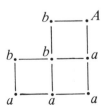

ISBN 0-201-02930-8 / 0-201-02931-6, pbk

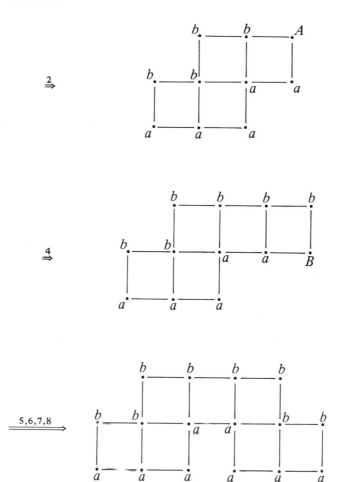

As in our earlier discussions, we write $\theta \Rightarrow \gamma$ (or $\theta \Rightarrow \gamma$ for short) to indicate that γ is derivable from θ by using productions from the set P in G_w.

It is noted that the patterns generated by this grammar consist of sets of stacked square structures. The patterns shown above represent a subset of $L(G_w)$ characterized by the property that no diagonal connections exist between nodes. It is also of interest to note that G_w only generates structures in which the upper edges are labeled with b's and the lower edges with a's. □

ISBN 0-201-02930-8/0-201-02931-6, pbk

3.4 PLEX GRAMMARS

As an additional example of higher-dimensional syntactic patterns we consider in this section structures having an arbitrary number n of attaching points for joining to other symbols. A structure of this type is called an *n attaching-point entity* (NAPE). Structures formed by interconnecting such entities are called *plex structures*.[‡] These structures are quite general in nature and include strings, trees, and webs as subcases.

3.4.1 Formulation

A *plex grammar* is a six-tuple $G_p = (N, \Sigma, P, S, I, i_0)$ where

N is a finite nonempty set of NAPEs called the *nonterminal vocabulary*;

Σ is a finite nonempty set of NAPEs called the *terminal vocabulary*;
P is a finite set of *productions* or *replacement rules*;
S in N is a special NAPE called the *initial* NAPE;
I is a finite set of symbols called *identifiers*; and
i_0 in I is a special identifier called the *null identifier*.

As usual, we require that $\Sigma \cap N = \varnothing$. We also assume in this case that $I \cap (\Sigma \cup N) = \varnothing$. The symbols of I are used to identify the attaching points of NAPEs. Every attaching point of a NAPE has an identifier in I, and no two attaching points of the same NAPE have the same identifier. The null identifier i_0 serves as a place marker and is not associated with any attaching points. Interconnections of NAPEs can only be made through the specified attaching points; "imaginary" connections using the null identifier are not permitted. A set of NAPEs is said to be *connected* if a path exists between any two NAPEs in the set.

As in the grammars previously discussed, several types of plex grammars may be defined by imposing restrictions on the production rules. An *unrestricted plex grammar* has productions of the form

$$\psi \Gamma_\psi \Delta_\psi \rightarrow \omega \Gamma_\omega \Delta_\omega$$

where ψ is called the *left-side component list*; ω the *right-side component list*; Γ_ψ the *left-side joint list*; Γ_ω the *right-side joint list*; Δ_ψ the *left-side tie-point list*; and Δ_ω the *right-side tie-point list*.

The component lists are strings of the form $\psi = a_1 a_2 \ldots a_i \ldots a_m$ and $\omega = b_1 b_2 \ldots b_j \ldots b_n$, where a_i and b_j are single NAPEs called *components*; ψ and ω list and provide an ordering for the groups of connected NAPEs that comprise the respective component lists. The connection of

---

[‡]The word "plex" is derived from the word "plexus," meaning an interwoven arrangement of parts.

ISBN 0-201-02930-8/0-201-02931-6, pbk

attaching points of two or more NAPEs forms a *joint*, and Γ_ψ and Γ_ω specify the way in which the NAPEs of their respective component lists interconnect. The joint lists, which are unordered, are divided into *fields* that specify which attaching points of which NAPEs connect at each joint. Exactly one field is required per joint. The lengths of the fields for the left and right sides of a production are given by $l(\psi)$ and $l(\omega)$, respectively, where l denotes the length of its string argument. An entry i_k in the jth position of a field indicates that attaching point i_k of the jth element (i.e., NAPE) of the component list preceding Γ connects at the joint associated with that field. If the jth NAPE is not involved in that particular joint, the null identifier appears in the jth position of the field.

The component and joint lists $\psi\Gamma_\psi$ and $\omega\Gamma_\omega$, when taken as pairs, define the structures involved in a rewriting rule. These structures attach to the remainder of the plex at a finite number of joints called *tie points*. The tie-point lists Δ_ψ and Δ_ω give the correspondence between these external connections for the left and right sides of a production. The tie-point lists are also divided into fields, with exactly one field specifying each tie point. Since the number of tie points for the left and right sides of a production must be the same, the number of fields in each tie-point list is the same. Moreover, the tie-point lists are ordered, with the kth field on the left corresponding to the kth field on the right.

Example: Before proceeding, let us clarify the preceding definitions with a simple example. Consider a plex production of the form

$$A(1, 2, 3) \rightarrow bc(41)(10, 20, 30)$$

where A is a single nonterminal NAPE and b and c are terminal NAPEs describing the structures

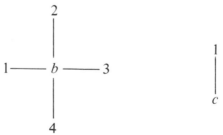

In this case,

$$\psi = A, \qquad\qquad \omega = bc,$$

$$\Gamma_\psi = \phi \qquad\qquad \Gamma_\omega = (41),$$

$$\Delta_\psi = (1, 2, 3), \qquad \Delta_\omega = (10, 20, 30).$$

Γ_ψ is not needed because ψ consists of a single NAPE. The right-side joint list indicates that the joint labeled 4 in the first NAPE of ω connects to the joint labeled 1 in the second. There is only one joint specified, so only one field is required in Γ_ω. When the production is applied, A is rewritten as the structure

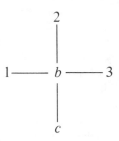

The left-side tie-point list, $\Delta_\psi = (1, 2, 3)$, has three fields; they indicate that A can be connected to a plex at any of the points labeled 1, 2, or 3. The right-side tie-point list also has three fields, but each field contains two identifiers corresponding to tie points in the two structures of ω. Letting 0 represent the null identifier, we see that $\Delta_\omega = (10, 20, 30)$ indicates that b can be connected to a plex at any of the points labeled 1, 2, or 3, and that c is not involved in any of the connections. This production is considered again in the next section in a more complete illustration. $\square$

The following restrictions are placed on all plex productions in order to avoid ambiguity:

1. A NAPE cannot connect to itself. In other words, a NAPE appearing more than once in a component list refers to distinct occurrences of the same structure.

2. No interconnections between the NAPEs in the component definition lists other than those specified in the joint lists can exist.

3. Every attaching point of every NAPE in the left (right) side of a production must either connect to another NAPE in the left (right) side or be one of the tie points. It follows that every attaching point of every NAPE in the left (right) side must be referenced in at least one field of the left (right) side of a plex production.

The general definition of an unrestricted plex grammar given above is too broad to be of much practical use, just as, analogously, there is limited use for string grammars in which arbitrary rewriting rules are allowed. Plex grammars are further classified according to the forms of their rewriting rules.

ISBN 0-201-02930-8/0-201-02931-6, pbk

A *context-sensitive* plex grammar has rewriting rules of the form

$$A\psi_1\Gamma_{\psi_1}\Gamma_{A\psi_1}\Delta_A \rightarrow \chi\psi_1\Gamma_\chi\Gamma_{\psi_1}\Gamma_{\chi\psi_1}\Delta_\chi$$

where A is a single NAPE and χ and ψ_1 are arbitrary lists of NAPEs. It is assumed that χ is not null. The other modifiers in the production rule have a meaning similar to the ones described before:

Γ_{ψ_1} is a joint list whose fields describe the interconnection of the NAPEs listed in ψ_1;

Γ_χ is a joint list whose fields describe the interconnection of the NAPEs listed in χ;

$\Gamma_{A\psi_1}$ is a joint list whose fields give the interconnection of A and the components of ψ_1 by listing the joints connecting A to the structure $\psi_1\Gamma_{\psi_1}$;

$\Gamma_{\chi\psi_1}$ is a joint list whose fields give the interconnection of the structures $\chi\Gamma_\chi$ and $\psi_1\Gamma_{\psi_1}$.

Δ_A and Δ_χ are the tie-point lists that give the correspondence between the attaching points of A and the tie points of $\chi\Gamma_\chi$.

The foregoing rewriting rule indicates that a NAPE A can be replaced by the subplex $\chi\Gamma_\chi$, provided that A is embedded in the substructure specified by $\psi_1\Gamma_{\psi_1}$. Although rules of this type represent a considerable limitation when compared to unrestricted plex productions, they still are of limited use. As will be seen in what follows, context-free rules are much simpler to define and, at the same time, are capable of generating plex structures of adequate complexity.

If ψ_1 is empty in the foregoing rule, we obtain the *context-free* plex production

$$A\Delta_A \rightarrow \chi\Gamma_\chi\Delta_\chi$$

which states that a single NAPE A, appearing in any context, can be replaced by the subplex given by $\chi\Gamma_\chi$. Context-free plex grammars and languages, which are obtained by using only productions of this type, are illustrated in detail in the following section.

3.4.2 Some Examples

In the following illustrations of context-free plex grammars, positive integers are used as identifiers, with 0 being reserved for the null identifier i_0. Parentheses are used to enclose the fields of Γ and Δ; distinct fields are separated by commas, and empty fields are denoted by ( ). In order to clarify the notation, NAPE names are enclosed by brackets of the form $\langle \; \rangle$.

ISBN 0-201-02930-8/0-201-02931-6, pbk

Letters

The following plex grammar generates patterns for the letters A and H:
$G_p = (N, \Sigma, P, S, I, i_0)$ where

$$N = \{\langle A\rangle, \langle H\rangle, \langle SIDE\rangle, \langle LETTER\rangle\}, \qquad \Sigma = \{\langle SL\rangle\},$$

$$S = \langle LETTER\rangle, \qquad\qquad\qquad\qquad I = \{0, 1, 2\},$$

$$i_0 = 0,$$

and P:

$$\langle LETTER\rangle \to \langle A\rangle | \langle H\rangle$$

$$\langle A\rangle \to \langle SIDE\rangle\langle SIDE\rangle\langle SL\rangle(110, 201, 022)(\ )$$

$$\langle H\rangle \to \langle SIDE\rangle\langle SIDE\rangle\langle SL\rangle(201, 022)(\ )$$

$$\langle SIDE\rangle(1, 2) \to \langle SL\rangle\langle SL\rangle(21)(10, 21)$$

The only terminal NAPE in this grammar is $\langle SL\rangle$; it represents a straight line segment defined without regard to orientation, and with attaching points denoted by identifiers 1 and 2 at each end. All the other NAPEs are nonterminals.

The fourth production indicates that $\langle SIDE\rangle$ is composed of two $\langle SL\rangle$s. In this case $\Delta_A = (1, 2)$, $\Delta_x = (10, 21)$, and $\Gamma_x = (21)$. The interpretation of these lists is as before. Thus, Δ_A indicates that $\langle SIDE\rangle$ is connected to the rest of the plex at points labeled 1 and 2. The first field of Δ_x, 10, indicates that point 1 of the first $\langle SL\rangle$ connects to the rest of the plex, while the second $\langle SL\rangle$ is not involved in that connection. The connection is made at the point corresponding to point 1 in $\langle SIDE\rangle$, as indicated by the first entry in Δ_A. The other field of Δ_x, 21, indicates that point 2 of the first $\langle SL\rangle$ and point 1 of the second connect to the plex at the point corresponding to 2 in $\langle SIDE\rangle$. Since $\Gamma_x = (2, 1)$, point 2 of the first $\langle SL\rangle$ is connected to point 1 of the second. Graphically, this production may be interpreted as follows:

It is noted that point 2 of the second (bottom) $\langle SL\rangle$ is not shown because it is not used for any connections, and that we denote the junction of the

ISBN 0-201-02930-8/0-201-02931-6, pbk

two $\langle SL \rangle$s by the label 2 in $\langle SIDE \rangle$. It is equally valid to call the junction 1 (or any other symbol), as long as this is taken into account in Δ_A.

The third production corresponds to construction of the letter H by connecting two $\langle SIDE \rangle$s and one $\langle SL \rangle$ according to the fields 201 and 022 of Γ_X; that is,

Note that only two fields corresponding to the two connections are required: field 201 indicates one connection made between point 2 of the first $\langle SIDE \rangle$ and point 1 of $\langle SL \rangle$, with the second $\langle SIDE \rangle$ not being involved. Field 022 describes a similar situation involving the second $\langle SIDE \rangle$ and the other point of $\langle SL \rangle$. No tie-point lists are specified because the structure created by this production is "final" and does not connect to any other plex.

The second production generates a letter A as follows:

Since three connections are involved in this production, Γ contains three fields. As in the case of H, no tie-point lists are specified.

Finally, the first production simply allows us to rewrite the starting symbol $\langle LETTER \rangle$ as either $\langle A \rangle$ or $\langle H \rangle$. $\qquad\square$

Natural rubber molecules

The grammar given in the previous example is capable of generating only two patterns. By contrast, a plex grammar that can generate a structure of arbitrary length is $G_p = (N, \Sigma, P, S, I, i_0)$, with

$N = \{\langle CH \rangle, \langle CH_2 \rangle, \langle CH_3 \rangle, \langle SECTION \rangle, \langle CHAIN \rangle\}$, $\Sigma = \{\langle C \rangle, \langle H \rangle\}$,

$S = \langle CHAIN \rangle$, $\qquad\qquad\qquad\qquad\qquad I = \{0, 1, 2, 3, 4\}$,

$i_0 = 0$,

ISBN 0-201-02930-8/0-201-02931-6, pbk

and productions

$$\langle CHAIN \rangle (1, 3) \rightarrow \langle SECTION \rangle \langle CHAIN \rangle (31)(10, 03)|$$

$$\langle SECTION \rangle ( )(1, 3)$$

$$\langle SECTION \rangle (1, 3) \rightarrow \langle CH_2 \rangle \langle C \rangle \langle CH_3 \rangle \langle CH \rangle \langle CH_2 \rangle (31000,$$

$$02100, 03020, 04010, 00031)(10000, 00003)$$

$$\langle CH_3 \rangle (1) \rightarrow \langle CH_2 \rangle \langle H \rangle (31)(10)$$

$$\langle CH_2 \rangle (1, 3) \rightarrow \langle CH \rangle \langle H \rangle (21)(10, 30)$$

$$\langle CH \rangle (1, 2, 3) \rightarrow \langle C \rangle \langle H \rangle (41)(10, 20, 30)$$

The terminal NAPEs $\langle C \rangle$ and $\langle H \rangle$ represent, respectively, a carbon atom with four attaching points and a hydrogen atom with one attaching point. These structures are of the form

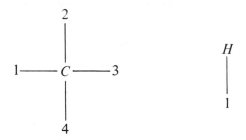

The last production indicates that nonterminal $\langle CH \rangle$, which has three attaching points, can be replaced by a structure composed of $\langle C \rangle$ and $\langle H \rangle$. This structure is formed by connecting point 4 of $\langle C \rangle$ to point 1 of $\langle H \rangle$. Connections of the entity $\langle C \rangle \langle H \rangle (41)$ are made through points 1, 2, and 3 of $\langle C \rangle$, with $\langle H \rangle$ not being involved, as indicated by the tie-point list (10, 20, 30). The graphical interpretation of this production is

ISBN 0-201-02930-8/0-201-02931-6, pbk

Nonterminal NAPEs $\langle CH_2 \rangle$ and $\langle CH_3 \rangle$ are similarly interpreted as follows:

$$
\langle CH_2 \rangle \rightarrow 1 \!\!-\!\! \overset{\displaystyle H}{\underset{\displaystyle H}{\overset{|}{\underset{|}{C}}}} \!\!-\!\! 3
$$

$$
\langle CH_3 \rangle \rightarrow 1 \!\!-\!\! \overset{\displaystyle H}{\underset{\displaystyle H}{\overset{|}{\underset{|}{C}}}} \!\!-\!\! H
$$

The composition of $\langle SECTION \rangle$ is a bit more complicated. As indicated by the second production, this NAPE is formed by connecting point 3 of $\langle CH_2 \rangle$ to point 1 of $\langle C \rangle$, point 2 of $\langle C \rangle$ to point 1 of $\langle CH_3 \rangle$, point 3 of $\langle C \rangle$ to point 2 of $\langle CH \rangle$, point 4 of $\langle C \rangle$ to point 1 of $\langle CH \rangle$, and point 3 of $\langle CH \rangle$ to point 1 of $\langle CH_2 \rangle$; in other words,

$$
\langle SECTION \rangle \rightarrow 1 - \overset{H}{\underset{H}{C}} - \overset{H-\overset{II}{C}-H}{\underset{H}{C}} = \overset{}{\underset{H}{C}} - \overset{H}{\underset{II}{C}} - 3
$$

The dual lines indicate the connections of points 3 and 4 of $\langle C \rangle$ to points 2 and 1 of $\langle CH \rangle$. The tie points of $\langle SECTION \rangle$ are the end points 1 and 3 of the overall structure.

The first production introduces iterative regularity and can be used to generate any number of connected $\langle SECTION \rangle$s. In other words, this production yields structures of the form shown in Fig. 3.8. □

ISBN 0-201-02930-8/0-201-02931-6, pbk

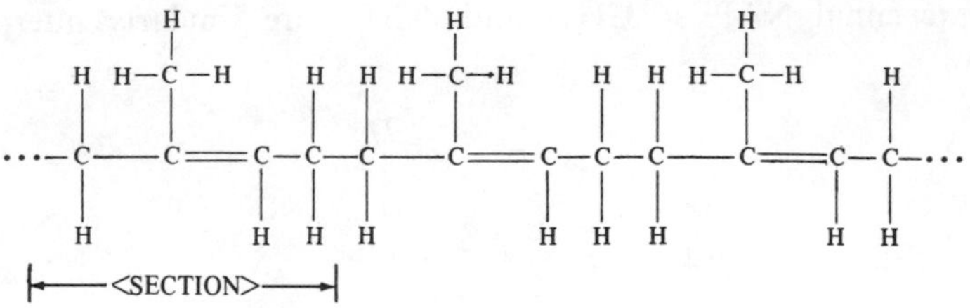

Figure 3.8. Natural rubber molecule structure generated by a context-free plex grammar. (From Feder [1971].)

Shift registers

As a final illustration, let us consider a plex grammar for generating shift registers of arbitrary length: $G_p = (N, \Sigma, P, S, I, i_0)$, with

$$N = \{\langle \text{SHFT STGE}\rangle, \langle \text{SHFT RGSTR}\rangle\}, \quad \Sigma = \{\langle \text{FF}\rangle, \langle \text{A}\rangle, \langle \text{D}\rangle\},$$

$$S = \langle \text{SHFT RGSTR}\rangle, \qquad\qquad\qquad I = \{0, 1, 2, 3, 4, 5\},$$

$$i_0 = 0,$$

and productions

$$\langle \text{SHFT RGSTR}\rangle(1, 2, 3, 4, 5) \rightarrow \langle \text{SHFT STGE}\rangle\langle \text{SHFT RGSTR}\rangle$$

$$(41, 52, 33)(10, 20, 33, 04, 05)$$

$$\langle \text{SHFT STGE}\rangle(\ )(1, 2, 3, 4, 5)$$

$$\langle \text{SHFT STGE}\rangle(1, 2, 3, 4, 5) \rightarrow \langle \text{FF}\rangle\langle \text{A}\rangle\langle \text{A}\rangle\langle \text{D}\rangle\langle \text{D}\rangle$$

$$(31000, 40100, 02200, 03010, 00301)$$

$$(10000, 20000, 02200, 00020, 00002)$$

The terminal NAPEs in this grammar correspond to flip-flops, AND gates, and delay lines:

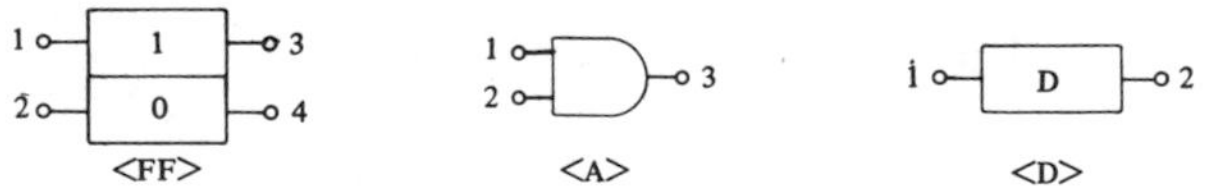

ISBN 0-201-02930-8/0-201-02931-6, pbk

The second production generates one shift register stage by connecting point 3 of ⟨FF⟩ to point 1 of ⟨A⟩, point 4 of ⟨FF⟩ to point 1 of a second ⟨A⟩, points 2 of the two ⟨A⟩s, point 3 of the first ⟨A⟩ to point 1 of a ⟨D⟩, and point 3 of the second ⟨A⟩ to point 1 of a another ⟨D⟩. These connections yield the structure

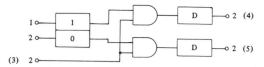

The numbers in parentheses are renamings of the tie-points to avoid ambiguous connections.

As in the previous example, the first production introduces iterative regularity and can be used to generate any number of connected stages. The form of these structures is illustrated in Fig. 3.9.

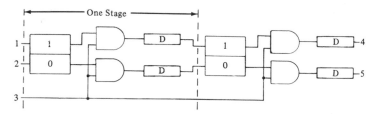

Figure 3.9. Two stages of a shift register generated by a context-free plex grammar. (From Feder [1971].)

3.5 SHAPE GRAMMARS

The grammars discussed thus far generate sentences that, through proper definition of the primitives, represent patterns of some class. In this section, we consider grammars that generate patterns directly. A grammar of this type, called a *shape grammar*, is defined as a four-tuple $G_h = (N, \Sigma, R, I)$ for which

> N is a finite set of nonterminal shape elements called *markers*,
> Σ a finite set of pattern primitives called *terminal shape elements*,
> R a finite set of replacement shape rules given as a binary relation with elements (θ, ψ), and
> I the initial shape containing element θ such that (θ, ψ) is in R.

A shape grammar is similar to a string grammar. It is required that N and Σ be disjoint. A rule (θ, ψ) in R is written $\theta \rightarrow \psi$ to indicate that the replacement of left-hand shape θ by right-hand shape ψ is allowed. To generate shapes, one begins with I and applies rules in R according to the following specifications:

1.　Locate a part of the current shape that has a one-to-one correspondence with θ in a rule $\theta \rightarrow \psi$. There must be an exact correspondence between the terminals and markers in θ and the terminals and markers in the part of the current shape to be replaced.

2.　Find the geometric transformations necessary to make θ identical to this part of the current shape. These transformations may be adjustment of scales, rotations, translations, or formation of mirror images.

3.　Apply the *same* set of transformations to shape element ψ in rule $\theta \rightarrow \psi$.

4.　Replace the part of the shape by the transformed version of ψ.

We write $\alpha \overset{*}{\underset{G_h}{\Rightarrow}} \beta$ iff shape β is derivable from shape α by a finite number of rules. It is noted that this method of using a rule for replacement resembles the use of a production in a string grammar; however, the provision for geometric transformations is necessary because shapes or figures are directly generated by G_h. Rules are applied until no more replacements are possible. The *language of a shape grammar* G_h is the set of derivable shapes that contain only terminal elements:

$$L(G_h) = \{ x | x \text{ consist of shapes in } \Sigma \text{ only, } x \text{ is derivable from}$$

$$I \text{ using geometric transformations on rules in } R \}$$

$$= \{ x | x \text{ consists of terminals only, } I \overset{*}{\underset{G_h}{\Rightarrow}} x \}.$$

Expressing this in another way, we say that any shape of terminals and markers derivable from initial shape I by the method above is a *sentential shape* of G_h. The language $L(G_h)$ is the set of sentential shapes consisting only of terminals.

Two types of shape grammars are defined by placing restrictions on the forms of the rules. A *nonerasing shape grammar* is one in which, for each rule $\theta \rightarrow \psi$, all terminal elements in θ appear identically in ψ. In the generation of shapes with a nonerasing grammar, once a terminal is introduced into a sentential shape, it cannot be deleted or erased.

A *unimarker shape grammar* is a special kind of nonerasing grammar in which:

1.　the initial shape I contains exactly one marker;

ISBN 0-201-02930-8/0-201-02931-6, pbk

2. The left-hand side of each rule contains exactly one marker; and
3. the right-hand side of each rule contains either one marker or no marker.

Each sentential shape generated by a unimarker grammar contains either a single marker or no marker at all.

Example: The following shape grammar generates structures resembling snowflakes: $G_h = (N, \Sigma, R, I)$, with

$$N = \{ \; \circ \; \}, \qquad \Sigma = \{ \; \text{—} \; \},$$

initial shape I,

and five rules,

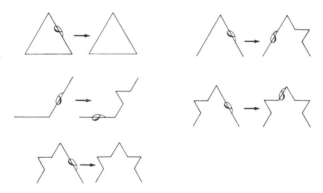

An illustrative derivation applying the sequence of rules 2, 2, 5 yields a simple, symmetric pattern:

It is noted that $\curvearrowright$ identifies the correspondence between the left side of a production rule and the subshape being replaced. For instance, in order to derive the third shape from the second, it is necessary to rotate the left side of rule 2 so that it will line up with the proper substructure in the second shape. A rotation is also required on the left side of rule 5 to generate the fourth shape from the third. A more elaborate snowflake form is obtained by the rule sequence 2, 2, 4, 3, 2, 3, 2, 3, 2, 3, 2, 3, 2, 3, 5:

The language $L(G_h)$ is countably infinite. Its elements are well formed, balanced shapes, as indicated by the two samples derived above. G_h is a unimarker grammar.   □

3.6 CONCLUDING REMARKS

The grammars presented in this chapter are representative generalizations of string grammars. The principal advantage of higher-dimensional grammars is their capability for expressing syntactic relationships at a level considerably more complex than that afforded by string representations. The disadvantage inherent in the added complexity of higher-dimensional grammars is their relative lack of a formal theoretical background. Tree grammars are perhaps the best compromise between string grammars and more general formalisms, such as web or plex grammars. In terms of syntactic pattern recognition, the theory of tree grammars has been developed to a reasonably practical level. This will become evident in Chapters 4 and 6 when we discuss recognition and learning models based on tree representations of pattern classes.

ISBN 0-201-02930-8/0-201-02931-6, pbk

REFERENCES

Interest in tree grammars as generating systems may be traced to the work of Brainerd [1967, 1969]. Additional references on this topic are Fu and Bhargava [1973], and Gonzalez and Thomason [1974].

The material on graph theory presented in Section 3.3.1 is based on the book by Harary [1969]. Web grammars were first introduced by Pfaltz and Rosenfeld [1969]. Additional references on this topic are Pfaltz [1970, 1972], Montanary [1970], Milgram [1972], and Rosenfeld and Milgram [1972]. The material in Section 3.4 is based on the paper by Feder [1971]. For additional details on shape grammars see Gips [1975], and Stiny [1975].

Other references dealing with concepts related to the material in this chapter are Narasimhan [1966], Miller and Shaw [1968], Rounds [1969], Montanary [1970], Milgram and Rosenfeld [1970, 1971], Pavlidis [1972], and C. R. Cook [1974].

ISBN 0-201-02930-8/0-201-02931-6, pbk

ISBN 0-201-02930-8/0-201-02931-6, pbk

4

RECOGNITION AND TRANSLATION OF SYNTACTIC STRUCTURES

One brought me happiness;
the other, recognition.
Anonymous

4.1 INTRODUCTION

In the previous chapters, grammars were developed as finite systems that define pattern languages by providing rules for the generation of the members of the languages. In this chapter, attention is focused on the development of mathematical models of computing machines, called *automata*, which, given an input pattern, have the capability of recognizing whether or not the pattern belongs to a specified language or pattern class.

There is a one-to-one correspondence between the four types of string-generation grammars in the Chomsky hierarchy defined in Chapter 2 and four kinds of automata as recognizers:

type 0	Turing machine
type 1	linear-bounded automaton
type 2	push-down automaton
type 3	finite automaton

In fact, this hierarchy is preserved when the general capabilities of these automata as computing devices are studied; thus, the Turing machine is, by Church's Thesis, equivalent to the most powerful computing devices conceivable (cf. Davis [1968]), while the finite automaton is the least powerful machine of the four. Attention is restricted in this text to finite and push down automata used to accept or reject input strings and to frontier-to-root automata as generalized finite automata for tree recognition. These are the models that have thus far proved to be the most useful and interesting for syntactic pattern recognition tasks.

In order to study the recognition of languages, we first define the string-recognizing automata formally and examine these machines in order to develop an understanding of this kind of language processing. These formal models provide the theoretical foundations for the recognition task. Subsequently, recognition methods stated directly as algorithms without specific references to the automata are also considered. These algorithms provide some insight into the practical problems encountered.

Also presented in this chapter are automata for recognizing and translating strings, a formal model of syntax-directed correction of errors in strings, and tree automata for recognition of trees.

4.2 STRING LANGUAGE RECOGNIZERS

4.2.1 Finite Automata

We shall introduce first the simplest language-processing automata, which are capable of handling only those languages generated by the most restricted grammars, the regular languages. A (*nondeterministic*) *finite automaton* is a system specified as a five-tuple $\mathcal{C}_f = (Q, \Sigma, \delta, q_0, F)$ where

Q is a finite set of *states*,
Σ is a finite *input alphabet*,
δ is a *mapping* from $Q \times \Sigma$ into 2^Q, the collection of all subsets of Q;
q_0 in Q is the *starting state*, and
F is a set of "*final*" or "*accepting*" *states*, a subset of Q.

Figure 4.1 gives a general representation of this type of automaton, which operates in the following way. The starting state is always q_0. An input string x from Σ^+ is placed on the tape, to be scanned symbol by symbol beginning at the leftmost tape cell.[‡] As the scanning proceeds to the right across the tape, the state transition mapping δ defines the operation of $\mathcal{C}_f$ by giving, for the current state and input symbol, the set from which the next state must be selected. String x is said to be *accepted* or *recognized by* $\mathcal{C}_f$ if it is possible for the automaton, starting in q_0, to scan all of x and follow a sequence of states so as to halt in one of the states in F.

It is noted that this machine is *not* stochastic and *must* accept its input string if there is any possible way to do so; that is, the convention for using $\mathcal{C}_f$ as a recognizer requires that it always follow a sequence of states

---

[‡]Reference to a "tape" in the model of an automaton is a convention to facilitate description. In reality, the input may be supplied in any of a number of ways.

ISBN 0-201-02930-8/0-201-02931-6, pbk

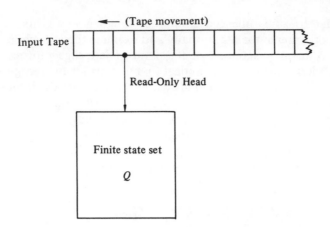

Figure 4.1. General representation of a finite automaton.

leading to acceptance of the string if any such sequence is allowed by the δ mapping, even though for a specified current state and input symbol there may be several potential next states from which to choose.

The *language recognized by finite automaton* $\mathcal{Q}_f$ is the set

$$L(\mathcal{Q}_f) = \{x \mid x \text{ in } \Sigma^+, \mathcal{Q}_f \text{ starts in } q_0 \text{ and can halt in a}$$
$$\text{state of } F \text{ when all of } x \text{ is scanned}\}.$$

$L(\mathcal{Q}_f)$ is also called the set of "accepted tapes," to suggest that the input is read from a tape moving past a read-only head. Normally the machine halts after an entire string is scanned; however, if a state–input combination, say (q, a), occurs for which $\delta(q, a) = \emptyset$, then $\mathcal{Q}_f$ is unable to complete its scan and halts, rejecting the string.

Example: Consider the set of primitives and corresponding pattern terminals shown in Fig. 4.2. The pattern class is described by the regular language $\{x \mid x = a^n b, n \geqslant 0\}$ in which the concatenation of two terminals means that they are adjacent in the pattern. A finite automaton capable of recognizing these patterns is the machine $\mathcal{Q}_f = (Q, \Sigma, \delta, q_0, F)$ where

$$Q = \{q_0, q_1\}, \qquad \Sigma = \{a, b\}, \qquad F = \{q_1\},$$

and δ is defined as

$$\delta(q_0, a) = \{q_0\}, \delta(q_0, b) = \{q_1\}, \delta(q_1, a) = \delta(q_1, b) = \emptyset.$$

ISBN 0-201-02930-8/0-201-02931-6, pbk

Pattern Primitive   Terminal

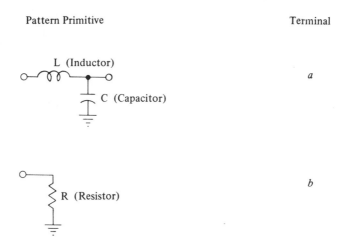

Figure 4.2. Pattern primitives and terminals.

Any string of the form a^n, $n \geqslant 0$, causes $\mathcal{Q}_f$ to remain in starting state q_0; a single occurrence of symbol b causes a transition from q_0 to q_1, and q_1 is an accepting state. Hence, strings of the form $a^n b$ are recognized, but strings of any other form are rejected. For example, input bba is not accepted because $\delta(q_0, b) = \{q_1\}$ and $\delta(q_1, b) = \varnothing$, causing $\mathcal{Q}_f$ to halt because it is unable to scan the entire input. String a^3 is rejected because $\mathcal{Q}_f$ can only reach state q_0 while scanning this input, and q_0 is not a final state used to accept a sentence.   □

A finite automaton is conveniently represented by giving its *state transition diagram*, a directed graph with nodes for the states connected by arcs labeled with input symbols causing transitions. By convention, all final states appear as double circles, and the starting state is indicated by an entering arrow. The diagram for the automaton in the example just given is shown in Fig. 4.3.

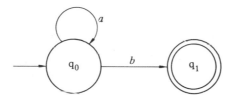

Figure 4.3. Finite automaton state transition diagram.

ISBN 0-201-02930-8/0-201-02931-6, pbk

It follows from the discussion in Section 2.2.1 that the language $\{x \mid x = a^n b, n \geq 0\}$ is generated by the regular grammar $G = (\{S\}, \{a, b\}, P, S)$ with productions $P = \{S \rightarrow aS, S \rightarrow b\}$. The fact that this language is both recognized by a finite automaton and generated by a regular grammar is an instance of the following fundamental result.

Theorem: A language is recognized by a finite automaton iff it is generated by a regular grammar.   □

In order to prove this theorem, it must be shown that, given a finite automaton $\mathcal{C}_f$, a regular grammar G can be constructed such that $L(\mathcal{C}_f) = L(G)$,[‡] and given a regular grammar G, a finite automaton $\mathcal{C}_f$ can be constructed such that $L(\mathcal{C}_f) = L(G)$.[‡] The proof, which may be outlined as follows, is important because it describes the way to obtain a finite automaton from a regular grammar, and vice versa.

Given a regular grammar $G = (N, \Sigma, P, X_0)$, the corresponding finite automaton $\mathcal{C}_f = (Q, \Sigma, \delta, q_0, F)$ is specified as follows. Suppose the non-terminal set N is composed of the starting symbol (labeled X_0 for reference here) and n additional nonterminals $X_1, X_2, \ldots, X_n$; then the state set Q is formed by introducing $n + 2$ states, $\{q_0, q_1, \ldots, q_n, q_{n+1}\}$, such that q_i corresponds to X_i for $0 \leq i \leq n$, and q_{n+1} is an *additional* state. The set F in this case is simply $\{q_{n+1}\}$, and the set of input symbols is identical to the set of terminals in G. The δ mapping is defined by two rules based on the productions of G; namely, for each i and j, $0 \leq i \leq n, 0 \leq j \leq n$:

(i)   if $X_i \rightarrow aX_j$ is in P, then $\delta(q_i, a)$ contains q_j; and
(ii) if $X_i \rightarrow a$ is in P, then $\delta(q_i, a)$ contains q_{n+1}.

The sequence of states entered by $\mathcal{C}_f$ in accepting an input string corresponds to the sequence of nonterminals appearing in a derivation of the same string in G. In accepting a string, the automaton simulates a derivation of the string in the grammar G; if a string is rejected by $\mathcal{C}_f$, it is because no derivation of that string using the productions in G is possible.

On the other hand, given a finite automaton $\mathcal{C}_f = (Q, \Sigma, \delta, q_0, F)$, we specify a regular grammar $G = (N, \Sigma, P, X_0)$ by letting N be identified with the state set Q, with starting symbol X_0 corresponding to q_0, and productions of G obtained as follows:

(i)   if q_j is in $\delta(q_i, a)$, there is a production $X_i \rightarrow aX_j$; and,
(ii) if a state in F is in $\delta(q_i, a)$, there is a production $X_i \rightarrow a$.

Productions introduced by rule (i) allow generation of a string in G to follow the state sequence taken by $\mathcal{C}_f$ in responding to the string; produc-

---

[‡]The reader should recognize that this proof requires establishing the equality of sets of strings.

ISBN 0-201-02930-8/0-201-02931-6, pbk

tions introduced by rule (ii) terminate a derivation in correspondence with entry of $\mathcal{C}_f$ into an accepting state. Formal proof by induction establishes that, for the construction either of $\mathcal{C}_f$ from G or of G from $\mathcal{C}_f$, it will be the case that $L(G)$ is identical to $L(\mathcal{C}_f)$.

Example: Consider the regular grammar $G = (\{S\}, \{a, b\}, P, S)$ with productions

$$S \rightarrow aS \qquad S \rightarrow b$$

A finite automaton $\mathcal{C}_f = (Q, \Sigma, \delta, q_0, F)$ to recognize $L(G)$ is constructed as follows. Since S is the only nonterminal in N, the automaton state set Q is $\{q_0, q_1\}$, where q_1 is the additional state introduced to be the accepting state. The set of input symbols Σ is $\{a, b\}$. In obtaining the δ mapping, production $S \rightarrow aS$ requires that $\delta(q_0, a)$ contain q_0, and production $S \rightarrow b$ means that $\delta(q_0, b)$ must contain q_1. Since there are no other productions, we also have $\delta(q_1, a) = \delta(q_1, b) = \varnothing$. The state transition diagram of this machine is shown in Fig. 4.3. □

Example: Consider the finite automaton $\mathcal{C}_f = (\{q_0, q_1, q_2\}, \{0, 1\}, \delta, q_0, \{q_2\})$ with the state transition diagram given in Fig. 4.4. The state transition mapping is

$$\delta(q_0, 0) = \{q_2\}, \qquad \delta(q_0, 1) = \{q_1\},$$
$$\delta(q_1, 0) = \{q_2\}, \qquad \delta(q_1, 1) = \{q_0\},$$
$$\delta(q_2, 0) = \{q_2\}, \qquad \delta(q_2, 1) = \{q_1\}.$$

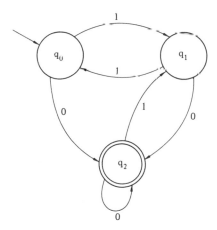

Figure 4.4. Finite automaton.

ISBN 0-201-02930-8/0-201-02931-6, pbk

The method for obtaining a regular grammar from $\mathcal{C}_f$ yields the grammar $G = (\{X_0, X_1, X_2\}, \{0, 1\}, P, X_0)$ with productions

$$X_0 \to 1X_1 \qquad X_0 \to 0X_2 \qquad X_0 \to 0$$

$$X_1 \to 1X_0 \qquad X_1 \to 0X_2 \qquad X_1 \to 0$$

$$X_2 \to 1X_1 \qquad X_2 \to 0X_2 \qquad X_2 \to 0$$

$\mathcal{C}_f$, for example, accepts the input string 1100 by the sequence

$$\delta(q_0, 1) = \{q_1\}, \quad \delta(q_1, 1) = \{q_0\}, \quad \delta(q_0, 0) = \{q_2\}, \quad \delta(q_2, 0) = \{q_2\},$$

beginning in state q_0 and reaching accepting state q_2 when all symbols in the string are scanned. G generates this same string by the sequence of sentential forms

$$X_0 \Rightarrow 1X_1 \Rightarrow 11X_0 \Rightarrow 110X_2 \Rightarrow 1100. \qquad \square$$

Machine $\mathcal{C}_f$ in Fig. 4.4 illustrates the special class of finite automata that are *completely specified* and *deterministic*. A completely specified, deterministic finite automaton is one in which, for each state and input symbol combination, there is exactly one next state specified by the δ mapping; that is, δ is a function from $Q \times \Sigma$ to Q. Such a machine operates deterministically because it is never forced to select the next state from among several possibilities; furthermore, there is no state–input combination (q, a) such that $\delta(q, a) = \varnothing$, so the machine is able to scan any input string completely. It should be noted that a completely specified, deterministic finite automaton is a conventional sequential logic network realizable in hardware with flip-flops and combinational logic gates. We simply assign output 1 to each final state and output 0 to each nonfinal state.

It can be shown that, given any finite automaton $\mathcal{C}_f$, there exists a completely specified, deterministic finite automaton $\mathcal{C}_f'$, such that $L(\mathcal{C}_f') = L(\mathcal{C}_f)$. The basic idea is to make the state set of $\mathcal{C}_f'$ correspond to subsets of the state set of $\mathcal{C}_f$; in this way, $\mathcal{C}_f'$ can keep track of all possible states that $\mathcal{C}_f$ might have entered at a given time.

Specifically, given a nondeterministic or incompletely specified finite automaton $\mathcal{C}_f = (Q, \Sigma, \delta, q_0, F)$, we define a deterministic automaton $\mathcal{C}_f' = (Q', \Sigma, \delta', q_0', F')$, the state set of which is a collection of labels for the subsets of Q; that is, $Q' \equiv 2^Q$. For the new starting state, we let q_0' be $\{q_0\}$. The set of final states is

$$F' = \{q' | q' \text{ in } 2^Q, q' \text{ contains at least one state in } F\};$$

thus, F' consists of all the subsets that, taken individually, contain one or

ISBN 0-201-02930-8/0-201-02931-6, pbk

more of the final states of $\mathcal{Q}_f$. The δ' mapping from $Q' \times \Sigma$ to Q' must be constructed to allow $\mathcal{Q}_f'$ to keep track of any possible state that $\mathcal{Q}_f$ may have entered in response to the input so far scanned; therefore, the δ' mapping is specified for each q' in Q' and a in Σ as

$$\delta'(q', a) = \{ p \mid p \text{ in } Q, p \text{ in } \delta(q, a) \text{ for some state } q \text{ in the subset } q' \}.$$

In words, if $\mathcal{Q}_f$ is residing in one of the states in q' and the input symbol is a, then it is certain that the next state of $\mathcal{Q}_f$ will be selected from $\delta'(q', a)$. Recalling that an input string will be accepted by $\mathcal{Q}_f$ iff there is an allowable sequence of states leading to F, we see that for the same input $\mathcal{Q}_f'$ will halt in one of the elements of F'; also, if a given input is accepted by $\mathcal{Q}_f'$, then there is at least one state sequence for $\mathcal{Q}_f$ leading to F in response to this same sentence. $\mathcal{Q}_f'$ deterministically recognizes the identical set of sentences as $\mathcal{Q}_f$.

Example: We will illustrate the method for obtaining a deterministic automaton from an incompletely specified finite automaton in this example. Consider the incompletely specified automaton $\mathcal{Q}_f = (\{q_0, q_1\}, \{a, b\}, \delta, q_0, \{q_1\})$ given in Fig. 4.3. To obtain a deterministic finite automaton $\mathcal{Q}_f' = (Q', \{a, b\}, \delta', q_0', F')$ such that $L(\mathcal{Q}_f') = L(\mathcal{Q}_f)$, first let $Q' = \{\emptyset, \{q_0\}, \{q_1\}, \{q_0, q_1\}\}$ with starting state $q_0' = \{q_0\}$ and with final states $F' = \{\{q_1\}, \{q_0, q_1\}\}$. For convenience in reference, let us relabel the states in Q' in the following way:

$$q_\phi = \emptyset, \qquad q_0' = \{q_0\}, \qquad q_A = \{q_1\}, \qquad q_B = \{q_0, q_1\}.$$

The set of accepting states F' is $\{q_A, q_B\}$. The δ' mapping becomes

$$\delta'(q_0', a) = q_0', \qquad \delta'(q_0', b) = q_A,$$

$$\delta'(q_A, a) = q_\phi, \qquad \delta'(q_A, b) = q_\phi,$$

$$\delta'(q_B, a) = q_0', \qquad \delta'(q_B, b) = q_A,$$

$$\delta'(q_\phi, a) = q_\phi, \qquad \delta'(q_\phi, b) = q_\phi.$$

The state transition diagram for $\mathcal{Q}_f'$ is shown in Fig. 4.5.

Suppose the input string aab is applied; $\mathcal{Q}_f'$ accepts this sentence via the sequence

$$\delta'(q_0', a) = q_0', \qquad \delta'(q_0', a) = q_0', \qquad \delta'(q_0', b) = q_A$$

since q_A is in F'. Suppose the input string is now abb; the state sequence

ISBN 0-201-02930-8/0-201-02931-6, pbk

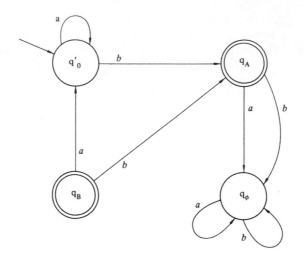

Figure 4.5. Deterministic finite automaton.

for $\mathcal{Q}'_f$ is

$$\delta'(q'_0, a) = q'_0, \qquad \delta'(q'_0, b) = q_A, \qquad \delta'(q_A, b) = q_\phi,$$

and this string is rejected because q_ϕ is not one of the accepting states.   □

It should be noted that for the automaton $\mathcal{Q}'_f$ in the preceding example, the state q_B is never entered because $\mathcal{Q}'_f$ always starts in q'_0 and there is no input string that will cause it to reach q_B. Therefore, q_B is called an *inaccessible state* and is like an inaccessible nonterminal in a grammar; it may be removed from Q' to give a simpler automaton without changing $L(\mathcal{Q}'_f)$. The state q_ϕ is called a *trap state*; $\mathcal{Q}'_f$ can never leave this state once it has been entered because

$$\delta'(q_\phi, a) = \delta'(q_\phi, b) = q_\phi.$$

Suppose there are two completely specified, deterministic, finite automata $\mathcal{Q}_{f1}$ and $\mathcal{Q}_{f2}$ such that $L(\mathcal{Q}_{f1})$ is identical to $L(\mathcal{Q}_{f2})$; then $\mathcal{Q}_{f1}$ and $\mathcal{Q}_{f2}$ are *equivalent machines*. Since additional states increase cost and complexity, we should select the machine with fewer states as our recognizer. This leads to the question whether there is a third automaton, $\mathcal{Q}_{f3}$, equivalent to $\mathcal{Q}_{f1}$ and $\mathcal{Q}_{f2}$ but with even fewer states. For finite automata, there is the following important result.

Theorem: For any completely specified, deterministic finite automaton $\mathcal{Q}_f$ there is an equivalent finite automaton $\mathcal{Q}_{fm}$ that has as few states as any

ISBN 0-201-02930-8/0-201-02931-6, pbk

other deterministic recognizer of $L(\mathcal{Q}_f)$ and that is unique up to a relabeling of its states.   □

This theorem indicates that there is a unique, minimal-state, deterministic recognizer associated with each finite automaton. Any other finite automaton accepting exactly the same set of strings must either have more states or have the same number of states and an identical state transition diagram (except that its states may have different labels). The proof of this theorem involves the construction of the *minimal machine* $\mathcal{Q}_{fm}$ from a given automaton $\mathcal{Q}_f = (Q, \Sigma, \delta, q_0, F)$. The minimization technique is as follows.

First, it is necessary to eliminate all inaccessible states. Second, it is necessary to find all sets of equivalent states, where two states q_i and q_j are said to be *equivalent* iff $L(\mathcal{Q}_f)$ is exactly the same language with q_i designated to be the starting state as with q_j designated to be the starting state. Three or more states are equivalent if they are all pairwise equivalent. It should be noted that "state equivalence" is an equivalence relation on Q; that is, it is reflexive, symmetric, and transitive as defined in Section 2.2.1. A set of equivalent states can be replaced in $\mathcal{Q}_f$ by a single state representing the merged equivalent states. The minimal machine $\mathcal{Q}_{fm}$ is obtained by locating and merging all equivalent sets of states.

Two states q_i and q_j may be tested for equivalence by checking two conditions:

(i) q_i, q_j must both be in F or both be in $\overline{F}$; and
(ii) for each input symbol a in Σ, $\delta(q_i, a)$ must be equivalent to $\delta(q_j, a)$.

Condition (i) is easily checked by inspection. Condition (ii) states that for each symbol a in Σ, $\delta(q_i, a)$ must be equivalent to $\delta(q_j, a)$. A check for this aspect of equivalence can be conveniently organized by preparing a *merger table* that has a block for each pair of states in Q. We first cross out the blocks for all pairs of states established as being not equivalent by condition (i); in each remaining block we then enter those states which condition (ii) indicates must be equivalent. The blocks are now examined for nonequivalent next-state entries, and any block for which a next-state pair is not equivalent is itself crossed out. This process continues until no more crossings off are possible, at which point the sets of equivalent states can be extracted from the table. This technique is illustrated by the following example.

Example: Suppose that the seven-state, completely specified, deterministic automaton $\mathcal{Q}_f = (\{q_0, q_A, q_B, q_C, q_D, q_E, q_F\}, \{0, 1\}, \delta, q_0, \{q_B, q_C, q_D, q_E, q_F\})$ with the state transition diagram in Fig. 4.6 has been designed as the recognizer of a pattern class and must be minimized. By

ISBN 0-201-02930-8/0-201-02931-6, pbk

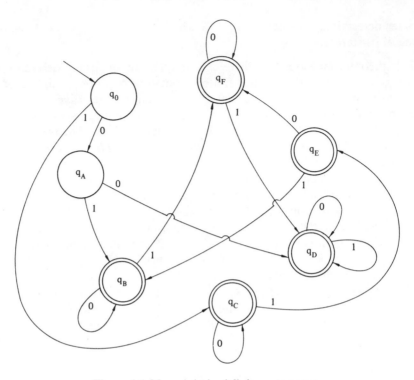

Figure 4.6. Nonminimized finite automaton.

inspection, it is seen that there are no inaccessible states. State equivalence must now be checked. The first step is the creation of the merger table in Fig. 4.7(a), in which blocks for pairs of states not equivalent by condition (i) have been crossed out and the next states required to be equivalent by condition (ii) have been entered in the remaining blocks. To see how this is done, consider the block for testing equivalence of q_0 and q_A. For input 0, we have $\delta(q_0, 0) = q_A$ and $\delta(q_A, 0) = q_D$, indicating that q_A must be equivalent to q_D; and for input 1, we have $\delta(q_0, 1) = q_C$ and $\delta(q_A, 1) = q_B$, indicating that q_C must be equivalent to q_B. This is the information entered into the q_0–q_A block by writing "A–D" "C–B."

The next stage in the merger table is shown in Fig. 4.7(b), in which the block for q_0 and q_A has been crossed out because q_A and q_D are not equivalent. No other crosses occur. The remaining blocks are consistent and establish that the sets of equivalent states are $\{q_0\}$, $\{q_A\}$, and $\{q_B, q_C, q_D, q_E, q_F\}$. We therefore, have the minimal machine $\mathcal{Q}_{fm} = (\{q_0, q_A, q_{BCDEF}\}, \{0, 1\}, \delta, q_0, \{q_{BCDEF}\})$ with only three states and the state transition diagram given in Fig. 4.8.   □

ISBN 0-201-02931-6, pbk   0-201-02930-8 /0-201-02931-6, pbk

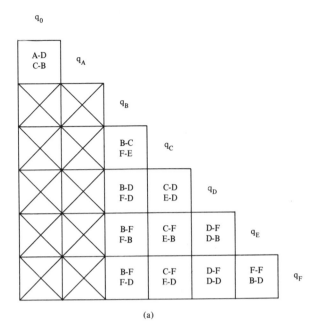

(a)

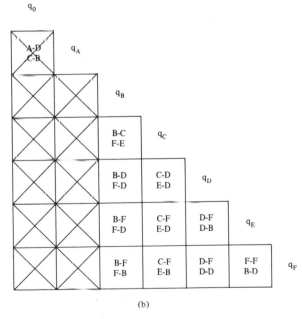

(b)

Figure 4.7. Merger table for minimization. (a) Initial table. (b) Final table.

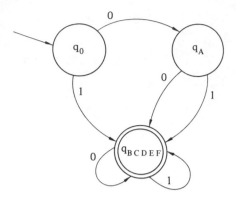

Figure 4.8. Minimized finite automaton.

4.2.2   Pushdown Automata

Although finite automata are computing devices powerful enough to be used as recognizers of regular languages, these machines are unable to recognize languages that are context free but not regular. The languages in this category are generated by context-free grammars that have at least one self-embedding nonterminal as defined in Section 2.2.2. Let us suppose that A is a self-embedding nonterminal in grammar G for which

$$S \overset{*}{\underset{G}{\Rightarrow}} uAy, \qquad A \overset{*}{\underset{G}{\Rightarrow}} vAx, \qquad \text{and} \qquad A \overset{*}{\underset{G}{\Rightarrow}} w$$

represent the possible derivations; then the language $L(G)$ is exactly the countably infinite set $\{uv^iwx^iy \mid i \geqslant 0\}$ because derivations of terminal strings are of the form

$$S \overset{*}{\Rightarrow} uAy \overset{*}{\Rightarrow} uvAxy \overset{*}{\Rightarrow} uvvAxxy \overset{*}{\Rightarrow} uv^iAx^iy \overset{*}{\Rightarrow} uv^iwx^iy.$$

But no finite automaton can recognize this set because the occurrences of substring v must exactly balance the occurrences of substring x, yet there are sentences in $L(G)$ with a greater number of v's and x's than any automaton with a finite fixed amount of memory is able to count.

In order to develop a recognizer for context-free languages, a new automaton must be designed with a mechanism for handling strings with derivations in which self-embedding is used. Essentially, this machine is a finite automaton with a pushdown list of unlimited storage provided as auxiliary memory. The pushdown list is a "last-in, first-out" stack in which the symbol most recently stored pushes down all others previously placed

ISBN 0-201-02930-8/0-201-02931-6, pbk

in the stack and must be the first symbol retrieved; there is access only to the topmost symbol on the stack at any time.

This computing device, called a (*nondeterministic*) *pushdown automaton*, or PDA, is formally defined as a seven-tuple $\mathcal{C}_p = (Q, \Sigma, \Gamma, \delta, q_0, Z_0, F)$ where Q, Σ, q_0, and F are the same as for a finite automaton, Γ is a finite *pushdown list alphabet*, δ is a *mapping* from $Q \times (\Sigma \cup \{\lambda\}) \times \Gamma$ into finite subsets of $Q \times \Gamma^*$, and Z_0 in Γ is the *initial pushdown list symbol*.

Figure 4.9 is a general representation of this type of automaton. The machine is operated by starting in state q_0 with only Z_0 on the stack and with the input tape holding a string x from Σ^+ to be scanned symbol by symbol from left to right. For the triple combination of current state, current input symbol or empty string λ, and single symbol currently on top of the stack, the δ mapping specifies what the next state can be *and* which string in Γ^* can replace the single topmost stack symbol. The PDA has access only to the single symbol on top of the stack, and the string in Γ^* that replaces this symbol pushes down the other stack contents. In the event that the topmost symbol is replaced by the empty string λ, this symbol is said to be "popped out of the stack"; the symbol that was residing immediately below the top then becomes accessible. A string x is accepted by the PDA if it is possible for the machine, starting in q_0 with Z_0 on the stack, to scan all of x and halt in a state of F. Note that, if

ISBN 0-201-02930-8/0-201-02931-6, pbk

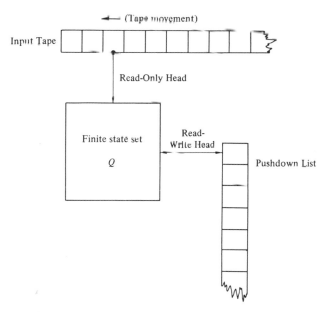

Figure 4.9. General representation of a pushdown automaton.

$\delta(q, \lambda, Z)$ is not null for state q and stack symbol Z, the PDA may change state or stack contents without actually reading another input symbol; this permits a PDA to manipulate the stack contents independently of the input, an action that is sometimes required.

In Section 4.2.1 it was stated that for any nondeterministic finite automaton $\mathcal{Q}_f$ there is a deterministic finite automaton that also recognizes the regular language $L(\mathcal{Q}_f)$. This result does not generalize to nondeterministic pushdown automata; there exist nondeterministic PDA's without deterministic equivalents. This implies that the language recognized by such a PDA has properties that make processing the language inherently nondeterministic in nature, and that in developing algorithms to operate on a string from such a language one must be prepared to use techniques to recover from an earlier incorrect choice or action. In the nondeterministic PDA model, however, the same assumption is made as for a nondeterministic finite automaton; namely, at each step in scanning an input string, a PDA *always* selects an action that will lead to acceptance of the string if there is any way this can occur.

Since a PDA can have a set F of final or accepting states, the *language recognized by pushdown automaton $\mathcal{Q}_p$ by final state* is defined as

$$L(\mathcal{Q}_p) = \{x \mid x \text{ in } \Sigma^+, \mathcal{Q}_p \text{ starts in state } q_0 \text{ with symbol}$$
$$Z_0 \text{ on its stack and can halt in a state in } F$$
$$\text{when } x \text{ is entirely scanned}\}.$$

A variation of this method of accepting a string by final state is provided by a PDA that signals recognition of a string by halting with the stack empty, that is, with λ being the string of Γ^* that is left on the stack when the machine halts. This *language accepted by empty stack* is the set

$$L_\lambda(\mathcal{Q}_p) = \{x \mid x \text{ in } \Sigma^+, \mathcal{Q}_p \text{ starts in } q_0 \text{ with } Z_0 \text{ on the stack}$$
$$\text{and can halt with the stack empty when } x \text{ is}$$
$$\text{scanned}\}.$$

When a PDA accepts strings in this way, it is convenient to let F be the null set $\emptyset$. It can be established that $L = L(\mathcal{Q}_p)$ for some pushdown automaton $\mathcal{Q}_p$ iff $L = L_\lambda(\mathcal{Q}_p')$ for a second PDA, $\mathcal{Q}_p'$. We shall assume in the following discussions that acceptance by empty stack is used.

Example: Consider the set of pattern primitives and the patterns generated from them in Fig. 4.10. This pattern class is represented by the nonregular, context-free language $\{x \mid x = ca^n db^n, n \geqslant 0\}$, which cannot be recognized by any finite automaton. A PDA that accepts exactly this set of

ISBN 0-201-02930-8/0-201-02931-6, pbk

Pattern   String Representation

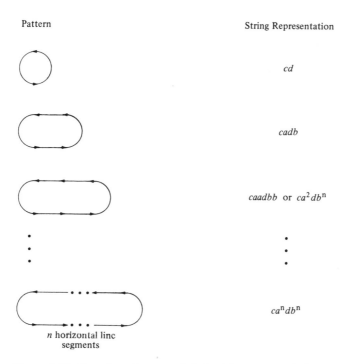

cd

$cadb$

$caadbb$ or $ca^2 db^n$

$ca^n db^n$

n horizontal line
segments

Figure 4.10. Sample patterns and their string representations.

sentences by empty stack is the nondeterministic machine $\mathcal{C}_p =$ ($\{q_0\}$, $\{a, b, c, d\}$, $\{S, A, B, C, D\}$, δ, q_0, S, $\varnothing$) with the δ mapping defined as follows:

$$\delta(q_0, c, S) = \{(q_0, DAB), (q_0, C)\}, \qquad \delta(q_0, d, C) = \{(q_0, \lambda)\},$$

$$\delta(q_0, a, D) = \{(q_0, \lambda)\}, \qquad \delta(q_0, b, B) = \{(q_0, \lambda)\},$$

$$\delta(q_0, a, A) = \{(q_0, AB), (q_0, CB)\}.$$

This δ mapping shows, for instance, that when $\mathcal{C}_p$ is in state q_0 scanning input symbol a with A on top of its stack, one of two actions will occur: $\mathcal{C}_p$ will either enter state q_0 and replace A by AB on the stack or enter state q_0 and replace A by CB on the stack; then move to the next symbol on the input tape. By contrast, when $\mathcal{C}_p$ is in state q_0 scanning input symbol a with D on top of its stack, the δ mapping allows only one action, specifically, replacing D by λ to pop D from the stack. In specifying the δ mapping, we have followed the convention that any combination of [state,

ISBN 0-201-02930-8/0-201-02931-6, pbk

λ or input symbol, stack symbol] not explicitly listed is a combination for which δ is null; if $\mathcal{C}_p$ encounters such a combination, it halts, rejecting the input string. Note that $\mathcal{C}_p$ is a single-state machine that depends entirely on its stack as its memory during string processing.

Suppose the input string is *caadbb*. $\mathcal{C}_p$ proceeds in the following way. The starting state is q_0, the initial stack symbol is S, and the first input symbol scanned is c; the mapping entry is

$$\delta(q_0, c, S) = \{(q_0, DAB), (q_0, C)\}.$$

The correct action at this point is the first of these two alternatives; therefore, $\mathcal{C}_p$ reenters state q_0, replaces S by DAB on the stack so that symbol D is now accessible on top, and moves to read the next input symbol. The remaining actions of $\mathcal{C}_p$ are as follows:

$\delta(q_0, a, D) = \{(q_0, \lambda)\}$ D is popped from the stack, which now holds the string AB with A on top.

$\delta(q_0, a, A) = \{(q_0, AB), (q_0, CB)\}$ The machine correctly selects (q_0, CB) and the stack contents become CBB.

$\delta(q_0, d, C) = \{(q_0, \lambda)\}$ C is popped from the stack, which now holds BB.

$\delta(q_0, b, B) = \{(q_0, \lambda)\}$ B is popped from the stack, which now holds B.

$\delta(q_0, b, B) = \{(q_0, \lambda)\}$ B is popped from the stack, which now holds the empty string λ.

Since the entire string is scanned and $\mathcal{C}_p$ halts with empty stack, this input is accepted as representing a well-formed pattern of the class defined in Fig. 4.10. It is instructive to examine the consequences of an incorrect choice on the machine's third step:

$\delta(q_0, a, A) = \{(q_0, AB), (q_0, CB)\}$ Suppose $\mathcal{C}_p$ selects (q_0, AB) here. The stack contents become ABB.

$\delta(q_0, d, A) = \varnothing$ With no action defined, $\mathcal{C}_p$ must halt and reject the input.

Since by definition an automaton must accept an input string if any sequence of actions permits it to do so, the assumption is that $\mathcal{C}_p$ always makes a correct selection. It is recommended that the actions of $\mathcal{C}_p$ in

ISBN 0-201-02930-8/0-201-02931-6, pbk

accepting input string *caaadbbb* be examined at this time, for this demon-strates that (q_0, AB) is the proper choice at one point while (q_0, CB) is correct at another.

As a final illustration, suppose the input is string *ca*; the actions of $\mathcal{Q}_p$ are

$\delta(q_0, c, S)$ contains (q_0, DAB) S is replaced by DAB; D is now on top of the stack.

$\delta(q_0, a, D) = \{(q_0, \lambda)\}$ D is popped from the stack which now holds AB.

$\mathcal{Q}_p$ scans the entire input string but halts with a nonempty stack; therefore, the sentence *ca* is rejected.   □

The following theorem is a fundamental result concerning the capability of pushdown automata to recognize languages.

Theorem: A language is recognized by a PDA iff it is generated by a context-free grammar.   □

In order to prove this theorem it must be shown that, given a context-free grammar G, a pushdown automaton $\mathcal{Q}_p$ can be constructed such that $L_\lambda(\mathcal{Q}_p) = L(G)$, and vice versa. The construction of a grammar from a PDA is somewhat complex. Since in syntactic pattern recognition the problem usually is that of constructing a recognizer from a grammar that is given or has been inferred, we shall describe only the algorithm for obtaining $\mathcal{Q}_p$ from a context-free grammar G.

Let $G = (N, \Sigma, P, S)$ be a context-free pattern grammar. A pushdown automaton such that $L_\lambda(\mathcal{Q}_p) = L(G)$ is constructed by defining the machine to be $\mathcal{Q}_p = (\{q_0\}, \Sigma, N \cup \Sigma, \delta, q_0, S, \varnothing)$ with its δ mapping ob-tained from the productions in P as follows:

(i) if $A \rightarrow \alpha$ is in P, then $\delta(q_0, \lambda, A)$ contains (q_0, α); and
(ii) $\delta(q_0, a, a) = \{(q_0, \lambda)\}$ for each terminal a in Σ.

This single-state machine uses its stack as its memory to simulate a leftmost derivation of an acceptable string. Nonterminals are pushed down and subsequently popped out of the stack in the same order as they occur left to right in a derivation in G. The actions arising from rule (i) permit $\mathcal{Q}_p$ to replace a nonterminal on top of the stack by the right-hand side of a production for rewriting that nonterminal; the actions arising from rule (ii) pop terminals from the stack in the same order as their appearance in the input string. Proof of set inclusion both ways by induction on the length of strings establishes that $L_\lambda(\mathcal{Q}_p) = L(G)$.

ISBN 0-201-02930-8/0-201-02931-6, pbk

Example: The grammar $G = (\{S, A\}, \{a, b, c, d\}, P, S)$ with productions $\{S \to cA, A \to aAb, A \to d\}$ generates the strings for the class of patterns in Fig. 4.10. Application of the construction technique described earlier gives the pushdown automaton $\mathcal{Q}_p = (\{q_0\}, \{a, b, c, d\}, \{S, A, a, b, c, d\}, \delta, q_0, S, \varnothing)$ where, by rule (i),

$$\delta(q_0, \lambda, S) = \{(q_0, cA)\},$$

$$\delta(q_0, \lambda, A) = \{(q_0, aAb), (q_0, d)\},$$

and by rule (ii),

$$\delta(q_0, a, a) = \delta(q_0, b, b) = \delta(q_0, c, c) = \delta(q_0, d, d) = \{(q_0, \lambda)\}.$$

Suppose the sentence *caadbb* is applied as the input string. The actions taken by $\mathcal{Q}_p$ in accepting this string are the following:

$\delta(q_0, \lambda, S) = \{(q_0, cA)\}$	cA replaces S on the stack.
$\delta(q_0, c, c) = \{(q_0, \lambda)\}$	c is popped from the stack, since it matches the input symbol; the stack now holds A.
$\delta(q_0, \lambda, A) = \{(q_0, aAb), (q_0, d)\}$	$\mathcal{Q}_p$ selects (q_0, aAb); the stack now holds aAb.
$\delta(q_0, a, a) = \{(q_0, \lambda)\}$	a is popped from the stack, which now holds Ab.
$\delta(q_0, \lambda, A)$ contains (q_0, aAb)	The stack contents become $aAbb$.
$\delta(q_0, a, a) = \{(q_0, \lambda)\}$	The stack now holds Abb.
$\delta(q_0, \lambda, A)$ contains (q_0, d)	The stack now holds dbb.
$\delta(q_0, d, d) = \{(q_0, \lambda)\}$	d is popped and the stack contents become bb.
$\delta(q_0, b, b) = \{(q_0, \lambda)\}$	The stack now holds b.
$\delta(q_0, b, b) = \{(q_0, \lambda)\}$	The stack is now empty and the input has been entirely scanned.

ISBN 0-201-02931-6, pbk

It is noted that the leftmost derivation of this same string can be taken directly from the response of $\mathcal{Q}_p$; specifically, S is rewritten as cA, A is then rewritten as aAb, A is rewritten as aAb, then A is rewritten as d.   □

If the original context-free grammar G is in Greibach normal form, the construction of the recognizing automaton $\mathcal{Q}_p$ can be simplified somewhat by merging rules (i) and (ii) above into one rule. Recalling that the Greibach normal form productions will all have the form $A \rightarrow a\alpha$ for A in N, a in Σ, α in N^*, we construct the pushdown automaton $\mathcal{Q}_p = (\{q_0\}, \Sigma, N, \delta, q_0, S, \varnothing)$ for which $\delta(q_0, a, A)$ contains (q_0, α) if there is a production $A \rightarrow a\alpha$ in P. Thus, this PDA is able to match an input symbol at the same time as it replaces a nonterminal on its stack.

Example: A Greibach normal form grammar for the language $\{x | x = ca^n db^n, n \geqslant 0\}$ is $G_G = (\{S, A, B\}, \{a, b, c, d\}, P, S)$ with productions

$$S \rightarrow cA \qquad A \rightarrow aAB \qquad A \rightarrow d \qquad B \rightarrow b$$

The pushdown automaton obtained from these productions by the construction just described is $\mathcal{Q}_p = (\{q_0\}, \{a, b, c, d\}, \{S, A, B\}, \delta, q_0, S, \varnothing)$ where

$$\delta(q_0, c, S) = \{(q_0, A)\},$$

$$\delta(q_0, a, A) = \{(q_0, AB)\},$$

$$\delta(q_0, d, A) = \{(q_0, \lambda)\},$$

$$\delta(q_0, b, B) = \{(q_0, \lambda)\}.$$

This PDA accepts the sentence $caadbb$ via the sequence

$$\delta(q_0, c, S) = \{(q_0, A)\}, \delta(q_0, a, A) = \{(q_0, AB)\},$$

$$\delta(q_0, a, A) = \{(q_0, AB)\}, \delta(q_0, d, A) = \{(q_0, \lambda)\}, \delta(q_0, b, B) = \{(q_0, \lambda)\},$$

$$\delta(q_0, b, B) = \{(q_0, \lambda)\}.$$ □

As the final topic in this section, we consider pushdown automata that operate deterministically. As previously pointed out, there are context-free languages that cannot be recognized by deterministic pushdown machines; thus, the set of languages that can be recognized by these automata forms a proper subset of the set of all context-free languages.

ISBN 0-201-02930-8/0-201-02931-6, pbk

A *deterministic pushdown automaton*, or DPDA, is a machine with only one action possible for a given combination of current state, current input symbol or empty string λ, and single symbol currently on top of the stack. Additionally, it must always be clear whether the automaton is to make a spontaneous move or read another input symbol. Specifically, a DPDA is a seven-tuple $\mathcal{Q}_{dp} = (Q, \Sigma, \Gamma, \delta, q_0, Z_0, F)$ where $Q, \Sigma, \Gamma, q_0,$ and Z_0 are the same as before, and δ is restricted such that for all q in Q, a in Σ, and Z in Γ:

(i) $\delta(q, a, Z)$ contains at most one element;
(ii) $\delta(q, \lambda, Z)$ contains at most one element; and
(iii) if $\delta(q, \lambda, Z)$ is not empty, then $\delta(q, a, Z)$ is empty for all a in Σ.

Identical conventions for string recognition by empty stack are followed for a DPDA as for a general (nondeterministic) PDA. Note that the third restriction on δ eliminates any confusion as to whether an input symbol is to be scanned or a spontaneous action using λ is to occur.

A *deterministic context-free language* is one recognized by a DPDA. Such languages form an important class of context-free languages because their sentences can be recognized efficiently in a straightforward way.

Example: The PDA obtained directly from the Greibach normal form grammar in the preceding example is deterministic and takes no spontaneous actions.

4.3   AUTOMATA FOR SIMPLE SYNTAX-DIRECTED TRANSLATION

The finite and pushdown automata that are used as recognizers of regular and context-free languages may be generalized to obtain machines for *simple* syntax-directed translations. These new automata not only recognize a correct input string but also map it into an output string.

It is necessary first to classify a simple syntax-directed translation schema (see Section 2.5) as regular or context-free, according to the underlying grammars in the SDTS's rules. A *context-free SDTS* is a simple schema, the rules of which have the general form $A \rightarrow \alpha, \beta$ for A in N, α in $(\Sigma \cup N)^*$, and β in $(\Delta \cup N)^*$, subject of course to the requirement that the α nonterminals occur in the same left-to-right order as their associates in β. A *regular SDTS* is a special type of context-free SDTS in which each rule is of the form $A \rightarrow aB, bB$ or $A \rightarrow a, b$ for A, B in N, a in $\Sigma \cup \{\lambda\}$, and b in $\Delta \cup \{\lambda\}$.

ISBN 0-201-02930-8/0-201-02931-6, pbk

4.3.1 Finite Transducers

The simplest translation device is a direct generalization of a nondeterministic finite automaton obtained by including an output alphabet. Specifically, a (*nondeterministic*) *finite transducer* is a system given as a six-tuple $\mathcal{T}_f = (Q, \Sigma, \Delta, \delta, q_0, F)$ where Q, Σ, q_0, and F are the same as for a finite automaton, Δ is a finite *output alphabet*, and δ is a *mapping* from $Q \times (\Sigma \cup \{\lambda\})$ into subsets of $Q \times (\Delta \cup \{\lambda\})$.

Figure 4.11 gives a general representation of a finite transducer, which functions in the following way. The starting state is always q_0 and the output tape is blank initially. An input string x from Σ^+ is placed on the input tape to be scanned symbol by symbol beginning at the leftmost tape cell; as this scanning proceeds, the state transition/output mapping δ defines the operation of $\mathcal{T}_f$ by giving, for the combination of current state and input symbol or empty string, the set from which the next state and the output substring must be selected. The output string is written on the output tape in as many adjacent cells as required, and the writing head moves over to the next blank cell to accommodate the next output. Input string x is accepted by $\mathcal{T}_f$ if it is possible for the transducer, starting in q_0, to scan all of x and follow a sequence of states so as to halt in one of the accepting states in F. If x is accepted, the string y that has been placed on

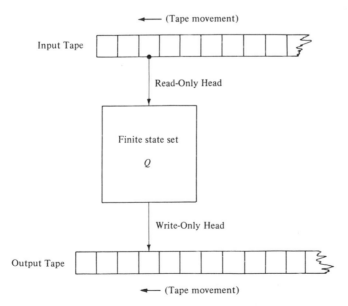

Figure 4.11. General representation of a finite transducer.

the output tape is a *regular translation* of x, so that (x, y) forms a translation pair. If input x is not recognized by $\mathfrak{I}_f$, no translation is accomplished.

The operation of a finite transducer parallels that of a finite automaton with the additional complexity of the δ mapping and the output tape used for translating. It should be noted that a finite transducer is allowed to make spontaneous changes of state or generations of output; that is, if $\delta(q, \lambda)$ is not null for some state q, the automaton may change this state or generate an output substring without actually reading another input symbol. Furthermore, the empty string λ may be generated as the output substring at times; if $\delta(q, a)$ contains (q', λ) and this is selected as the action for $\mathfrak{I}_f$ to take, then state q is changed into q', the input tape head advances one cell past a, but no output symbols are emitted. The ability of a finite transducer to take spontaneous actions or to read an input symbol without generating an output symbol allows the machine to perform translations in which the lengths of the input and output strings are different.

The *translation from* Σ^* *to* Δ^* *defined by finite transducer* $\mathfrak{I}_f$ is the set

$$\tau(\mathfrak{I}_f) = \{(x, y) | x \text{ in } \Sigma^*, y \text{ in } \Delta^*, y \text{ is output as } x \text{ is recognized by } \mathfrak{I}_f\}.$$

The same convention concerning nondeterminism in the recognition process applies to a finite transducer as to a finite automaton: input string x must be recognized by termination in a state in F if there is any way at all that the machine can do this. In the most general case, a given input x can have several recognition sequences, some of which produce different output strings.

A finite transducer is conveniently represented by its *state transition/output diagram*, a directed graph with nodes for the states that are connected by arcs labeled with input/output symbols. All final states in F appear as double circles, and the starting state is indicated by an entering but unattached arrow.

Example: The electrical activity of human heart muscle stimulation can be monitored by sensors whose output produces an electrocardiogram (ECG). A normal ECG appears in Fig. 4.12. The smaller of the heart's muscles, the *atria*, are stimulated first with a p pulse; the subsequent stimulation of the larger muscles, the *ventricles*, produces a larger r pulse followed by a t pulse as the ventricles repolarize after the pumping action.

The regularity of this normal ECG waveform may be described by a regular grammar. The waveform primitives are p, r, and t for the pulses

ISBN 0-201-02930-8/0-201-02931-6, pbk

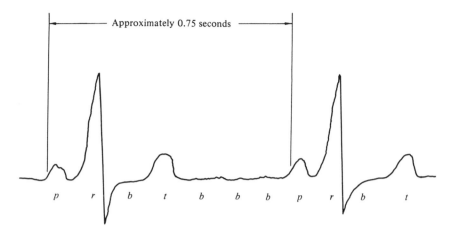

Figure 4.12. Normal human ECG.

and b for the quiescent times. A normal ECG sequence consists of concatenations of the substrings *prbtb*, *prbtbb*, and *prbtbbb*, in which the variable number of b's allows for variations in basically healthy heart rates. A regular grammar generating concatenations of these three substrings as its language is $G = (\{S, A, B, C, D, E, H\}, \{p, r, t, b\}, P, S)$ with productions

$$S \rightarrow pA \qquad A \rightarrow rB \qquad B \rightarrow bC$$

$$C \rightarrow tD \qquad D \rightarrow b \qquad D \rightarrow bE$$

$$E \rightarrow b \qquad E \rightarrow bH \qquad E \rightarrow pA$$

$$H \rightarrow b \qquad H \rightarrow bS \qquad H \rightarrow pA$$

An example of a derivation of a well-formed ECG wave using this grammar is

$$S \Rightarrow pA \Rightarrow prB \Rightarrow prbC \Rightarrow prbtD \Rightarrow prbtbE \Rightarrow prbtbbH$$

$$\Rightarrow prbtbbbS \Rightarrow prbtbbbpA \Rightarrow prbtbbbprB \Rightarrow prbtbbbprbC$$

$$\Rightarrow prbtbbbprbtD \Rightarrow prbtbbbprbtbE \Rightarrow prbtbbbprbtbb.$$

A deterministic finite automaton $\mathcal{C}_f$ that recognizes the language $L(G)$ is shown in Fig. 4.13. Because the starting state q_0 is designated to be a final state here, the empty string λ is actually accepted also; the precise

ISBN 0-201-02930-8/0-201-02931-6, pbk

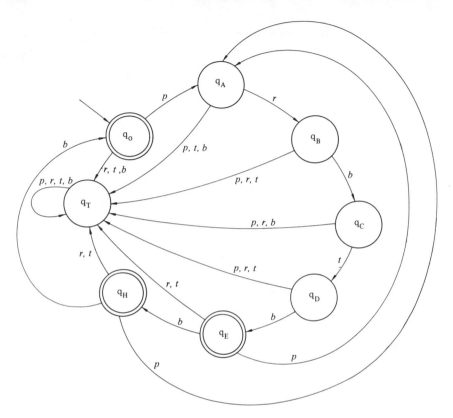

Figure 4.13. Finite automaton for recognizing normal ECG strings.

definition of $L(\mathcal{Q}_f)$ is therefore

$$L(\mathcal{Q}_f) = L(G) \cup \{\lambda\}.$$

Suppose that the requirement, however, is for a machine to serve as an ECG monitor in a situation in which a real-time alarm must be sounded immediately if the ECG becomes *abnormal*. The ECG sensors attached to the human will always provide a signal of p, r, t, or b to the automaton; thus, an abnormal ECG in this case means a sequence causing the machine in Fig. 4.13 to enter the trap state q_T. In the new situation, this set of abnormal ECG waveforms must be recognized; furthermore, the monitor must translate its input into an appropriate output message.

We assign output 0 to a normal or a potentially normal ECG subsequence and output 1 to a subsequence clearly identified as abnormal.

ISBN 0-201-02930-8/0-201-02931-6, pbk

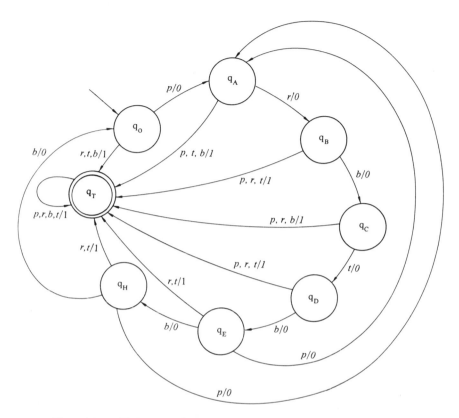

Figure 4.14. Finite transducer for recognizing abnormal ECG strings.

(Assume the output drives an audible alarm that is silent for a 0 and activated by a 1.) Then the finite automaton $\mathcal{C}_f$ in Fig. 4.13 is replaced by the finite transducer $\mathcal{T}_f$ in Fig. 4.14. The trap state q_T has been made the only accepting state for this machine. The outputs associated with the machine's transitions are such that a sequence of 0's will be produced as long as the input defines a normal or potentially normal ECG waveform, but a sequence of 1's will start as soon as the input becomes abnormal.

For instance, the normal waveform sequence *prbtbbbprbtbb* derived by using grammar G causes the transducer $\mathcal{T}_f$ to follow the state sequence $q_0, q_A, q_B, q_C, q_D, q_E, q_H, q_0, q_A, q_B, q_C, q_D, q_E, q_H$, and produce the output sequence 0^{13}. Note that this input string cannot be said to be translated into the output string because the input is not accepted by $\mathcal{T}_f$, and a translation occurs only when the input is an accepted sentence.

Suppose, however, that the input string applied to the machine is *prbtbprbtbbbbbb* .... The state sequence that $\mathcal{T}_f$ follows for this string is

ISBN 0-201-02930-8/0-201-02931-6, pbk

$q_0, q_A, q_B, q_C, q_D, q_E, q_A, q_B, q_C, q_D, q_E, q_H, q_0, q_T, q_T, q_T, \ldots$. The output string produced is $0^{12}1111 \ldots$. A translation of the input sentence into the output sentence does occur in this case because the input is accepted by the finite transducer as representing an abnormal ECG waveform. Output 1 is the alert signal.   □

It should be observed that the machine obtained by ignoring the output of a finite transducer is simply a finite automaton serving as a recognizer of a regular language. If this underlying automaton is nondeterministic, an equivalent deterministic finite-state recognizer may be constructed. A transducer, however, performs translation as well as recognition of an acceptable input string; and, in the most general case, this operation of translating is inherently nondeterministic because there are input sentences with multiple translations.

A fundamental relationship between simple syntax-directed translation schemata and finite transducers is given by the following theorem.

Theorem: A set T in $\Sigma^* \times \Delta^*$ is the translation set of a finite transducer iff T is the translation set generated by a regular SDTS.   □

In order to prove this theorem, it must be shown that, given a finite transducer $\mathfrak{I}_f$, a regular SDTS $\mathfrak{I}_r$ can be constructed such that $\tau(\mathfrak{I}_f) = \tau(\mathfrak{I}_r)$, and vice versa. These constructions are very similar to the procedures given in Section 4.2.1 relating regular grammars and finite automata.

Given a regular SDTS $\mathfrak{I}_r = (N, \Sigma, \Delta, R, X_0)$, the corresponding finite transducer $\mathfrak{I}_f = (Q, \Sigma, \Delta, \delta, q_0, F)$ is specified as follows. Suppose the set N consists of starting symbol X_0 and n additional nonterminals $X_1, X_2, \ldots, X_n$; then the state set Q is formed by introducing $n + 2$ states $\{q_0, q_1, \ldots, q_n, q_{n+1}\}$, where q_i corresponds to X_i for $i = 0, 1, 2, \ldots, n$, and q_{n+1} is an additional state. The set of final states is simply $\{q_{n+1}\}$. The δ mapping is developed from the rules in R such that for all i and j, $0 \leqslant i \leqslant n, 0 \leqslant j \leqslant n$:

   (i) if $X_i \to aX_j, bX_j$ is in R, then $\delta(q_i, a)$ contains (q_j, b) for a in $\Sigma \cup \{\lambda\}$, b in $\Delta \cup \{\lambda\}$; and
   (ii) if $X_i \to a, b$ is in R, then $\delta(q_i, a)$ contains (q_{n+1}, b) for a in $\Sigma \cup \{\lambda\}$, b in $\Delta \cup \{\lambda\}$.

Thus, the sequence of states entered by $\mathfrak{I}_f$ in translating an input string into an output string corresponds to the sequence of nonterminals appearing in the translation forms producing the identical translation using $\mathfrak{I}_r$. If an input string cannot be recognized and translated by $\mathfrak{I}_f$, it is because that string is not in the language of the input grammar of $\mathfrak{I}_r$.

On the other hand, given a finite transducer $\mathfrak{I}_f = (Q, \Sigma, \Delta, \delta, q_0, F)$, we

ISBN 0-201-02930-8/0-201-02931-6, pbk

specify a regular SDTS $\mathfrak{I}_r = (N, \Sigma, \Delta, R, X_0)$ by letting N be identified with the state set Q, with starting symbol X_0 corresponding to q_0, and rules obtained as follows:

(i) if (q_j, b) is in $\delta(q_i, a)$, then there is a rule $X_i \rightarrow aX_j, bX_j$ for a in $\Sigma \cup \{\lambda\}$, b in $\Delta \cup \{\lambda\}$; and

(ii) if (q_j, b) is in $\delta(q_i, a)$ and q_j is in F, then there is a rule $X_i \rightarrow a, b$ for a in $\Sigma \cup \{\lambda\}$, b in $\Delta \cup \{\lambda\}$.

Rules introduced by (i) allow translation forms of $\mathfrak{I}_r$ to follow the state sequence taken by $\mathfrak{I}_f$ in translating a string; rules introduced by (ii) terminate a $\mathfrak{I}_r$ translation in correspondence with entry of $\mathfrak{I}_f$ into an accepting state. Formal proof by induction establishes that for either construction, it will be the case that $\tau(\mathfrak{I}_f)$ is identical to $\tau(\mathfrak{I}_r)$.

Example: We wish to obtain a regular schema $\mathfrak{I}_r$ to generate the same set of translations from $\{p, r, t, b\}^*$ to $\{0, 1\}^*$ defined by the finite transducer $\mathfrak{I}_f$ in Fig. 4.14. The state set Q of this machine is $\{q_0, q_A, q_B, q_C, q_D, q_E, q_H, q_T\}$, so the set N of nonterminals for the schema becomes $\{S, A, B, C, D, E, H, T\}$ with starting symbol S. The input alphabet Σ for both $\mathfrak{I}_f$ and $\mathfrak{I}_r$ is $\{p, r, t, b\}$, and the output alphabet Δ for both is $\{0, 1\}$. The δ mapping represented by the state transition/output diagram in Fig. 4.14 has, for example,

$$\delta(q_0, p) = \{(q_A, 0)\},$$

$$\delta(q_0, r) = \delta(q_0, t) = \delta(q_0, b) = \{(q_T, 1)\}$$

as the possible transitions from state q_0. By part (i) in obtaining the schema's rules as described earlier, these transitions introduce the following:

$$S \rightarrow pA, 0A \qquad S \rightarrow rT, 1T$$

$$S \rightarrow tT, 1T \qquad S \rightarrow bT, 1T$$

Additionally, because q_T is a final state, there are rules

$$S \rightarrow r, 1 \qquad S \rightarrow t, 1$$

$$S \rightarrow b, 1$$

The entire set of rules for $\mathfrak{I}_r$ obtained in this way includes these rules for

ISBN 0-201-02930-8/0-201-02931-6, pbk

rewriting S together with the following rules for rewriting the other nonterminals:

$A \rightarrow rB, 0B$	$C \rightarrow rT, 1T$	$E \rightarrow cT, 1T$
$A \rightarrow tT, 1T$	$C \rightarrow p, 1$	$E \rightarrow t, 1$
$A \rightarrow p, 1$	$C \rightarrow b, 1$	$H \rightarrow bS, 0S$
$A \rightarrow b, 1$	$C \rightarrow pT, 1T$	$H \rightarrow rT, 1T$
$A \rightarrow pT, 1T$	$C \rightarrow r, 1$	$H \rightarrow r, 1$
$A \rightarrow bT, 1T$	$D \rightarrow pT, 1T$	$H \rightarrow pA, 0A$
$A \rightarrow t, 1$	$D \rightarrow tT, 1T$	$H \rightarrow tT, 1T$
$B \rightarrow pT, 1T$	$D \rightarrow r, 1$	$H \rightarrow t, 1$
$B \rightarrow tT, 1T$	$D \rightarrow bE, 0E$	$T \rightarrow pT, 1T$
$B \rightarrow r, 1$	$D \rightarrow rT, 1t$	$T \rightarrow tT, 1T$
$B \rightarrow bC, 0C$	$D \rightarrow p, 1$	$T \rightarrow p, 1$
$B \rightarrow rT, 1T$	$D \rightarrow t, 1$	$T \rightarrow t, 1$
$B \rightarrow p, 1$	$E \rightarrow pA, 0A$	$T \rightarrow rT, 1T$
$B \rightarrow t, 1$	$E \rightarrow rT, 1T$	$T \rightarrow bT, 1T$
$C \rightarrow tT, 1T$	$E \rightarrow r, 1$	$T \rightarrow r, 1$
$C \rightarrow tD, 0D$	$E \rightarrow bH, 0H$	$T \rightarrow b, 1$

An example of a translation produced by $\mathfrak{T}_r$ is the sequence of translation forms

$(S, S) \Rightarrow (pA, 0A) \Rightarrow (prB, 00B) \Rightarrow (prbC, 000C)$

$\Rightarrow (prbtD, 0000D) \Rightarrow (prbtbE, 00000E) \Rightarrow (prbtbbH, 000000H)$

$\Rightarrow (prbtbbbS, 0000000S) \Rightarrow (prbtbbbb, 00000001).$

ISBN 0-201-02930-8/0-201-02931-6, pbk

The fact that this input sentence can be derived and translated into an output string in which a 1 appears means that the same input sentence would be accepted and translated by $\mathcal{T}_f$. The input represents an abnormal ECG waveform, and the output introduces a 1 as soon as it is clear that the input could not be a normal subsequence.   □

4.3.2 Pushdown Transducers

In order to develop a transducer for a nonregular, context-free syntax-directed translation, a pushdown list of finite but unbounded capacity must be provided, just as was done in constructing an automaton for recognition of a context-free language. A (*nondeterministic*) *pushdown transducer* is a system given as an eight-tuple $\mathcal{T}_p = (Q, \Sigma, \Gamma, \Delta, \delta, q_0, Z_0, F)$ where $Q, \Sigma, \Gamma, q_0, Z_0, F$ are the same as in the definition of a pushdown automaton, Δ is a finite *output alphabet*, and δ is a *mapping* from $Q \times (\Sigma \cup \{\lambda\}) \times \Gamma$ to finite subsets of $Q \times \Gamma^* \times \Delta^*$.

Figure 4.15 gives the general representation of this kind of machine, which operates in the following way. The automaton is started in state q_0 with an empty output tape, the single symbol Z_0 on the stack, and input string x from Σ^+ on the input tape. x is scanned symbol by symbol from left to right. For the triple combination of current state, current input symbol or the empty string, and single symbol currently on top of the

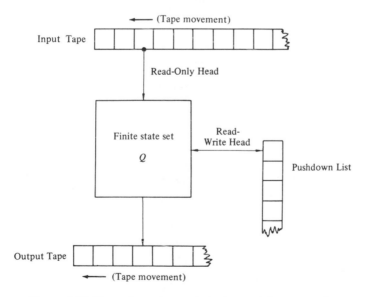

Figure 4.15. General representation of a pushdown transducer.

ISBN 0-201-02930-8/0-201-02931-6, pbk

stack, the δ mapping specifies the allowed combinations of next state, output substring in Δ^* to be placed on the next segment on the output tape, and string in Γ^* to replace the single topmost stack symbol. The operation of a pushdown transducer is therefore similar to that of a pushdown automaton, with the addition that an output string is generated as part of the processing.

Since a pushdown transducer can have a set of final states used for acceptance, the *translation set produced by* $\mathcal{T}_p$ *by final state* is defined to be

$$\tau(\mathcal{T}_p) = \{(x, y)| x \text{ in } \Sigma^*, y \text{ in } \Delta^*, y \text{ is on the output tape,}$$
$$\mathcal{T}_p \text{ starts in } q_0 \text{ with } Z_0 \text{ on its stack and can}$$
$$\text{halt in a state in } F \text{ when input } x \text{ is entirely}$$
$$\text{scanned}\}.$$

If F is the null set, the *translation set produced by empty stack* is defined as

$$\tau_\lambda(\mathcal{T}_p) = \{(x, y)| x \text{ in } \Sigma^*, y \text{ in } \Delta^*, y \text{ is on the output tape,}$$
$$x \text{ is recognized by empty stack}\}.$$

We shall assume acceptance by empty stack in the following discussions. It is noted that the machine obtained by ignoring the output of a pushdown transducer is a conventional pushdown automaton which is the recognizer of a context-free language (the input language of the transducer). In general, both recognition and translation are nondeterministic for pushdown machines.

A fundamental relationship between context-free schemata and pushdown transducers is given in the following theorem.

Theorem: A set T in $\Sigma^* \times \Delta^*$ is the translation set produced by a pushdown transducer by empty stack iff T is the translation set of a (simple) context-free SDTS. $\square$

The proof of this theorem is to show that, given a transducer $\mathcal{T}_p$, we can construct a context-free SDTS $\mathcal{T}_{cf}$ such that $\tau_\lambda(\mathcal{T}_p) = \tau(\mathcal{T}_{cf})$, and vice versa. Since the usual problem in syntactic pattern processing is the construction of a transducer from a SDTS, we describe only this portion of the construction.

Let $\mathcal{T}_{cf} = (N, \Sigma, \Delta, R, S)$ be a simple schema. It is necessary for the machine's stack to use a version of the output alphabet that is disjoint from Σ to guarantee that input and output symbols will not be mixed; so a new alphabet,

$$\Delta' = \{b'|b \text{ in } \Delta\},$$

ISBN 0-201-02930-8/0-201-02931-6, pbk

the symbols of which carry primes, is introduced.[‡] The pushdown transducer is the single-state machine $\mathcal{T}_p = (\{q_0\}, \Sigma, N \cup \Sigma \cup \Delta',$ $\Delta, \delta, q_0, S, \varnothing)$ with the δ mapping defined from R as follows:

(i) if $A \to x_0 B_1 x_1 \ldots x_{k-1} B_k x_k, y_0 B_1 y_1 \ldots y_{k-1} B_k y_k$ is a rule in R for $A, B_1, \ldots, B_k$ in N, x_i in Σ^*, and y_i in Δ^*, $0 \leqslant i \leqslant k$, then $\delta(q_0, \lambda, A)$ contains $(q_0, x_0 y_0' B_1 x_1 y_1' \ldots B_k x_k y_k', \lambda)$ where y_i' is y_i with each symbol of Δ replaced by its primed version;

(ii) $\delta(q_0, a, a) = \{(q_0, \lambda, \lambda)\}$ for each a in Σ; and

(iii) $\delta(q_0, \lambda, b') = \{(q_0, \lambda, b)\}$ for each b' in Δ'.

This transducer nondeterministically simulates the translation process of $\mathcal{T}_{cf}$ by replacing a nonterminal on the top of its stack by a list of symbols corresponding to the right side of a rule, then popping symbols of Σ from the stack as they match up with the input string, and removing symbols of Δ' from the stack to form the output string. A formal proof by induction establishes that $\tau_\lambda(\mathcal{T}_p)$ is identical to $\tau(\mathcal{T}_{cf})$.

Example: A context-free grammar G for string descriptions of submedian and telocentric chromosomes (due to Ledley *et al.*, [1965]) has the five primitive line segments in Fig. 4.16(a) as its five terminals. The set N of nonterminals is $\{S, S_1, S_2, A, B, C, D, E, F\}$, and the productions are

$$S \to S_1 \qquad\qquad S \to S_2$$

$$S_1 \to AA \qquad\qquad S_2 \to BA$$

$$A \to CA \qquad\qquad A \to AC$$

$$A \to DE \qquad\qquad A \to FD$$

$$B \to bB \qquad\qquad B \to Bb$$

$$B \to e \qquad\qquad C \to bC$$

$$C \to Cb \qquad\qquad C \to b$$

$$C \to d \qquad\qquad D \to bD$$

$$D \to Db \qquad\qquad D \to a$$

$$E \to cD \qquad\qquad F \to Dc$$

[‡]The primes need not be used when Σ and Δ are already disjoint; the changes in the way the pushdown transducer is constructed in this case are obvious.

ISBN 0-201-02930-8/0-201-02931-6, pbk

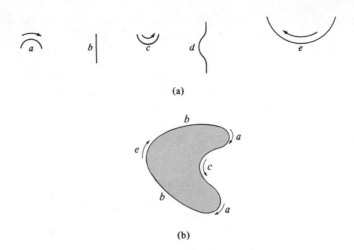

(a)

(b)

Figure 4.16. (a) Chromosome grammar primitives.   (b) Telocentric chromosome.

An example derivation of the string description of a telocentric chromosome from starting symbol S is

$$S \Rightarrow S_2 \Rightarrow BA \Rightarrow BbA \Rightarrow ebA \Rightarrow ebDE \Rightarrow ebaE$$

$$\Rightarrow ebacD \Rightarrow ebacDb \Rightarrow ebacab.$$

The chromosome pattern represented by this string appears in Fig. 4.16(b).

An approximate English-language interpretation of the nine nonterminals is that

S	means	⟨chromosome⟩
S_1	means	⟨submedian⟩
S_2	means	⟨telocentric⟩
A	means	⟨armpair⟩
B	means	⟨bottom⟩
C	means	⟨side⟩
D	means	⟨arm⟩
E	means	⟨rightpart⟩
F	means	⟨leftpart⟩

ISBN 0-201-02930-8/0-201-02931-6, pbk

Approximate descriptions in English for the five terminals are that

a means ⟨clockwise⟩ or ⟨cw⟩

b means ⟨straight line⟩ or ⟨st⟩

c means ⟨counterclockwise⟩ or ⟨ccw⟩

d means ⟨bulge line⟩ or ⟨bl⟩

e means ⟨broad clockwise⟩ or ⟨bcw⟩

With these interpretations, the production $E \rightarrow cD$, for example, means that a chromosome ⟨rightpart⟩ consists of a counterclockwise line segment followed by an ⟨armpair⟩.

Let us treat the last 8 nonterminal descriptions and 5 terminal descriptions in English as a set of 13 symbols in an output alphabet Δ. Each of these 13 items is an approximate word description of a physical characteristic of a chromosome outline or makeup.

The chromosome grammar $G = (N, \Sigma, P, S)$ may be converted into a simple schema $\mathcal{T} = (N, \Sigma, \Delta, R, S)$ with the following rules:

$S \rightarrow S_1, \langle\text{sub}\rangle S_1$ $S \rightarrow S_2, \langle\text{telo}\rangle S_2$

$S_1 \rightarrow AA, \langle\text{armpair}\rangle A \langle\text{armpair}\rangle A$ $S_2 \rightarrow BA, \langle\text{bottom}\rangle B \langle\text{armpair}\rangle A$

$A \rightarrow CA, \langle\text{side}\rangle CA$ $A \rightarrow AC, A \langle\text{side}\rangle C$

$A \rightarrow DE, \langle\text{arm}\rangle D \langle\text{rightpart}\rangle E$ $A \rightarrow FD, \langle\text{leftpart}\rangle F \langle\text{arm}\rangle D$

$B \rightarrow bB, \langle\text{st}\rangle B$ $B \rightarrow Bb, B \langle\text{st}\rangle$

$B \rightarrow e, \langle\text{bcw}\rangle$ $C \rightarrow bC, \langle\text{st}\rangle C$

$C \rightarrow Cb, C \langle\text{st}\rangle$ $C \rightarrow b, \langle\text{st}\rangle$

$C \rightarrow Cd, \langle\text{bl}\rangle$ $D \rightarrow bD, \langle\text{st}\rangle D$

$D \rightarrow Db, D \langle\text{st}\rangle$ $D \rightarrow a, \langle\text{cw}\rangle$

$E \rightarrow cD, \langle\text{ccw}\rangle \langle\text{arm}\rangle D$ $F \rightarrow Dc, \langle\text{arm}\rangle D \langle\text{ccw}\rangle$

This schema can be used to derive a string representation of a chromosome in terms of the primitive line segments and, simultaneously, to

ISBN 0-201-02930-8/0-201-02931-6, pbk

translate it into an approximate description in English. For instance, the sentence just derived using grammar G is translated by the sequence of translation forms

$(S, S) \Rightarrow (S_2, \langle \text{telo} \rangle S_2) \Rightarrow (BA, \langle \text{telo} \rangle \langle \text{bottom} \rangle B \langle \text{armpair} \rangle A)$

$\Rightarrow (BbA, \langle \text{telo} \rangle \langle \text{bottom} \rangle B \langle \text{st} \rangle \langle \text{armpair} \rangle A)$

$\Rightarrow (ebA, \langle \text{telo} \rangle \langle \text{bottom} \rangle \langle \text{bcw} \rangle \langle \text{st} \rangle \langle \text{armpair} \rangle A)$

$\Rightarrow (ebDE, \langle \text{telo} \rangle \langle \text{bottom} \rangle \langle \text{bcw} \rangle \langle \text{st} \rangle \langle \text{armpair} \rangle \langle \text{arm} \rangle D \langle \text{rightpart} \rangle E)$

$\Rightarrow (ebaE, \langle \text{telo} \rangle \langle \text{bottom} \rangle \langle \text{bcw} \rangle \langle \text{st} \rangle \langle \text{armpair} \rangle \langle \text{arm} \rangle \langle \text{cw} \rangle \langle \text{rightpart} \rangle E)$

$\Rightarrow (ebacD, \langle \text{telo} \rangle \langle \text{bottom} \rangle \langle \text{bcw} \rangle \langle \text{st} \rangle \langle \text{armpair} \rangle \langle \text{arm} \rangle \langle \text{cw} \rangle \langle \text{rightpart} \rangle$

$\qquad \langle \text{ccw} \rangle \langle \text{arm} \rangle D)$

$\Rightarrow (ebacDb, \langle \text{telo} \rangle \langle \text{bottom} \rangle \langle \text{bcw} \rangle \langle \text{st} \rangle \langle \text{armpair} \rangle \langle \text{arm} \rangle \langle \text{cw} \rangle \langle \text{rightpart} \rangle$

$\qquad \langle \text{ccw} \rangle \langle \text{arm} \rangle D \langle \text{st} \rangle)$

$\Rightarrow (ebacab, \langle \text{telo} \rangle \langle \text{bottom} \rangle \langle \text{bcw} \rangle \langle \text{st} \rangle \langle \text{armpair} \rangle \langle \text{arm} \rangle \langle \text{cw} \rangle \langle \text{rightpart} \rangle$

$\qquad \langle \text{ccw} \rangle \langle \text{arm} \rangle \langle \text{cw} \rangle \langle \text{st} \rangle).$

The output sentence provides a complete analysis of the input sentence *ebacab*; specifically, it states that the input string defines a telocentric chromosome with a bottom $\langle \text{bcw} \rangle \langle \text{st} \rangle$ attached to an armpair consisting of an arm $\langle \text{cw} \rangle$ and a rightpart that is a $\langle \text{ccw} \rangle$ line followed by an arm $\langle \text{cw} \rangle \langle \text{st} \rangle$.

This example is completed with the construction of a pushdown transducer $\mathfrak{T}_p = (\{q_0\}, \Sigma, \Gamma, \Delta, \delta, q_0, S, \varnothing)$ to define the same translation set as the schema $\mathfrak{T}$. The transducer is the formal specification of a machine that can recognize a pattern string as produced, for example, by an automatic chromosome outline scanner, and translate it into an approximate description in the English language. Since Σ and Δ are already disjoint, no new symbols are needed for the stack alphabet. The transducer has a single state, q_0; the initial stack symbol is S; and there are no final states because recognition is by empty stack. The alphabets are

$\Sigma = \{a, b, c, d, e\},$

$\Delta = \{\langle \text{sub} \rangle, \langle \text{telo} \rangle, \langle \text{armpair} \rangle, \langle \text{bottom} \rangle, \langle \text{side} \rangle, \langle \text{arm} \rangle, \langle \text{rightpart} \rangle,$

$\qquad \langle \text{leftpart} \rangle, \langle \text{cw} \rangle, \langle \text{st} \rangle, \langle \text{ccw} \rangle, \langle \text{bl} \rangle, \langle \text{bcw} \rangle\},$

ISBN 0-201-02930-8/0-201-02931-6, pbk

and

$$\Gamma = N \cup \Sigma \cup \Delta$$

$$= \{S, S_1, S_2, A, B, C, D, E, F\} \cup \Sigma \cup \Delta.$$

The δ mapping is obtained from the schema rules R by the three steps presented earlier:

(i) $\delta(q_0, \lambda, S) = \{(q_0, \langle\text{sub}\rangle S_1, \lambda), (q_0, \langle\text{telo}\rangle S_2, \lambda)\}$,

$\delta(q_0, \lambda, S_1) = \{(q_0, \langle\text{armpair}\rangle A\langle\text{armpair}\rangle A, \lambda)\}$,

$\delta(q_0, \lambda, S_2) = \{(q_0, \langle\text{bottom}\rangle B\langle\text{armpair}\rangle A, \lambda)\}$,

$\delta(q_0, \lambda, A) = \{(q_0, \langle\text{side}\rangle CA, \lambda), (q_0, A\langle\text{side}\rangle C, \lambda), (q_0, \langle\text{arm}\rangle$
$\qquad\qquad\qquad D\langle\text{rightpart}\rangle E, \lambda), (q_0, \langle\text{leftpart}\rangle F\langle\text{arm}\rangle D, \lambda)\}$,

$\delta(q_0, \lambda, B) = \{(q_0, b\langle\text{st}\rangle B, \lambda), (q_0, Bb\langle\text{st}\rangle, \lambda),$
$\qquad\qquad\qquad (q_0, e\langle\text{bcw}\rangle, \lambda)\}$,

$\delta(q_0, \lambda, C) = \{(q_0, b\langle\text{st}\rangle C, \lambda), (q_0, Cb\langle\text{st}\rangle, \lambda),$
$\qquad\qquad\qquad (q_0, b\langle\text{st}\rangle, \lambda), (q_0, d\langle\text{bl}\rangle, \lambda)\}$,

$\delta(q_0, \lambda, D) = \{(q_0, b\langle\text{st}\rangle D, \lambda), (q_0, Db\langle\text{st}\rangle, \lambda),$
$\qquad\qquad\qquad (q_0, a\langle\text{cw}\rangle, \lambda)\}$,

$\delta(q_0, \lambda, E) = \{(q_0, c\langle\text{ccw}\rangle\langle\text{arm}\rangle D, \lambda)\}$,

$\delta(q_0, \lambda, F) = \{(q_0, \langle\text{arm}\rangle Dc\langle\text{ccw}\rangle, \lambda)\}$.

(ii) For each input alphabet symbol a in Σ,

$\delta(q_0, a, a) = \{(q_0, \lambda, \lambda)\}$.

(iii) For each output alphabet symbol $\langle s\rangle$ in Δ,

$\delta(q_0, \lambda, \langle s\rangle) = \{(q_0, \lambda, \langle s\rangle)\}$.

Suppose the input string applied to $\mathfrak{I}_p$ is *ebacab*. $\mathfrak{I}_p$ proceeds in the following way. The starting state is q_0 and the initial stack symbol is S. Before any input symbol is scanned, $\mathfrak{I}_p$ must select an action from

$$\delta(q_0, \lambda, S) = \{(q_0, \langle\text{sub}\rangle S_1, \lambda), (q_0, \langle\text{telo}\rangle S_2, \lambda)\}.$$

In this case, the machine selects the second option, reenters state q_0, replaces S by $\langle\text{telo}\rangle S_2$ on the stack, and does not emit any output symbols. The remaining actions of $\mathfrak{I}_p$ are these:

$\delta(q_0, \lambda, \langle\text{telo}\rangle) = \{(q_0, \lambda, \langle\text{telo}\rangle)\}$ The output generated is $\langle\text{telo}\rangle$. The stack now contains S_2.

$\delta(q_0, \lambda, S_2) =$
$\{(q_0, \langle\text{bottom}\rangle B\langle\text{armpair}\rangle A, \lambda)\}$ The stack now holds the string $\langle\text{bottom}\rangle B\langle\text{armpair}\rangle A$.

$\delta(q_0, \lambda, \langle\text{bottom}\rangle) =$
$\{(q_0, \lambda, \langle\text{bottom}\rangle)\}$ Output $\langle\text{bottom}\rangle$ is emitted. The stack now contains $B\langle\text{armpair}\rangle A$.

$\delta(q_0, \lambda, B)$ contains $(q_0, Bb\langle\text{st}\rangle, \lambda)$.   The stack holds $Bb\langle\text{st}\rangle \langle\text{armpair}\rangle A$.

ISBN 0-201-02930-8/0-201-02931-6, pbk

$\delta(q_0, \lambda, B)$ contains $(q_0, e\langle bcw \rangle, \lambda)$.

The stack holds $e\langle bcw \rangle$ $b\langle st \rangle \langle armpair \rangle A$.

$\delta(q_0, e, e) = \{(q_0, \lambda, \lambda)\}$

The first input symbol is scanned and popped from the stack, which now holds $\langle bcw \rangle$ $b\langle st \rangle \langle armpair \rangle A$.

$\delta(q_0, \lambda, \langle bcw \rangle) = \{(q_0, \lambda, \langle bcw \rangle)\}$

Output $\langle bcw \rangle$ is emitted. The stack contains $b\langle st \rangle \langle armpair \rangle A$.

$\delta(q_0, b, b) = \{(q_0, \lambda, \lambda)\}$

The second input symbol is scanned and the stack holds $\langle st \rangle \langle armpair \rangle A$.

$\delta(q_0, \lambda, \langle st \rangle) = \{(q_0, \lambda, \langle st \rangle)\}$
$\delta(q_0, \lambda, \langle armpair \rangle) = \{(q_0, \lambda, \langle armpair \rangle)\}$

These two consecutive actions emit output $\langle st \rangle \langle armpair \rangle$. The stack holds A.

$\delta(q_0, \lambda, A)$ contains $(q_0, \langle arm \rangle D \langle rightpart \rangle E, \lambda)$.

The stack now holds $\langle arm \rangle D \langle rightpart \rangle E$.

$\delta(q_0, \lambda, \langle arm \rangle) = \{(q_0, \lambda, \langle arm \rangle)\}$

Output $\langle arm \rangle$ is emitted. The stack contains $D\langle rightpart \rangle E$.

$\delta(q_0, \lambda, D)$ contains $(q_0, a\langle cw \rangle, \lambda)$

The stack holds $a\langle cw \rangle \langle rightpart \rangle E$.

$\delta(q_0, a, a) = \{(q_0, \lambda, \lambda)\}$

The third input symbol is popped, and the stack holds $\langle cw \rangle \langle rightpart \rangle E$.

$\delta(q_0, \lambda, \langle cw \rangle) = \{(q_0, \lambda, \langle cw \rangle)\}$
$\delta(q_0, \lambda, \langle rightpart \rangle) = \{(q_0, \lambda, \langle rightpart \rangle)\}$

These two consecutive actions emit output $\langle cw \rangle \langle rightpart \rangle$. The stack holds E.

$\delta(q_0, \lambda, E) = \{q_0, c\langle cw \rangle \langle arm \rangle D, \lambda)\}$

The stack holds $c\langle ccw \rangle \langle arm \rangle D$.

$\delta(q_0, c, c) = \{(q_0, \lambda, \lambda)\}$
$\delta(q_0, \lambda, \langle ccw \rangle) = \{(q_0, \lambda, \langle ccw \rangle)\}$
$\delta(q_0, \lambda, \langle arm \rangle) = \{(q_0, \lambda, \langle arm \rangle)\}$

These three actions scan one more input symbol and emit output $\langle ccw \rangle \langle arm \rangle$. The stack now contains D.

$\delta(q_0, \lambda, D)$ contains $(q_0, Db\langle st \rangle, \lambda)$.

The stack holds $Db\langle st \rangle$.

$\delta(q_0, \lambda, D)$ contains $(q_0, a\langle cw \rangle, \lambda)$.

The stack holds $a\langle cw \rangle b\langle st \rangle$.

ISBN 0-201-02930-8/0-201-02931-6, pbk

The last four actions of $\mathcal{T}_p$ complete the input string scan, emit the last output symbols, and empty the stack:

$$\delta(q_0, a, a) = \{(q_0, \lambda, \lambda)\},$$

$$\delta(q_0, \lambda, \langle \text{cw} \rangle) = \{(q_0, \lambda, \langle \text{cw} \rangle)\},$$

$$\delta(q_0, b, b) = \{(q_0, \lambda, \lambda)\},$$

$$\delta(q_0, \lambda, \langle \text{st} \rangle) = \{(q_0, \lambda, \langle \text{st} \rangle)\}.$$

A review of the entire output sentence that $\mathcal{T}_p$ places on the output tape will confirm that this translation of input string *ebacab* agrees with the one produced by the simple schema $\mathcal{T}$. □

4.4 PARSING IN STRING LANGUAGES

4.4.1 Introduction

The finite and pushdown automata discussed in Section 4.2 are formal models of machines used for recognition of regular and context-free languages, respectively. These machines essentially reconstruct a leftmost derivation of an acceptable sentence as their computation; in other words, they perform the function of analyzing the syntax of an input string to reach a binary decision about the string's grammatical correctness. The formal models establish many important characteristics of this analysis, such as the requirement for a pushdown list or its equivalent to handle context-free languages. However, it is possible to study syntax analysis in a general way by considering techniques and algorithms that may or may not be implemented directly in the form of automata designed expressly for the purpose. This kind of algorithm is called a *parsing algorithm*.

4.4.2 Parsing

To parse a string x, which is a sentence in a language $L(G)$ with a known regular or context-free grammar $G = (N, \Sigma, P, S)$, means to determine a sequence of productions used to derive x. If G is ambiguous and x has more than one derivation, the environment in which G is used determines whether all derivations of x are required. Any string not in $L(G)$, of course, cannot be parsed using G.

There are two general approaches to parsing. First, given G and x in $L(G)$, we may begin with starting symbol S and attempt to derive x by

ISBN 0-201-02930-8/0-201-02931-6, pbk

applying productions in P. In this first case, the syntax analysis proceeds *top-down* from S through intermediate sentential forms until x is obtained and a leftmost derivation of x is found. Second, given G and x in $L(G)$, we may begin with x itself and, by applying productions in a reverse fashion, attempt to reduce x to the starting symbol S. In this second case, the syntax analysis proceeds *bottom-up* from x to S to yield the reverse of the sequence of productions in a rightmost derivation of x.

Both approaches have been implemented in practice. The general algorithm for either method is simply an exhaustive enumeration that follows all alternatives simultaneously until an input string either is completely parsed or is rejected because it has become clear that the string is not in $L(G)$.

4.4.2.1 Bottom-Up Parsing

In "brute force" bottom-up parsing, given string x in Σ^+ and grammar G, we begin with x and construct strings in $(N \cup \Sigma)^+$ that *might* occur in a derivation of x by applying the reverses of productions. To apply a production $A \rightarrow \alpha$ "in reverse" means that an occurrence of the right-hand side α must be located in a string and reduced to the single nonterminal, A, to get a new element of $(N \cup \Sigma)^+$. Since it is not known in advance which series of strings is potentially correct, all the possible series must be developed in parallel.

Example: Consider the grammar $G = (\{S, A\}, \{a, b\}, P, S)$ with productions

$$S \rightarrow Ab \qquad S \rightarrow ASb \qquad A \rightarrow a$$

Its language is

$$L(G) = \{x \mid x = a^n b^n, n > 0\}.$$

Suppose $x = aabb$ is to be parsed bottom-up. The following series of sentential forms is obtained by reversing the indicated productions:

$\underline{a}abb$ becomes $Aabb$ via $A \rightarrow a$ in reverse;

$A\underline{a}bb$ becomes $AAbb$ via $A \rightarrow a$ in reverse;

$A\underline{Ab}b$ becomes ASb via $S \rightarrow Ab$ in reverse;

$\underline{ASb}$ becomes S via $S \rightarrow ASb$ in reverse.

Two other series found by different choices of replacement are *aabb, aAbb, aSb, ASb, S* and *aabb, aAbb, AAbb, ASb, S*.   □

ISBN 0-201-02930-8/0-201-02931-6, pbk

In a derivation of the form

$$S \overset{*}{\Rightarrow} \beta A \gamma \Rightarrow \beta \alpha \gamma \overset{*}{\Rightarrow} x,$$

in which production $A \rightarrow \alpha$ is used, the substring α is a *handle* of the sentential form $\beta \alpha \gamma$. The bottom-up technique, having reduced x to $\beta \alpha \gamma$ (and possibly to several additional strings of terminals and nonterminals), would locate handle α (and all other potential handles), then generate the new string $\beta A \gamma$ (with others possibly generated as well). The same operation would then be applied to all currently existing strings, including $\beta A \gamma$. Termination occurs for a series of strings whenever starting symbol S is reached or no further reductions are possible. In the former case, the strings are sentential forms in a legitimate derivation of x.

It is desirable to organize the bottom-up method to produce a specific type of derivation for each recognizable input string. A *rightmost derivation* will be found by requiring that when a sentential form $\beta \alpha \gamma$ is reduced to $\beta A \gamma$ by virtue of production $A \rightarrow \alpha$, the substring γ must consist only of terminals. It should be noted that, in the preceding example, only the first of the three series meets this requirement. Its production sequence is the reverse of the rightmost derivation

$$S \Rightarrow ASb \Rightarrow AAbb \Rightarrow Aabb \Rightarrow aabb.$$

The need to carry out all developing series in parallel is a serious problem in practice. An alternative is to produce a single series of strings by making an arbitrary choice for handle reduction whenever necessary, but to provide for backtracking to decision points to try other possibilities if the reduction stalls.

4.4.2.2 Top-Down Parsing

In brute force top-down parsing, given string x in Σ^+ and grammar G, we begin with starting symbol S and derive sentential forms simultaneously by applying productions rewriting leftmost nonterminals. Since the number of symbols in a sentential form cannot be decreased when a production is applied, all the forms exceeding x in length can be abandoned. Only the finite set of sentential forms with length equal to or less than x need be developed.

Example: Consider the grammar $G = (\{S, A\}, \{a, b\}, P, S)$ with productions

$$S \rightarrow Ab \qquad S \rightarrow ASb \qquad A \rightarrow a$$

Suppose $x = aabb$ must be parsed top-down. Beginning with S, the following

ISBN 0-201-02930-8/0-201-02931-6, pbk

three derivation sequences are found:

$$S \Rightarrow Ab \Rightarrow ab,$$

$$S \Rightarrow ASb \Rightarrow aSb \Rightarrow aAbb \Rightarrow aabb,$$

$$S \Rightarrow ASb \Rightarrow aSb \Rightarrow aASbb.$$

The first of these terminates before producing x. The third is abandoned because a sentential form with five symbols has appeared. The second is therefore the only leftmost derivation of x.   □

In practice, it is usually more attractive to implement a top-down parser with backtracking than with parallel development of all conceivable sentential forms. The number of production choices can sometimes be reduced at a given step by recognizing that in going from sentential form $yA\beta$ to $yzB\gamma\beta$ by application of production $A \to zB\gamma$, the terminal prefix yz must agree with a terminal prefix of x. A production causing disagreement is known to be incorrect and need not be used.

The fact that the underlying pushdown automaton of a pushdown transducer simulates a leftmost derivation of an acceptable input string makes this machine the standard model of a top-down parser for a context-free language. The assumption that a pushdown transducer always takes a correct action when presented with alternatives is a mathematical fiction eliminating the need for backtracking or parallel development.

To construct the *parsing pushdown transducer* for a given context-free grammar $G = (N, \Sigma, P, S)$, one first assigns a reference number to each production in P. A simple syntax-directed translation schema $\mathfrak{T}_G = (N, \Sigma, \Delta, R, S)$ is then defined such that Δ is the set of production reference numbers and

$$R = \{A \to x_0 B_1 x_1 \ldots x_{k-1} B_k x_k, n \, B_1 \ldots B_k | n \text{ is the}$$
$$\text{reference number for production } A \to x_0 B_1 \ldots B_k x_k$$
$$\text{with nonterminals } B_1, \ldots, B_k \text{ in the right-hand}$$
$$\text{side}\}.$$

The nondeterministic pushdown transducer corresponding to schema $\mathfrak{T}_G$ is the natural leftmost parser of $L(G)$. The translation set of this machine is

$$\tau_\lambda(\mathfrak{T}_G) = \{(x, y) | x \text{ in } L(G_i), y \text{ is the number sequence of the}$$
$$\text{productions in a leftmost derivation of } x\}.$$

Example: Consider the grammar $G = (\{S, A\}, \{a, b\}, P, S)$ with numbered productions,

$$[1]S \to Ab \qquad [2]S \to ASb \qquad [3]A \to a$$

The schema is $\mathfrak{T}_G = (\{S, A\}, \{a, b\}, \{1, 2, 3\}, R, S)$ with rules

$$S \to Ab, 1A \qquad S \to ASb, 2AS \qquad A \to a, 3$$

ISBN 0-201-02930-8/0-201-02931-6, pbk

The pushdown transducer obtained from $\mathfrak{T}_G$ by the method discussed in Section 4.3.2 is the machine $\mathfrak{T}_p = (\{q_0\}, \{a, b\}, \{S, A, a, b, 1, 2, 3\}, \{1, 2, 3\}, \delta, q_0, S, \varnothing)$ with the following δ mapping:

$$\delta(q_0, \lambda, S) = \{(q_0, 1Ab, \lambda), (q_0, 2ASb, \lambda)\},$$

$$\delta(q_0, \lambda, A) = \{(q_0, a3, \lambda)\},$$

$$\delta(q_0, a, a) = \delta(q_0, b, b) = \{(q_0, \lambda, \lambda)\},$$

$$\delta(q_0, \lambda, 1) = \{(q_0, \lambda, 1)\},$$

$$\delta(q_0, \lambda, 2) = \{(q_0, \lambda, 2)\},$$

$$\delta(q_0, \lambda, 3) = \{(q_0, \lambda, 3)\}.$$

Primes are not required on any symbols of the stack alphabet because Σ and Δ are disjoint.

Suppose the input string is *aabb*. The first action of $\mathfrak{T}_p$ is a replacement of S on the stack selected from

$$\delta(q_0, \lambda, S) = \{(q_0, 1Ab, \lambda), (q_0, 2ASb, \lambda)\}.$$

The correct action at this point is the second of these alternatives, giving *2ASb* on the stack and output λ. The remaining actions of $\mathfrak{T}_p$ are

$(\delta(q_0, \lambda, 2) = \{(q_0, \lambda, 2)\}$ giving stack contents *ASb* and output *2*;

$\delta(q_0, \lambda, A) = \{(q_0, a3, \lambda)\}$ giving stack *a3Sb* and output *2*;

$\delta(q_0, a, a) = \{(q_0, \lambda, \lambda)\}$ giving stack *3Sb* and output *2*;

$\delta(q_0, \lambda, 3) = \{(q_0, \lambda, 3)\}$ giving stack *Sb* and output *23*;

$\delta(q_0, \lambda, S)$ has $(q_0, 1Ab, \lambda)$ giving stack *1Abb* and output *23*;

$\delta(q_0, \lambda, 1) = \{(q_0, \lambda, 1)\}$ giving stack *Abb* and output *231*;

$\delta(q_0, \lambda, A) = \{(q_0, a3, \lambda)\}$ giving stack *a3bb* and output *231*;

$\delta(q_0, a, a) = \{(q_0, \lambda, \lambda)\}$ giving stack *3bb* and output *231*;

$\delta(q_0, \lambda, 3) = \{(q_0, \lambda, 3)\}$ giving stack *bb* and output *2313*;

$\delta(q_0, b, b) = \{(q_0, \lambda, \lambda)\}$ giving stack *b* and output *2313*;

$\delta(q_0, b, b) = \{(q_0, \lambda, \lambda)\}$ giving stack contents λ and output *2313*.

ISBN 0-201-02930-8/0-201-02931-6, pbk

Since the entire string is scanned and $\mathcal{T}_p$ halts with empty stack, the input is accepted; and the output of the translation, *2313*, is the sequence of productions in the leftmost derivation,

$$S \Rightarrow ASb \Rightarrow aSb \Rightarrow aAbb \Rightarrow aabb. \qquad \square$$

4.4.3   The Cocke–Younger–Kasami Parsing Algorithm

Two ways to specify the methods for syntax analysis of a context-free language are the pushdown automaton and the top-down/bottom-up parsing techniques. Both of these specifications provide insight into various aspects of the problem. A third description is provided by the statement of algorithms in which information is organized and processed in ways differing from the straightforward top-down/bottom-up methods.

One of the outstanding examples of an algorithm of this nature is the tabular method of Cocke (Cocke and Schwartz, [1970]), Younger [1967], and Kasami [1965]. This algorithm requires that the grammar to be used for parsing, $G = (N, \Sigma, P, S)$, be given in Chomsky normal form (Section 2.4.3). It is assumed, therefore, that each production in P is either of the form $A \to BC$ or of the form $A \to a$. No empty string production like $A \to \lambda$ is allowed.

Given input string $x = a_1 a_2 \ldots a_n$ to be parsed, a triangular table with elements t_{ij}, $1 \leqslant i \leqslant n$, $1 \leqslant j \leqslant (n - i + 1)$, is constructed where i and j are the column and row indices, respectively, and the origin ($i = 1, j = 1$) is located at the bottom left corner. Each table entry t_{ij} must be constructed to contain a subset of N, with a nonterminal A entered into t_{ij} if the substring of x beginning with a_i and extending for j symbols can be derived from A; in other words, if

$$A \overset{*}{\underset{G}{\Rightarrow}} a_i \ldots a_{i+j-1}.$$

Ultimately, x is in $L(G)$ iff S is in t_{1n} when the table is completed. In the case that S is in t_{1n}, a leftmost derivation can also be extracted from the table.

The table is built up left to right from the lowest row to the upper entry, t_{1n}. The requirement that G be in Chomsky normal form allows construction of the table for an input string of length n to proceed as follows:

Step 1.   Set $j = 1$. Compute t_{i1} as i ranges from 1 to n by placing A in t_{i1} exactly when there is a production $A \to a_i$ in P.

Step 2.   Assuming $t_{i,j-1}$ has been formed for $1 \leqslant i \leqslant n$, compute t_{ij}

ISBN 0-201-02930-8/0-201-02931-6, pbk

where A is placed in t_{ij} when, for any k such that $1 \leqslant k < j$, there is a production $A \to BC$ in P with B in t_{ik} and C in $t_{i+k, j-k}$. Observe that this recursive step is based on a decomposition of the substring $a_i \ldots a_{i+j-1}$ into prefix $a_i \ldots a_{i+k-1}$ and suffix $a_{i+k} \ldots a_{j-k}$ such that

$$B \overset{*}{\Rightarrow} a_i \ldots a_{i+k-1}, \quad C \overset{*}{\Rightarrow} a_{i+k} \ldots a_{j-k}, \quad \text{and} \quad A \overset{*}{\Rightarrow} BC.$$

Step 3.   Repeat step 2 until the table is completed or until an entire row has only null entries. x is in $L(G)$ iff S is in t_{1n}.

For parsing a string of length n, the amount of storage required by this algorithm in the worst case is proportional to n^2 and the number of elementary operations (such as assigning a value to a variable or testing two variables for equality) is proportional to n^3.

Example: Let $G = (\{S, A, B, C\}, \{a, b\}, P, S)$ have productions

$$S \to AB \qquad S \to AC \qquad A \to a \qquad B \to b \qquad C \to SB$$

This grammar is in Chomsky normal form with no empty string productions. Its language is $\{x | x = a^m b^m, m \geqslant 1\}$.

Let $x = aabb$ be the input string to be parsed. Table construction proceeds as follows:

Step 1.   Set $j = 1$ and compute t_{ij} for $1 \leqslant i \leqslant 4$.
For $a_1 = a$ we have $t_{11} = \{A\}$, since there is a production $A \to a$.
For $a_2 = a$, $t_{21} = \{A\}$.
For $a_3 = b$, $t_{31} = \{B\}$, since $B \to b$ is a production in P.
For $a_4 = b$, $t_{41} = \{B\}$.

(The bottom row of the table in Fig. 4.17(a) is filled in with these entries.)

Step 2.   (i)   First iteration: Set $j = 2$ and compute t_{i2} for $1 \leqslant i \leqslant 3$.
For $a_1 a_2 = aa$, we find $t_{12} = \varnothing$ because there is no nonterminal X such that $X \to YZ$, $Y \to a$, $Z \to a$.
For $a_2 a_3 = ab$, $t_{22} = \{S\}$ since there are productions $S \to AB$, $A \to a$, $B \to b$.
For $a_3 a_4 = bb$, $t_{32} = \varnothing$.
If at this point t_{22} were also null, the algorithm would be terminated and the input string would be rejected; however, t_{22} is not null, so there is another iteration of this step.

(ii)   Second iteration: Set $j = 3$, and compute t_{i3} for $1 \leqslant i \leqslant 2$.
For $a_1 a_2 a_3 = aab$, we have $t_{13} = \varnothing$ because for neither decomposition of substring aab, namely, as *(a)(ab)* or as *(aa)(b)*, is it found that there is a

ISBN 0-201-02930-8/0-201-02931-6, pbk

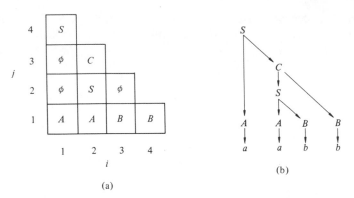

(a)

(b)

Figure 4.17. Cocke–Younger–Kasami parsing algorithm. (a) Parse table. (b) Leftmost derivation.

nonterminal X such that $X \to YZ$ where Y derives the prefix and Z derives the suffix.

For $a_2 a_3 a_4 = abb$, we find $t_{23} = C$ since $C \to SB$, $S \overset{*}{\Rightarrow} ab$, and $B \overset{*}{\Rightarrow} b$.

(iii) Third iteration: Set $j = 4$ and compute t_{14}.

For $a_1 a_2 a_3 a_4 = aabb$, we find $t_{14} = \{S\}$ because $S \to AC$, $A \overset{*}{\Rightarrow} a$, and $C \overset{*}{\Rightarrow} abb$.

Step 3.   Halt. The table is complete.

It is concluded that sentence *aabb* is in $L(G)$. Its leftmost derivation is the production sequence $S \to AC$, $A \to a$, $C \to SB$, $S \to AB$, $A \to a$, $B \to b$, $B \to b$, extracted from the table as shown in Fig. 4.17(b). □

4.4.4 The Transition Diagram Method

The transition diagram method of parsing with a context-free grammar was introduced by Conway [1963] and studied more formally by Lomet [1973]. It has been used as a practical, effective algorithm (cf. Button [1977], Moore [1977], Wilcox *et al.* [1976], to produce top-down parses of well-formed input strings in context-free languages generated by deterministic grammars.

In this parsing technique, a set of transition diagrams resembling those used for finite automata is constructed from the grammar's productions. There is one transition diagram for each nonterminal, and the diagram for a specific nonterminal embodies all productions rewriting that nonterminal. The nodes in a diagram are distinctly labeled states, and the arcs are labeled with single elements of the set $N \cup \Sigma \cup \{\lambda\}$ for grammar $G = (N, \Sigma, P, S)$. The parser produces a top-down parse of an acceptable input

ISBN 0-201-02930-8/0-201-02931-6, pbk

string by first invoking the diagram for starting symbol S, then tracing through the diagrams according to the individual terminals and nonterminals encountered. The parser must match the current input symbol with the label of an arc leaving the current node in order to make a transition within the same diagram, and must invoke a new copy of the appropriate diagram whenever an arc with a nonterminal label is traced.

The parser's *current status* is defined to be its location in each diagram so far invoked *and* the order in which the diagrams were invoked. (This corresponds roughly to knowledge of the current state and current stack contents in a pushdown automaton or pushdown transducer.) If the language is deterministic, the appropriate action for the parser is uniquely determined by its current status and one additional input terminal or the empty string.

To construct the diagram for nonterminal A, we introduce an initial (starting) state and an exit (return) state. (In the case of the starting symbol S, the exit state also serves as an accepting state for the entire parser.) Then for each production $A \rightarrow \theta_1 \theta_2 \ldots \theta_n$ with right-hand side consisting of symbols θ_i in $N \cup \Sigma$, $1 \le i \le n$, we provide a path from the initial to the exit state via arcs with labels $\theta_1, \theta_2, \ldots, \theta_n$.

The transition diagram method is usually employed in conjunction with a deterministic context-free grammar without cycles and without left-recursion. This means that no two different arcs leaving the same node can have the same label and that there cannot be an arc with label A leaving the initial node in A's own diagram. Determinism in the grammar's productions implies deterministic operation of the parser as it traverses and manipulates the diagrams for a specific input string. The parser "recursively descends" through copies of the diagrams as nonterminals are encountered, but follows transitions between nodes in the same diagram in response to input string terminals matching arc labels. The parser is never required to backtrack or take other corrective actions.

These constructions and the parsing procedure are illustrated in the following example.

Example: We consider the deterministic Greibach normal form grammar $G_G = (\{S, A, B\}, \{a, b, c, d\}, P, S)$ with productions

$$S \rightarrow cA \qquad A \rightarrow aAB \qquad A \rightarrow d \qquad B \rightarrow b$$

The transition diagram for nonterminal S is

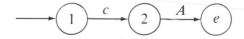

with initial node 1 and exit node *e*. The diagram for *A* is

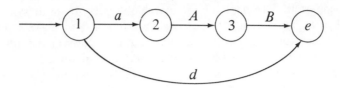

and the diagram for *B* is

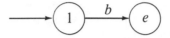

Suppose the input sentence is *x* = *caadbb*. The parser commences its trace by invoking a copy of the diagram for the starting symbol *S*. The first input symbol in *x* matches the arc labeled *c* in the diagram, so a transition to node 2 occurs and the next input symbol becomes available. The transition out of node 2 is labeled as nonterminal *A*; the parser invokes a copy of *A*'s transition diagram. The current status of the parser is represented by the dotted lines in Fig. 4.18.

Upon entering *A*'s diagram, the parser finds the second input terminal, *a*, to match an arc and thereby produce a transition to node 2 in the currently active diagram. The arc leaving this node 2 is labeled with nonterminal *A*, so the parser invokes a second copy of *A*'s diagram, as shown in Fig. 4.19.

Upon entering this new diagram, the parser finds the third input symbol, *a*, to match an arc and produce a transition. Once again, the arc leaving

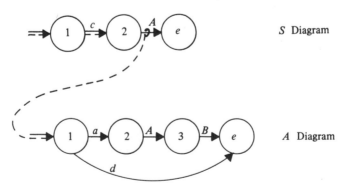

Figure 4.18. Partially completed parse for transition diagram method.

ISBN 0-201-02930-8/0-201-02931-6, pbk

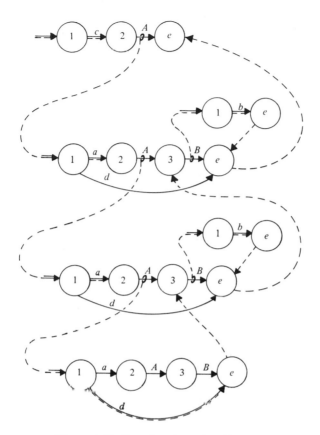

Figure 4.19. Completed parsing diagram.

the current node is labeled *A*, so a third copy of *A*'s diagram is invoked
and entered. The fourth input terminal, *d*, causes a transition from node 1
to node *e* in this third copy. Entry into exit node *e* causes the parser to
return to the diagram immediately preceding and to complete the transition from node 2 to node 3 along arc *A*.

The arc leaving current node 3 is labeled with nonterminal *B*, so the
parser creates and enters a copy of *B*'s diagram. The fifth input symbol, *b*,
matches the arc in *B*'s diagram and causes a transition to exit node *e*.

The remaining parser actions invoke one more copy of *B*'s diagram and
ultimately complete the transition to the exit node in *S*'s diagram with all
the input string scanned. This signals a successful parse, the entire history
of which is given by Fig. 4.19. Note that the explicit order of productions
in a leftmost derivation is immediately obtained by examination of the

ISBN 0-201-02930-8/0-201-02931-6, pbk

paths followed in transition diagrams. In the case just described, the productions in order are $S \to cA$, $A \to aAB$, $A \to aAB$, $A \to d$, $B \to b$, $B \to b$.   □

Many useful grammars are in the deterministic class for which the transition diagram method is an effective parsing technique. In syntactic pattern processing, it is often possible to construct such a grammar by careful design.

4.4.5 Operator Precedence Grammars

As an illustration of an efficient parsing algorithm for a special subset of the context-free grammars, we shall consider the *operator precedence technique*, which can be used to produce a so-called skeletal bottom-up parse of a sentence generated by an operator precedence grammar. This is a "shift-reduce" parsing method in which certain relations in the current sentential form are checked to determine whether the handle has been located or not. If it has, the sentential form is reduced by application of a production in reverse at the handle; if not, the algorithm shifts along to another terminal in the input string and checks again for the handle. A unique end marker symbol must be attached to the beginning and the end of the input string; by convention, the dollar sign $ is used, and the sentence to be parsed has the form $\$x\$$ for x in Σ^+. The relations are denoted by $\doteq$, $\lessdot$, and $\gtrdot$.

An *operator precedence grammar* is a context-free grammar $G = (N, \Sigma, P, S)$ with these properties:

(i) G has no cycles, no useless symbols or productions, no empty-string productions of the form $A \to \lambda$, and no productions with two adjacent nonterminals in the right-hand side.

(ii) At most one of the following three operator precedence relations on $\Sigma \cup \{\$\}$ holds for any pair of symbols:

1. If $A \to \alpha a B b \beta$ or $A \to \alpha a b \beta$ is in P, then $a \doteq b$.
2. If $A \to \alpha a B \beta$ is in P, and $B \overset{+}{\Rightarrow} Cb\delta$ or $B \overset{+}{\Rightarrow} b\delta$, then $a \lessdot b$.
3. If $A \to \alpha B a \beta$ is in P, and $B \overset{+}{\Rightarrow} \delta b C$ or $B \overset{+}{\Rightarrow} \delta b$, then $b \gtrdot a$.
4. If $S \overset{+}{\Rightarrow} a\beta$ or $S \overset{+}{\Rightarrow} Ba\beta$, then $\$ \lessdot a$.
5. If $S \overset{+}{\Rightarrow} \alpha a$ or $S \overset{+}{\Rightarrow} \alpha a B$, then $a \gtrdot \$$.

Thus, the relation $\doteq$ exists between two terminals if they are introduced into a sentential form at the same step by the same production. If a is introduced earlier than b in a rightmost derivation and b is located right of

ISBN 0-201-02930-8/0-201-02931-6, pbk

a in the string, then $a \lessdot b$; if *a* is introduced before *b* but is located right of *b* in the string, then $b \gtrdot a$. The end marker is a special terminal that brackets the entire sentence. The reader should observe that relations $\lessdot$ and $\gtrdot$ are not in general obtainable from one another and are not to be thought of as inverse relations.

The operator precedence parsing method is based on the fact that if there is a rightmost derivation

$$\$ S \$ \overset{*}{\underset{G}{\Rightarrow}} \alpha A w \underset{G}{\Rightarrow} \alpha \beta w$$

with the end markers treated as terminals and placed as shown, then the relation $\lessdot$ holds between the last terminal in α and the first terminal in β,[‡] the relation $\doteq$ holds between consecutive terminals in β,[‡] the relation $\gtrdot$ holds between the last terminal in β and the first symbol in w,[‡] and no other relations hold between these symbols. This means that the handle β of the sentential form $\alpha \beta w$ is isolated and enclosed by a relation sequence like $\lessdot \gtrdot$ or like $\lessdot \doteq \ldots \doteq \gtrdot$. We note, however, that the handle may be the right-hand side of more than one production, and in this case the relations do not provide any information about which production is appropriate for reducing $\alpha \beta w$ to the correct sentential form. For this reason, operator precedence parsing uses the "skeletal grammar" of G rather than G itself.

Given operator precedence grammar $G = (N, \Sigma, P, S)$, its *skeletal grammar* is $G' = (\{S\}, \Sigma, P', S)$, in which all nonterminals in all productions are replaced by the single nonterminal S and from which production $S \to S$ is removed. In general, the language $L(G')$ is larger than, and properly contains, the language $L(G)$; however, when operator precedence parsing is done with G' and a rightmost derivation of a sentence in $L(G)$ is found, there is a legitimate rightmost derivation in G that "looks like" the skeletal one. This G derivation is recovered by substituting appropriate nonterminals for S and filling in productions of the form $A \to B$ where needed.

The following example illustrates operator precedence parsing.

Example: The grammar $G = (\{S, A, B\}, \{(,), +, *, a\}, P, S)$ has productions

$$S \to S + A \qquad S \to A$$

$$A \to A * B \qquad A \to B$$

$$B \to (S) \qquad B \to a$$

[‡]Any intervening nonterminals are ignored in order to evaluate the relations between terminals only.

ISBN 0-201-02930-8/0-201-02931-6, pbk

The language $L(G)$ consists of well-formed strings of balanced parentheses enclosing expressions with a as the operand and $+$ and $*$ as binary operators. Application of the appropriate algorithms of Section 2.4 establishes that G has no cycles or useless nonterminals. By inspection, there are neither empty string productions nor productions with adjacent nonterminals on the right-hand side.

To complete the verification that G is operator precedence, we compute the relations $<\!\cdot$, $\doteq$, $\cdot\!>$ between terminals. The only production introducing two terminals that are adjacent or are separated by one nonterminal is $B \rightarrow (S)$; thus, symbol (has relation $\doteq$ to symbol) via condition (1). There is a production $S \rightarrow S + A$ and a derivation $A \overset{+}{\Rightarrow} (S)$; thus, $+$ has relation $<\!\cdot$ to (via condition (2).

When all the relations have been computed by applying the definitions in this way, it is convenient to summarize them in a matrix format:

	a	$+$	$*$	$($	$)$	$\$$
a		$\cdot\!>$	$\cdot\!>$		$\cdot\!>$	$\cdot\!>$
$+$	$<\!\cdot$	$\cdot\!>$	$<\!\cdot$	$<\!\cdot$	$\cdot\!>$	$\cdot\!>$
$*$	$<\!\cdot$	$\cdot\!>$	$\cdot\!>$	$<\!\cdot$	$\cdot\!>$	$\cdot\!>$
$($	$<\!\cdot$	$<\!\cdot$	$<\!\cdot$	$<\!\cdot$	$\doteq$	
$)$		$\cdot\!>$	$\cdot\!>$		$\cdot\!>$	$\cdot\!>$
$\$$	$<\!\cdot$	$<\!\cdot$	$<\!\cdot$			

The definition of operator precedence does not require that some relation exist between each pair of elements in $\Sigma \cup \{\$\}$, so the matrix does not have to be completely filled in. The definition does require that at most one relation hold between two symbols, and the matrix shows that there are no conflicts; therefore, G is an operator precedence grammar.

The skeletal grammar is $G' = (\{S\}, \{(,),+, *, a\}, P', S)$ with productions

$$S \rightarrow S + S \qquad S \rightarrow S * S$$

$$S \rightarrow (S) \qquad S \rightarrow a$$

(Two appearances of production $S \rightarrow S$ have been deleted.)

Suppose the input string is $\$a + (a * a)\$$. The handle for reduction of this sentential form will be found by scanning the string from left to right and evaluating relations between adjacent terminals until the relation $\cdot\!>$ holds and brackets the desired substring; that is, the parser can be viewed as shifting the string along from left to right until the handle is located within a sequence $<\!\cdot$ $\cdot\!>$ or $<\!\cdot$ $\doteq$ $\cdots$ $\doteq$ $\cdot\!>$ for reduction. An

ISBN 0-201-02930-8/0-201-02931-6, pbk

evaluation of relations for the input sentence gives

$$\$ \quad a \quad +(a * a)\$.$$
$$\lessdot \quad \gtrdot$$

This sentence is therefore of the form $\alpha\beta w$ with $\alpha = \$$, $\beta = a$, and $w = +(a * a)\$$. The reduction by production $S \to a$ in reverse gives new sentential form $\$S + (a * a)\$$. The relations for this form are

$$\$ S + \quad (\quad a \quad * a)\$,$$
$$\lessdot \quad \lessdot \quad \lessdot \quad \gtrdot$$

as found by ignoring the nonterminal S to evaluate the relation between $\$$ and $+$. The remaining sentential forms and reductions are as follows:

$$\$ \quad S + \quad (\quad S * \quad a \quad) \$ \qquad \text{Reduce by } S \to a$$
$$\lessdot \quad \lessdot \quad \lessdot \quad \lessdot \quad \gtrdot$$

$$\$ \quad S + \quad (\quad S * S) \$ \qquad \text{Reduce by } S \to S * S$$
$$\lessdot \quad \lessdot \quad \lessdot \quad \gtrdot$$

$$\$ \quad S + \quad (\quad S) \quad \$ \qquad \text{Reduce by } S \to (S)$$
$$\lessdot \quad \lessdot \quad \doteq \quad \gtrdot$$

$$\$ \quad S + S \$ \qquad \text{Reduce by } S \to S + S$$
$$\lessdot \quad \gtrdot$$

$$\$S\$ \qquad \qquad \text{Parse completed}$$

This parse provides the productions of a rightmost derivation in reversed order. The rightmost derivation of the input string in G' is

$$\$S\$ \Rightarrow \$S + S\$ \Rightarrow \$S + (S)\$ \Rightarrow \$S + (S * S)\$$$
$$\Rightarrow \$S + (S * a)\$ \Rightarrow \$S + (a * a)\$$$
$$\Rightarrow \$a + (a * a)\$.$$

The corresponding rightmost derivation in G is recovered by tracking down the proper nonterminal substitutions for S and the places in which productions like $A \to B$ must be used. By quick inspection, we find, for

ISBN 0-201-02930-8/0-201-02931-6, pbk

operator precedence grammar G,

$$\$S\$ \Rightarrow \$S + A\$ \Rightarrow \$S + B\$ \Rightarrow \$S + (S)\$$$

$$\Rightarrow \$S + (A * B)\$ \Rightarrow \$S + (A * a)\$ \Rightarrow \$S + (B * a)\$$$

$$\Rightarrow \$S + (a * a)\$ \Rightarrow \$A + (a * a)\$ \Rightarrow \$B + (a * a)\$$$

$$\Rightarrow \$a + (a * a)\$. \qquad\qquad \square$$

4.5 RECOGNITION OF IMPERFECT STRINGS

In syntactic pattern recognition, a string grammar G defines a class of patterns represented by strings in $L(G)$. The recognizing and translating automata of the types discussed thus far will accept perfectly formed strings, but will reject any strings that are in any way imperfect. Since pattern processing systems often receive noisy or ill-formed inputs for which a classification must be attempted, it is of interest to consider techniques for nonideal situations.

One approach to processing erroneous strings is to apply error correction, which transforms an unacceptable input into a recognizable string. Such a system may not be able to handle all errors and cannot be expected always to recover the intended input, but its performance can be significantly better than that of a system that simply rejects all imperfect inputs.

We consider in this section the correction of three common types of corrupting errors in the syntactic string description of a pattern. The errors are a CH error, where one terminal (usually representing a pattern primitive or a relationship among primitives) is changed into another; a DE error, where one terminal is deleted; and an IN error, where one extra symbol is inserted. Multiple occurrences of various combinations of these errors can also be handled at the cost of increased complexity of the system.

The correction process is a transformation of an input string that may contain errors into an error-free output string. A language-theoretic model of a string-to-string mapping for context-free languages is the syntax-directed translation schema developed in Section 2.5. We shall describe the construction of schemata to correct the error types explained in the preceding paragraph.

Suppose a context-free grammar $G = (N, \Sigma, P, S)$ for the pattern class is available. To provide for the occurrence of errors of changed symbols, we define an operator CH such that for any terminal a in Σ

$$CH(a) = \Sigma - \{a\}.$$

ISBN 0-201-02930-8/0-201-02931-6, pbk

CH represents an error changing a into any other symbol in Σ. By extension, for string x in Σ^*,

$$CH(x) = \{y | y \text{ in } \Sigma^*, y \text{ obtained from } x \text{ by changing exactly}$$
$$\text{one terminal into another}\}.$$

A single CH error affects a single terminal location in string x. For the general case of n errors, $n \geqslant 0$, let

$$CH^n(x) = \begin{cases} \varnothing & \text{if } |x| < n, \\ \{y | y \text{ in } \Sigma^*, y \text{ is obtained from } x \text{ by } CH \text{ errors in} \\ n \text{ distinct locations in } x\} & \text{otherwise}. \end{cases}$$

To develop a new grammar G_{CH} deriving the set of strings obtained from $L(G)$ by CH errors, we first write the productions in G in an equation form in which a nonterminal is equated to the union of its possible replacements.[‡] In this notation, the productions for nonterminal A, say $A \to \alpha_1, A \to \alpha_2, \ldots, A \to \alpha_m$, are represented by the equation

$$A = \alpha_1 + \alpha_2 + \ldots + \alpha_m,$$

in which the equal sign means "replacement by" and the plus sign denotes "or". Then, for each term α_i, $1 \leqslant i \leqslant m$, we compute $CH(\alpha_i)$, $CH^2(\alpha_i), \ldots, CH^{n(i)}(\alpha_i)$ where $n(i)$ is the number of terminals in α_i. Note that CH only affects terminals and is not applied to nonterminals in α_i. The new grammar is $G_{CH} = (N, \Sigma, P_{CH}, S)$, in which each production equation like the one displayed above is replaced by the expanded equation

$$A = \alpha_1 + \cdots + \alpha_m + CH(\alpha_1) + \cdots$$

$$+ CH(\alpha_m) + \cdots + CH^{n(m)}(\alpha_m).$$

This construction simply expands the set of productions in the original grammar G so that strings with errors of changed terminals can be derived. The language generated by G_{CH} is

$$L(G_{CH}) = \{y | y \text{ in } \Sigma^*, y \text{ in } CH^n(x), x \text{ in } L(G), n \geqslant 0\}.$$

Example: Consider the grammar $G = (\{S, A\}, \{a, b\}, P, S)$ with productions

$$S \to aA \qquad S \to aSa \qquad A \to b$$

[‡]This use of equations for representing productions is not mandatory but is convenient in explaining the method for obtaining the augmented grammars to handle errors in strings.

ISBN 0-201-02930-8/0-201-02931-6, pbk

Here,

$$L(G) = \{x | x = a^n aba^n, n \geqslant 0\}.$$

The production equations are

$$S = aA + aSa \qquad A = b$$

For CH errors, we compute

$$CH(aA) = [CH(a)]A = bA,$$

$$CH(aSa) = [CH(a)]Sa + aS[CH(a)] = bSa + aSb,$$

$$CH^2(aSa) = [CH(a)]S[CH(a)] = bSb,$$

$$CH(b) = a.$$

The expanded equations in $G_{CH} = (\{S, A\}, \{a, b\}, P_{CH}, S)$ are

$$S = aA + aSa + bA + bSa + aSb + bSb \qquad A = b + a,$$

from which we get the productions $S \rightarrow aA$, $S \rightarrow aSa$, $S \rightarrow bA$, $S \rightarrow bSa$, $S \rightarrow aSb$, $S \rightarrow bSb$, $A \rightarrow b$, $A \rightarrow a$. As an example, the sentence $aaba$ is in $L(G)$; the sentences $aaba$, $baba$, $abba$, $aaaa$, $aabb$, $bbba$, $baaa$, $babb$, $abaa$, $abbb$, $aaab$, $bbaa$, $bbbb$, $baab$, $abab$, and $bbab$ are in $L(G_{CH})$, and these represent all possible CH errors in $aaba$. $\qquad\square$

In order to correct CH errors, a simple syntax-directed translation schema $\mathfrak{T}_{CH} = (N, \Sigma, \Delta, R, S)$ is constructed with properties that

(i)   its translations are length preserving;
(ii) $L(G_i) = L(G_{CH})$; and
(iii) $L(G_0) = L(G)$.

The input and output alphabets are equal, $\Delta = \Sigma$; and, for each production equation in P_{CH}, there are rules in R of the forms

$A \rightarrow \alpha_i, \alpha_i$	for no error
$A \rightarrow \mu, \alpha_i$	for each term μ in $CH(\alpha_i)$ to correct one error
$A \rightarrow \rho, \alpha_i$	for each term ρ in $CH^2(\alpha_i)$ to correct two errors
$\vdots$	$\vdots$
$A \rightarrow \psi, \alpha_i$	for each term ψ in $CH^{n(i)}(\alpha_i)$ to correct $n(i)$ errors

ISBN 0-201-02930-8/0-201-02931-6, pbk

It is straightforward to verify that $\mathfrak{T}_{CH}$ defines a length-preserving translation from $L(G_{CH})$ to $L(G)$ and thereby provides a nondeterministic
correction of CH errors.

Example: For the grammars G and G_{CH} in the previous example, the
schema constructed as indicated is $\mathfrak{T}_{CH} = (\{S, A\}, \{a, b\}, \{a, b\}, R, S)$
with rules:

for no error $S \rightarrow aA, aA$
$S \rightarrow aSa, aSa$
$A \rightarrow b, b$

for one error $S \rightarrow bA, aA$
$S \rightarrow bSa, aSa$
$S \rightarrow aSb, aSa$
$A \rightarrow a, b$

for two errors $S \rightarrow bSb, aSa$

Suppose input $x = abba$ is applied to $\mathfrak{T}_{CH}$ to be translated; the single
resulting sequence of translation forms is

$$(S, S) \Rightarrow (aSa, aSa)$$

$$\Rightarrow (abAu, aaAa)$$

$$\Rightarrow (abba, aaba).$$

This produces a translation of input string $x = abba$ into output string
$y = aaba$ by changing the first b into a. Note that y is in $L(G)$.   □

For instances of errors that delete terminals, we define an operator DE
to remove single terminals, that is, for a in Σ,

$$DE(a) = \lambda.$$

By extension to x in Σ^*, and to multiple errors,

$$DE^n(x) = \begin{cases} \varnothing & \text{if } |x| < n, \\ \{y \mid y \text{ in } \Sigma^*, y \text{ is obtained from } x \text{ by deletion} \\ \text{of } n \text{ terminals}\} & \text{otherwise}. \end{cases}$$

It is noted that these errors, unlike CH errors, cause a change in the length

ISBN 0-201-02930-8/0-201-02931-6, pbk

of a string. An SDTS to correct *DE* errors is constructed by a method analogous to that used for *CH* errors; that is, a set of rules of the form $A \to \alpha$, β, such that $A \to \alpha$ reflects a finite number of *DE* errors and $A \to \beta$ reflects a correction of those errors, is created.

Example: For the grammar $G = (\{S, A\}, \{a, b\}, P, S)$ with production equations $S = aA + aSa$ and $A = b$, we obtain for deletion of terminals

$$DE(aA) = \left[DE(a)\right]A = \lambda A = A,$$

$$DE(aSa) = aS + Sa,$$

$$DE(b) = \lambda,$$

$$DE^2(aSa) = S.$$

The SDTS for nondeterministic correction of deletion errors is $\mathfrak{T}_{DE} = (\{S, A\}, \{a, b\}, \{a, b\}, R, S)$ with rules:

for no error	$S \to aA,\ aA$
	$S \to aSa,\ aSa$
	$A \to b,\ b$
for one error	$S \to A,\ aA$
	$S \to Sa,\ aSa$
	$S \to aS,\ aSa$
	$A \to \lambda,\ b$
for two errors	$S \to S,\ aSa$

Note that we are forced to allow a rule introducing the empty string λ into an input sentence in order to handle an error in which terminal b is deleted. As an example, for input $x = aba$, $\mathfrak{T}_{DE}$ gives the translation forms

$$(S, S) \Rightarrow (aSa, aSa) \qquad \text{and} \qquad (S, S) \Rightarrow (Sa, aSa)$$

$$\Rightarrow (aAa, aaAa) \qquad\qquad\qquad \Rightarrow (aAa, aaAa)$$

$$\Rightarrow (aba, aaba) \qquad\qquad\qquad \Rightarrow (aba, aaba).$$

These two sequences identify two different errors, but both map the input string x into the same output string, *aaba*. Other translations can also occur.   □

To incorporate errors of inserted terminals that cause an increase in string lengths, an *IN* operator applied to an element of the alphabet

ISBN 0-201-02930-8/0-201-02931-6, pbk

$\Sigma = \{a_1, \ldots, a_l\}$ is defined as

$$IN(a) = \Sigma a + a\Sigma$$

$$= (a_1 + \cdots + a_l)a + a(a_1 + \cdots + a_l)$$

$$= a_1 a + \cdots + a_l a + aa_1 + \cdots + aa_l.$$

This handles a maximum of one extra symbol insertion associated with each terminal in a string, so the IN operator must be reapplied if insertion of a greater number of terminals is a possibility.

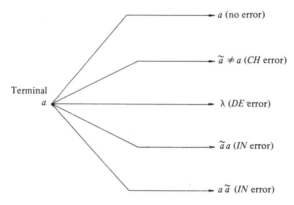

Figure 4.20. *CH, DE*, and *IN* errors on a terminal-by-terminal basis.

Suppose that these *CH, DE*, and *IN* errors affect single terminals on a terminal-by-terminal basis as shown in Fig. 4.20. To construct a composite SDTS for these three error categories, let the grammar $G = (N, \Sigma, P, S)$ be given in Greibach normal form for notational convenience and to avoid considering multiple error occurrences and types in one production. The rules in one SDTS $\mathcal{T}_E = (N, \Sigma, \Sigma, R, S)$, to correct these errors are such that for each production $A \to a\alpha$ in G, there are rules:

for no error	$A \to a\alpha,\ a\alpha$
for *DE* error	$A \to \alpha,\ a\alpha$
for *CH* errors	$A \to \tilde{a}\alpha,\ a\alpha$ for each $\tilde{a}$ in $\Sigma - \{a\}$
for *IN* errors	$A \to \tilde{a}a\alpha,\ a\alpha$
	$A \to a\tilde{a}\alpha,\ a\alpha$ for each $\tilde{a}$ in Σ

ISBN 0-201-02930-8/0-201-02931-6, pbk

Example: Consider the Greibach normal form grammar $G = (\{S, A, B\}, \{a, b\}, P, S)$ with production equations

$$S = aA + aSB \qquad A = b \qquad B = a.$$

This grammar generates the language $\{x \mid x = a^n aba^n, n \geqslant 0\}$. The rules in error-correcting schema $\mathcal{T}_E = (\{S, A, B\}, \{a, b\}, \{a, b\}, R, S)$ are

for no error
$$S \rightarrow aA, aA$$
$$S \rightarrow aSB, aSB$$
$$A \rightarrow b, b$$
$$B \rightarrow a, a$$

for DE errors
$$S \rightarrow A, aA$$
$$S \rightarrow SB, aSB$$
$$A \rightarrow \lambda, b$$
$$B \rightarrow \lambda, a$$

for CH errors
$$S \rightarrow bA, aA$$
$$S \rightarrow bSB, aSB$$
$$A \rightarrow a, b$$
$$B \rightarrow b, a$$

for IN errors
$$S \rightarrow aaA, aA \qquad A \rightarrow ab, b$$
$$S \rightarrow baA, aA \qquad A \rightarrow ba, b$$
$$S \rightarrow abA, aA \qquad A \rightarrow bb, b$$
$$S \rightarrow aaSB, aSB \qquad B \rightarrow aa, a$$
$$S \rightarrow baSB, aSB \qquad B \rightarrow ba, a$$
$$S \rightarrow abSB, aSB \qquad B \rightarrow ab, a$$

Suppose that the input string is $x = aba$; the translation forms produced by $\mathcal{T}_E$ are the following with the error correction as indicated.

$$(S, S) \Rightarrow (aA, aA)$$
$$\Rightarrow (aba, ab) \qquad \text{[one } IN \text{ error]}$$

$$(S, S) \Rightarrow (abA, aA) \qquad \text{[one } IN \text{ error]}$$
$$\Rightarrow (aba, ab) \qquad \text{[one } CH \text{ error]}$$

$$(S, S) \Rightarrow (aSB, aSB)$$
$$\Rightarrow (aBA, aaAB) \qquad \text{[one } DE \text{ error]}$$
$$\Rightarrow (abB, aabB)$$
$$\Rightarrow (aba, aaba)$$

ISBN 0-201-02930-8/0-201-02931-6, pbk

$$(S, S) \Rightarrow (SB, aSB) \qquad \text{[one } DE \text{ error]}$$
$$\Rightarrow (aAB, aaAB)$$
$$\Rightarrow (abB, aabB)$$
$$\Rightarrow (aba, aaba)$$

Among the corrections of this input sentence *aba* are therefore the output strings $y_1 = ab$ and $y_2 = aaba$. The first, y_1, is the result of correcting one insertion error or one insertion and one change error; the second, y_2, is the result of correcting one deletion error in either of two locations. □

Example: The five pattern primitives shown in Fig. 4.16(a) are used in the chromosome pattern grammar to describe submedian and telocentric chromosomes. The grammar is $G = (\{S, S_1, S_2, A, B, C, D, E, F\}, \{a, b, c, d, e\}, P, S)$ with production equations

$$S = S_1 + S_2 \qquad\qquad\qquad C = bC + Cb + b + d$$

$$S_1 = AA \qquad\qquad\qquad\qquad D = bD + Db + a$$

$$S_2 = BA \qquad\qquad\qquad\qquad E = cD$$

$$A = CA + AC + DE + FD \qquad F = Dc$$

$$B = bB + Bb + e$$

Applying the CH operator to the production equations yields, for B as one example,

$$CH(bB + Bb + e) = CH(bB) + CH(Bb) + CH(e)$$

$$= [CH(b)]B + B[CH(b)] + CH(e)$$

$$= aB + cB + dB + eB + Ba + Bc$$

$$+ Bd + Be + a + b + c + d$$

where we use the fact that an unrestricted CH error on terminal b implies that b could be incorrectly identified as any of the other four terminals; that is,

$$CH(b) = a + c + d + e.$$

In practice, it is not always necessary to provide for all errors; for example, if the errors in string representations of chromosomes are known to arise from primitives improperly identified during the process of obtaining a string representation of a chromosome, two of the most likely errors are $CH(b) = d$ and $CH(d) = b$. Let us make the assumption that the mislabeling of b as a, c, or e cannot occur, so the rules to correct these errors need not be provided. Suppose also that an error on a, c, or e is precluded. With these simplifications, the expanded production equation for non-

ISBN 0-201-02930-8/0-201-02931-6, pbk

terminal B becomes

$$B = bB + Bd + e + dB + Bd$$

Similarly, for other production equations under the same assumptions,

$$C = bC + Cb + b + d + dC + Cd$$
$$D = bD + Db + a + dD + Dd$$

The complete set of productions for the new grammar that handles the two errors $CH(b) = d$ and $CH(d) = b$ is now given by the equations

$$S = S_1 + S_2 \qquad\qquad C = bC + Cb + b + d + dC + Cd$$

$$S_1 = AA \qquad\qquad D = bD + Db + a + dD + Dd$$

$$S_2 = BA \qquad\qquad E = cD$$

$$A = CA + AC + DE + FD \qquad F = Dc$$

$$B = bB + bB + e + dB + Bd$$

The rules in an SDTS to correct these two kinds of CH errors are constructed as previously described; for example, the rules for nonterminal B are

$$\text{for no error} \qquad B \to bB,\, bB$$
$$B \to Bb,\, Bb$$
$$B \to e,\, e$$

$$\text{for } CH \text{ error} \qquad B \to dB,\, bB$$
$$B \to Bd,\, Bb$$

Suppose that the process of obtaining a string description produces the sentence *ebadcbad* for the chromosome in Fig. 4.21(a). One translation of this input that the SDTS produces is obtained by the sequence of translation forms

$$(S, S) \Rightarrow (S_2, S_2) \Rightarrow (BA, BA) \Rightarrow (BbA, BbA) \Rightarrow (ebA, ebA)$$

$$\Rightarrow (ebDE, ebDE) \Rightarrow (ebDdE, ebDbE)$$

$$\Rightarrow (ebadD, ebabD) \Rightarrow (ebadcD, ebabcD)$$

$$\Rightarrow (ebadcbD, ebabcbD) \Rightarrow (ebadcbDb, ebabcbDb)$$

$$\Rightarrow (ebadcbad, ebabcbab).$$

ISBN 0-201-02930-8/0-201-02931-6, pbk

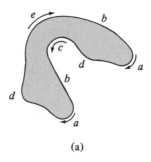

(a)

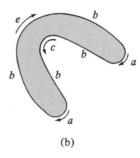

(b)

Figure 4.21. (a) Imperfect telocentric chromosome.   (b) Corrected telocentric chromosome.

Due to the ambiguity in the original grammar, a second way in which this same translation pair may occur is

$$(S, S) \Rightarrow (S_2, S_2) \Rightarrow (BA, BA) \Rightarrow (eCA, eCA)$$

$$\Rightarrow (ebA, ebA) \Rightarrow (ebDE, ebDE) \Rightarrow (ebDdD, ebDbE)$$

$$\Rightarrow (ebadE, ebabE) \Rightarrow (ebadcD, ebabcD)$$

$$\Rightarrow (ebadcbD, ebabcbD) \Rightarrow (ebadcbDb, ebabcbDb)$$

$$\Rightarrow (ebadcbad, ebabcbab).$$

Thus, this input would have two *CH* errors corrected and would be classified as a telocentric chromosome with standard representation in Fig. 4.21(b).   ☐

We shall consider probabilistic error correction in Section 5.5.

ISBN 0-201-02930-8/0-201-02931-6, pbk

4.6 TREE AUTOMATA

Expansive-form tree grammars and the structures they generate were discussed in Section 3.2.2. Since it is possible to represent a tree by a unique string in the language of a structural description context-free grammar, the recognition problem for trees may be studied in terms of pushdown automata; however, we gain insight into the power of tree representations and the processors of trees by defining a generalized finite automaton that operates on input trees directly. Whereas a conventional finite automaton scans an input string symbol by symbol from left to right, a tree automaton must begin simultaneously at each node on the frontier of the input tree and proceed along parallel paths toward the root.

Specifically, a *frontier-to-root tree automaton* is a system $\mathcal{Q}_t = (Q, F, \{f_a | a \text{ in } \Sigma\})$ where

> Q is a finite set of *states*,
> F is a set of *final states*, a subset of Q, and
> f_a is a relation in $Q^n \times Q$ such that n is a rank of a.

Note that Q^n is the Cartesian product of Q with itself n times. $\mathcal{Q}_t$ is a nondeterministic machine, parallel in nature, that represents the process of tree recognition in the following way. Using the relations defined for the symbols in alphabet Σ, $\{f_a | a \text{ in } \Sigma\}$, the automaton assigns an initial state to *each* leaf node on the frontier of the input tree T (T is an element of T_Σ); then, as paths upward toward the root are simultaneously scanned, $\mathcal{Q}_t$ assigns a state to *each* node in T by examining the relation defined by the label of that node and the states already assigned to its offspring. Alternatively, one may think of $\mathcal{Q}_t$ as compactly representing the actions of several conventional finite automata concurrently scanning the individual strings that make up the various paths from the frontier to the root of T. An input tree is accepted by $\mathcal{Q}_t$ if the automaton can enter a final state upon encountering the root.

The *language recognized by* $\mathcal{Q}_t$ is the set

$$T(\mathcal{Q}_t) = \{T | T \text{ in } T_\Sigma, \mathcal{Q}_t \text{ can halt in a state in } F \text{ when the root of } T \text{ is reached}\}.$$

Given an expansive tree grammar $G_t = (V, r, S, P)$ as a generator of a set $L(G_t)$ of trees with nodes labeled with elements in Σ, we may construct a tree automaton $\mathcal{Q}_t$ that recognizes $L(G_t)$ as follows. Let $Q = N$ with $F = \{S\}$; and, for each symbol a in Σ, define a relation f_a such that

ISBN 0-201-02930-8/0-201-02931-6, pbk

$(X_1, \ldots, X_n, X)$ is in f_a iff there is in G_t a production

$$X \to a$$
$$X_1 \cdots X_n$$

4.6.1 A Simple Illustration

Let us consider the construction of the recognizer for trees generated by the expansive tree grammar $G_t = (\{S, A, x, y, z, \$\}, r, S, P)$ with non-terminals S, A; terminals $x, y, z, \$$; and productions

$$A \to x \qquad A \to y \qquad A \to z \qquad S \to \$$$
$$\qquad\qquad\qquad\qquad\qquad\quad A \qquad\quad A \quad A$$

The automaton $\mathcal{Q}_t$ is specified as $(\{S, A\}, \{S\}, \{f_x, f_y, f_z, f_\$\})$ with its four relations defined as follows:

$f_x = \{(\emptyset, A)\}$, arising from production $A \to x$

$f_y = \{(\emptyset, A)\}$, arising from production $A \to y$

$f_z = \{(A, A)\}$, arising from production $A \to z$
$$\qquad\qquad\qquad\qquad\qquad\qquad\qquad\qquad A$$

$f_\$ = \{(A, A, S)\}$, arising from production $S \to \$$
$$\qquad\qquad\qquad\qquad\qquad\qquad\qquad\qquad\qquad\qquad A \quad A$$

The interpretation of relation f_x is that a node labeled x with no offspring (a leaf on the frontier) is assigned state A. The interpretation of relation $f_\$$ is that a node labeled $\$$ with offspring having states A, A is to be assigned state S.

Suppose the input tree is the one shown in Fig. 4.22(a). $\mathcal{Q}_t$ first assigns initial states to frontier nodes x and y via relations f_x and f_y, respectively; in this case, A is assigned to both these leaves, as shown in Fig. 4.22(b). The automaton next makes a state assignment to node z on the basis of relation f_z and the state of this node's offspring; once again, state A is selected, and the status of the recognition process is given in Fig. 4.22(c). Since states have now been associated with the two offspring of root $\$$, $\mathcal{Q}_t$ uses relation $f_\$$ to assign a state to the root; the offspring states A, A here dictate assignment of state S to the root, and the tree is accepted because S is in F. The final representation of the state sequences followed along the frontier-to-root paths is Fig. 4.22(d).

ISBN 0-201-02930-8/0-201-02931-6, pbk

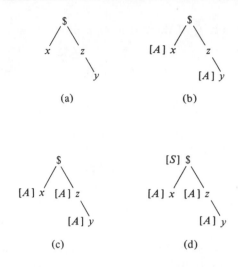

Figure 4.22. Tree automaton processing stages. (a) Input tree. (b) State assignment to frontier nodes. (c) State assignment to offspring of root. (d) State assignment to root.

It should be noted that the set of state-assignment relations for automaton $\mathcal{Q}_t$ in this example is less complex than those which appear in the construction of recognizers for more elaborate tree languages. In the general case, the automaton is nondeterministic and the relations have more than one entry.

4.6.2   An Example

An extended illustration of the use of tree grammars and automata in syntactic pattern recognition is provided by a tree system approach to fingerprint recognition developed by Moayer and Fu [1974, 1976b]. Since this system is in fact a sequence of several pattern processing techniques, it also illustrates the power of a careful combination of algorithms and the importance of empirical knowledge about the pattern classes. The objective was to develop a system to enhance the existing manual procedure for matching or classifying fingerprints by having a print automatically assigned to one of a finite number of basic classes. It was recognized that final matching of patterns would probably remain a manual operation, and it was desired to have a balance among the basic classes, with each having roughly the same number of members for the sake of efficiency.

The features that uniquely identify a fingerprint are called *minutiae*. These serve as the pattern primitives and are essentially properties of the

ISBN 0-201-02930-8/0-201-02931-6, pbk

ridges, such as abrupt endings, branching, mergings, dots, cuts, and disconnected segments, together with the relative locations of these physical characteristics. The number of possible fingerprints is taken to be virtually infinite by the following argument. There are some 50 to 100 minutiae in each print (as few as a dozen is considered sufficient for identification); but suppose conservatively that only 50 occur, each being either a ridge termination or a ridge branching at the same 50 possible locations. Even in this restricted case, there would be 2^{50}, or approximately 10^{15}, different fingerprints. Since a typical print has more than 50 minutiae, each with several possible characteristics, and their relative locations vary, the actual number of combinations is much larger than 10^{15}. The FBI alone has more than 20×10^6 distinct fingerprints currently on file. Types and locations of minutiae are sufficiently well mixed to support the argument that identical prints will not occur on different individuals.

The tree-oriented fingerprint processing system developed by Moayer and Fu performs the following sequence of operations on an input print: digitization and segmentation of the fingerprint image, picture enchancement, preprocessing, ridge tracing and coding, postprocessing, feature extraction, representation as a tree, and classification into one of the basic classes. In the digitization phase, the image is scanned and converted into a 256×256 matrix with each matrix point assigned a grey scale value in the range 0 to 255. Since up to 100 minutiae can appear in a fingerprint, it is desirable to reduce the complexity of representation by partitioning a pattern into smaller segments, subject to the constraints that the segments not be too small to contain a relevant number of primitives nor too large to defeat the goal of reducing complexity to manageable levels. To this end, the image boundaries (which provide little or no useful information) are eliminated and the fingerprint is decomposed into a 4×4 matrix of windows, each window being an array of 48×48 points located by their x–y coordinates. Classification of each of these 16 windows is done separately. Since fingerprints seem to have no natural decomposition, it appears that this approach is potentially as good as any other. Any shift in the orientation of the pattern may cause primitives to move from one window to another and result in a different classification; it is argued, however, that a set of rules could be developed for positioning the sample matrix for each pattern class and that buffer zones of nonzero thickness could be used to separate the windows to allow inclusion of primitives on a border in more than one window.

The picture enhancement phase is the repetitive application of the Laplacian operator

$$\nabla^2 = \partial^2/\partial x^2 + \partial^2/\partial y^2$$

ISBN 0-201-02930-8/0-201-02931-6, pbk

to the grey level values within a small region in order to approximate each point by a weighted sum of the grey levels in its immediate area. The actual calculation transforms the grey level f_{ij} at coordinates i and j into a value

$$f'_{ij} = 1.92f_{ij} + 0.154(f_{i+3,j} + f_{i-3,j} + f_{i+2,j+2} + f_{i+2,j-2}$$

$$+f_{i-2,j+2} + f_{i-2,j-2}).$$

The weighting factors, 1.92 and 0.154, were determined experimentally. The final representation as a binary value is computed as

$$f''_{ij} = \begin{cases} 1 & \text{if } f'_{ij} \geqslant t_1, \\ 0 & \text{if } f'_{ij} \leqslant t_2, \end{cases}$$

where the threshold functions $t_1(n)$ and $t_2(n)$ control convergence to a binary value by reflecting the number n of repetitive applications of the Laplacian operator (see Fig. 4.23). The end result of this phase is an image composed of 16 square windows, each with 2304 binary-valued points. As an illustration, Fig. 4.24 shows a typical fingerprint with a whorl pattern. An enlargement of the window indicated on this print, after digitization, enhancement by 15 applications of the Laplacian operator, and conversion to binary, is shown in Fig. 4.25.

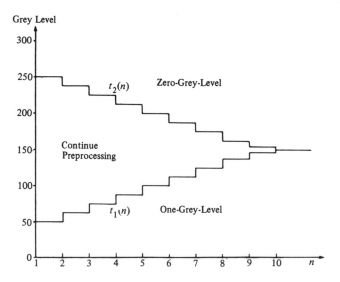

Figure 4.23. Convergence function for repetitions of the Laplacian operator. (From Moayer and Fu [1976b].)

ISBN 0-201-02930-8/0-201-02931-6, pbk

Figure 4.24. Whorl pattern fingerprint. (From Moayer and Fu [1976b].)

The functions of the preprocessing and ridge-coding phases are to scan the binary window, locate the ridges, suppress variations in ridge thickness, and provide an encoding of the ridge skeletons according to the directional code shown in Fig. 4.26. In the preprocessor, overlapping pairs of adjacent lines are scanned to attempt the identification of true ridges and the elimination of false primitives that are not a part of the underlying fingerprint (false primitives here are usually due to excess ink or smearing). The ridge-encoding routine takes this skeletal image and applies the directional code to generate a chain code for each ridge that has been found. Its output is a chain-encoded representation in which the directional codes appear along with the symbols +, • , * , and B, which define starting, terminating, merging, and branching points, respectively, of ridges. Preprocessing and ridge encoding of the window in Fig. 4.25 yield the chain-coded representation in Fig. 4.27.

The postprocessing phase is considered the most critical operation in the sequence because it attempts further removal of erroneous features that are due to noise, excess ink flow, or insufficient ink when the original fingerprint was made. This phase has the specific task of examining the chain-coded ridges and deciding whether pairs of ridges that terminate near each other should be connected—an extremely important function because the tree grammars employed subsequently for classification use

ISBN 0-201-02930-8/0-201-02931-6, pbk

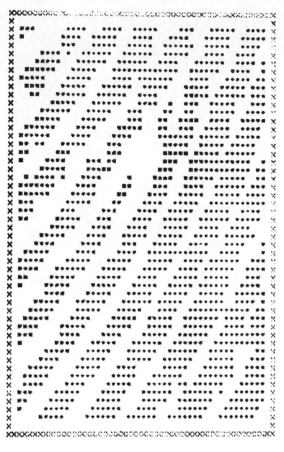

Figure 4.25. Fingerprint window converted to binary. (From Moayer and Fu [1976b].)

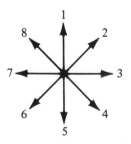

Figure 4.26. Directional code.

ISBN 0-201-02930-8 / 0-201-02931-6, pbk

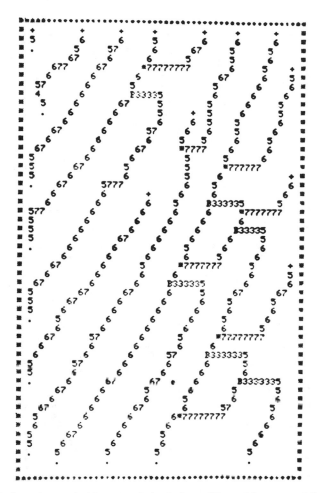

Figure 4.27. Preprocessed ridge-encoded window. (From Moayer and Fu [1976b].)

minutiae such as the branching points as their primitives. Design of the postprocessing routine reflects the facts that:

1. ridges are continuous lines;
2. ridges generally run in parallel;
3. the beginning or terminating point of a ridge generally is located between two continuous parallel ridges; and
4. the degree of variation of curvature is gradual except around deltas, the centers of loops, and the centers of whorls.

ISBN 0-201-02930-8/0-201-02931-6, pbk

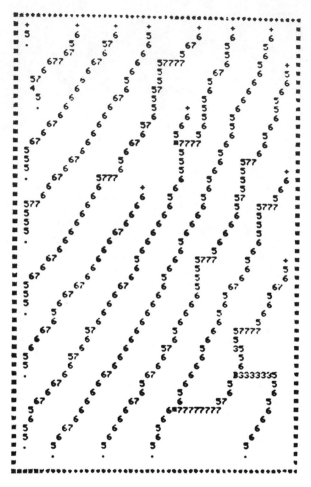

Figure 4.28. Postprocessed ridge-enclosed window. (From Moayer and Fu [1976b].)

These four "global" considerations are used in postprocessing particularly to fill in small gaps in the ink flow for a single ridge. A detailed description of the routine may be found in Moayer and Fu [1974]. Postprocessing converts the window in Fig. 4.27 into the one in Fig. 4.28.

In the feature extraction phase, the valid minutiae in the window being processed are identified by type and location. The ridge configurations for a given window reflect the following aspects:

1. There are continuous ridges passing through windows from one to another. There are no minutiae in these.

ISBN 0-201-02930-8/0-201-02931-6, pbk

2. There are ridge terminations, branchings, mergings, and segments. These are rich in primitives.

3. There is information in the relative positions of ridges.

These considerations led to the set of pattern primitives in Fig. 4.29. Note that the terminals R and L are used as information about relative locations. A ridge termination is identified as a "sudden ending" if its coordinates i and j satisfy the relations

$$3 \leqslant i \leqslant 48, \qquad 3 \leqslant j \leqslant 48;$$

otherwise, a termination is taken to be a continuation from adjacent

Terminal	Interpretation	Description
A		Directional Code
B		Directional Code
C		Directional Code
D		Directional Code
X		Branching Point
*		Merging Point
–		Loop
$		Sudden Ending
$–$		Segment
L	Left Side	Left
R	Right Side	Right
●	Starting Point	Starting Ridge

Figure 4.29. Fingerprint pattern primitives. (From Moayer and Fu [1976b].)

ISBN 0-201-02930-8/0-201-02931-6, pbk

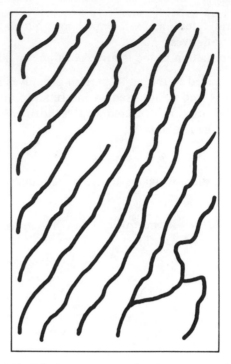

Figure 4.30. Window representation by pattern primitives.

windows. Figure 4.30 shows how the window of Fig. 4.28 would be represented by the pattern primitives (the relative location primitives, L and R, are not yet necessary).

The tree representation of a window is actually generated as a set of nodes in the form of a triple-linked list. Each node is represented by four items called, respectively, the *Symbol, B, S,* and *C* fields. The *Symbol* field contains the primitive selected from Fig. 4.29 as the physical description of part of a ridge or a relative location. The *B* field is a pointer or link to the preceding node in the tree. The *S* field links to the next adjacent ridge or to a second ridge that merges with or branches from the one under consideration. The *C* field is a pointer to the node that contains the next primitive for the ridge under consideration. These node descriptions are automatically extracted from the window by a routine that proceeds generally from left to right and top to bottom, while tracing each ridge through its chain code and expressing the primitives for each ridge as a set of nodes.

As an illustration of a portion of this representation, consider the first six ridges encountered in moving left to right across Fig. 4.30. The four

ISBN 0-201-02930-8/0-201-02931-6, pbk

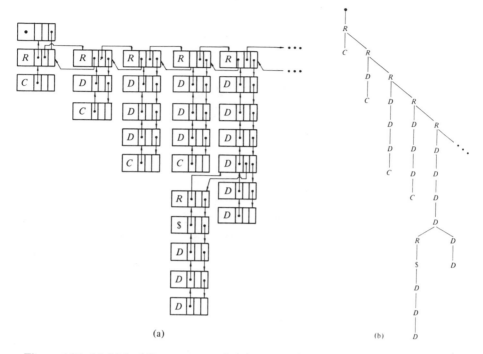

ISBN 0-201-02930-8/0-201-02931-6, pbk

(a)   (b)

Figure 4.31. (a) Linked list representation for part of window. (b) Portion of tree defined by linked list.

field nodes for these ridges and their relative locations are given in Fig. 4.31(a) in which the links are directly indicated. The portion of the tree actually described by these nodes appears in Fig. 4.31(b).

The final phase of this classification system is the recognition of the tree representation of a window. An expansive-form tree grammar must be provided for each one of the basic classification categories, and a window must be placed in the class of the language whose grammar generates its tree representation. As an example of the form these grammars take, consider a fingerprint consisting of ridges that sweep from the left upward continuously through a window, together with ridge segments entirely contained in the window or entering from the left, then terminating, such as the subsection of a print in Fig. 4.31. A tree grammar deriving the tree in Fig. 4.31(b) (among an infinite number of other trees) is $G_t = (V, r, S, P)$ for which

$$N = \{S, T1, T2, T3\},$$
$$\Sigma = \{\cdot, \$, R, C, D\},$$

with ranks

$$r(\cdot) = \{1\}, \; r(\$) = \{1\}, \; r(R) = \{1, 2\}, \; r(C) = r(D) = \{0, 1\},$$

$$r(S) = r(T1) = r(T2) = r(T3) = \{0\},$$

and with the following expansive productions:

$$S \to \begin{array}{c} \cdot \\ | \\ T3 \end{array} \qquad T1 \to C \qquad T1 \to D \qquad T1 \to \begin{array}{c} C \\ | \\ T1 \end{array} \qquad T1 \to \begin{array}{c} D \\ | \\ T1 \end{array}$$

$$T2 \to \begin{array}{c} \$ \\ | \\ T1 \end{array} \qquad T3 \to \begin{array}{c} R \\ \diagup \diagdown \\ T1 \quad T3 \end{array} \qquad T3 \to \begin{array}{c} R \\ | \\ T2 \end{array} \qquad T3 \to C \qquad T3 \to D$$

The formal model of the recognizer of this class of trees is the frontier-to-root tree automaton obtained from G_T. This automaton is $\mathcal{A}_t = (Q, F, \{f \cdot f_\$, f_R, f_C, f_D\})$ with state set $Q = \{S, T1, T2, T3\}$, set of final states $F = \{S\}$, and relations

$$f_\cdot = \{(T3, S)\},$$

$$f_\$ = \{(T1, T2)\},$$

$$f_R = \{(T2, T3), (T1, T2, T3)\},$$

$$f_R f_C = f_D = \{(\varnothing, T3), (\varnothing, T1), (T1, T1)\}.$$

It was realized in designing this fingerprint processing system that there would be too many basic classes of windows for all the important tree grammars and corresponding automata to be generated by hand; therefore, an inference procedure was included. A window rejected by all existing tree automata is taken to define a new basic class, and an expansive-form tree grammar is inferred. These new grammars are also analyzed for possible combinations with existing similar ones in order not to create more grammars than can reasonably be handled and to attempt to get balanced classes with neither too many nor too few members to be useful. A description of this aspect of the system may be found in Moayer and Fu [1974]. The following is an example of a tree grammar and automaton defining a basic class of windows that occur in sample fingerprints.

Example: One basic class consists of windows that have continuous ridges together with *one* ridge with *one* branching minutiae. An expansive-

ISBN 0-201-02930-8/0-201-02931-6, pbk

form tree grammar for this class is $G_t = (V, r, S, P)$ where

$$N = \{N1, N2, N3, N4, N5, N6, N7\};$$

$$\Sigma = \{\bullet, X, A, B, C, D, R, L\};$$

S is a single nonterminal, $N1$; the ranks of the terminals are

$$r(R) = r(L) = r(X) = \{2\},$$

$$r(\bullet) = \{1, 2\},$$

$$r(A) = r(B) = r(C) = r(D) = \{0, 1, 2\};$$

and the productions are

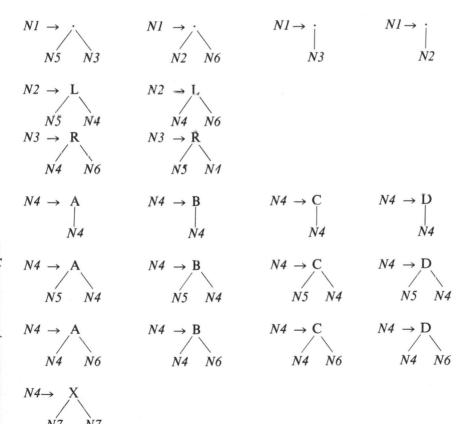

ISBN 0-201-02930-8/0-201-02931-6, pbk

$N5 \rightarrow L$ over ($N5$, $N7$) $N5 \rightarrow L$ over ($N7$, $N5$) $N5 \rightarrow L$ over ($N7$, $N7$)

$N6 \rightarrow R$ over ($N5$, $N7$) $N6 \rightarrow R$ over ($N7$, $N5$) $N6 \rightarrow R$ over ($N7$, $N7$)

$N7 \rightarrow A$ over ($N7$) $N7 \rightarrow B$ over ($N7$) $N7 \rightarrow C$ over ($N7$) $N7 \rightarrow D$ over ($N7$)

$N7 \rightarrow A$ over ($N5$, $N7$) $N7 \rightarrow B$ over ($N5$, $N7$) $N7 \rightarrow C$ over ($N5$, $N7$) $N7 \rightarrow D$ over ($N5$, $N7$)

$N7 \rightarrow A$ over ($N7$, $N7$) $N7 \rightarrow B$ over ($N7$, $N7$) $N7 \rightarrow C$ over ($N7$, $N7$) $N7 \rightarrow D$ over ($N7$, $N7$)

$N7 \rightarrow A$ over ($N7$, $N6$) $N7 \rightarrow B$ over ($N7$, $N6$) $N7 \rightarrow C$ over ($N7$, $N6$) $N7 \rightarrow D$ over ($N7$, $N6$)

$N7 \rightarrow B$ over ($N7$, $N7$) $N7 \rightarrow B$ over ($N7$, $N7$) $N7 \rightarrow C$ over ($N7$, $N7$) $N7 \rightarrow D$ over ($N7$, $N7$)

$N7 \rightarrow A$ $N7 \rightarrow B$ $N7 \rightarrow C$ $N7 \rightarrow D$

An example derivation using G_t is the following:

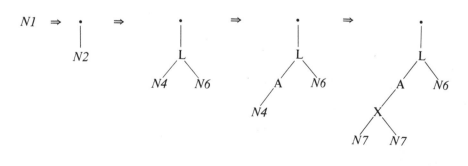

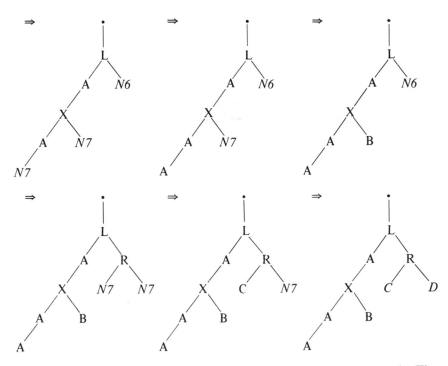

The pattern of fingerprint primitives defined by this tree appears in Fig. 4.32.

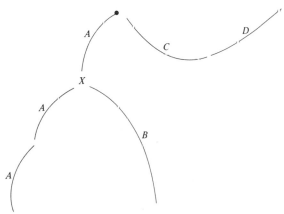

Figure 4.32. Example pattern generated by one fingerprint grammar.

In an experiment with 92 sample fingerprints, this system generated 193 window classes, as summarized in Table 4.1. No attempt was made to find a better-balanced system due to the small number of samples available.

☐

ISBN 0-201-02930-8/0-201-02931-6, pbk

Table 4.1. Populations of Fingerprint Window Classes[a]

Population	Class Numbers		Population
1	93	2	193
3	52	5	11
6	67	9	26
10	24	12	101
13	40	21	56
22	23	24	45
25	16	27	17
71	12	28, 35	10
69, 101	8	11, 107	14
7, 56, 57, 73, 93 106, 167	5	26, 38, 177	7
17, 61, 63, 65, 102 109, 112	6	44, 54, 66, 123	9
4, 8, 51, 68, 77, 78 88, 89, 94, 124, 141 143, 145, 176, 187	4	14, 18, 20, 41, 43 52, 55, 62, 70, 139 142, 146, 158	3
16, 31, 36, 37, 42, 47 50, 53, 58, 60, 74, 79 81, 82, 86, 92, 96, 97 100, 105, 108, 110, 122, 126, 140, 150, 151, 153, 155, 165, 174, 175, 182, 185, 189, 190	2	19, 30, 32, 33, 59, 80 85, 103, 116, 117, 125 128, 131, 138, 152, 161 168, 178, 181, 188	0
		Misconnected windows	61
Noisy windows	176	Other classes	1

[a]From Moayer and Fu [1976b].

The differentiation between left–right positions of features and their curvatures was also supressed due to the large number of classes being created; it was observed, however, that the rate of inferring new grammars fell off significantly as the number of processed fingerprints increased. Of the windows, 4.2% caused problems in the postprocessor, while 11.9% were too dark or too light to be handled. The overall result indicated that this method has potential for processing fingerprints, a recognition problem for patterns that are complex and have an extremely large number of classes.

ISBN 0-201-02930-8/0-201-02931-6, pbk

4.7 CONCLUDING REMARKS

Mathematical models of machines that recognize or both recognize and translate the sentences in a string language have been an important part of formal language theory since its inception. An understanding of the *types* of automata and transducers corresponding to the *types* of grammars in the Chomsky hierarchy (i.e., finite-state machines for the regular, or type 3, grammars; pushdown machines for the context-free, or type 2, grammars) reveals a great deal about the constraints encountered in actually processing the languages generated.

One turns naturally from these mathematical models to parsing algorithms of some practicality. The Cocke–Younger–Kasami parsing algorithm is an example of a technique powerful enough to handle all context-free grammars in Chomsky normal form with no empty string productions. In many specific applications, however, greater efficiency in the use of time and storage is gained by tailoring a parser to the *specific* grammar or set of grammars used. The transition diagram method is available for the class of deterministic context-free grammars. The operator precedence technique is restricted to operator precedence grammars.

Formal syntax at times seems almost too structured, because only those sentences totally without error are acceptable. Flexible or fault-tolerant parsing is a desirable feature for syntactic pattern recognition. This chapter describes syntax-directed translations to correct errors as an illustration of one approach to this problem. Finally, recognition of trees by frontier-to-root tree automata is discussed. These machines are generalized finite automata.

The following chapter introduces probabilities into the models already developed, that is, into grammars, machines, and translation schemata. With this generalization, the models reflect an uncertainty that is stochastic in nature, as contrasted with the "linguistic nondeterminism" encountered thus far.

REFERENCES

Recognizing automata as an integral part of formal language theory are discussed in formal language texts such as Hopcroft and Ullman [1969] and Kain [1972]. The classic paper of Rabin and Scott [1959] is an excellent reference on finite automata in language theory. Minimization techniques and other aspects of finite automata may be found in Booth [1968]. Pushdown and finite automata are also discussed in Lewis *et al.* [1976] and in many other books dealing with computer programming

ISBN 0-201-02930-8/0-201-02931-6, pbk

languages and their processing. Transducers are covered in Aho and Ullman [1972] and in the original source paper cited therein.

Parsing algorithms, both general and restricted in nature, are extensively covered in Aho and Ullman [1972] and Lewis *et al.* [1976]. The Cocke–Younger–Kasami parsing algorithm is the subject of Cocke and Schwartz [1970], Kasami [1965], Kasami and Torii [1969], and Younger [1967]. The top-down, recursive descent method based on transition diagrams is introduced by Conway [1963] and formalized by Lomet [1973]. Descriptions of its implementation in various programming systems may be found in Button [1977], Moore [1977], and Wilcox *et al.* [1976]. Floyd [1961] presents the concepts of shift-reduce parsing, and Floyd [1963] introduces the operator precedence method.

Error detection and correction in formal languages is a subject of intense study, and recent references include Aho and Peterson [1972], Fung and Fu [1974], Hopcroft and Ullman [1966], Leinius [1970], Lyons [1974], Thompson [1976], and Wagner and Fischer [1974]. Syntax-directed error correction is described by Thomason [1975] and Thomason and Gonzalez [1975].

Trees are discussed by Knuth [1968] and in other books on data structures. Tree automata are surveyed by Thatcher [1973] and discussed in more detail by Thatcher and Wright [1965, 1969], Brainerd [1967, 1968], and Doner [1970]. Tree grammars and automata for pattern recognition are introduced by Fu and Bhargava [1973] and are also discussed by Bhargava and Fu [1974] and Gonzalez and Thomason [1974a, b]. Moayer and Fu [1974, 1975, 1976b] describe the fingerprint classification system of Section 4.6.1.

ISBN 0-201-02930-8/0-201-02931-6, pbk

5

STOCHASTIC GRAMMARS, LANGUAGES, AND RECOGNIZERS

> Variety's the very spice of life
> That gives it all its flavour.
> *Cowper*

5.1 INTRODUCTION

In our discussion thus far, attention has been focused on nonstochastic approaches to syntactic pattern recognition. Implicit in these approaches is the assumption that all patterns under consideration are equally likely to occur. The recognition methods discussed in the previous chapters, therefore, place the same degree of importance on all inputs classified into a particular pattern class.

In practice, some patterns may occur more frequently than others and certain pattern variations may be more likely than other deviations; in these cases, the quality of recognition is often improved by employing probabilities in the classification process. An important application of stochastic grammars in syntactic pattern recognition occurs in situations in which there is a finite number of pattern classes, each defined by a distinct pattern grammar, but with random errors possible in the strings or with the generated languages not all disjoint. In these cases, a given string x to be recognized and classified may be an element of more than one language and the appropriate classification may not be clear. If probabilities can be assigned to the grammars in a way that reflects the a priori likelihoods of the classes and the individual sentences in them, stochastic decision theory can be employed to make the final assignment of the string into a pattern class. Thus, if the pattern grammars are $G_1, G_2, \ldots, G_M$, and the candidate string is x, the value $p(x|G_i)$ would be computed for each grammar G_i, $1 \leqslant i \leqslant M$; and the string would be classified according to the maximum value of $p(G_i|x)$ where $p(G_i)$ is the a priori probability (often as determined by relative frequency of occurrence) of pattern class i and

$$p(G_i|x) = \frac{p(x|G_i)p(G_i)}{p(x)}$$

$$= \frac{p(x|G_i)p(G_i)}{\sum\limits_{i=1}^{M} p(x|G_i)p(G_i)} .$$

It will be shown in the following sections that the introduction of probabilities into the syntactic recognition process can be handled in a formal way by employing stochastic grammars, languages, and automata. The development of these concepts, as well as of stochastic parsing techniques, closely parallels the development of their nonstochastic counterparts given in Chapters 2 and 4. We shall restrict all detailed discussions in this chapter to context-free and regular stochastic systems. Methods for inferring certain relevant probabilities from finite sample sets are given in Chapter 6.

5.2 STOCHASTIC GRAMMARS AND LANGUAGES

A context-free grammar is defined in Section 2.2.2 as the four-tuple $G = (N, \Sigma, P, S)$ with P a finite set of productions of the general form $A_i \rightarrow \beta_j$ for nonterminal A_i and β_j in $(N \cup \Sigma)^+$. A meaningful generalization of this definition is the assignment of probabilities to the productions of P. To introduce this concept, we consider a leftmost derivation of a terminal string x starting from S and using the productions in a non-stochastic grammar G:

$$S = \alpha_0 \Rightarrow \alpha_1 \Rightarrow \ldots \Rightarrow \alpha_{m-1} \Rightarrow \alpha_m = x.$$

The replacement of string α_k by string α_{k+1} is accomplished by applying one of the productions from P. For purpose of reference to the productions, let us assign a distinct label to each production in P, and let r_{k+1} be the label identifying the particular production used to obtain α_{k+1} from α_k. Then the preceding derivation may be written as

$$S = \alpha_0 \overset{r_1}{\Rightarrow} \alpha_1 \overset{r_2}{\Rightarrow} \alpha_2 \ldots \overset{r_{m-1}}{\Rightarrow} \alpha_{m-1} \overset{r_m}{\Rightarrow} \alpha_m = x.$$

If the derivation is now viewed as a sequence of stochastic events, the probability of generating α_1 from S is equal to the probability of applying

ISBN 0-201-02930-8/0-201-02931-6, pbk

the production labeled r_1. Denote this probability as $p(r_1)$. The probability of generating α_2 from S by applying productions r_1 and r_2 is the *product* of $p(r_1)$ and the probability of applying the production r_2, given that r_1 was applied; that is,

$$P_{r_1 r_2}(\alpha_2) = p(r_1)p(r_2|r_1).$$

Continuing along these lines yields the *probability of generation of x by the production sequence* $r_1, \ldots, r_m$ is

$$P_{r_1 \ldots r_m}(x) = p(r_1)p(r_2|r_1)p(r_3|r_1, r_2) \ldots p(r_m|r_1, \ldots, r_{m-1})$$

where $p(r_j|r_1, r_2, \ldots, r_{j-1})$, for $1 < j \leqslant m$, is the conditional probability of applying the production identified by label r_j, given that the productions $r_1, r_2, \ldots, r_{j-1}$ have been applied.

By specifying probabilities for all the productions of P in the manner just described, we may define a *stochastic grammar* as the five-tuple $G_s = (N, \Sigma, P, D, S)$ where N, Σ, and P are finite sets of nonterminals, terminals, and productions, respectively; S is the starting symbol; and D is the set of probabilities assigned to the productions of P.

We will be concerned in subsequent discussions only with unconditional probabilities for which, using the notation above,

$$p(r_j|r_1, r_2, \ldots, r_{j-1}) = p(r_j).$$

In other words, the probability of applying any particular production from P will be assumed to be independent of the sequence of previously applied productions. A stochastic grammar for which the probability assignment D satisfies this condition is said to be *unrestricted*[‡]. In this case, the probability of generating a terminal string x by applying production sequence $r_1, \ldots, r_m$ is

$$P_{r_1 \ldots r_m}(x) = p(r_1)p(r_2) \ldots p(r_m).$$

Since the problem is one of specifying the probability of each production independently of the others, it is convenient to write the productions of an unrestricted stochastic context-free grammar in the form $p_{ij}: A_i \rightarrow \beta_j$ where A_i is in N, β_j is in $(N \cup \Sigma)^+$, and p_{ij} is in D. This *stochastic production* indicates that nonterminal A_i is rewritten as β_j with probability p_{ij}. $A_i \rightarrow \beta_j$ is an element of P, and D assigns probability p_{ij} to the production.

[‡]Use of the word *unrestricted* in this context is often found in the literature; it should not be confused with use of the same term for nonstochastic type 0 grammars.

ISBN 0-201-02930-8/0-201-02931-6, pbk

Let the set of all productions for rewriting a specific nonterminal A_i be denoted as $\{A_i \rightarrow \beta_1, A_i \rightarrow \beta_2, \ldots, A_i \rightarrow \beta_n\}$. It will be assumed that the sum of the probabilities assigned to the productions $A_i \rightarrow \beta_j, j = 1, 2, \ldots, n$, is one; that is,

$$\sum_{j=1}^{n} p_{ij} = 1.$$

A grammar for which this assumption holds for each nonterminal A_i is called a *proper* stochastic grammar. That a grammar be proper is a reasonable requirement from the point of view that the function of the grammar is to describe the generation of terminal strings; hence, a derivation by a stochastic grammar is a sequence of random events rewriting a single nonterminal in each step and continuing until a terminal string is obtained.

Aside from the probability assignments, stochastic productions are of exactly the same form as the productions introduced in Sections 2.2.1 and 2.2.2. In fact, the Chomsky hierarchy defined in the latter section can be extended directly to stochastic grammars. The *characteristic grammar* G_{sc} of a stochastic grammar G_s is obtained by deleting D from G_s; thus,

$$G_{sc} = G_s - D$$

$$= (N, \Sigma, P, S).$$

Then G_s is of type 0, 1, 2, or 3 if G_{sc} is, respectively, of type 0, 1, 2, or 3. Other concepts based on the form of the productions, such as the Chomsky and Greibach normal forms, are similarly extendable to stochastic grammars.

It is possible to have in a grammar productions that allow more than one derivation of the same terminal string. A stochastic grammar is said to be *ambiguous* if there are n_x distinct leftmost derivations of a terminal string x with respective probabilities $p_1(x), p_2(x), \ldots, p_{n_x}(x), n_x > 1$. For an ambiguous stochastic grammar, the probability of generation of $x^{\ddagger}$ is given by

$$p(x) = \sum_{i=1}^{n_x} p_i(x),$$

which is the sum of the probabilities of a finite number of mutually exclusive events.

---

‡In an environment in which more than one grammar might be the source of string x, this probability must be denoted as $p(x|G_s)$ and must be computed for each grammar G_s.

ISBN 0-201-02930-8/0-201-02931-6, pbk

The *stochastic language* $L(G_s)$ *generated by a stochastic grammar* G_s is the set of derivable terminal strings together with their probabilities of generation:

$$L(G_s) = \left\{ [x, p(x)] | x \text{ in } \Sigma^+, S \underset{p_i(x)}{\overset{*}{\Rightarrow}} x, i = 1, 2, \ldots, n_x \right\}$$

where n_x is the number of distinct leftmost derivations of x and the fact that there is a specific leftmost derivation with probability $p_i(x)$ is indicated by writing

$$S \underset{p_i(x)}{\overset{*}{\Rightarrow}} x.$$

If the grammar is unambiguous, there is the simpler definition

$$L(G_s) = \left\{ [x, p(x)] | x \text{ in } \Sigma^+, S \underset{p(x)}{\overset{*}{\Rightarrow}} x \right\}$$

Two stochastic grammars G_{s1} and G_{s2} are *equivalent* if $L(G_{s1}) = L(G_{s2})$.

It should be noted that the strings generated by a stochastic grammar G_s and its nonstochastic characteristic grammar G_{sc} are exactly the same. All that has been done to modify the previous concept of a string grammar is to associate a probability of generation $p(x)$ with each terminal string x and to make the derivation process stochastic.

Example: Consider the proper stochastic context-free grammar $G_s = (N, \Sigma, P, D, S)$ where $N = \{S\}$, $\Sigma = \{a, b\}$, and the productions with their probabilities are

$$p : S \rightarrow aSb \qquad 1 - p : S \rightarrow ab$$

The terminal string $x = aaabbb$, for example, is obtained by the single derivation

$$S \Rightarrow aSb \Rightarrow aaSbb \Rightarrow aaabbb,$$

for which

$$p(x) = (p)(p)(1 - p) = p^2(1 - p).$$

In general, G_s generates strings of the form $a^t b^t$ with probability $p^{t-1}(1 - p)$ for $t \geqslant 1$. The stochastic language is

$$L(G_s) = \{ [a^t b^t, p^{t-1}(1 - p)] | t \geqslant 1 \}.$$

ISBN 0-201-02930-8/0-201-02931-6, pbk

It is noted that this stochastic grammar is not ambiguous, since the sequence of productions leading to each terminal string is unique.   □

One use of a stochastic grammar is as a source of patterns produced randomly according to a known probability law. The patterns themselves might then be used as test sequences or for various other applications. The following example illustrates this idea.

Example: We wish to define a proper stochastic PDL grammar G_s to generate stylized versions of the capital letters E, F, J, and T with the same relative frequencies of occurrence that the four letters have in random English text. We first develop the characteristic grammar $G_{sc} =$ (N, Σ, P, S), then assign probabilities to its productions.

PDL's and their grammars were discussed in Section 2.3.2. For this example, let the terminals of G_{sc} consist of the left and right parentheses, the four directed line segments in Fig. 5.1 as pattern primitives, and the two connection operations + for "join head to tail" and × for "join tail to tail." It is recalled that joins of primitive structures in a PDL can be made because the connection points are well defined; for instance, the joining of structure X to structure Y to form $(X + Y)$ joins the head of structure X to the tail of structure Y.

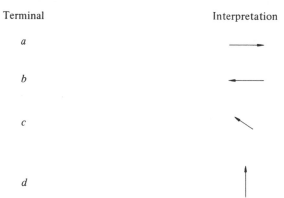

Figure 5.1. PDL terminals and pattern primitives.

We let the nonterminals be S, A, B, C, H, K, L, and M. The following productions, which provide unambiguous derivations of PDL representations of the four letters, introduce one join operation in a sentential form at a time:

$S \rightarrow (a \times (A))$ $S \rightarrow (A)$ $S \rightarrow ((M) \times (H))$ $S \rightarrow (H)$

$A \rightarrow d + (B)$ $B \rightarrow a \times (C)$ $C \rightarrow d + a$

$M \rightarrow b + c$ $H \rightarrow d + (K)$ $K \rightarrow d + (L)$ $L \rightarrow a \times b$

ISBN 0-201-02930-8/0-201-02931-6, pbk

An example derivation of a sentence in $L(G_{sc})$ is

$$S \Rightarrow (a \times (A)) \Rightarrow (a \times (d + (B))) \Rightarrow (a \times (d + (a \times (C))))$$
$$\Rightarrow (a \times (d + (a \times (d + a)))).$$

The pattern represented by this string is shown in Fig. 5.2. The three additional derivations for this language yield the sentences

$$(d + (a \times (d + a))), ((b + c)(d + (d + (a \times b)))),$$

and

$$(d + (d + (a \times b)));$$

the patterns they represent are also shown in Fig. 5.2.

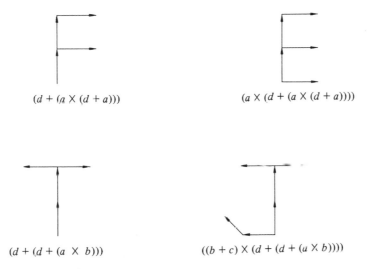

$(d + (a \times (d + a)))$ $(a \times (d + (a \times (d + a))))$

$(d + (d + (a \times b)))$ $((b + c) \times (d + (d + (a \times b))))$

Figure 5.2. PDL sentences and letter patterns.

ISBN 0-201-02930-8/0-201-02931-6, pbk

Standard tables of letter counts (cf. Pratt [1942]) provide the information that in 1000 letters in random English words, it is expected that there will be 131 E's, 29 F's, 1.3 J's, and 105 T's. Using relative frequencies of occurrence as our estimates of probabilities, we find that G_s should generate the string for E with probability 0.492, the string for F with probability 0.109, the string for J with probability 0.005, and the string for T with probability 0.394.

It is seen by inspection that the only nonterminal for which there is a choice of rewriting rules is the starting symbol S. The letter E is derived if the first production is $S \rightarrow (a \times (A))$; similarly, $S \rightarrow (A)$ generates letter F, $S \rightarrow ((M) \times (H))$ generates letter J, and $S \rightarrow (H)$ generates letter T.

The stochastic grammar $G_{sc} = (N, \Sigma, P, D, S)$ must therefore have the following stochastic productions:

$0.492: S \to (a \times (A))$ 　　 $0.109: S \to (A)$ 　　 $0.005: S \to ((M) \times (H))$

$0.394: S \to (H)$ 　　 $1: A \to d + (B)$ 　　 $1: B \to a \times (C)$

$1: C \to d + a$ 　　 $1: H \to d + (K)$ 　　 $1: K \to d + (L)$

$1: L \to a \times b$ 　　 $1: M \to b + c$

It is straightforward to extend this grammar to a stochastic generator of all 26 capital letters such that each letter is generated with a probability corresponding to the relative frequency of occurrence of that letter in random English text. Such a grammar preserves at least the first moment of the alphabet probabilities. 　　　　　　　　　　　　　　　　　□

5.3　CONSISTENCY OF STOCHASTIC CONTEXT-FREE GRAMMARS

A stochastic context-free grammar (abbreviated SCFG) is *consistent* if

$$\sum_{x \text{ in } \Sigma^*} p(x) = 1.$$

An important aspect of a stochastic grammar G_s is whether or not it has this property because a consistent grammar induces a probability measure on Σ^* as a sample space in which an event is an appearance of a terminal string. In syntactic pattern processing, a stochastic grammar is a mathematical model of a random source of individual pattern description strings; therefore, a requirement for consistency in this case is a requirement that the sum of the probabilities of all patterns arising from the source be 1.

We shall assume G_s is proper, but a proper SCFG need not be consistent (see Section 5.3.2 for a counterexample). In looking for the specific conditions for consistency to hold, it is convenient first to classify a grammar as *linear* or *nonlinear*. A *linear* SCFG has productions only of the forms $p : A_i \to xA_jy$ or $p : A_i \to x$ for nonterminals A_i, A_j and strings x, y in Σ^*; otherwise, the grammar is *nonlinear*. Note that all regular stochastic grammars are linear. The theory of Markov chains provides a test for consistency of linear grammars; the theory of multitype branching processes must be used for nonlinear grammars.

ISBN 0-201-02930-8/0-201-02931-6, pbk

5.3.1 Consistency of Linear Grammars

A discrete-parameter Markov process can be defined in general terms to be a stochastic process in which transitions among elements in a set of states occur at discrete points in time with probabilities dependent only on the current state and not on any past states. A discrete-parameter Markov process with a finite or denumerably infinite state set is called a *Markov chain*. A state of a Markov chain with the property that once the process enters this state, it will forever remain there, is called an *absorbing state*. Extensive discussion of Markov chains is available in the literature (cf. Kemeny and Snell [1960]; Parzen [1962]).

A linear stochastic context-free grammar $G_L = (N, \Sigma, P, D, S)$ is an example of an absorbing Markov chain with state set $N \cup \{H\}$. H is an absorbing state, and entry of the process into H represents termination of a derivation of G_L. The initial state of the Markov process is S, the state corresponding to the grammar's starting symbol. There is a transition with probability $\hat{p}$ from state A_i directly to state A_j iff $\hat{p}$ is the sum of the probabilities of all productions of the form $p : A_i \to xA_jy$; there is a transition with probability $\hat{p}$ from state A_i directly to state H iff $\hat{p}$ is the sum of the probabilities of all productions of the form $p : A_i \to x$. There is a transition from H back to itself with probability 1.

The Markov chain is completely described by a transition matrix $\mathbf{M}$ defined in the following way. Let the states be ordered such that the initial state S is first and the terminal state H is last. For n states, $\mathbf{M}$ is an $n \times n$ matrix with element m_{ij} being the probability of a one-step transition from state A_i to state A_j. The element m_{1n} is therefore the probability of reaching state H from state S in one step, which is exactly the probability of deriving a terminal string from starting symbol S by applying one production. When the square of $\mathbf{M}$ is computed, its element m_{1n}^2 is the sum of the probabilities of all derivations of terminal strings that use one or two productions and take either one or two steps; and, in general, element m_{1n}^k in $\mathbf{M}^k$ is the sum of the derivation probabilities for all strings in Σ^+ that are obtained from starting symbol S in no more than k steps. The essential result for consistency is the following theorem.

Theorem: Suppose G_L is a linear grammar; then G_L is consistent iff

$$\lim_{k \to \infty} m_{1n}^k = 1.$$

Proof: Suppose $\lim_{k \to \infty} m_{1n}^k = 1$; since this element of the limiting matrix, $\lim_{k \to \infty} \mathbf{M}^k$, gives the sum of the probabilities of all derivations, it follows that G_L is consistent.

ISBN 0-201-02930-8/0-201-02931-6, pbk

On the other hand, if G_L is consistent, then by definition, the sum of all terminal string derivation probabilities must be 1; hence, $\lim_{k \to \infty} m_{1n}^k = 1$.

□

This test may be stated in somewhat different, but equivalent, terms. An *open set* $\mathcal{O}$ in a Markov chain is defined to be a subset of its states with the property that, from each state in $\mathcal{O}$, there is nonzero probability of reaching some state not in $\mathcal{O}$ in a finite number of steps. By contrast, a *closed set* $\mathcal{C}$ has the property that, for each state in $\mathcal{C}$, the probability is 1 that a transition to a state outside $\mathcal{C}$ will never occur. These definitions lead to the following test for consistency.

Theorem: Let G_L be a linear grammar, and consider N, the set containing all states in the Markov chain except state H. G_L is consistent iff N is an open set.

Proof: Suppose G_L is consistent; then, in the powers of matrix $\mathbf{M}$, we have $\lim_{k \to \infty} m_{1n}^k = 1$. This implies that $\{H\}$ is the only closed set in the Markov chain, since the probability that the process is in an absorbing subset after k steps tends to 1 as k tends to infinity.

On the other hand, if N is an open set, it contains no closed subsets and the probability that the Markov chain vacates N tends to 1 as k tends to infinity; hence, $\lim_{k \to \infty} m_{1n}^k = 1$ and G_L is consistent.

□

It is noted that N is an open set iff for each state A_i in N

$$\sum_{k=1}^{n-1} m_{in}^k > 0.$$

For the case in which N is open, the $(n - 1) \times (n - 1)$ matrix $\hat{\mathbf{M}}$ is formed by deleting the nth row and column from $\mathbf{M}$. It is well known that the *fundamental matrix* $\mathbf{M}_f$ of the Markov process, defined by

$$\mathbf{M}_f = \sum_{k=0}^{\infty} \hat{\mathbf{M}}^k = (\mathbf{I} - \hat{\mathbf{M}})^{-1}$$

where $\mathbf{I}$ is the $(n - 1) \times (n - 1)$ identity matrix, is bounded and yields various properties of the process. Specifically, its element f_{1i}, $1 \leqslant i \leqslant (n - 1)$, is the expected number of occurrences of state A_i before termination in absorbing state H; and this is the expected number of occurrences of nonterminal A_i in a derivation using stochastic grammar G_L.

ISBN 0-201-02930-8/0-201-02931-6, pbk

Example: We wish to investigate the linear grammar G_L, which has terminals a and b, nonterminals S and A, starting symbol S, and the following stochastic productions:

$$0.6: S \to aSb \qquad 0.4: S \to Abb$$

$$0.2: A \to abS \qquad 0.7: A \to aA \qquad 0.1: A \to b$$

The one-step transition matrix for the associated Markov chain with states ordered as S, A, and H is

$$\mathbf{M} = \begin{bmatrix} 0.6 & 0.4 & 0 \\ 0.2 & 0.7 & 0.1 \\ 0 & 0 & 1 \end{bmatrix}.$$

That m_{13} is 0 indicates that there is no single step derivation of a terminal string in this grammar. Squaring this matrix yields

$$\mathbf{M}^2 = \begin{bmatrix} 0.44 & 0.52 & 0.04 \\ 0.26 & 0.57 & 0.17 \\ 0 & 0 & 1 \end{bmatrix}.$$

The sum of the probabilities of all derivations of terminal strings taking one or two steps is 0.04, the value of m_{13}^2. It is easy to establish that the only two-step derivation for grammar G_L is

$$S \Rightarrow Abb \Rightarrow bbb,$$

which occurs with probability

$$p(bbb) = (0.4)(0.1) = 0.04.$$

The elements in $\mathbf{M}^2$ also establish that the set of states $\{S, A\}$ is open for this Markov chain because there is nonzero probability of reaching state H from A and from S in no more than two steps. In terms of the grammar, this means that both S and A can be used to derive at least one terminal string with nonzero probability and that G_L is consistent. It is also seen that $\{H\}$ is a closed set.

The third column and row corresponding to absorbing state H are deleted from $\mathbf{M}$ to get matrix $\hat{\mathbf{M}}$, used to compute the fundamental matrix $\mathbf{M}_f$; thus,

$$\hat{\mathbf{M}} = \begin{bmatrix} 0.6 & 0.4 \\ 0.2 & 0.7 \end{bmatrix}$$

ISBN 0-201-02930-8/0-201-02931-6, pbk

and

$$M_f = \left(I - \begin{bmatrix} 0.6 & 0.4 \\ 0.2 & 0.7 \end{bmatrix} \right)^{-1}$$

$$= \left(\begin{bmatrix} 1 & 0 \\ 0 & 1 \end{bmatrix} - \begin{bmatrix} 0.6 & 0.4 \\ 0.2 & 0.7 \end{bmatrix} \right)^{-1}$$

$$= \begin{bmatrix} 0.4 & -0.4 \\ -0.2 & 0.3 \end{bmatrix}^{-1}$$

$$= \begin{bmatrix} 7.5 & 10 \\ 5 & 10 \end{bmatrix}.$$

The values in the first row of M_f show that the expected number of occurrences of nonterminal S in a derivation is 7.5 and the expected number of occurrences of nonterminal A in a derivation is 10. If the grammar were redefined to have the same terminals, nonterminals, and productions, but A as its starting symbol, then the second row (indexed by A) would provide these expectations and show that the expected number of occurrences of S is 5 and of A is 10.　　　□

5.3.2　Consistency of Nonlinear Grammars

A *linear* stochastic grammar G_L may be investigated by employing Markov chain theory because at most one nonterminal appears in a G_L sentential form and there is a direct correspondence between the nonterminals and the states in a Markov chain (with the exception that the chain has one more state for absorption). This Markov model is not appropriate for a *nonlinear* stochastic context-free grammar because an arbitrary number of nonterminals may appear in a sentential form.

A nonlinear grammar $G_{NL} = (N, \Sigma, P, D, S)$ is an instance of a more general random process known as a *multitype branching process*. In this description, each nonterminal is one of the so-called "types" of symbols in the process, and the probabilities assigned to the productions determine the ways in which a symbol of one type is stochastically rewritten as, or branches into, itself or other symbol types. For example, the stochastic context-free productions $p: S \rightarrow aSbS$ and $\hat{p}: S \rightarrow bXb$ indicate that S branches into two symbols of its same type with probability p or into one symbol of type X with probability $\hat{p}$. Terminal symbols are also produced as these branchings occur.

An extensive coverage of multitype branching processes is beyond the scope of this discussion; however, we will make use of certain results of

ISBN 0-201-02930-8/0-201-02931-6, pbk

this theory (Harris [1963]) to find a test for consistency of nonlinear SCFG's. The critical factor in this test is the largest-magnitude eigenvalue of the grammar's first-moment matrix.

The *first-moment matrix* **B** for grammar G_{NL} is a matrix with rows and columns labeled as nonterminals. Let A_i and A_j be nonterminals; the element b_{ij} in **B** is the expected number of A_j's appearing in one rewriting of A_i. To compute the elements of **B**, let the set of stochastic productions in P for which A_i is the left-hand side be $\{p_{i1}: A_i \to \alpha_1, \ldots, p_{im} : A_i \to \alpha_m\}$; then

$$b_{ij} = \sum_{k=1}^{m} (p_{ik}) \#j(\alpha_k)$$

where $\#j(\alpha_k)$ denotes the number of occurrences of nonterminal A_j in α_k.

The *characteristic equation of* B is obtained by setting the determinant of the matrix $(\mathbf{B} - \rho\mathbf{I})$ to 0; that is, for n nonterminals,

$$\begin{vmatrix} b_{11} - \rho & b_{12} & \cdots & b_{1n} \\ b_{21} & b_{22} - \rho & \cdots & b_{2n} \\ \vdots & \vdots & & \vdots \\ b_{n1} & b_{n2} & \cdots & b_{nn} - \rho \end{vmatrix} = 0.$$

The *characteristic roots* (also called the *eigenvalues*) of **B** are the roots $\rho_1, \rho_2, \ldots, \rho_n$ of this equation. Let ρ denote the principal (i.e., largest-magnitude) eigenvalue. The following theorem is obtained from the general theory of multitype branching processes.

Theorem: Let ρ be the largest eigenvalue of the first-moment matrix for grammar G_{NL}. G_{NL} is consistent if $|\rho| < 1$ and inconsistent if $|\rho| > 1$, where $|\rho|$ is the absolute value of ρ. ☐

The case where $|\rho| = 1$ requires additional analysis and a new definition. Let us define a *final class FC of types* to be a subset of the nonterminals with the property that each nonterminal in *FC*, when rewritten, will produce at least one nonterminal also in *FC* (nonterminals not in *FC* and terminals may also appear when an element of *FC* is rewritten). The following theorem completes the test for consistency.

Theorem: Suppose the largest eigenvalue of the first-moment matrix for grammar G_{NL} is $|\rho| = 1$; then G_{NL} is consistent iff there is no final class of nonterminals. ☐

ISBN 0-201-02930-8/0-201-02931-6, pbk

Example: Consider the nonlinear SCFG $G_{NL} = (\{S, X, Y\}, \{a, b\},$ $P, D, S)$ with stochastic productions

$$4/7: S \rightarrow aSbS \qquad\qquad 3/7: S \rightarrow bXb$$

$$1/35: X \rightarrow aba \qquad\qquad 16/35: X \rightarrow aSbYb$$

$$18/35: X \rightarrow XbXb$$

$$3/7: Y \rightarrow abX \qquad\qquad 4/7: Y \rightarrow YabY$$

With the nonterminals ordered as S, X, Y for row and column labels in the 3×3 matrix **B**, the entry b_{23} becomes, for example,

$$b_{23} = \sum_{k=1}^{3} p_{2k} \#3(\alpha_k)$$

$$= (1/35)(0) + (16/35)(1) + (18/35)(0)$$

$$= 16/35.$$

The entire matrix is

$$\mathbf{B} = \begin{bmatrix} \dfrac{8}{7} & \dfrac{3}{7} & 0 \\[2mm] \dfrac{16}{35} & \dfrac{36}{35} & \dfrac{16}{35} \\[2mm] 0 & \dfrac{3}{7} & \dfrac{8}{7} \end{bmatrix}.$$

Its principal eigenvalue is found to be $\rho = 12/7$. Since $|\rho| > 1$, G_{NL} is inconsistent. Evidently, this occurs because the probability of the only production that can terminate a derivation, $X \rightarrow aba$, is too low compared to other production probabilities. □

5.4 STOCHASTIC RECOGNIZERS

5.4.1 Stochastic Finite Automata

Since the derivations of a regular or context-free grammar can be made stochastic by assigning probabilities to the productions, it is natural to ask whether there are equivalent recognizers that also operate in a probabilistic

ISBN 0-201-02930-8/0-201-02931-6, pbk

way. It should be recalled that an important relationship discussed in Section 4.2.1 is the equality of the set of languages generated by nondeterministic regular grammars with the set of languages accepted by nondeterministic finite automata, and that this relationship is based on establishing a one-to-one correspondence between the productions in a regular grammar and the state transitions in a finite automaton. This correspondence may be extended to stochastic models by making the state transitions of a finite automaton probabilistic in a manner similar to the way in which selection of the productions is made a random event in a stochastic grammar.

Specifically, a *stochastic finite automaton* is a machine defined by a six-tuple $\mathcal{Q}_{sf} = (Q, \Sigma, \delta, q_0, F, D)$ in which Q, Σ, and F are finite sets of states, input symbols, and final states, respectively; q_0 is the starting state; and δ is a mapping from $Q \times \Sigma$ into 2^Q to which D assigns a set of probabilities.

A stochastic finite automaton operates in the following way. An input string x from Σ^+ is placed on the input tape, the tape head is located on the leftmost tape cell for scanning movement to the right, and $\mathcal{Q}_{sf}$ is placed in starting state q_0. Thereafter, the selection of the next state of $\mathcal{Q}_{sf}$ is a random event governed by a set of probabilities assigned by D to combinations of current state and current input symbol. For instance, if $\mathcal{Q}_{sf}$ has reached state q and is scanning symbol a, then $\delta(q, a)$ is the set of potential next states, any one of which the machine could enter; and D assigns the probability law by which one element of $\delta(q, a)$ is actually selected. Analogous to the way in which a stochastic regular grammar provides for probabilistic derivations in a regular language, a stochastic finite automaton provides for probabilistic recognition as a random state sequence in response to an input string.

A stochastic finite automaton for which all probabilities are unconditional (i.e., for which the next state is a function only of the current state and input symbol, and not a function of any previous states or symbols) is said to be *unrestricted*. In this case the combination of current state, input symbol, and probability assignment D establishes a set of probabilities on sample space Q for selection of the machine's transition to the next state. *The probability of acceptance of terminal string x by following state sequence $q_0, q_1, \ldots, q_f$* (with q_f in F reached as all of x is scanned) is the product of the probabilities of the transitions that actually occur as $\mathcal{Q}_{sf}$ goes from q_0 to q_f. Since $\mathcal{Q}_{sf}$ is unrestricted, this definition simply indicates that this probability is to be computed as the product of the probabilities of a set of independent events.

ISBN 0-201-02930-8/0-201-02931-6, pbk

We shall consider only unrestricted stochastic automata and shall also require that D be a *proper* assignment in the following sense. Suppose for a given current state q and input symbol a that the set of potential next states is $\{q_1, \ldots, q_n\}$. Let $p(q_i|a, q)$ denote the probability of selecting state q_i from this set; then $\mathcal{Q}_{sf}$ is a *proper machine* if

$$\sum_{q_i \text{ in } \delta(q, a)} p(q_i|a, q) = 1$$

holds for all combinations (q, a) in $Q \times \Sigma$.

Recognition is a random event for a stochastic automaton, so there is associated with each string x in Σ^+ a probability $p(x)$ that x will be accepted by $\mathcal{Q}_{sf}$. In general, there will be alternate sequences of states by which string x can cause $\mathcal{Q}_{sf}$ to enter a final state in F; therefore, if there are n_x distinct paths from starting state q_0 through the states in Q by which string x can lead $\mathcal{Q}_{sf}$ to an accepting state, and if these paths occur with respective probabilities $p_1(x), \ldots, p_{n_x}(x)$, then the *probability of recognition of x by $\mathcal{Q}_{sf}$* is

$$p(x) = \sum_{i=1}^{n_x} p_i(x),$$

which is simply the sum of the probabilities of a finite number of mutually exclusive events.

The *language recognized by* $\mathcal{Q}_{sf}$ in its stochastic operation is

$$L(\mathcal{Q}_{sf}) = \left\{ [x, p(x)] | x \text{ in } \Sigma^+, p(x) = \sum_{i=1}^{n_x} p_i(x), \right.$$

$p_i(x)$ is the probability of one of the n_x distinct ways in which $\mathcal{Q}_{sf}$ can start in q_0 and halt in a

state in F when all of x is scanned $\left. \vphantom{\sum} \right\}$.

Two stochastic automata $\mathcal{Q}_{sf1}$ and $\mathcal{Q}_{sf2}$ are *equivalent* if $L(\mathcal{Q}_{sf1}) = L(\mathcal{Q}_{sf2})$.

Example: Consider the four-state stochastic finite automaton $\mathcal{Q}_{sf} = (Q, \Sigma, \delta, q_0, F, D)$ for which $Q = \{q_0, q_1, q_2, q_3\}$, $\Sigma = \{a, b\}$, $F = \{q_2\}$,

ISBN 0-201-02930-8/0-201-02931-6, pbk

and the stochastic state transitions defined by δ and D are as follows:

$$\delta(q_0, a) = \{q_0, q_1, q_3\} \quad \text{with} \quad p(q_0|a, q_0) = p_1, p(q_1|a, q_0) = p_2,$$
$$p(q_3|a, q_0) = p_3;$$

$$\delta(q_0, b) = \{q_1\} \qquad \text{with} \quad p(q_1|b, q_0) = 1;$$

$$\delta(q_1, a) = \{q_3\} \qquad \text{with} \quad p(q_3|a, q_1) = 1;$$

$$\delta(q_1, b) = \{q_1, q_2\} \qquad \text{with} \quad p(q_1|b, q_1) = p_4, p(q_2|b, q_1) = p_5;$$

$$\delta(q_2, a) = \{q_3\} \qquad \text{with} \quad p(q_3|a, q_2) = 1;$$

$$\delta(q_2, b) = \{q_3\} \qquad \text{with} \quad p(q_3|b, q_2) = 1;$$

$$\delta(q_3, a) = \{q_3\} \qquad \text{with} \quad p(q_3|a, q_3) = 1;$$

$$\delta(q_3, b) = \{q_3\} \qquad \text{with} \quad p(q_3|b, q_3) = 1.$$

A representation of $\mathcal{C}_{sf}$ as a weighted state transition diagram is given in Fig. 5.3. The nodes of the diagram correspond to the states of $\mathcal{C}_{sf}$ and the

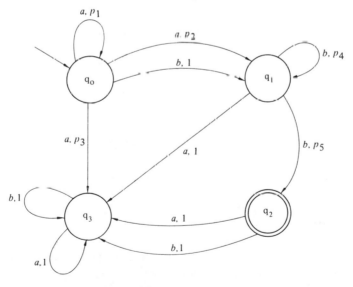

Figure 5.3. Stochastic finite automaton.

ISBN 0-201-02930-8/0-201-02931-6, pbk

arcs are labeled with input symbols and probabilities. The final state, q_2, appears as a double circle, and starting state q_0 is indicated by an unconnected entering arrow.

Since we are requiring that all stochastic automata be proper, it is known that

$$p_1 + p_2 + p_3 = p_4 + p_5 = 1.$$

Suppose that input string $x = aabb$ is applied to $\mathcal{Q}_{sf}$. The eight state sequences that can occur as x is scanned, together with their probabilities, are

$$q_0, q_0, q_0, q_1, q_1 \quad \text{with probability} \quad (p_1 p_1 p_4);$$

$$q_0, q_0, q_0, q_1, q_2 \quad \text{with probability} \quad (p_1 p_1 p_5);$$

$$q_0, q_0, q_1, q_1, q_1 \quad \text{with probability} \quad (p_1 p_2 p_4 p_4);$$

$$q_0, q_0, q_1, q_1, q_2 \quad \text{with probability} \quad (p_1 p_2 p_4 p_5);$$

$$q_0, q_0, q_1, q_2, q_3 \quad \text{with probability} \quad (p_1 p_2 p_5);$$

$$q_0, q_0, q_3, q_3, q_3 \quad \text{with probability} \quad (p_1 p_3);$$

$$q_0, q_1, q_3, q_3, q_3 \quad \text{with probability} \quad (p_2);$$

$$q_0, q_3, q_3, q_3, q_3 \quad \text{with probability} \quad (p_3).$$

The second and fourth of these sequences terminate in final state q_2 for acceptance of the input string; therefore,

$$p(x) = p_1^2 p_5 + p_1 p_2 p_4 p_5$$

is the probability that a random application of x will be accepted. The probability that x will be rejected by $\mathcal{Q}_{sf}$ is $1 - p(x)$, the sum of the probabilities of the remaining six state sequences, each of which ends in a nonfinal state. □

The capability of stochastic finite automata as probabilistic recognizers is given by the following fundamental result.

Theorem: A stochastic language L is generated by a stochastic regular grammar iff $L = L(\mathcal{Q}_{sf})$ for a stochastic finite automaton $\mathcal{Q}_{sf}$. □

ISBN 0-201-02930-8/0-201-02931-6, pbk

In order to prove this claim, it is necessary to show that, given a stochastic machine $\mathcal{Q}_{sf}$, a stochastic regular grammar G_s can be constructed such that $L(\mathcal{Q}_{sf}) = L(G_s)$, and vice versa. The proof, which may be outlined as follows, contains the rules for obtaining G_s from $\mathcal{Q}_{sf}$ or $\mathcal{Q}_{sf}$ from G_s.

Suppose first that a proper stochastic regular grammar $G_s = (N, \Sigma, P, D, X_0)$ is given. The stochastic finite automaton $\mathcal{Q}_{sf} = (Q, \Sigma, \delta, q_0, F, \hat{D})$ is constructed in the following manner. Let the set of G_s nonterminals be $\{X_0, X_1, \ldots, X_n\}$, where X_0 represents the starting symbol; then the state set Q is formed by introducing $n + 3$ states $\{q_0, q_1, \ldots, q_n, q_{n+1}, q_{n+2}\}$ where q_i corresponds to X_i for $i = 0, 1, 2, \ldots, n$, and q_{n+1} and q_{n+2} are two additional states. The set of final states is simply $F = \{q_{n+1}\}$, and q_{n+2} is a nonfinal (rejecting) state used to normalize the probabilities to make $\mathcal{Q}_{sf}$ proper. G_s and $\mathcal{Q}_{sf}$ have the same alphabet Σ. The δ mapping and probability assignment $\hat{D}$ are defined as follows. For $0 \leqslant i \leqslant n, 0 \leqslant j \leqslant n$,

  (i) if $p: X_i \to aX_j$ is in P, then $\delta(q_i, a)$ contains q_j and $p(q_j|a, q_i)$ is p;
  (ii) if $p: X_i \to a$ is in P, then $\delta(q_i, a)$ contains q_{n+1} and $p(q_{n+1}|a, q_i)$ is p;

  (iii) q_{n+2} is a trap state such that, for each terminal a in Σ, $\delta(q_{n+2}, a)$ is $\{q_{n+2}\}$ and $p(q_{n+2}|a, q_{n+2}) = 1$; and
  (iv) in order to make $\mathcal{Q}_{sf}$ a proper machine, for each combination of state q and terminal a, we place q_{n+2} in $\delta(q, a)$ where

$$p(q_{n+2}|a, q) = 1 - \sum_{i=0}^{n+1} p(q_i|a, q).$$

Thus, $\mathcal{Q}_{sf}$ will move stochastically through its states to accept a string in a way that is a direct correspondence with the sequence of nonterminals appearing in a derivation of the same string. $\mathcal{Q}_{sf}$ is made to be proper by introducing transitions to the trap state q_{n+2}.

On the other hand, given a proper stochastic finite automaton $\mathcal{Q}_{sf} = (Q, \Sigma, \delta, q_0, F, \hat{D})$, we seek a stochastic regular grammar $G_s = (N, \Sigma, P, D, X_0)$, the derivations of which parallel the state sequences of $\mathcal{Q}_{sf}$ leading to recognition of strings. Even though $\mathcal{Q}_{sf}$ is a proper automaton, G_s will not in general be a proper grammar. (A method that attempts to obtain a proper grammar equivalent to one not proper is described later in this section.)

To obtain G_s directly from $\mathcal{Q}_{sf}$, let N be identified with the state set Q, with starting symbol X_0 corresponding to q_0, and productions as follows:

  (i) if q_j is in $\delta(q_i, a)$ and $p(q_j|a, q_i)$ is p, then there is a stochastic production $p: X_i \to aX_j$ in P; and

ISBN 0-201-02930-8/0-201-02931-6, pbk

(ii) if q_j is in $\delta(q_i, a)$, q_j is a final state, and $p(q_j|a, q_i)$ is p, then there is in P a stochastic production $p:X_i \to a$.

A formal proof by induction establishes that there is a one-to-one correspondence between the state sequences in $\mathcal{C}_{sf}$ leading to acceptance of a string and the derivations in G_s, and that the relevant probabilities are preserved.

Example: Suppose we wish to construct a stochastic recognizer for the language of the proper grammar $G_s = (\{X_0, X_1\}, \{a, b\}, P, D, X_0)$ with stochastic productions

$$p_1: X_0 \to aX_0 \qquad p_2: X_0 \to aX_1 \qquad p_3: X_0 \to bX_1$$

$$p_4: X_1 \to bX_1 \qquad p_5: X_1 \to h$$

The automaton is constructed as $\mathcal{C}_{sf} = (Q, \Sigma, \delta, q_0, F, D)$ having states $\{q_0, q_1, q_2, q_3\}$ with q_0 identified with X_0, q_1 identified with X_1, final state q_2, and trap state q_3 to be used for normalization. Σ is the set $\{a, b\}$. The partial specification of δ and $\hat{D}$ that arises from the productions is as follows:

$$\delta(q_0, a) = \{q_0, q_1, q_3\} \text{ with } p(q_0|a, q_0) = p_1, p(q_1|a, q_0) = p_2,$$

$$p(q_3|a, q_0) = 1 - p_1 - p_2;$$

$$\delta(q_0, b) = \{q_1, q_3\} \text{ with } p(q_1|b, q_0) = p_3, p(q_3|b, q_0) = 1 - p_3;$$

$$\delta(q_1, a) = \{q_3\} \text{ with } p(q_3|a, q_1) = 1;$$

$$\delta(q_1, b) = \{q_1, q_2, q_3\} \text{ with } p(q_1|b, q_1) = p_4, p(q_2|b, q_1) = p_5,$$

$$p(q_3|b, q_1) = 1 - p_4 - p_5.$$

The δ and $\hat{D}$ specifications are completed by making q_3 a trap state:

$$\delta(q_2, a) = \{q_3\} \quad \text{with} \quad p(q_3|a, q_2) = 1;$$

$$\delta(q_2, b) = \{q_3\} \quad \text{with} \quad p(q_3|b, q_2) = 1;$$

$$\delta(q_3, a) = \{q_3\} \quad \text{with} \quad p(q_3|a, q_3) = 1;$$

$$\delta(q_3, b) = \{q_3\} \quad \text{with} \quad p(q_3|b, q_3) = 1.$$

The state transition diagram for $\mathcal{C}_{sf}$ is shown in Fig. 5.4.   □

ISBN 0-201-02930-8 / 0-201-02931-6, pbk

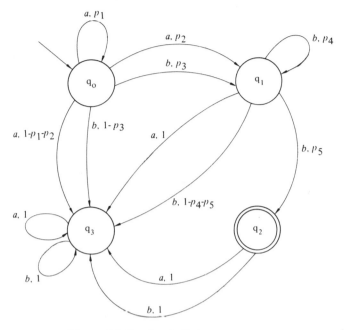

Figure 5.4. Stochastic finite automaton.

Example: Consider the proper automaton $\mathcal{Q}_{sf} = (\{q_0, q_1, q_2, q_3\},$ $\{a, b\}, \delta, q_0, \{q_2\}, \hat{D})$ with the state transition diagram in Fig. 5.3. A stochastic grammar G_s such that $L(G_s) = L(\mathcal{Q}_{sf})$ is required. Following the construction outlined in the preceding example, we let $N = \{X_0, X_1, X_2, X_3\}$ with X_0 being the starting symbol. The stochastic productions from rule (i) are

$$p_1: X_0 \to aX_0 \qquad p_2: X_0 \to aX_1 \qquad p_3: X_0 \to aX_3$$

$$1: X_0 \to bX_1$$

$$1: X_1 \to aX_3 \qquad p_4: X_1 \to bX_1 \qquad p_5: X_1 \to bX_2$$

$$1: X_2 \to aX_3 \qquad 1: X_2 \to bX_3$$

$$1: X_3 \to aX_3 \qquad 1: X_3 \to bX_3$$

The production arising from rule (ii) is $p_5: X_1 \to b$.   □

It should be noted that the productions in the preceding example that rewrite the nonterminal X_3 (the nonterminal associated with the trap state

q_3) are useless in the same sense as defined in Section 2.4.2. They cannot be used in any derivation that yields a terminal string with nonzero probability, so they can be eliminated without changing $L(G_s)$. G_s is *not* proper; in particular, the fact that $\mathcal{C}_{sf}$ is a proper automaton implies

$$p_1 + p_2 + p_3 = 1,$$

so that the sum of the probabilities for rewriting X_0 in the grammar is

$$p_1 + p_2 + p_3 + 1 = 2.$$

However, G_s does preserve recognition probabilities. As an illustration, a previous example demonstrates that string $x = aabb$ is accepted by $\mathcal{C}_{sf}$ with probability

$$p(x) = p_1^2 p_5 + p_1 p_2 p_4 p_5.$$

Corresponding derivations in G_s are

$$X_0 \Rightarrow aX_0 \Rightarrow aaX_0 \Rightarrow aabX_1 \Rightarrow aabb$$

with probability $(p_1^2 p_5)$, and

$$X_0 \Rightarrow aX_0 \Rightarrow aaX_1 \Rightarrow aabb$$

with probability $(p_1 p_2 p_4 p_5)$.

As pointed out earlier, the stochastic regular grammar G_s obtained from a stochastic finite automaton $\mathcal{C}_{sf}$ is not in general a proper grammar. In some circumstances, however, we may find for G_s an equivalent proper regular grammar $\tilde{G}_s$ using a method described by Thompson [1974]. The method attempts to find a set of normalizing factors that can be applied to the G_s production probabilities in D so as to produce a proper grammar that has the same string derivation probabilities; that is, given $G_s = (N, \Sigma, P, D, S)$, only D is changed to get grammar $\tilde{G}_s$.

In order to use this method, it is necessary first to obtain the transition matrix $\hat{\mathbf{M}}$ for the G_s Markov chain as defined in Section 5.3.1. In addition, we define the *final vector* $\mathbf{f}$ for a grammar with n nonterminals to be the $n \times 1$ column matrix in which element f_i, $0 \leq i \leq n - 1$, is the sum of the probabilities of all productions of the form $X_i \to a$, a in Σ. The *normalizing vector* $\mathbf{n}$ is then computed as

$$\mathbf{n} = (\mathbf{I} - \hat{\mathbf{M}})^{-1}\mathbf{f}$$

$$= \mathbf{M}_f \mathbf{f}$$

where $\mathbf{I}$ is the $n \times n$ unit diagonal matrix. The elements of $\mathbf{n}$ may be used to adjust D by multiplying the probability for each production of the form

ISBN 0-201-02930-8/0-201-02931-6, pbk

$X_i \to aX_j$ by (n_j/n_i) and the probability for each production of the form $X_i \to a$ by $(1/n_i)$. It is shown by Thompson [1974] that this normalization also preserves derivation probabilities.

The method fails if any of the following occur:

(i) $(\mathbf{I} - \hat{\mathbf{M}})$ is singular, so $(\mathbf{I} - \hat{\mathbf{M}})^{-1}$ does not exist.

(ii)   Some n_i is negative, so its use as a multiplier causes negative values in D.

(iii)   Some n_i is 0, so $(1/n_i)$ cannot be used.

(iv) $n_0 \neq 1$ where X_0 is the starting symbol. The new grammar probabilities are such that string derivation probabilities are multiplied by $(1/n_0)$ as compared with the original; thus, n_0 must be equal to 1 to preserve these values.

The conditions under which the last two of these problems can appear are unresolved at this time.

Example: Consider the nonproper stochastic grammar $G_s = (\{S, A, B\}, \{a, b\}, P, D, S)$ with stochastic productions

$$0.3: S \to aA \qquad 0.4: S \to aB$$

$$0.3: A \to bA \qquad 8/9: A \to b$$

$$0.4: B \to aB \qquad 13/14: B \to a$$

The transition matrix for the Markov chain of G_s is

$$\hat{\mathbf{M}} = \begin{bmatrix} 0 & 0.3 & 0.4 \\ 0 & 0.3 & 0 \\ 0 & 0 & 0.4 \end{bmatrix}$$

and the final vector is

$$\mathbf{f} = \begin{bmatrix} 0 \\ 8/9 \\ 13/14 \end{bmatrix}.$$

The normalizing vector giving factors by which to adjust the grammar probabilities is

$$\mathbf{n} = (\mathbf{I} - \hat{\mathbf{M}})^{-1}\mathbf{f}$$

$$= \begin{bmatrix} 1 \\ 80/63 \\ 65/42 \end{bmatrix},$$

ISBN 0-201-02930-8/0-201-02931-6, pbk

from which $n_S = 1$, $n_A = 80/63$, and $n_B = 65/42$. None of these factors is 0 or negative, and n_S is 1. The stochastic productions in the new *proper* grammar are

$$[(0.3)(1)(80/63) = 8/21]: S \rightarrow aA$$

$$[(0.4)(1)(65/42) = 13/21]: S \rightarrow aB$$

$$[(0.3)(63/80)(80/63) = 0.3]: A \rightarrow bA$$

$$[(8/9)(63/80) = 0.7]: A \rightarrow b$$

$$[(0.4)(42/65)(65/42) = 0.4]: B \rightarrow aB$$

$$[(13/14)(42/65) = 0.6]: B \rightarrow a$$

The set of terminal string derivations and their probabilities obtained via this new grammar is equal to that for the original grammar G_s.   □

5.4.2 Stochastic Pushdown Automata

A stochastic pushdown automaton, or SPDA, is a generalization of a nondeterministic pushdown automaton with a stack (see Section 4.2.2). For an SPDA, manipulation of the stack and occurrence of state transitions are probabilistic in nature. The function of this machine is to serve as a stochastic recognizer of a context-free language.

A *stochastic pushdown automaton* is defined formally as an eight-tuple, $\mathcal{Q}_{sp} = (Q, \Sigma, \Gamma, \delta, q_0, Z_0, F, D)$, where Q, Σ, Γ, and F are finite sets of states, input symbols, stack symbols, and final states, respectively; q_0 is the starting state; Z_0 the initial stack symbol; and δ a mapping from $Q \times (\Sigma \cup \{\lambda\}) \times \Gamma$ into finite subsets of $Q \times \Gamma^*$. D assigns a probability measure to the elements of $\delta(q, a, Z)$ for each triple combination of state, input symbol or empty string λ, and stack symbol. This type of stochastic automaton operates somewhat like its nondeterministic counterpart, with the exception that the δ mapping is governed by probabilities rather than by the assumption that a "correct action" is always taken. (A "correct action" in this context is a change of stack contents or a change of state, either spontaneously or as the result of reading an input symbol, which can lead to acceptance of the input string.)

An SPDA is started in state q_0, with Z_0 on its stack and with the input tape head scanning the leftmost symbol of the input string. For state q in Q, symbol a in $\Sigma \cup \{\lambda\}$, and Z in Γ, $\delta(q, a, Z)$ defines the elements of $Q \times \Gamma^*$ from which the next state and stack string to replace Z must be selected, and D assigns the probabilities by which one element of $\delta(q, a, Z)$ is actually selected.

ISBN 0-201-02930-8/0-201-02931-6, pbk

An SPDA is *unrestricted* if the probabilities given by D are unconditional. Suppose for a given triple in $Q \times (\Sigma \cup \{\lambda\}) \times \Gamma$, say (q, a, Z), that the finite set of potential next states and replacements of Z is $\{(q_1, x_1), \ldots, (q_n, x_n)\}$. Let $p(i|q, a, Z)$ denote the probability of selecting (q_i, x_i), $1 \le i \le n$, that is provided by D; then an SPDA is *proper* iff

$$\sum_{i=1}^{n} p(i|q, a, Z) = 1$$

for all triples (q, a, Z) in $Q \times (\Sigma \cup \{\lambda\}) \times \Gamma$.

Two modes of string acceptance by an SPDA are possible. First, if F is not null, an input string x is recognized by halting in a final state when all of x is scanned. The *probability of final state acceptance of x by a specific sequence of actions allowed by the δ mapping* is the product of the probabilities of those actions actually executed. Let $p_j(x)$ denote this product for the specific machine response represented by j. If there are m_x distinct ways for x to be accepted, the *probability of recognition of x by final state* is

$$p(x) = \sum_{j=1}^{m_x} p_j(x).$$

The *language recognized by $\mathcal{C}_{sp}$ by final state* is

$$L(\mathcal{C}_{sp}) = \left\{ [x, p(x)] | x \text{ in } \Sigma^+, p(x) = \sum_{j=1}^{m_x} p_j(x), p_j(x) \text{ is} \right.$$
$$\left. \begin{array}{l} \text{the probability of one of the } m_x \text{ ways in which } \mathcal{C}_{sp} \\ \text{can start in } q_0 \text{ with } Z_0 \text{ on its stack and halt in} \\ \text{a state in } F \text{ when all of } x \text{ is scanned} \end{array} \right\}.$$

The second mode of string recognition is by empty stack. Let $p_{l\lambda}(x)$ denote the product of the probabilities of a specific sequence of actions taken by $\mathcal{C}_{sp}$ so as to halt with empty stack when x is scanned. If there are n_x distinct sequences, the *probability of recognition of x by empty stack* is

$$p_\lambda(x) = \sum_{l=1}^{n_x} p_{l\lambda}(x).$$

The *language recognized by $\mathcal{C}_{sp}$ by empty stack* is

$$L_\lambda(\mathcal{C}_{sp}) = \left\{ [x, p_\lambda(x)] | x \text{ in } \Sigma^+, p_\lambda(x) = \sum_{l=1}^{n_x} p_{l\lambda}(x), p_{l\lambda}(x) \right.$$
$$\left. \begin{array}{l} \text{is the probability of one of the } n_x \text{ ways for } \mathcal{C}_{sp} \\ \text{to start in } q_0 \text{ with } Z_0 \text{ on its stack and halt with} \\ \text{empty stack when all of } x \text{ is scanned} \end{array} \right\}.$$

ISBN 0-201-02930-8/0-201-02931-6, pbk

We shall assume in the following discussion that acceptance by empty stack is used. The set F of final states will be null.

The following theorem characterizes the ability of stochastic pushdown automata to recognize languages.

Theorem: A stochastic language L generated by a stochastic context-free grammar is recognized by a stochastic pushdown automaton by empty stack.   □

As with the previous theorems of this nature that have been presented, the proof is constructive: given a stochastic context-free grammar G_s, it must be possible to construct a stochastic pushdown automaton $\mathcal{Q}_{sp}$ such that $L_\lambda(\mathcal{Q}_{sp}) = L(G_s)$. Since the problem in syntactic pattern processing is generally the construction of a recognizer from a known grammar, we shall outline the appropriate algorithm for doing this.

Let $G_s = (N, \Sigma, P, D, S)$ be a stochastic context-free grammar. The automaton will be defined as $\mathcal{Q}_{sp} = (\{q_0\}, \Sigma, \Sigma \cup N, \delta, q_0, S, \varnothing, \hat{D})$; that is, $\mathcal{Q}_{sp}$ is a single-state machine that will use its stack to simulate stochastically a leftmost derivation in G_s in such a way that relevant probabilities will be preserved. The δ mapping and probability assignment $\hat{D}$ are obtained from P and D in G_s as follows:

(i) If $p: A \to \alpha$ is a stochastic production of G_s, then $\delta(q_0, \lambda, A)$ contains (q_0, α). Hence (q_0, α) will be selected with probability p whenever nonterminal A is on top of the stack; and

(ii) $\delta(q_0, a, a) = \{(q_0, \lambda)\}$ for each terminal a in Σ. The action of reading symbol a from the input string together with popping a from the stack occurs with probability one.

The construction of a stochastic pushdown automaton from a stochastic context-free grammar is illustrated by the following example.

Example: Consider the SCFG $G = (\{S, X, Y\}, \{a, b\}, P, D, S)$ with stochastic productions

$4/7: S \to aSbS$	$3/7: S \to bXb$

$1/35: X \to aba$ $16/35: X \to aSbYb$ $18/35: X \to XbXb$

$3/7: Y \to abX$ $4/7: Y \to YabY$

The automaton is $\mathcal{Q}_{sp} = (\{q_0\}, \{a, b\}, \{a, b, S, X, Y\}, \delta, q_0, S, \varnothing, \hat{D})$ with the δ mapping and probability assignment $\hat{D}$ obtained from P and D

ISBN 0-201-02930-8/0-201-02931-6, pbk

as follows:

From rule (i):$\delta(q_0, \lambda, S) = \{(q_0, aSbS), (q_0, bXb)\}$. The first option, $(q_0, aSbS)$, is selected with probability 4/7; the second, (q_0, bXb), with probability 3/7.

$\delta(q_0, \lambda, X) = \{(q_0, aba), (q_0, aSbYb), (q_0, XbXb)\}$. The first of these options is selected with probability 1/35, the second with probability 16/35, and the third with probability 18/35.

$\delta(q_0, \lambda, Y) = \{(q_0, abX), (q_0, YabY)\}$. The first option occurs with probability 3/7, the second with probability 4/7.

From rule (ii): $\delta(q_0, a, a) = \delta(q_0, b, b) = \{(q_0, \lambda)\}$ with probability 1.

Suppose the string input to $\mathcal{Q}_{sp}$ is *babab*. The sequence of machine actions and their probabilities leading to acceptance of the input is tabulated as follows:

$\delta(q_0, \lambda, S) = \{(q_0, aSbS), (q_0, bXb)\}$	The second of these occurs with probability 3/7. The stack now holds *bXb* with the first *b* scanned as the topmost symbol.
$\delta(q_0, b, b) = \{(q_0, \lambda)\}$	The popping of *b* from the stack occurs with probability 1. The stack now holds *Xb*.
$\delta(q_0, \lambda, X) = \{(q_0, aba), (q_0, aSbYb), (q_0, XbXb)\}$	The first occurs with probability 1/35. The stack contains *abab*.
$\delta(q_0, a, a) = \{(q_0, \lambda)\}$ with probability 1.	The stack now holds *bab*.
$\delta(q_0, b, b) = \{(q_0, \lambda)\}$ with probability 1.	The stack now holds *ab*.
$\delta(q_0, a, a) = \{(q_0, \lambda)\}$ with probability 1.	The stack contains *b*.
$\delta(q_0, b, b) = \{(q_0, \lambda)\}$ with probability 1.	The stack is empty.

ISBN 0-201-02930-8/0-201-02931-6, pbk

The input string *babab* is therefore recognized by empty stack by this sequence of actions with probability

$$p_\lambda(x) = (3/7)(1)(1/35)(1)(1)(1)(1)$$

$$= 3/245. \qquad \square$$

5.5   STOCHASTIC SYNTAX-DIRECTED TRANSLATIONS

Analogous to the way in which probabilities are incorporated into formal grammars and their derivation processes, we also generalize the definitions and concepts of syntax-directed translations discussed in Section 2.5. In order to describe probabilistic translations, a *stochastic syntax-directed translation schema*, or SSDTS, is defined to be a system $\mathfrak{T}_s = (N, \Sigma, \Delta, R, S, D)$ where N, Σ, Δ, and R are, as before, finite sets of nonterminals, input string terminals, output string terminals, and rules, respectively, and S is the starting symbol. Additionally, D is an assignment of probabilities to the rules in R.

The same terminology used to describe a stochastic context-free grammar is used to describe an SSDTS. A schema is *unrestricted* if all probabilities assigned by D are unconditional and is *proper* if, for each nonterminal A in N, the sum of the probabilities of all rules for rewriting A is equal to one. A rule $A \rightarrow \alpha, \beta$ with probability p assigned to it by D is written $p : A \rightarrow \alpha, \beta$.

A *translation form* for an unrestricted stochastic schema is defined as follows:

(i) $1:(S, S)$ is a form with the S's associated; and
(ii)   if $p:(\gamma A\omega, \rho A\psi)$ is a form and $\hat{p}: A \rightarrow \alpha, \beta$ is a rule, then $p \cdot \hat{p}:(\gamma\alpha\omega, \rho\beta\psi)$ is also a translation form.

To say that $p :(x, y)$ is a translation form for schema $\mathfrak{T}_s$ therefore means that there is a sequence of rules that change (S, S) into (x, y) for which p is the product of their probabilities. An SSDTS is *ambiguous* if there is at least one translation (x, y), x in Σ^*, y in Δ^*, produced by two or more distinct leftmost sequences of rules. Suppose that there are n ways to translate input sentence x to output sentence y and that these ways have probabilities $p_1(x, y), p_2(x, y), \ldots, p_n(x, y)$, respectively; then the probability of translation pair (x, y) for schema $\mathfrak{T}_s$ is

$$p(x, y) = \sum_{i=1}^{n} p_i(x, y)$$

$$= \sum_{i=1}^{n} \prod_{j=1}^{k(i)} p_{ij}(x, y)$$

ISBN 0-201-02930-8/0-201-02931-6, pbk

where there are $k(i)$ rules used in the ith translation sequence, and $p_{ij}(x, y)$ is the probability assigned to the jth rule in the ith translation.

An SSDTS describes both the syntactic structure and the probability law for a stochastic mapping between context-free languages. The model is useful in a pattern processing environment in which probabilities of strings representing patterns and of errors corrupting those strings are known or are computable. The value of SSDTS used as a corrector of errors is as a model of the process, not as a technique for direct implementation.

We consider the same three common types of errors defined in Section 4.5. These are a CH error changing one terminal into another; a DE error deleting one terminal; and an IN error, which inserts an extra terminal into the string. Suppose initially that only CH errors can happen; that is, DE and IN errors have zero probability, but CH errors occur independently on a terminal-by-terminal basis with known probability p_{CH}. If there are l different terminals and if a CH error is as likely to change a given terminal a into any one element of $\Sigma - \{a\}$ as any other, Fig. 5.5 represents the CH error probabilities. The probability q that a terminal is unchanged is $1 - p_{CH}$, a value that must be much larger than p_{CH} for realistic error correction.

Assume that the pattern string representations are generated by an unrestricted, proper, stochastic context-free grammar $G_s = (N, \Sigma, P, D, S)$. The characteristic grammar of G_s derives the pattern representations, and the probabilities assigned to P by D reflect the relative frequencies of occurrence of productions as determined by the statistics of the pattern class. In an environment in which pattern scanning noise or other random factors induce CH errors on individual terminals in the strings, as in Fig. 5.5, a stochastic schema $\mathcal{T}_s = (N, \Sigma, \Sigma, R, S, \hat{D})$

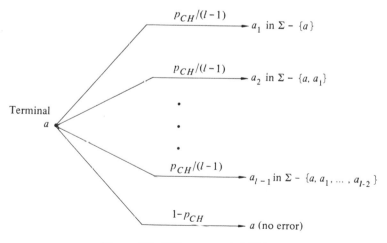

Figure 5.5. CH error probabilities.

must be constructed to correct these errors. Suppose there is a production $p : A \rightarrow \gamma$ in G_s for which γ has m terminals; then the use in a correcting translation of a rule of the form $A \rightarrow \pi, \gamma$ for π in $CH^k(\gamma), 0 \leqslant k \leqslant m$, must reflect the probability of the event "production $A \rightarrow \gamma$ used in G_s, CH error in k terminals occurred" with the specific errors indicated by the difference between π and γ. The following probabilities can, therefore, be assigned to the SSDTS rules obtained from the productions:

$$pq^n : A \rightarrow \gamma, \gamma$$

$$pq^{n-1}(p_{CH}/(l-1)): A \rightarrow \mu, \gamma \text{ for } \mu \text{ in } CH(\gamma)$$

$$pq^{n-2}(p_{CH}/(l-1))^2: A \rightarrow \rho, \gamma \text{ for } \rho \text{ in } CH^2(\gamma)$$

$$\vdots$$

$$p(p_{CH}/(l-1))^n : A \rightarrow \psi, \gamma \text{ for } \psi \text{ in } CH^m(\gamma)$$

The probability

$$p(x, y) = \sum_{i=1}^{n} \prod_{j=1}^{k(i)} p_{ij}(x, y)$$

computed for schema $\mathfrak{T}_s$ then describes the event "y generated by G_s, y changed to x by CH errors." The unrestricted schema with rules determined in this way is proper because G_s is proper and any stochastic production $p : A \rightarrow \gamma$ gives rise to a collection of rules whose probabilities sum to

$$\sum_{r=0}^{n} \binom{n}{r} pq^{n-r} \left(\frac{p_{CH}}{l-1} \right)^r (l-1)^r = p(q + p_{CH})^n$$

$$= p(1)^n$$

$$= p.$$

Independent DE and IN errors are accounted for by similar methods. For example, consider again the case of single CH, DE, and IN errors occurring independently from one terminal to the next, as shown in Fig. 4.11, but at this point with known probabilities, respectively, of p_{CH}, p_{DE}, and p_{IN}, as shown in Fig. 5.6. With these probabilities, the probability of no error is

$$q = 1 - p_{CH} - p_{DE} - p_{IN}.$$

ISBN 0-201-02930-8/0-201-02931-6, pbk

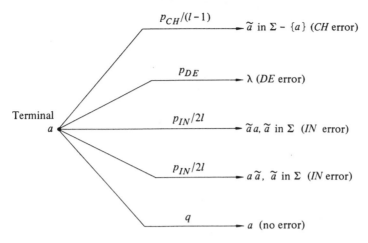

Figure 5.6. *CH*, *DE*, and *IN* error probabilities.

Assume that G_s is in Greibach normal form; then probabilities are associated with rules in $\mathcal{T}_s$ in the following way: for each production $p : A \rightarrow a\xi$,

$$pq : A \rightarrow a\xi, a\xi, \qquad pp_{DE} : A \rightarrow \xi, a\xi;$$

for each $\tilde{a}$ in $\Sigma - \{a\}$,

$$p(p_{CH}/(l - 1)): A \rightarrow \tilde{a}\xi, a\xi;$$

and for each $\tilde{a}$ in Σ,

$$p(p_{IN}/2l): A \rightarrow \tilde{a}a\xi, a\xi, \qquad p(p_{IN}/2l): A \rightarrow a\tilde{a}\xi, a\xi.$$

Whenever possible, one must use information about errors and strings to eliminate rules that will not be used or to adjust rule probabilities. For instance, all *CH* errors may not be equally likely, and there are environments that prevent the occurrences of certain error types. There is no reason to make an SSDTS more complex than necessary by carrying along rules with no value.

Example: Consider the Greibach normal form grammar $G = (\{S, A, B\}, \{a, b\}, P, S)$ with production equations

$$S = aA + aSB \qquad A = b \qquad B = a.$$

As indicated in an example in Chapter 4, this grammar generates the language

$$L(G) = \{x \mid x = a^n aba^n, n \geqslant 0\}$$

as the set of representatives of a pattern class with primitives a and b. Let G be the characteristic grammar for stochastic grammar $G_s = (\{S, A, B\}, \{a, b\}, P, D, S)$ in which the probabilities reflect the statistics of the pattern class, and let the stochastic productions be written as

$$p : S \to aA \qquad (1 - p): S \to aSB$$

$$1: A \to b \qquad\qquad 1: B \to a$$

Suppose it has also been determined that CH, DE, and IN errors occur with respective probabilities p_{CH}, p_{DE}, and p_{IN}, as shown in Fig. 5.6. The rules in stochastic error-correcting schema $\mathfrak{T}_s = (\{S, A, B\}, \{a, b\}, \{a, b\}, R, D, S)$ are,

for no error
$$pq : S \to aA, aA$$
$$(1 - p)q : S \to aSB, aSB$$
$$q : A \to b, b$$
$$q : B \to a, a$$

for DE errors
$$pp_{DE} : S \to A, aA$$
$$(1 - p)p_{DE} : S \to SB, aSB$$
$$p_{DE} : A \to \lambda, b$$
$$p_{DE} : B \to \lambda, a$$

for CH errors
$$pp_{CH} : S \to bA, aA$$
$$(1 - p)p_{CH} : S \to bSB, aSB$$
$$p_{CH} : A \to a, b$$
$$p_{CH} : B \to b, a$$

for IN errors
$$p(p_{IN}/2): S \to aaA, aA$$
$$p(p_{IN}/4): S \to baA, aA$$
$$p(p_{IN}/4): S \to abA, aA$$
$$(1 - p)(p_{IN}/2): S \to aaSB, aSB$$
$$(1 - p)(p_{IN}/4): S \to baSB, aSB$$
$$(1 - p)(p_{IN}/4): S \to abSB, aSB$$
$$(p_{IN}/2): A \to bb, b$$
$$(p_{IN}/4): A \to ab, b$$
$$(p_{IN}/4): A \to ba, b$$
$$(p_{IN}/2): B \to aa, a$$
$$(p_{IN}/4): B \to ab, a$$

ISBN 0-201-02930-8/0-201-02931-6, pbk

Suppose that the input string is $x = aba$; four stochastic translation forms produced by $\mathfrak{T}_s$ are

$$1:(S, S) \Rightarrow pq :(aA, aA)$$

$$\Rightarrow pq(p_{IN}/4):(aba, ab);$$

$$1:(S, S) \Rightarrow p(p_{IN}/4):(abA, aA)$$

$$\Rightarrow p(p_{IN}/4)p_{CH} :(aba, ab);$$

$$1:(S, S) \Rightarrow (1 - p)q :(aSB, aSB)$$

$$\Rightarrow (1 - p)q\,pp_{DE} :(aAB, aaAB)$$

$$\Rightarrow (1 - p)q\,pp_{DE}q :(abB, aabB)$$

$$\Rightarrow (1 - p)q\,pp_{DE}qq :(aba, aaba);$$

$$1:(S, S) \Rightarrow (1 - p)p_{DE} :(SB, aSB)$$

$$\Rightarrow (1 - p)p_{DE}pq :(aAB, aaAB)$$

$$\Rightarrow (1 - p)p_{DE}pqq :(abB, aabB)$$

$$\Rightarrow (1 - p)p_{DE}pqqq :(aba, aaba).$$

The translation pairs for input string $x = aba$, together with their probabilities, are (aba, ab) with probability

$$p(aba, ab) = \frac{pqp_{IN}}{4} + \frac{pp_{IN}p_{CH}}{4}$$

$$= \frac{pp_{IN}}{4}(q + p_{CH})$$

and $(aba, aaba)$ with probability

$$p(aba, aaba) = (1 - p)pq^3p_{DE} + (1 - p)p_{DE}pq^3$$

$$= 2(1 - p)pq^3p_{DE}.$$

It is determined by inspection that these are the two most likely translations of aba that can be produced by $\mathfrak{T}_s$. By definition,

$$p(ab|aba) = \frac{p(aba, ab)}{p(aba)} \quad \text{and} \quad p(aaba|aba) = \frac{p(aba, aaba)}{p(aba)}.$$

ISBN 0-201-02930-8/0-201-02931-6, pbk

Based on these conditional probabilities, we would select the more likely of these two corrections for the given input aba; that is, we would select ab if $p(ab|aba) > p(aaba|aba)$; select $aaba$ if $p(ab|aba) < p(aaba|aba)$; and select either if $p(ab|aba) = p(aaba|aba)$. In terms of the joint probabilities actually computed, the decision can be to output ab if $p(aba, ab) \geqslant p(aba, aaba)$ and output $aaba$ otherwise.   □

5.6 MODIFIED COCKE–YOUNGER–KASAMI PARSING ALGORITHM FOR STOCHASTIC ERRORS OF CHANGED SYMBOLS

Fung and Fu [1975] have described a modification of the tabular parsing method of Cocke–Younger–Kasami (Section 4.4.3) to incorporate probabilities of errors that preserve the length of a string but can cause terminals to be changed from one to another. These CH errors occur frequently in pattern processing when a primitive is misidentified because it is ill formed or distorted by noise.

In the following discussion, the conditional probability that terminal a is changed into terminal b (or remains unchanged when $b = a$) is denoted $r(b|a)$ and is assumed known for all a and b in Σ; furthermore, for each terminal a,

$$\sum_{b \text{ in } \Sigma} r(b|a) = 1.$$

These errors of changed symbols are assumed to occur independently from one terminal to the next in a string; thus, the probability that sentence $x = a_1 a_2 \cdots a_n$ is deformed into sentence $y = b_1 b_2 \cdots b_n$ is

$$p(y|x) = r(b_1|a_1)r(b_2|a_2) \cdots r(b_n|a_n).$$

A possibly erroneous sentence y is an input to this parsing algorithm, which is essentially the Cocke–Younger–Kasami technique modified to carry information about probabilities along in the table entries. When the table is complete, table entry t_{1n} is examined; if starting symbol S is in t_{1n}, the logarithm of the probability $p(y|x)$ that has the largest value for all sentences x in $L(G)$ is also available.

The motivation for this kind of stochastic syntactic decoding is to enable maximum-likelihood classification of deformed patterns. For suppose that sentence y must be classified as representing a pattern in one of the classes defined by Chomsky normal form grammars $G_1, G_2, \ldots, G_M$. The modified algorithm to be described can be used for each grammar to compute

ISBN 0-201-02930-8/0-201-02931-6, pbk

in turn the maximum values of

$$p(y|x_1) \text{ for any string } x_1 \text{ in } L(G_1)$$

$$p(y|x_2) \text{ for any string } x_2 \text{ in } L(G_2)$$

$$\vdots$$

$$p(y|x_M) \text{ for any string } x_M \text{ in } L(G_M)$$

The algorithm will also indicate if, for grammar G_i, there is no string x_i in $L(G_i)$ that could be erroneously read as y. On the basis of these probabilities, a maximum-likelihood classification of y into one of the M pattern classes can be made.

The modified algorithm requires a grammar $G = (N, \Sigma, P, S)$ in Chomsky normal form with no productions of the form $A \to \lambda$. Given input string $y = b_1 \cdots b_n$ to be considered for classification in $L(G)$, a right-triangular table with element t_{ij}, $1 \leqslant i \leqslant n$, $1 \leqslant j \leqslant (n - i + 1)$, is constructed with table entries that are elements of $N \times (0, \infty)$. Let

$$f(b, a) = -\log_B r(b|a)$$

where any convenient base B can be used. Table construction proceeds as follows:

Step 1. Set $j = 1$. Compute t_{i1} for $1 \leqslant i \leqslant n$ as
$t_{i1} = \{(A, u)|u = \min (e_1, e_2, \ldots, e_{n_A}), e_m = f(b_i, a_m) \text{ for each}$
production $A \to a_m$ in $P\}$
where n_A is the number of productions having nonterminal A on the left side.

Step 2. Assuming $t_{i, j-1}$ has been found for $1 \leqslant i \leqslant n$, compute t_{ij} as
$t_{ij} = \{(A, k)| \text{ there is an index } m, 1 < m < j, \text{ such that } A \to BC \text{ is in } P,$
$(B, k_1) \text{ is in } t_{im}, (C, k_2) \text{ is in } t_{i+m, j-m}\}$
where $k = k_1 + k_2$ and, if $(A, \hat{k})$ is already in t_{ij} but $k < \hat{k}$, then (A, k) replaces $(A, \hat{k})$ as a table entry.

Step 3. Repeat step 2 until the table is completed or until an entire row has only null entries. If (S, k_e) is not in t_{1n}, $L(G)$ has no sentence of length n that could be changed by CH errors into y; if (S, k_e) is in t_{1n}, then B^{-k_e} is the maximum value of the probability $p(y|x)$ for any sentence x in $L(G)$. Termination with an entire row of null entries indicates failure of the parse (the string cannot be derived with the grammar, no matter which nonterminal is used as the starting symbol).

ISBN 0-201-02930-8/0-201-02931-6, pbk

It is seen that this modified version of the Cocke–Younger–Kasami algorithm does not directly correct an input string with errors but does obtain the maximum value of $p(y|x)$ for $L(G)$. This allows maximum-likelihood classification of pattern string y in the case that several Chomsky normal form grammars for several classes must be considered.

Example: The following example is from the article of Fung and Fu [1975]. We consider two context-free grammars for two pattern classes. The grammars themselves are not stochastic. The first is $G_1 = (\{S, A, B\}, \{a, b\}, P_1, S)$ with productions

$$S \rightarrow aB \qquad S \rightarrow bA$$

$$A \rightarrow bAA \qquad A \rightarrow aS$$

$$A \rightarrow a \qquad B \rightarrow aBB$$

$$B \rightarrow bS \qquad B \rightarrow b$$

$L(G_1)$ is the set of strings in $\{a, b\}^+$ that have an equal number of a's and b's. The second grammar is $G_2 = (\{S_2, A_1, A_2, B_1, B_2\}, \{a, b\}, P_2, S_2)$ with productions

$$S_2 \rightarrow aB_2 \qquad S_2 \rightarrow bA_2$$

$$A_1 \rightarrow a \qquad A_1 \rightarrow aS_2$$

$$A_1 \rightarrow bA_2A_1 \qquad A_1 \rightarrow bA_1A_2$$

$$A_2 \rightarrow aA_1 \qquad A_2 \rightarrow bA_2A_2$$

$$B_1 \rightarrow aB_2B_1 \qquad B_1 \rightarrow aB_1B_2$$

$$B_1 \rightarrow bS_2 \qquad B_1 \rightarrow b$$

$$B_2 \rightarrow bB_1 \qquad B_2 \rightarrow aB_2B_2$$

$L(G_2)$ is the set of strings in $\{a, b\}^+$ that have twice as many a's as b's; thus, the two pattern classes are disjoint.

ISBN 0-201-02930-8/0-201-02931-6, pbk

The probabilities of CH errors and of no errors are the following:

$$r(a|a) = 0.9, \qquad r(b|a) = 0.1,$$

$$r(a|b) = 0.2, \qquad r(b|b) = 0.8.$$

Suppose the string input to the parser is $y = bababbababab$. y has 5 a's and 7 b's, so it is in neither $L(G_1)$ nor $L(G_2)$; however, the 12 symbols of the original string could have contained 6 a's and 6 b's or 8 a's and 4 b's.

The parse table for string y and grammar G_1, constructed according to the method given earlier, is shown in Fig. 5.7. Base 10 logarithms are used.

j	1	2	3	4	5	6	7	8	9	10	11	12
12	S 1.81 C 2.72 D 0.91											
11	A 1.72 B 0.81	A 1.72 B 0.81										
10	S 1.67 C 2.57 D 0.77	S 0.72 C 1.62 D 1.37	S 1.67 C 2.57 D 0.77									
9	A 1.57 B 0.67	A 1.57 B 0.67	A 1.57 B 0.67	A 1.57 B 0.67								
8	S 1.53 C 2.43 D 0.62	S 0.57 C 1.48 D 1.23	S 1.53 C 2.43 D 0.62	S 0.57 C 1.48 D 1.23	S 1.53 C 2.43 D 0.62							
7	A 1.43 B 0.53	A 1.43 B 0.53	A 1.43 B 0.53	A 1.43 B 0.53	A 1.43 B 0.53	A 1.43 B 0.53						
6	S 1.38 C 2.29 D 0.48	S 0.43 C 1.33 D 1.08	S 1.38 C 2.29 D 0.48	S 0.43 C 1.33 D 1.08	S 1.38 C 2.29 D 0.48	S 0.43 C 1.33 D 1.08	S 0.43 C 1.33 D 1.08					
5	A 1.28 B 0.38	A 1.28 B 0.38	A 1.28 B 0.38	A 1.28 D 0.38	A 1.28 B 0.38	A 1.28 B 0.38	A 0.33 B 0.99	A 1.28 B 0.38				
4	S 0.29 C 1.19 D 0.94	S 0.29 C 1.19 D 0.94	S 1.24 C 2.14 D 0.34	S 0.29 C 1.19 D 0.94	S 1.24 C 2.14 D 0.34	S 0.29 C 1.19 D 0.94	S 0.29 C 1.19 D 0.94	S 0.29 C 1.19 D 0.94	S 0.29 C 1.19 D 0.94			
3	A 1.14 B 0.24	A 0.19 B 0.84	A 1.14 B 0.24	A 1.14 B 0.24	A 1.14 B 0.24	A 1.14 B 0.24	A 0.19 B 0.84	A 1.14 B 0.24	A 0.19 B 0.84	A 1.14 B 0.24		
2	S 0.14 C 1.05 D 0.80	S 0.14 C 1.05 D 0.80	S 0.14 C 1.05 D 0.80	S 0.14 C 1.05 D 0.80	S 1.10 C 2.00 D 0.19	S 0.14 C 1.05 D 0.80	S 0.14 C 1.05 D 0.80	S 0.14 C 1.05 D 0.80	S 0.14 C 1.05 D 0.80	S 0.14 C 1.05 D 0.80	S 0.14 C 1.05 D 0.80	
1	A 1.00 B 0.10	A 0.05 B 0.70	A 1.00 B 0.10	A 0.05 B 0.70	A 1.00 B 0.10	A 1.00 B 0.10	A 0.05 B 0.70	A 1.00 B 0.10	A 0.05 B 0.70	A 1.00 B 0.10	A 0.05 B 0.70	A 1.00 B 0.10
	1	2	3	4	5	6	7	8	9	10	11	12
						i						

Figure 5.7. Modified Cocke–Younger–Kasami parse table. (From Fung and Fu [1975].)

The appearance of entry $(S, 1.81)$ in table element $t_{1, 12}$ establishes that there is some sentence x_1 in $L(G_1)$ such that

$$p(y|x_1) = 10^{-1.81} = 0.0155.$$

If the parse table for string y and grammar G_2 is constructed, it is found that table element $t_{1, 12}$ contains entry $(S_2, 3.62)$; therefore, there is some sentence x_2 in $L(G_2)$ such that

$$p(y|x_2) = 10^{-3.62} = 0.00024.$$

Without additional information beyond the fact that $p(y|x_1)$ and $p(y|x_2)$ are the largest values obtainable for any sentences x_1 and x_2 in $L(G_1)$ and $L(G_2)$, respectively, we classify the input pattern string as a deformed element of $L(G_1)$.   □

5.7 CONCLUDING REMARKS

Stochastic systems theory plays an important role in syntactic pattern recognition because the uncertainties with which pattern processors must deal are often probabilistic in nature. The properties of stochastic grammars, automata, translators, and languages are important for their implications, both in theory and in applications. This chapter has shown ways in which probabilities can be incorporated into the derivations of a grammar, the transitions of an automaton, the syntax-directed mappings of an SDTS, and the execution of an error-tolerant parsing algorithm.

The uncertainties in pattern recognition that are due to vagueness or fuzziness in the generation of patterns or the recognition process can be described mathematically by *fuzzy set theory*. The impact of this theory on syntactic pattern processing has not been thoroughly investigated at this date. The interested reader is referred to the articles listed in the references for this chapter.

The next chapter is concerned with syntactic inference techniques, and discusses among other topics certain methods for estimation of probabilities in linguistic models.

REFERENCES

Discussions of stochastic grammars and languages may be found in many sources, including Booth [1969], Booth and Thompson [1973], Fu [1974], and Fu and Huang [1972]. Booth [1968] and Fu and Huang [1972] discuss stochastic automata. Applications of stochastic languages in syn-

ISBN 0-201-02930-8/0-201-02931-6, pbk

tactic pattern processing are topics in Fu [1971a, b, 1974] and Lee and Fu [1972a, b]. Stochastic syntax-directed translations are discussed in Thomason [1975] and Maryanski and Thomason [1977].

Booth [1968], Kemeny and Snell [1960], and Parzen [1962] are among the many texts presenting aspects of Markov chain theory. Harris [1963] is a standard reference for the theory of branching processes.

The method attempting to find a proper regular grammar given in Section 5.4.1 is due to Thompson [1974]. The modified Cocke–Younger–Kasami parsing algorithm is due to Fung and Fu [1975].

Readers interested in fuzzy set theory should see the classic paper of Zadeh [1965] for an introduction to the area. Fuzzy formal languages are discussed by Lee and Zadeh [1969] and Thomason and Marinos [1974], among others. Fuzziness in syntactic pattern recognition is briefly discussed in Lee [1975] and Thomason [1973].

ISBN 0-201-02930-8/0-201-02931-6, pbk

GRAMMATICAL INFERENCE

> No, no: I never guess. It is a shocking habit—
> destructive to the logical faculty. What seems
> strange to you is only so because you
> do not follow my train of thought or
> observe the small facts upon which
> large inferences may depend.
> *Sherlock Holmes*

6.1 INTRODUCTION

The syntactic recognition approaches presented in the previous chapters are based on the assumption that there is available at least one grammar that characterizes each pattern class under consideration. In some situations, one may be able to specify these grammars heuristically, based on the characteristics of a particular problem. Although this is not an unusual procedure, a systematic approach to the design of syntactic pattern recognition systems requires the use of algorithms capable of obtaining a grammar from a set of patterns that are representative of some pattern class of interest. This problem, commonly referred to as the *grammatical inference* problem, is a central issue in syntactic pattern recognition because of its machine-learning implications.

Suppose that all patterns of a class are generated by an *unknown* grammar G and that two finite sets of samples R^+ and R^- with the properties

$$R^+ \subseteq \{\alpha | \alpha \text{ in } L(G)\} \quad \text{and} \quad R^- \subseteq \{\beta | \beta \text{ in } \bar{L}(G)\}$$

are available. In other words, R^+ is a set of samples that belong to the language $L(G)$ while R^- is a set of samples from the complement of $L(G)$. The sample set R^+ is said to be *structurally complete* if each production rule of G is used in the generation of at least one element of R^+.

ISBN 0-201-02930-8/0-201-02931-6, pbk

ISBN 0-201-02930-8/0-201-02931-6, pbk

In its most general form, the inference problem is one of obtaining G from the information available in R^+ and R^-. In its simplest form, the problem is reduced to obtaining a limited grammar capable of generating only the sample set R^+. Clearly, a grammar with the property that $L(G) = R^+$ (called a *canonical grammar*) can be obtained by inspection. Although the general inference problem is considerably more difficult and has not been solved completely, techniques exist to infer limited classes of grammars. Several of these techniques are developed and illustrated in the following sections.

6.2 INFERENCE OF REGULAR GRAMMARS

Because of their relative simplicity, regular grammars are the easiest phrase-structure grammars for which to formulate an inference algorithm. Three inference approaches are discussed in this section. The first approach is based on an interactive procedure in which an operator (called a *teacher*) is asked to determine the validity and certain simple properties of strings. The second approach starts by generating a canonical grammar for the sample R^+; this grammar is then generalized by identifying the occurrence of iterative regularity in the strings of R^+. The third approach is based on the construction of a finite automaton that accepts R^+ plus other strings "similar" in structure.

Regular grammars have the advantage that their minimization is assured by using any of the many algorithms available for this purpose. The minimization procedure we will follow in this section is to obtain a finite automaton from the grammar we wish to reduce, and then use the algorithm discussed in Section 4.2.1. A grammar with the minimum number of nonterminals can then be obtained from the simplified machine. Although the procedure could be formulated directly in terms of a grammar, it is advantageous to consider the intermediate step of creating an automaton, not only because of its intuitive value, but also because most of the algorithms available in the literature are presented in this manner.

6.2.1 Inference with the Help of a Teacher

The procedure developed in this section is adapted from one of the first reported efforts in the area of grammatical inference. Given a positive sample R^+ from an unknown regular grammar, the strategy is to process each string separately with the help of a teacher. For each string x from R^+, the processing approach is to delete substrings from x. The substrings are deleted one at a time, and their length must always be less than the length of x. For each deletion, the teacher is asked if the remaining string is still a valid sentence. This is the only permissible question in the interactive procedure. If the answer is affirmative, then the substring, s, is reinserted in x and repeated a specified number of times (M); the teacher is asked each time if the new string is a valid sentence. If the answer is affirmative for a large enough value of M, s is said to be a *cycle*. The occurrence of a cycle in a string x is coded by enclosing s in parentheses. As will be seen in the following discussion, these cycles give rise to iterative regularity in the inferred grammar.

As a simple example of the processing method, consider the string abc, which we assume to be valid. The teacher is asked if bc, ac, ab, a, and c are valid sentences.[‡] Suppose that only bc is valid. The teacher is asked next if $aabc$, $aaabc$, . . . , $a^M bc$, are valid. If the answer is affirmative, then a is a cycle, and its occurrence is coded by using the notation $(a)bc$. Of course, it is possible to have longer cycles, as well as several cycles and subcycles in the same string. For instance, the string abc could have the cycle $(ab)c$. If the length of a cycle is greater than one, the cycle string must be examined for subcycles. This is done by processing each cycle string in the same manner as a string from R^+. Thus, if ab is a cycle, its substrings a and b are first examined for validity. If they are both valid, the teacher is asked if ab^M and $a^M b$ are also valid. If they are, a and b are subcycles of ab, and we use $(a)b$ and $a(b)$ to denote their presence. This indicates that strings of the form $ababab . . . abc$, $aaa . . . ab$, and $abbb . . . b$ are assumed to be valid sentences. The preprocessing algorithm yields two sets of strings, R_0^+ and R_c^+. The first set contains the strings from R^+ in which no cycles were found, while R_c^+ is the set of strings that have at least one cycle. Clearly $R_0^+ \cup R_c^+ = R^+$.

The next step in the procedure is to obtain a regular grammar using the strings in R_c^+ and R_0^+. The strings in R_c^+ are processed first; productions are formed as follows. Suppose that R_c^+ contains a coded string of the form $ab((c)(d))$. We form productions $S \rightarrow aA_2$ and $A_2 \rightarrow bA_3$ for the first two symbols that are not cycles. (We start numbering the productions with A_2 to simplify the notation in the generalization of the procedure.) For cycles cd, c, and d, we form the productions $\{A_3 \rightarrow cA_4, A_4 \rightarrow dA_3\}$, $\{A_3 \rightarrow cA_3\}$, and $\{A_4 \rightarrow dA_4\}$, respectively. The iterative regularity (cycling) is evident in these productions. Finally, we have $A_4 \rightarrow d$, $A_2 \rightarrow b$, $A \rightarrow bA_4$, and $A_3 \rightarrow c$. Note that the last four productions allow bypass and exit from a cycle. In general, a string with cycles and subcycles of the form $a_1 a_2 . . . a_{k-1}(a_k . . . a_{i-1}(a_i . . . a_j)a_{j+1} . . . a_m)a_{m+1} . . . a_{n-1}a_n$ yields

---

[‡]It is noted that b is not considered a proper string because to obtain b by itself would require deleting two disjoint substrings at the same time.

ISBN 0-201-02930-8/0-201-02931-6, pbk

productions $S \to a_1 A_2$, $A_2 \to a_2 A_3$, ..., $A_{k-1} \to a_{k-1} A_k$, $A_{k-1} \to a_{k-1} A_{m+1}$, $A_k \to a_k A_{k+1}$, ..., $A_{i-1} \to a_{i-1} A_i$, $A_{i-1} \to a_{i-1} A_{j+1}$, $A_i \to a_i A_{i+1}$, ..., $A_j \to a_j A_i$, $A_j \to a_j A_{j+1}$, ..., $A_m \to a_m A_k$, $A_m \to a_m A_{m+1}$, ..., $A_{n-1} \to a_{n-1} A_n$, $A_n \to a_n$. The looping productions are $A_m \to a_m A_k$ for the outer cycle and $A_j \to a_j A_i$ for its subcycle. More complex loops are handled in the same way.

After the strings in R_c^+ have been processed, the resulting set of production is augmented (if necessary) to generate all the strings in R_0^+. These productions, along with their terminals and nonterminals, constitute the inferred regular grammar. Finally, this grammar is reduced by using the procedure discussed in Section 4.2.1.

The inference procedure may be summarized as follows:

Step 1. Search for cycles and subcycles in the strings of R^+ with the help of a teacher and form the sets R_0^+ and R_c^+.

Step 2. Obtain a set of productions P using the strings of R_c^+.

Step 3. If necessary, augment P so that its productions are capable of generating the strings in R_0^+.

Step 4. Form a regular grammar using P and the terminals and nonterminals present in this set.

Step 5. Minimize the grammar obtained in Step 4.

Example: As an illustration of the inference algorithm, consider the sample set $R^+ = \{caaab, bbaab, caab, bbab, cab, bbb, cb\}$. The decomposition of *caaab* is:

1.	$\{c\}aaab = aaab$;	8.	$ca\{aa\}b = cab$;
2.	$c\{a\}aab = caab$;	9.	$caa\{ab\} = caa$;
3.	$ca\{a\}ab = caab$;	10.	$\{caa\}ab = ab$;
4.	$caa\{a\}b = caab$;	11.	$c\{aaa\}b = cb$;
5.	$caaa\{b\} = caaa$;	12.	$ca\{aab\} = ca$;
6.	$\{ca\}aab = aab$;	13.	$\{caaa\}b = b$;
7.	$c\{aa\}ab = cab$;	14.	$c\{aaab\} = c$;

where the deleted substrings are in brackets and the remaining strings to be examined are shown to the right of the equal signs.

At this point, the teacher is asked to identify the valid strings. Since the only information available is the sample set R^+ (which is small to simplify the example), each decision will be based on the structure of the strings in this set. Thus, we consider strings 1, 5, 6, 9, 10, and 12 invalid since no string in R^+ begins or ends with a. Similarly, strings 13 and 14 are treated as invalid because there are no instances of strings of length one in R^+. The remaining strings are represented in R^+ and are, therefore, treated as valid sentences. It is noted that if a cycle is discovered for a in strings 2, 3, or 4, all three cases will yield the same result. The same is true for aa in

ISBN 0-201-02930-8/0-201-02931-6, pbk

strings 7 and 8. By deleting strings 3, 4, and 8, this leaves us with strings 2, 7, and 11 to process further; that is, it must be established if $c[a]^M aab$, $c[aa]^M ab$, and $c[aaa]^M b$ are valid strings. This requires some knowledge of G or a much larger sample set than the one being considered. Since there are instances of repeated a's inside the string cb, however, let us assume for the purpose of illustration that $c[a]^M aab$ is valid. This produces the cycle a, which is denoted by $c(a)aab$.

The second string in R^+ has the following decomposition:

1.	$\{b\}baab = baab;$	8.	$bb\{aa\}b = bbb;$
2.	$b\{b\}aab = baab;$	9.	$bba\{ab\} = bba;$
3.	$bb\{a\}ab = bbab;$	10.	$\{bba\}ab = ab;$
4.	$bba\{a\}b = bbab;$	11.	$b\{baa\}b = bb;$
5.	$bbaa\{b\} = bbaa;$	12.	$bb\{aab\} = bb;$
6.	$\{bb\}aab = aab;$	13.	$\{bbaa\}b = b;$
7.	$b\{ba\}ab = bab;$	14.	$b\{baab\} = b.$

As before, we consider invalid all strings starting or ending with a and all strings of length one. Strings 1 and 7 are also treated as invalid because no string in R^+ starts with a single b. In addition, we choose to consider string bb invalid because it is not represented in R^+. Noting that string 4 is redundant leaves strings 3 and 8, so the strings $bb[a]^M ab$ and $bb[aa]^M b$ are evaluated next. The latter expression would yield cycles with an even number of a's bounded by bb and b. Since there are instances in R^+ of even and odd numbers of a's bounded by these two strings, let us choose the first expression as a valid string, which yields $bb(a)ab$.

By following the same approach as above, we have that the next three samples in R^+ result in the strings $c(a)ab$, $bb(a)b$, and $c(a)b$. String bbb has substrings b and bb, both of which are invalid. Finally, string cb has substrings c and b, which are also invalid.

From the foregoing results we have the sets $R_0^+ = \{bbb, cb\}$ and $R_c^+ = \{c(a)aab, bb(a)ab, c(a)ab, bb(a)b, c(a)b\}$. It is noted, however, that the loop in $c(a)b$ can generate exactly the same strings as those obtainable from $c(a)ab$ and $c(a)aab$. String $bb(a)ab$ is also redundant because of the presence of $bb(a)b$. The reduced set is then $R_c^+ = \{c(a)b, bb(a)b\}$, which yields the productions

$$
\begin{array}{ll}
S \to cA_2 & S \to bB_2 \\
S_1 \to cA_3 & B_2 \to bB_3 \\
A_2 \to aA_2 & B_2 \to bB_4 \\
A_2 \to aA_3 & B_3 \to aB_3 \\
A_3 \to b & B_3 \to aB_4 \\
& B_4 \to b
\end{array}
$$

ISBN 0-201-02930-8/0-201-02931-6, pbk

These productions, can generate of the two strings in R_0^+. The inferred grammar is then $G = (N, \Sigma, P, S)$, with

$$N = \{S, A_2, A_3, B_2, B_3, B_4\}, \qquad \Sigma = \{a, b, c\},$$

and productions

$$S \rightarrow cA_2 \qquad S \rightarrow bB_2$$

$$S_1 \rightarrow cA_3 \qquad B_2 \rightarrow bB_3$$

$$A_2 \rightarrow aA_2 \qquad B_2 \rightarrow bB_4$$

$$A_2 \rightarrow aA_3 \qquad B_3 \rightarrow aB_3$$

$$A_3 \rightarrow b \qquad B_3 \rightarrow aB_4$$

$$B_4 \rightarrow b$$

The final step in the algorithm is to simplify this grammar. As indicated in Section 4.2.1, we first construct a nondeterministic finite automaton (NDFA) from the given grammar; the NDFA is then converted to a deterministic finite automaton (DFA); the DFA is minimized; and the minimum grammar is finally obtained from the minimum DFA. The result in this case is the minimized regular grammar $G = (N, \Sigma, P, S)$ with $N = \{S, A, B\}$, $\Sigma = \{a, b, c\}$, and productions

$$S \rightarrow cA$$
$$S \rightarrow bB$$
$$A \rightarrow aA$$
$$B \rightarrow bA$$
$$A \rightarrow b \qquad \qquad \square$$

The foregoing example points out some shortcomings of the inference procedure. The most serious of these is the difficulty in establishing the validity of strings, a problem that is simplified if one has available a large sample set R^+. A large sample, however, creates another problem because the number of strings to be evaluated increases rapidly as a function of the

ISBN 0-201-02930-8/0-201-02931-6, pbk

number and length of the samples. Although many of the tedious aspects of the method can be handled by a computer, it is not difficult to visualize a situation where the number of decisions required from the teacher could become so large as to make the inference technique impractical. In spite of these shortcomings, this inference approach is important from a historical point of view and because it provides a systematic method for processing a given set of pattern sentences.

6.2.2 Inference Based on the Detection of Iterative Regularity in the Strings of R^+

The method developed in this section infers a regular grammar from the samples of R^+. As in the previous section, the approach is based on the detection of iterative regularity, but it uses only the information available in R^+ and does not employ the assistance of a teacher. Since the judgment and experience of a teacher are eliminated, the resulting grammar is quite dependent on the nature and completeness of the sample set.

The basic strategy of the method is to (1) construct a canonical grammar, (2) merge nonterminals to form a recursive grammar, and (3) minimize this grammar by using, for example, the algorithm presented in Section 4.2.1. The procedure can be summarized as follows.

Step 1.   A canonical grammar that generates exactly the given sample set is constructed. Sample strings are processed in order of decreasing length. Productions are constructed and added to the grammar as they are needed to generate each sample string. The final production used to generate the longest sample strings is a *residue production* with a right side of length 2. In general, a residue production of length n has the form

$$A \rightarrow a_1 a_2 \cdots a_n$$

where A is a nonterminal and $a_1, a_2, \ldots, a_n$ are terminals. It is assumed that the residue of each string of maximum length is the suffix of some shorter string. If this condition is not met for some residue, a string equal to the residue is added to the sample set. It will be evident from the following discussion that the choice of residues of length 2 is not a limiting factor in the algorithm. Longer residues may be chosen, but this requires a more complete sample set because of the condition that each residue must be the suffix of some shorter string.

Step 2.   A recursive regular grammar is obtained by merging each residue production of length 2 with a nonresidue production of the grammar. This is accomplished by merging each residue nonterminal with a nonresidue nonterminal that can generate the residue. Thus, if A_r is a

ISBN 0-201-02930-8 / 0-201-02931-6, pbk

residue nonterminal of the form $A_r \to a_1 a_2$, and A_n is a nonresidue non-terminal of the form $A_n \to a_1 A_r$, where $A_r \to a_2$, we replace all occurrences of A_r by A_n and delete the production $A_r \to a_1 a_2$. This technique produces a regular grammar that can generate the given sample set, and has the generalization power to generate an infinite set of other strings.

Step 3. The grammar resulting from Step 2 is minimized.

Example: Consider again the sample set of terminal strings $R^+ = \{caaab, bbaab, caab, bbab, cab, bbb, cb\}$. Applying the inference algorithm to these strings results in the following sequence of steps.

The first string of maximum length encountered in the sample set is *caaab*. The following productions are constructed to generate this string:

$$S \to cA_1$$

$$A_1 \to aA_2$$

$$A_2 \to aA_3$$

$$A_3 \to ab$$

where $A_3 \to ab$ is a residue production. The second string of length 5 is *bbaab*. The following productions are added to the grammar to generate this string:

$$S \to bA_4$$

$$A_4 \to bA_5$$

$$A_5 \to aA_6$$

$$A_6 \to ab$$

Another residue production of length 2 is required since *bbaab* is of the same length as the previous string. We also note that some redundant productions have been generated. For example, the second string could have been equally well accounted for by introducing the productions $S \to bA_4$ and $A_4 \to bA_2$. However, in the first step we are interested only in obtaining a canonical grammar for the given sample set without regard to redundancy.

To generate the third string, *caab*, we need only to add the production $A_3 \to b$ to the grammar. Considering the rest of the strings in R^+, we see that the final set of productions constructed to generate the sample set is

$$S \rightarrow cA_1 \qquad A_3 \rightarrow ab$$

$$S \rightarrow bA_4 \qquad A_4 \rightarrow bA_5$$

$$A_1 \rightarrow b \qquad A_5 \rightarrow b$$

$$A_1 \rightarrow aA_2 \qquad A_5 \rightarrow aA_6$$

$$A_2 \rightarrow b \qquad A_6 \rightarrow b$$

$$A_2 \rightarrow aA_3 \qquad A_6 \rightarrow ab$$

$$A_3 \rightarrow b$$

It is noted that these productions can generate only the strings in the sample set, as required.

In the second part of the inference technique we merge each residue nonterminal of length 2 with a nonresidue nonterminal that can generate the residue. In this example, the residue of A_3 can be generated from A_2 (i.e., $A_2 \rightarrow aA_3$ and $A_3 \rightarrow b$), and the residue of A_6 can be generated from A_5. Therefore, A_3 is merged with A_2, and A_6 is merged with A_5. After deletion of the residue productions, this yields the set

$$S \rightarrow cA_1 \qquad A_4 \rightarrow bA_5$$

$$S \rightarrow bA_4 \qquad A_5 \rightarrow b$$

$$A_1 \rightarrow b \qquad A_5 \rightarrow aA_5$$

$$A_1 \rightarrow aA_2 \qquad A_5 \rightarrow b$$

$$A_2 \rightarrow b$$

$$A_2 \rightarrow aA_2$$

$$A_2 \rightarrow b$$

The iterative productions are $A_2 \rightarrow aA_2$ and $A_5 \rightarrow aA_5$. It would have been equally valid to merge A_6 with A_2 and A_5 with A_3 since the residues are identical in this particular case.

The inferred grammar consists of the foregoing productions, the terminal set $\Sigma = \{a, b, c\}$, and the nonterminal set $N = \{S, A_1, A_2, A_4, A_5\}$. As in the example given in Section 6.2.1, we minimize this grammar by using the procedure discussed in Section 4.2.1. The result is $G = (N, \Sigma, P, S)$,

ISBN 0-201-02930-8/0-201-02931-6, pbk

with $N = \{S, A, B\}$, $\Sigma = \{a, b, c\}$, and productions

$$S \rightarrow cA$$
$$S \rightarrow bB$$
$$A \rightarrow aA$$
$$B \rightarrow bA$$
$$A \rightarrow b$$

This result agrees with the example given in Section 6.2.1 using a teacher.

□

6.2.3 Inference Via the Synthesis of Finite-State Automata

Given a positive sample set R^+, the problem considered in this section is the synthesis of a finite-state automaton that will accept the strings of R^+ and possibly some additional strings that "resemble" those of R^+. This approach is different from the methods of the previous sections in the sense that a recognizer (i.e., automaton) is obtained directly from the sample set. If desired, one can use the correspondence between regular grammars and finite automata to modify the procedure so that it will yield the inferred grammar directly.

The following definition plays a central role in the development of the synthesis procedure. Let $R^+ \subseteq \Sigma^*$ be a positive sample set and let z in Σ^* be a string such that zw is in R^+ for some w in Σ^*. Given a positive integer k, we define the k-tail of z with respect to R^+ as the set $h(z, R^+, k)$, where

$$h(z, R^+, k) = \{w | zw \text{ in } R^+, |w| \leqslant k\}.$$

In other words, the k-tail of z is the set of strings w with the properties (1) zw is in R^+, and (2) the length of w is less than, or equal to, k.

As indicated in Section 4.2.1, a nondeterministic finite automaton $\mathcal{Q}_f$ is a five-tuple $\mathcal{Q}_f = (Q, \Sigma, \delta, q_0, F)$, where Q is a finite nonempty set of states; Σ a finite nonempty set of input symbols; δ a mapping from $Q \times \Sigma$ to 2^Q; q_0 in Q is the initial state; and $F \subseteq Q$ is the set of final states.

A procedure has been suggested by Biermann and Feldmann [1970] for obtaining an automaton from a sample set R^+ and a given value of k. Using $\mathcal{Q}_f(R^+, k)$ to represent the inferred automaton $\mathcal{Q}_f(R^+, k) = (Q, \Sigma, \delta, q_0, F)$, the procedure is to let $Q = \{q | q = h(z, R^+, k)$ for z in $\Sigma^*\}$ and Σ be a finite set of input symbols. Also, for each a in Σ,

$$\delta(q, a) = \{q' \text{ in } Q | q' = h(z, a, R^+, k)$$
$$\text{where } q = h(z, R^+, k)\},$$

ISBN 0-201-02930-8/0-201-02931-6, pbk

$q_0 = h(\lambda, R^+, k)$, and $F = \{q | q +, k)$ in Q, λ in $q\}$. It is noted that $\mathcal{C}_f(R^+, k)$ has as states subsets of the set of all k-tails that can be constructed from R^+. The following example will clarify the notation.

Example: Suppose that $R^+ = \{a, ab, abb\}$ and $k = 1$. Using the foregoing definition, we have

$$z = \lambda, \qquad h(\lambda, R^+, 1) = \{w | \lambda w \text{ in } R^+, |w| \leq 1\}$$

$$= \{a\}$$

$$= q_0,$$

$$z = a, \qquad h(a, R^+, 1) = \{w | aw \text{ in } R^+, |w| \leq 1\}$$

$$= \{\lambda, b\}$$

$$= q_1;$$

$$z = ab, \qquad h(ab, R^+, 1) = \{\lambda, b\}$$

$$= q_1;$$

$$z = abb, \qquad h(abb, R^+, 1) = \{\lambda\}$$

$$= q_2.$$

Other strings z in Σ^* will yield, in this case, strings zw, that do not belong to R^+, giving rise to a fourth state, denoted by q_ϕ, which corresponds to the condition that h is the null set. The states, therefore, are $q_0 = \{a\}$, $q_1 = \{\lambda, b\}$, $q_2 = \{\lambda\}$, and q_ϕ, which give the set $Q = \{q_0, q_1, q_2, q_\phi\}$. It is noted that although the states are obtained as sets of symbols (i.e., k-tails), only the state labels $q_0, q_1, \ldots$ are used in forming the set Q.

The next step is to obtain the transition functions. Since $q_0 = h(\lambda, R^+, 1)$ then $\delta(q_0, a) = h(\lambda a, R^+, 1) = h(a, R^+, 1) = q_1$, and $\delta(q_0, b) = h(\lambda b, R^+, 1) = h(b, R^+, 1) = q_\phi$. Similarly, $q_1 = h(a, R^+, 1) = h(ab, R^+, 1)$ and $\delta(q_1, a) = h(aa, R^+, 1) = h(aba, R^+, 1) = q_\phi$. Also, $\delta(q, b) \supseteq h(ab, R^+, 1) = q$, and $\delta(q, b) \supseteq h(abb, R^+, 1) = q_2$, that is, $\delta(q, b) = \{q_1, q_2\}$. Following the procedure just described we obtain $\delta(q_2, a) = \delta(q_2, b) = \delta(q_\phi, a) = \delta(q_\phi, b) = q_\phi$.

The set of final states contains those states that have the empty string λ in their k-tail representation. In this case, $q_1 = \{\lambda, b\}$ and $q_2 = \{\lambda\}$, so it follows that $F = \{q_1, q_2\}$.

Based on these results, the inferred automaton is given by $\mathcal{C}_f(R^+, 1) = (Q, \Sigma, \delta, q_0, F)$, where $Q = \{q_0, q_1, q_2, q_\phi\}$, $\Sigma = \{a, b\}$, $F = \{q_1, q_2\}$, and the

ISBN 0-201-02930-8/0-201-02931-6, pbk

transition functions are given above. The state diagram is shown in Fig. 6.1. It is noted that the automaton accepts strings of the form a, ab, abb, ..., ab^n. In other words, the procedure has identified iterative regularity on the symbol b.

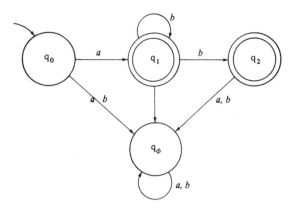

Figure 6.1. State diagram for the finite automaton $\mathcal{C}_f(R^+, 1)$ inferred from the sample set $R^+ = \{a, ab, abb\}$.

The automaton in Fig. 6.1 is nondeterministic. A deterministic minimized machine may be obtained by using the procedure discussed in Section 4.2.1. The result is shown in Fig. 6.2. The corresponding minimum grammar is $G = (N, \Sigma, P, S)$, with $N = \{S, A\}$, $\Sigma = \{a, b\}$, and productions $\{S \rightarrow aA, S \rightarrow a, A \rightarrow bA, A \rightarrow b\}$. □

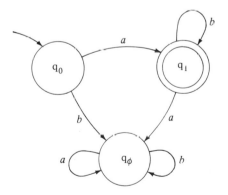

Figure 6.2. Minimized deterministic finite automaton corresponding to the machine shown in Fig. 6.1.

It is evident from the preceding example that the value of k controls the nature of the resulting automaton. The following properties exemplify the dependence of $\mathcal{C}_f(R^+, k)$ on this parameter.

ISBN 0-201-02930-8/0-201-02931-6, pbk

Property 1. $R^+ \subseteq L[\mathcal{A}_f(R^+, k)]$ for all $k \geqslant 0$, where $L[\mathcal{A}_f(R^+, k)]$ is the language accepted by $\mathcal{A}_f(R^+, k)$.

Property 2. $L[\mathcal{A}_f(R^+, k)] = R^+$ if k is equal to, or greater than, the length of the longest string in R^+; $L[\mathcal{A}_f(R^+, k)] = \Sigma^*$ if $k = 0$.

Property 3. $L[\mathcal{A}_f(R^+, k + 1)] \subseteq L[\mathcal{A}_f(R^+, k)]$.

Property 1 guarantees that $\mathcal{A}_f(R^+, k)$ will, as a minimum, accept the strings in the sample set R^+. If k is equal to, or greater than, the length of the longest string in R^+, then by Property 2 the automaton will accept *only* the strings in R^+. This corresponds to inferring a canonical regular grammar. If $k = 0$, $\mathcal{A}_f(R^+, 0)$ will consist of one state $q_0 = \{\lambda\}$, which will act as both the initial and final state. The transition functions will then be of the form $\delta(q_0, a) = q_0$ for a in Σ. It follows, therefore, that $L[\mathcal{A}_f(R^+, 0)] = \Sigma^*$ and the automaton will accept the empty string λ and all strings composed of symbols from Σ. Finally, Property 3 indicates that the scope of the language accepted by $\mathcal{A}_f(R^+, k)$ decreases as k increases.

Based on these three properties, it is evident that the nature of

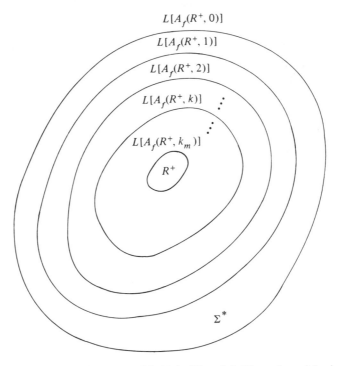

Figure 6.3. Relationship between $L[\mathcal{A}_f(R^+, k)]$ and k. The value of k_m is such that $k_m \geqslant$ (length of longest string in R^+).

ISBN 0-201-02930-8/0-201-02931-6, pbk

$Q_f(R^+, k)$ can be controlled simply by varying the parameter k. If we consider $L[Q_f(R^+, k)]$ to be a guess of the language L_0 from which the sample R^+ was chosen and if k is very small, then this guess of L_0 will constitute a very liberal inference that may include most or all of the strings in Σ^*. On the other hand, if k is equal to the length of the longest string in R^+, the inference will be very conservative in the sense that $Q_f(R^+, k)$ will accept only the strings contained in R^+. The situation is shown graphically in Fig. 6.3.

Example: Consider the set $R^+ = \{caaab, bbaab, caab, bbab, cab, bbb, cb\}$, which was used in two earlier examples. By using $k = 1$ and following the same procedure as in the previous example, we have the following results:

$$1.\ z = \lambda, \qquad h(\lambda, R^+, 1) = \{\phi\} = q_\phi;$$

$$2.\ z = c, \qquad h(z, R^+, 1) = \{b\} = q_1;$$

$$3.\ z = ca, \qquad h(z, R^+, 1) = \{b\} = q_1;$$

$$4.\ z = cb, \qquad h(z, R^+, 1) = \{\lambda\} = q_0;$$

$$5.\ z = caa, \qquad h(z, R^+, 1) = \{b\} = q_1;$$

$$6.\ z = cab, \qquad h(z, R^+, 1) = \{\lambda\} = q_0;$$

$$7.\ z = caaa, \qquad h(z, R^+, 1) = \{b\} = q_1;$$

$$8.\ z = caab, \qquad h(z, R^+, 1) = \{\lambda\} = q_0;$$

$$9.\ z = caaab, \qquad h(z, R^+, 1) = \{\lambda\} = q_0;$$

$$10.\ z = b, \qquad h(z, R^+, 1) = \{\phi\} = q_\phi;$$

$$11.\ z = bb, \qquad h(z, R^+, 1) = \{b\} = q_1;$$

$$12.\ z = bba, \qquad h(z, R^+, 1) = \{b\} = q_1;$$

$$13.\ z = bbb, \qquad h(z, R^+, 1) = \{\lambda\} = q_0;$$

$$14.\ z = bbaa, \qquad h(z, R^+, 1) = \{b\} = q_1;$$

$$15.\ z = bbab, \qquad h(z, R^+, 1) = \{\lambda\} = q_0;$$

$$16.\ z = bbaab, \qquad h(z, R^+, 1) = \{\lambda\} = q_0.$$

ISBN 0-201-02930-8 / 0-201-02931-6, pbk

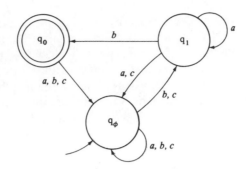

Figure 6.4. State diagram for the automaton $\mathcal{C}_f(R^+, 1)$ inferred from the sample set $R^+ = \{caaab, bbaab, caab, bbab, cab, bbb, cb\}$.

The automaton is $\mathcal{C}_f(R^+, 1) = (Q, \Sigma, \delta, q_0, F)$, with $Q = \{q_0, q_1, q_\phi\}$, $\Sigma = \{a, b, c\}$, $F = \{q_0\}$, and the transitions shown in the state diagram in Fig. 6.4. It is interesting to note that to be accepted by the automaton, a string must begin with a, b or c and end with a b. It is also evident that that strings with recursiveness in either a b or c are accepted by $\mathcal{C}_f(R^+, 1)$. These properties agree with the general structure of R^+ but are not fully in agreement with the previous results with this sample set, where recursiveness of the symbol b was not present in the inferred grammars.

The minimized deterministic machine is shown in Fig. 6.5. The corresponding regular grammar is $G = (N, \Sigma, P, S)$, with $N = \{S, A\}$, $\Sigma = \{a, b, c\}$, and productions $P = \{S \to aS|bA|cA, A \to aA|cA|bB|b, B \to aA|cA|bB|b\}$.   □

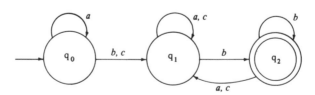

Figure 6.5. Minimized deterministic finite automaton corresponding to the machine shown in Fig. 6.4.

ISBN 0-201-02930-8/0-201-02931-6, pbk

The principal advantage of the preceding method is simplicity of implementation. The synthesis procedure can be simulated in a digital computer with a modest amount of effort. The main disadvantage is deciding on a proper value for k, although this problem is simplified to some degree by the three properties discussed above.

6.3 INFERENCE OF CONTEXT-FREE GRAMMARS

In this section, we present three techniques for inferring restricted classes of context-free grammars. The first procedure is an adaptation of the method discussed in Section 6.2.1 for regular grammars; the second deals with the inference of operator precedence grammars; and the third is a method for inferring pivot grammars.

As indicated in Section 2.2.2, context-free grammars have the advantage of being able to describe repetitions of substructures that require the concept of self-embedding. In terms of grammatical inference, however, the introduction of self-embedding complicates the problem of obtaining a grammer from a set of samples. In addition, the minimization problem, which is so easily handled for regular grammars, is known to have no solution in the general case for context-free grammars (see Section 2.4.2). The best we can do in this respect is to attempt to *simplify* a given grammar by trying to locate pairs of nonterminals that are equivalent in the sense that they generate exactly the same sets of strings. In practice, this involves comparing every pair of nonterminals and merging those for which it is possible to establish the foregoing condition. If useless nonterminals were somehow introduced in the inference process, they can be eliminated by using the procedure discussed in Section 2.4.2.

6.3.1 Inference with the Help of a Teacher

The inference procedure presented in this section is based on the approach developed in Section 6.2.1 for regular grammars. In the case of context-free languages, however, we are concerned with self-embedding in addition to iterative regularity. Based on the concept of self-embedding, cycles in strings from a context-free language may be pairs of disjoint substrings as well as single substrings. For example, the cycle b occurring in the form $a(b)c(b)d$ can be generated by a context-free grammar with productions $S \rightarrow aAd$, $A \rightarrow bAb$, and $A \rightarrow c$. It is noted that nonterminal A

ISBN 0-201-02930-8/0-201-02931-6, pbk

exhibits self-embedding, and that the double cycle is accounted for by a single production. This *simultaneous* cycling property cannot be achieved with a regular grammar.

Since context-free grammars can account for single and double cycles, the principal difficulty in using the methods of Section 6.2.1 to infer this type of grammars lies in the fact that strings must be processed by deleting single substrings *and* pairs of substrings in the validation process. The basic technique is the same, but the number of decisions required of the teacher is normally larger than in the case of regular grammars. Suppose, for example, that the string *abcdef* is a valid sentence. In the inference process for context-free grammars, the teacher is asked if the following strings are valid sentences:

$$
\left.
\begin{array}{lllll}
bcdef, & cdef, & def, & ef, & f \\
acdef & adef & aef & af & a \\
abdef & abef & abf & ab & \\
abcef & abcf & abc & & \\
abcdf & abcd & & & \\
abcde & & & &
\end{array}
\right\} \quad \text{deletion of single substrings}
$$

and

$$
\left.
\begin{array}{llll}
bdef, & acef, & abdf, & abce \\
bcef & acdf & abde & \\
bcdf & acde & & \\
bcde & & & \\
cef, & adf, & abe & \\
cdf & ade & & \\
cde & & &
\end{array}
\right\} \quad
\begin{array}{l}
\text{deletion of disjoint} \\
\quad \text{pairs of substrings}
\end{array}
$$

$$\vdots$$

The deletion routine is performed for all the sample sentences in R^+. Then, for each of the resulting acceptable sentences, several repetitions of the deleted portion(s) are reinserted, and the teacher is asked whether the resulting strings are acceptable sentences. In the above example, if *adef* were an acceptable sentence, the teacher would be asked to establish the validity of the sentences *abcbcdef*, *abcbcbcdef*, . . . , $a[bc]^M def$. If *cef* were

ISBN 0-201-02930-8/0-201-02931-6, pbk

an acceptable sentence, the reinsertion process would involve substrings ab and d. In this case, the teacher would be asked if the following are valid sentences: $ababcddef$, $ababababcdddef$, ..., $[ab]^M c[d]^M ef$. The number of repetitions (M) must be large enough to establish the validity of the sentences with an acceptable degree of accuracy. The value of M depends on the application and on the amount of prior knowledge possessed by the teacher.

As in Section 6.2.1, the deletion–insertion process is used to detect the presence of cycles. To avoid confusion with the material in that section, however, cycles will be denoted in the following discussion by means of *cycle markers* instead of parentheses. For instance, if the above repetition process for strings $adef$ and cef were found valid, we would denote the presence of cycle (bc) by the notation $a\alpha_1 def$ and the presence of the cycle pair (ab, d) by the notation $\alpha_2 c\alpha_2 ef$. In other words, $a\alpha_1 def$ denotes the presence of cycle (bc) in position α_1 and $\alpha_2 c\alpha_2 ef$ the presence of the cycle *pair* (ab, d) in position α_2. The symbol α_i will be used throughout this section as a cycle marker. It is noted that, in this case, the cycle (bc) in position α_1 implies productions of the form $S \to aAdef$, $S \to adef$, $A \to bcA$, and $A \to bc$, while the cycle pair (ab, d) in position α_2 implies productions of the form $S \to Bef$, $B \to abBd$, and $B \to c$. Cycle α_1 is an instance of iterative regularity on A and cycle α_2 an instance of self-embedding on B.

After all the sentences in R^+ have been subjected to the deletion–insertion process for single substrings and pairs of substrings, we divide the results into two sets. The first set, denoted by R_0^+, contains the strings from R^1 in which no cycles were found. The second set, denoted by R_c^+, contains the remaining strings, which are processed further to establish the presence of more cycles in the sentences and in the cycles themselves.

Suppose that $a\alpha_1 cd\alpha_1 f$ with loop (b, e) in the α_1 position was found acceptable in the first pass through R^+. We then try the deletion–insertion strategy again. For single substrings the approach is as before. The teacher is asked if the following are valid sentences with the cycle (b, e): $\alpha_1 cd\alpha_1 f$, $a\alpha_1 d\alpha_1 f$, $a\alpha_1 c\alpha_1 f$, $a\alpha_1 cd\alpha_1$, and $a\alpha_1 \alpha_1 f$. Suppose that $\alpha_1 cd\alpha_1 f$ is valid. The deleted substring (a in this case) is reinserted and repeated. If the results are valid for M repetitions, then (a) is a cycle in position α_2. This yields the string $\alpha_2 \alpha_1 cd\alpha_1 f$. All new strings generated in this manner are added to R_c^+. It is noted that cycles of this type cannot be discovered simultaneously with the basic deletion–insertion technique outlined previously. For example, to discover $\alpha_2 \alpha_1 cd\alpha_1 f$ with cycle (a) in position α_2 and cycle pair (b, e) in position α_1 would require the deletion of a, and the pair b, e simultaneously. This is invalid under the present approach because only single substrings *or* pairs of substrings can be deleted at any one time.

When we look for dual cycles, the strategy is more restricted. The string pairs deleted must both be between corresponding cycle markers or both not be between these markers. Other combinations are not valid generations for context-free grammars. In the case of string $a\alpha_1 cd\alpha_1 f$, this implies that the only valid pair deletions are (a, f) and (c, d), resulting in $\alpha_1 cd\alpha_1$ and $a\alpha_1\alpha_1 f$. If these were valid strings and, upon reinsertion and repetition of (a, f) and (c, d), results were also valid, we would have the string $\alpha_2\alpha_1\alpha_3\alpha_3\alpha_1\alpha_2$ with cycles (b, e), (a, f), and (c, d) in positions α_1, α_2, and α_3, respectively.

After all strings in $R_c{}^+$ have been analyzed for multiple cycles, the cycles themselves are analyzed for subcycles. For example, suppose that we have the cycle pair $(abcde, fghijk)$. We apply the deletion procedure to single, and pairs of, substrings. If all the resulting strings within the cycle remain valid, then we proceed with the reinsertion procedure to establish the presence of subcycles. If, for instance, we find (ade, ijk), $(abd, fghijk)$, and $(abcde, fgk)$ to be valid, and reinsertions of the deleted parts also result in valid cycles, then we have $(a\alpha_1 de, \alpha_1 ijk)$ with subcycles (bc, fgh) in the α_1 position, $(ab\alpha_2 d\alpha_2, fghijk)$ with subcycle (c, e) in the α_2 position, and $(abcde, fg\alpha_3 k)$ with subcycle (hij) in the α_3 position. All new subcycles discovered in this manner are added to $R_c{}^+$.

The resulting subcycles are successively broken down in an attempt to discover still more subcycles within subcycles. The evaluation process terminates when this is no longer possible. A context-free grammar is then obtained from the information available in R^+, as follows:

Step 1.   Search for single and pairs of cycles in the strings of R^+ with the help of a teacher and form the sets $R_0{}^+$ and $R_c{}^+$.

Step 2.   With the help of a teacher, analyze the strings of $R_c{}^+$ for further cycles and subcycles. Add to $R_c{}^+$ any strings (with their cycle markers) for which new cycles and subcycles are found.

Step 3.   Obtain a set of productions P using the strings of $R_c{}^+$. Table 6.1 contains a typical set of cycles associated with context-free grammars and their corresponding productions. Additional cases are formed in a similar manner.

Step 4.   If necessary, augment P so that its productions are capable of generating all the strings in $R_0{}^+$.

Step 5.   Form a context-free grammar using P and the terminals and nonterminals present in this set.

Step 6.   Simplify the inferred grammar.

Example: Suppose that the following sets were obtained by application of Steps 1 and 2 of the technique just discussed: $R_c{}^+ = \{\alpha_1 ba_1, a\alpha_2 c\}$ and $R_0{}^+ = \{acb, bac\}$, where the cycle in position α_1 is (a, c) and the cycle in

ISBN 0-201-02930-8/0-201-02931-6, pbk

Table 6.1. Some Basic Cycle Types and Corresponding Context-Free Productions

Cycles	Form of strings	Productions
1. Basic form: $a\alpha b\alpha c$ Cycle in α position: (d, e)	$ad^n be^n c$	$S \to aAc$ $A \to dAe$ $A \to b$
2. Basic form: $a\alpha_1\alpha_2 b\alpha_2\alpha_1 c$ Cycle in α_1 position: (f, g) Cycle in α_2 position: (d, e)	$af^n d^m be^m g^n c$	$S \to aBc$ $B \to fBg$ $B \to A$ $A \to dAe$ $A \to b$
3. Basic form: $a\alpha_1 b\alpha_1 c$ Cycle in α_1 position: $(d\alpha_2 f, g\alpha_2 e)$ Cycle in α_2 position: (h, k)	$a[dh^m f]^n b[gk^m e]^n c$	$S \to aAc$ $A \to dBe$ $B \to hBk$ $B \to fAg$ $A \to b$
4. Basic form: $a\alpha_1 b\alpha_1 c$ Cycle in α_1 position: $(f, g\alpha_2 h\alpha_2 k)$ Cycle in α_2 position: (d, e)	$af^n b[gd^m he^m k]^n c$	$S \to aAc$ $A \to fAgBk$ $A \to b$ $B \to dBe$ $B \to h$

position α_2 is (b). According to Step 3, we form the following productions to generate the strings in R_c^+: $P = \{S \to aSc, S \to ac, S \to b, S \to aAc, A \to bA, A \to b\}$. Since these productions cannot generate the strings in R_0^+, we add two productions, $S \to acb$ and $S \to bac$, to set P (Step 4). The augmented set $P = \{S \to aSc, S \to ac, S \to b, S \to aAc, A \to bA, A \to b, S \to acb, S \to bac\}$, together with the nonterminal set $N = \{S, A\}$ and terminal set $\Sigma = \{a, b, c\}$, constitutes the inferred grammar (Step 5). We see by inspection that no simplifications are possible (Step 6). □

6.3.2 Inference of Operator Precedence Grammars

As indicated in Section 4.4.5, operator precedence grammars (o.p.g.) are a special case of context-free grammars. The use of brackets in o.p.g. in this section establishes the order in which a string is evaluated, thus simplifying the inference process considerably The method discussed in this section utilizes this information and the concepts of the following definition to infer a restricted class of operator precedence grammars.

ISBN 0-201-02930-8/0-201-02931-6, pbk

Given a grammar $G = (N, \Sigma, P, S)$, let α be a nonempty string in $(N \cup \Sigma)^*$. The *left* and *right terminal sets* of α are defined as follows:

$$L_t(\alpha) = \left\{ a | \alpha \overset{*}{\Rightarrow} Aa\gamma \right\}, \qquad R_t(\alpha) = \left\{ a | \alpha \overset{*}{\Rightarrow} \gamma aA \right\}$$

with a in Σ, A in $(N \cup \lambda)$, and γ in $(N \cup \Sigma)^*$. The pair $[L_t(\alpha), R_t(\alpha)]$ is called the *terminal profile* of α.

For a string α, the set $L_t(\alpha)$ consists of the terminals that appear in the form $Aa\gamma$ or $a\gamma$ in the strings that can be derived from α by successive applications of the productions of G. For example, consider the string $\alpha = AaB$, and suppose that one valid derivation is $AaB \Rightarrow AbaB \Rightarrow dbaB \Rightarrow dbac$. In this case, $L_t(\alpha) = \{a, b, d\}$. Similarly, $R_t(\alpha) = \{a, c\}$. From the foregoing definition and this simple example, we note that $L_t(\alpha)$ is formed from the leftmost terminals in the strings that can be derived from α, and that only single terminals are considered at each derivation step. Similar comments hold for $R_t(\alpha)$. The terminal profile for this example is given by $[\{a, b, d\}, \{a, c\}]$.

Given a positive sample R^+ (in which all strings have been parenthesized to indicate the order of evaluation), the inference technique consists of the following sequence of steps:

Step 1. Obtain a canonical context-free grammar G_i for *each* string x_i in R^+.

Step 2. Obtain the left and right terminal sets $L_t(\alpha_j)$ and $R_t(\alpha_j)$ for each production $A_j \to \alpha_j$ in G_i.

Step 3. For any pair of values m and n, let $A_n = A_m$ in G_i if $L_t(\alpha_n) = L_t(\alpha_m)$ and $R_t(\alpha_n) = R_t(\alpha_m)$.

Step 4. After all strings in R^+ have been processed, form a composite grammar

$$G = \bigcup_{i=1}^{k} G_i$$

where k is the number of strings in R^+.

Step 5. Simplify the resulting grammar.

As a matter of convention, it will be assumed that strings are scanned from left to right, and that the first symbol considered is the one enclosed by the innermost pair of brackets encountered during the left-to-right scan.

The foregoing approach is characterized by the following properties (Crespi-Reghizzi [1970, 1971]):

(i)   There are no renaming rules (i.e., symbol-to-symbol mapping) in the grammar, except for rules of the form $S \to A_i$, having the starting symbol S as the left part.

ISBN 0-201-02930-8/0-201-02931-6, pbk

(ii)   There are no repeated right parts.

(iii)   All the right parts of the same nonterminal have identical terminal profiles.

(iv)   Two distinct nonterminals may not have identical terminal profiles.

The class of operator precedence grammars characterized by (i)–(iv), called *free grammars*, is more restricted than the class of operator precedence grammars defined in Section 4.4.5.

Example: As an illustration of the inference algorithm, let us consider syntactic structures composed of circles related by the relationship "inside of," which will be denoted by the symbol ∘ in conjunction with parentheses. The pattern shown in Fig. 6.6, for example, is represented by the string $c \circ (c \circ (c; c))$. According to the convention just adopted, this string represents two circles, $(c; c)$, inside a circle, $c \circ (c; c)$. The latter syntactic unit is in turn inside another circle, as indicated by the notation $c \circ (c \circ (c; c))$. In order to simplify the example, all circles will be denoted by the same symbol, c. That we are using an "inside of" relationship establishes a size hierarchy among the various circles in a pattern.

Let us begin by assuming that the set R^+ contains only the sample $r_1 = [[c] \circ [([c] \circ [([c]; [c])])]]$ where the square brackets (provided by the user) indicate the order in which the string is to be evaluated. We scan r_1 from left to right and stop at the innermost pair of brackets, which in this case enclose c. Any grammar that is compatible with r_1 must have a production of the form $A_1 \to c$ to account for the constituent $[c]$.[†] Using this production reduces r_1 to

$$\left[A_1 \circ \left[\left(A_1 \circ \left[(A_1; A_1) \right] \right) \right] \right]$$

since there are three other occurrences of c in r_1.

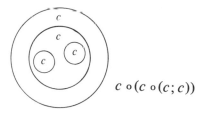

$$c \circ (c \circ (c; c))$$

Figure 6.6. A simple structure and its structural description.

[†]Strictly speaking, this production should be written as $A_1 \to [c]$. In order to simplify the notation, however, the brackets will be omitted, with the understanding that a production written as $A_i \to \alpha_i$ implicitly represents $A_i \to [\alpha_i]$.

ISBN 0-201-02930-8/0-201-02931-6, pbk

The innermost pair of brackets now contains $(A_1; A_1)$. A production $A_2 \rightarrow (A_1; A_i)$ is introduced to account for this term, which reduces the string to

$$[A_1 \circ [(A_1 \circ A_2)]].$$

The next scan produces the term $(A_1 \circ A_2)$, which requires a production of the form $A_3 \rightarrow (A_1 \circ A_2)$. We now have the string

$$[A_1 \circ A_3],$$

which can be generated by the production $A_4 \rightarrow A_1 \circ A_3$. This completes the scanning process.

Using the foregoing results, the canonical grammar for r_1 is given by $G_1 = (N_1, \Sigma_1, P_1, S)$ where $N_1 = \{A_1, A_2, A_3, S\}$, $\Sigma_1 = \{c, \circ, ;, (,)\}$, and $P_1 = \{S \rightarrow A_1 \circ A_3, A_3 \rightarrow (A_1 \circ A_2), A_2 \rightarrow (A_1; A_1), A_1 \rightarrow c\}$. It is noted that the brackets are not considered part of the terminal set, and that A_4 was renamed S to maintain consistency in notation for the starting symbol.

The next step in the algorithm involves computation of the right and left terminal sets for the right side of each production. For $A_1 \rightarrow c$ we have $L_t(c) = \{c\}$ and $R_t(c) = \{c\}$. To obtain L_t and R_t for the right side of A_2 we note that $(A_1; A_1)$ produces the following derivation: $(A_1; A_1) \Rightarrow (c; A_1) \Rightarrow (c; c)$. Only the first term satisfies the definition of L_t with $B = \lambda$, $a = ($, and $x = A_1; A_1)$. Thus, we have that $L_t((A_1; A_1)) = \{(\}$. Similarly, only the first and second steps satisfy the definition for R_t. Both of these steps yield the result $R_t((A_1; A_1)) = \{)\}$. We also have $L_t((A_1 \circ A_2)) = \{(\}$, $R_t((A_1 \circ A_2)) = \{)\}$, $L_t(A_1 \circ A_3) = \{\circ\}$, $R_t(A_1 \circ A_3) = \{\circ\}$.

Since the right sides of A_2 and A_3 have identical right and left terminal sets, we let $A_3 = A_2$. This yields the following grammar for r_1: $G_1 = (N_1, \Sigma_1, P_1, S)$, with $N_1 = \{A_1, A_2, S\}$, $\Sigma_1 = \{c, \circ, ;, (,)\}$, and $P_1 = \{S \rightarrow A_1 \circ A_2, A_2 \rightarrow (A_1 \circ A_2), A_2 \rightarrow (A_1; A_1), A_1 \rightarrow c\}$. The basic type of pattern generated by this grammar is shown in Fig. 6.7. It is noted that self-embed-

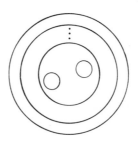

Figure 6.7. Type of pattern generated by grammar G_1.

ISBN 0-201-02930-8/0-201-02931-6, pbk

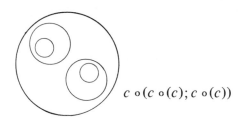

$$c \circ (c \circ (c); c \circ (c))$$

Figure 6.8. Second pattern added to the sample set.

ding was introduced in the second production as a consequence of two productions having right parts with identical terminals sets. This is the entire basis employed by this method for generating a grammar.

To continue the example, suppose that the sample $c\circ(c\circ(c); c\circ(c))$ is added to the learning set. This sample, which is shown in Fig. 6.8, may be bracketed as follows: $r_2 = [[c]\circ[([c]\circ[([c])]]; [[c]\circ[([c])]])]]$. The canonical grammar G_2 for this string has productions

$$S \to B_1 \circ B_4$$

$$B_4 \to (B_3; B_3)$$

$$B_3 \to B_1 \circ B_2$$

$$B_2 \to (B_1)$$

$$B_1 \to c$$

The terminal sets are

$$L_t(B_1 \circ B_4) = \{\circ, c\}, \qquad R_t(B_1 \circ B_4) = \{\circ,)\},$$

$$L_t((B_3; B_3)) = \{(\}, \qquad R_t((B_3; B_3)) = \{)\},$$

$$L_t(B_1 \circ B_2) = \{\circ, c\}, \qquad R_t(B_1 \circ B_2) = \{\circ,)\},$$

$$L_t((B_1)) = \{(\}, \qquad R_t((B_1)) = \{)\},$$

$$L_t(c) = \{c\}, \qquad R_t(c) = \{c\}.$$

Since L_t and R_t are equal for the right sides of B_2 and B_4, and B_3 and S, we

ISBN 0-201-02930-8/0-201-02931-6, pbk

let $B_4 = B_2$ and $B_3 = S$. This results in the following productions for G_2:

$$S \to B_1 \circ B_2$$
$$B_2 \to (S; S)$$
$$S \to B_1 \circ B_2$$
$$B_2 \to (B_1)$$
$$B_1 \to c$$

Since the first and third productions are identical, we have $G_2 = (N_2, \Sigma_2, P_2, S)$ with $N_2 = \{B_1, B_2, S\}$, $\Sigma_2 = \{c, \circ, ;, (,)\}$, and productions

$$S \to B_1 \circ B_2$$
$$B_2 \to (S; S)$$
$$B_2 \to (B_1)$$
$$B_1 \to c$$

Some generations of G_2 are shown in Fig. 6.9.

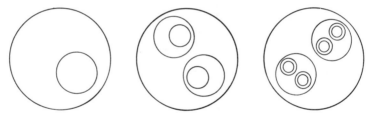

Figure 6.9. Some generations of grammar G_2.

By noting that $\Sigma_1 = \Sigma_2$ and $A_1 \equiv B_1$, we obtain the following results for Steps 4 and 5 of the inference technique: $G = (N, \Sigma, P, S)$ with $N = \{A_1, A_2, A_3, S\}$, $\Sigma = \{c, \circ, ;, (,)\}$, and productions

$$S \to A_1 \circ A_2$$
$$S \to A_1 \circ A_3$$
$$A_2 \to (A_1 \circ A_2)$$
$$A_2 \to (A_1; A_1)$$
$$A_3 \to (S; S)$$
$$A_3 \to (A_1)$$
$$A_1 \to c$$

where $A_3 = B_2$. $\square$

ISBN 0-201-02930-8/0-201-02931-6, pbk

6.3.3 Inference of Pivot Grammars

A *pivot grammar* is a grammar $G = (N, \Sigma, P, S)$ in which the set of terminal symbols Σ is partitioned into two sets, Σ_1 and Σ_2, such that

(i) a in Σ_1 implies that a (called a *pivot terminal*) appears only in productions of the form $A \rightarrow BaC$, and

(ii) b in Σ_2 implies that b appears only in productions of the form $A \rightarrow bB$, $A \rightarrow Bb$, or $A \rightarrow b$

for a, b in Σ, and A, B, C in N. Only productions of the form shown in (i) and (ii) are allowed. Since we do not allow context-free productions of the form $B \rightarrow \lambda$ or $C \rightarrow \lambda$, it is noted from (i) that a pivot terminal cannot be the first or last symbol in a string; also, occurrences of pivot terminals must be separated by at least one nonpivot terminal in each string.

Since no production in a pivot grammar has a right side with two adjacent nonterminals, we see that these grammars are included in the category of operator grammars (see Section 4.4.5). In addition, a pivot grammar for which $\Sigma_1 = \emptyset$ reduces to a context-free grammar with mixed right and left linear forms, as defined in Section 2.2.2.

The principal strategy of the following technique is to find self-embedding in the strings of R^+. A special nonterminal, X, is set aside for this purpose. The inference approach may be summarized as follows.

Step 1. Each string in R^+ is examined to see if it has substrings that are also in R^+. If a string does not satisfy this condition, it is simply copied onto a working set, denoted by W^+. If a string has substrings in R^+, the longest of these substrings is replaced by X and the new string is placed in the working set.

Step 2. Each string in W^+ is examined independently. If it contains a pivot terminal, the test and substitution procedure outlined in Step 1 is repeated for the symbols on the side of the pivot not containing X. All results are placed in W^+.

Step 3. A pivot grammar is constructed to generate the samples in W^+. Nonterminal X is used as the starting symbol.

Step 4. The grammar obtained in Step 3 is simplified.

Example: Consider the set R^+ shown in Table 6.2. The longest valid substrings are shown in the second column, and execution of Step 1 of the foregoing algorithm yields the set W^+ shown in the third column.

The pivot terminal in this case is the symbol $*$. Only the fourth string in W^+ satisfies the conditions of Step 2, so this string is changed to $(X) * (X)$ and placed in W^+. After deletion of duplicate strings, we obtain the set $W^+ = \{a * a, a * (X), (X) * a, (X) * (X)\}$.

ISBN 0-201-02930-8/0-201-02931-6, pbk

Table 6.2

R^+	Longest valid substring	W^+
$a * a$	*none*	$a * a$
$a * (a * a)$	$a * a$	$a * (X)$
$(a * a) * a$	$a * a$	$(X) * a$
$(a * a) * (a * a)$	$a * a$	$(X) * (a * a)$
$(a * (a * a)) * a$	$a * (a * a)$	$(X) * a$
$((a * a) * a) * a$	$(a * a) * a$	$(X) * a$
$a * (a * (a * a))$	$a * (a * a)$	$a * (X)$
$a * ((a * a) * a)$	$(a * a) * a$	$a * (X)$

In Step 3 of the algorithm, we construct a pivot grammar. To generate the string $a * a$ we start with X and introduce the following productions:

$$X \rightarrow A_1 * A_2$$

$$A_1 \rightarrow a$$

$$A_2 \rightarrow a$$

To generate $a * (X)$ the productions

$$A_2 \rightarrow (A_3$$

$$A_3 \rightarrow X)$$

must be added. To generate $(X) * a$ we add the productions

$$A_1 \rightarrow (A_4$$

$$A_4 \rightarrow X)$$

The productions are now

$$X \rightarrow A_1 * A_2$$

$$A_1 \rightarrow a|(A_4$$

$$A_2 \rightarrow a|(A_3$$

$$A_3 \rightarrow X)$$

$$A_4 \rightarrow X)$$

The string $(X) * (X)$ can be generated with these productions,

ISBN 0-201-02930-8/0-201-02931-6, pbk

so no additional rewriting rules are required. The inferred grammar, therefore, consists of the foregoing productions, nonterminals $N = \{X, A_1, A_2, A_3, A_4\}$, and $\Sigma = \{a, *, (,)\}$.

In the last step, we simplify the grammar obtained in Step 3. First we note that nonterminals A_3 and A_4 are equivalent, so the production $A_4 \rightarrow X)$ is eliminated and A_3 is substituted for all occurrences of A_4. The resulting productions are

$$X \rightarrow A_1 * A_2$$

$$A_1 \rightarrow a|(A_3$$

$$A_2 \rightarrow a|(A_3$$

$$A_3 \rightarrow X)$$

Clearly, A_1 and A_2 are also equivalent, so we have

$$X \rightarrow A_1 * A_1$$

$$A_1 \rightarrow a|(A_3$$

$$A_3 \rightarrow X)$$

No further simplifications are possible. The simplified grammar is $G = (N, \Sigma, P, S)$ with $N = \{X, A_1, A_3\}$, $\Sigma = \{a, *, (,)\}$, and productions $P = \{X \rightarrow A_1 * A_1, A_1 \rightarrow a, A_1 \rightarrow (A_3, A_3 \rightarrow X)\}$. ☐

6.4 INFERENCE OF TREE GRAMMARS

As pointed out in Chapter 3, tree representations offer greater flexibility than strings in expressing certain types of pattern relationships. In this section, we consider a method for inferring an expansive tree grammar from a set of patterns that have been expressed in the form of tree structures. It is suggested that the reader review Section 3.2 before proceeding with the following development.

6.4.1 Preliminary Definitions

As indicated in Section 3.2, an expansive tree grammar has productions of the form

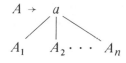

ISBN 0-201-02930-8/0-201-02931-6, pbk

for $A, A_1, A_2, \ldots, A_n$ in N and a in Σ. This is the only type of tree production considered in this section.

Let $\mathfrak{T}_i$ and $\mathfrak{T}_j$ be the sets of trees derivable by starting with nonterminals A_i and A_j, respectively. Then, A_i and A_j are *equivalent*, denoted $A_i \equiv A_j$, if $\mathfrak{T}_i = \mathfrak{T}_j$.

As an example, consider the set of expansive productions

$$S \to \$ \quad, \quad A \to a, \ A \to a, \ B \to a, \ B \to a$$

Nonterminals A and B are equivalent because each produces the set of trees

$$a, a, a, \ldots$$

The problem of determining whether or not A_i is equivalent to A_j is unsolved in the general case. However, if the sets generated by starting with A_i and A_j are finite, it is possible to test equivalence by enumeration of these sets. This is the approach that will be taken in the following discussion.

In order to reference nodes in a tree in a convenient and efficient manner, a formal addressing procedure is required. The following lexicographical ordering is due to Gorn [1967]. The *indices* or *Gorn addresses* of a tree are defined recursively by the conditions that the root has index 0, and if a node with index k has n offspring, they are assigned indices $k.1, k.2, \ldots, k.n$ in order from left to right. Given a tree with these indices assigned, there is a *lexicographical ordering relation* $<_L$ defined on the nodes as follows. Let r and s be indices; then $r <_L s$ if

(i)   there exists an index c such that $s = r.c$, or
(ii) $r = c.i.u$ and $s = c.j.v$, where c, u, and v are indices, and i and j are positive integers with i being less than j.

It is common practice to suppress leading zeros in the node addresses. Thus, the Gorn addresses of the root offspring are denoted by $1, 2, \ldots, n$, rather than $0.1, 0.2, \ldots, 0.n$.

The indexing procedure given by the preceding definition is illustrated in Fig. 6.10. Condition (i) establishes a top-to-bottom partial ordering along descendant paths. For instance, the node having label e and index $s = 2.2.1$ is a descendant of the node labeled f having index $r = 2.2$ since

ISBN 0-201-02930-8/0-201-02931-6, pbk

$s = r.c$ with $c = 1$. Similarly, condition (ii) establishes a left-to-right ordering among the descendants of any one node. Consider, for example, the nodes with indices $r = 2.2.2.1$ and $s = 2.2.2.2$ in Fig. 6.10. We find that $r <_L s$ since $r = c.i$ and $s = c.j$ where $c = 2.2.2$, $i = 1$, $j = 2$, and $i < j$. This indicates that the second node is positioned to the right of the first.

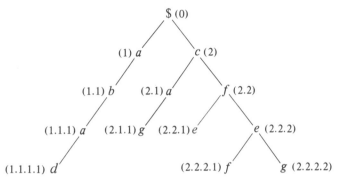

Figure 6.10. Illustration of the Gorn lexicographical ordering scheme. (From Gonzalez, Edwards, and Thomason [1976].)

A set of nodes $\{a_1, a_2, \ldots, a_n\}$ is said to be at the kth level of a tree if the Gorn address of each node in the set has exactly k integers. The root is defined to be at the 0th level.

Given two trees T_i and T_j with $N_i(k)$ and $N_j(k)$ nodes at level k, respectively, let $A(k)$ be the number of nodes at this level having the same Gorn address but different labels. We define the *distance* between T_i and T_j at the kth level as the quantity $B(k) = [A(k) + |N_i(k) - N_j(k)|]$.

In the following discussion we are concerned with *nonoverlapping* subtrees $\{T_1, T_2, \ldots, T_m\}$ of a tree T. It will be useful to characterize each subtree T_i by the normal Gorn addresses of T as well as by an *independent* set of Gorn addresses starting at its root $\$_i$. The following two definitions make use of this convention.

Two subtrees T_i and T_j of T with roots $\$_i$ and $\$_j$, and $r(\$_i) = r(\$_j) > 1$, respectively, are said to exhibit *self-embedding of depth* $D_S \geq 0$ if

(i)   the Gorn address of $\$_i$ in T is a prefix of the address of $\$_j$ in T;
(ii) $N_i(k) = N_j(k)$, $k = 0, 1, \ldots, D_S$;
(iii) $B(k) = 0$, $k = 0, 1, \ldots, D_S$.

It is noted that condition (i) makes use of the Gorn addresses of T, whereas conditions (ii) and (iii) make use of the independent Gorn addresses of T_i and T_j.

It will be useful in the following sections to consider different self-embedding depths in the same tree. We shall use the notation $D_S(\$_i)$ to denote that a subtree T_i with root $\$_i$ exhibits self-embedding in T with depth D_S.

Two subtrees T_i and T_j of T with roots $\$_i$ and $\$_j$, and $r(\$_i) = r(\$_j) = 1$, respectively, are said to exhibit *iterative regularity of depth* $D_R \geqslant 0$ if

   (i)   the Gorn address of $\$_i$ in T is a prefix of the address of $\$_j$ in T;
   (ii) $N_i(k) = N_j(k)$, $k = 0, 1, \ldots, D_R$;
   (iii) $B(k) = 0$, $k = 0, 1, \ldots, D_R$;
   (iv) there are no instances of self-embedding at level k of T_i and T_j, $k = 1, 2, \ldots, D_R$.

Condition (i) makes use of the Gorn addresses of T, whereas the other three conditions are based on the independent Gorn address of T_i and T_j.

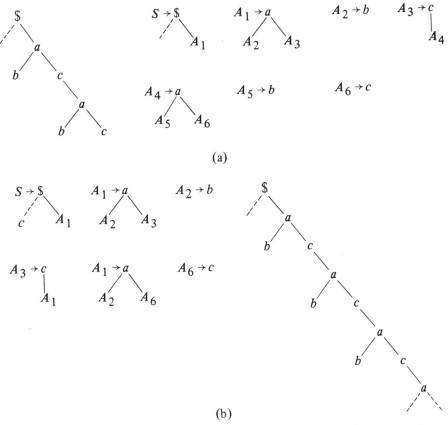

(a)

(b)

Figure 6.11. Illustration of self-embedding. (a) A sample tree and corresponding expansive productions. (b) Productions that exhibit self-embedding and a typical generation. (From Gonzalez, Edwards, and Thomason [1976].)

ISBN 0-201-02930-8/0-201-02931-6, pbk

Self-embedding and regularity play a central role in the algorithm developed in Section 6.4.2. These two properties allow generalization of tree grammars that can produce the samples used in the inference process as well as other samples similar in structure. The concept of self-embedding is illustrated in Fig. 6.11. It is noted in Fig. 6.11(a) that the substructure

exhibits self-embedding in T with depth $D_S(a) = 1$. Two instances are shown, and the nonterminals that point to the root of the self-embedding substructures are A_1 and A_4. By letting $A_4 = A_1$ and noting that A_2 and A_5 are equivalent, we obtain the productions shown in Fig. 6.11(b). The original productions can generate only the tree structure from which they were obtained. The second set of productions, on the other hand, can generate the same structure in addition to others with repetition of the self-embedding subtrees. The degree of acceptable similarity can be controlled by varying D_S.

Similar comments hold for regularity. The difference between these two properties lies in the fact that regularity allows generalization along single paths (because of the restriction placed on the number of offspring of the root of regular substructures), whereas self-embedding allows generalization along multiple paths. It should be noted that this is not an arbitrary restriction. Regular tree structures have an equivalent representation in regular or type 3 string languages, whereas self-embedding requires the added capability of context-free grammars.

6.4.2 Inference Approach

The method developed in this section produces a tree grammar from a set of input sample trees $\{T_1, T_2, \ldots, T_m\}$. The approach consists of the following seven steps.

Step 1. An expansive set of productions P_i is obtained for each sample tree T_i, $i = 1, 2, \ldots, m$. Each set P_i is capable of generating only T_i by starting with the root production.

Remarks. Since we are only considering expansive forms, the jth production in P_i is of the form

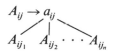

ISBN 0-201-02930-8/0-201-02931-6, pbk

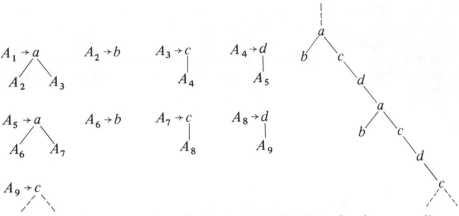

Figure 6.12. Two subtrees that self-embed with depth $D_S(a) = 2$ and corresponding expansive productions. (From Gonzalez, Edwards, and Thomason [1976].)

Although the use of expansive-form productions is not a basic requirement of the algorithm, their use greatly simplifies the implementation of the procedure. The union of all P_i will be denoted in what follows by P.

Step 2. The right part of each production in P is tested for self-embedding depth $D_S(a_{ij})$ and regularity depth $D_R(a_{ij})$. All right parts that are not instances of self-embedding or regularity are said to be of *degree* 0. The first occurrence of a right part that exhibits self-embedding of depth $D_S(a_{ij})$ or regularity of depth $D_R(a_{ij})$ is said to be of *degree* 1. All subsequent occurrences of the same right parts are said to be of *degree* 2.

Remarks. Because the right parts of expansive productions are subtrees of two levels, the statement, for example, that a right part exhibits self-embedding of depth $D_S(a_{ij})$ implies that a check on descendants of that right part must be carried out. This is illustrated in Fig. 6.12, in which two self-embedding substructures of depth 2 are present. To establish that the right part of A_1 exhibits self-embedding with $D_S(a) = 2$, it is also necessary to check the right parts of A_2, A_3, and A_4. This, of course, is in addition to checking the right parts of A_5, A_6, A_7, and A_8, since the combination of these two sets of productions is what gives rise to self-embedding in this particular case.

Step 3. All nonterminals in P having right parts of degree 1 are tested for equivalence using the definition given in Section 6.4.1. If a merging takes place, all descendant productions of a nonterminal that was merged are eliminated.

ISBN 0-201-02930-8/0-201-02931-6, pbk

Remarks.   It is noted that both Steps 3 and 5 deal with the merging of equivalent nonterminals. The reason for merging nonterminals associated with right parts of degree 1 in this step is as follows. It was pointed out in Section 6.4.1 that self-embedding and regularity are used as the basis for generalizing a grammar. This is accomplished by merging corresponding nonterminals associated with right parts that exhibit these properties. If generalization is allowed to take place before a test for equivalence is made in the first occurrence of self-embedding or regularity, serious logic loops can be introduced in the inference process. This phenomenon is easily illustrated by means of the following example, where for simplicity we use a self-embedding depth $D_S = 0$ on all nodes.

Consider the tree

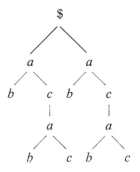

The expansive productions are

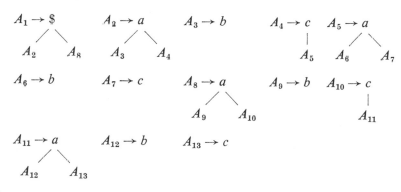

The right terminals of A_2 and A_5 exhibit self-embedding. This is also true of the right terminals of A_8 and A_{11}. If we let $A_5 = A_2$ and $A_{11} = A_8$, we

ISBN 0-201-02930-8/0-201-02931-6, pbk

have

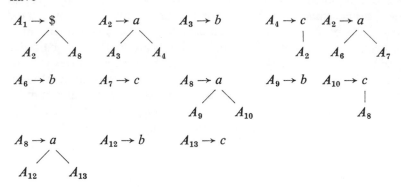

It is immediately evident that $A_3 \equiv A_6 \equiv A_9 \equiv A_{12}$ and $A_7 \equiv A_{13}$. Use of these results yields the productions

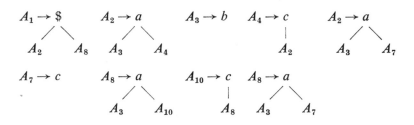

It is now noted that A_2 would be equivalent to A_8 if A_4 were equivalent to A_{10}. Conversely, A_4 would be equivalent to A_{10} if A_2 were equivalent to A_8. Although this is not a particularly difficult loop to resolve, it is clear that providing for more complex situations can in general present some very serious computational difficulties.

Suppose that, instead of merging as above, we first test for equivalence those nonterminals whose right parts have degree 1, as is done in Step 3 of the algorithm. In this case, we would find that $A_2 \equiv A_8$. Merging A_8 with A_2 and deleting the descendants of A_8 yields the productions

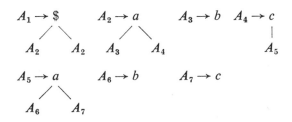

ISBN 0-201-02930-8/0-201-02931-6, pbk

Other types of logic loops can be handled in a similar manner. Generalization of the grammar takes place in the next step.

Step 4. All nonterminals in P having right parts of degree 1 are combined with corresponding nonterminals of degree 2.

Remarks. Applying Step 4 to the foregoing example yields the productions

$$A_1 \to \$ \qquad A_2 \to a \qquad A_3 \to b \quad A_4 \to c$$
$$\overset{A_2 \quad A_2}{} \qquad \overset{A_3 \quad A_4}{} \qquad \qquad \overset{A_2}{}$$

$$A_2 \to a \qquad A_6 \to b \qquad A_7 \to c$$
$$\overset{A_6 \quad A_7}{}$$

Note that the right side of A_4 allows generation back to A_2.

Step 5. Merge equivalent nonterminals with right parts of degree 0 to obtain a final set of reduced productions.

Remarks. Applying Step 5 to the productions obtained in the previous step, we find that $A_6 \equiv A_3$. The reduced set of productions is, therefore,

$$A_1 \to \$ \qquad A_2 \to a \qquad A_3 \to b \quad A_4 \to c$$
$$\overset{A_2 \quad A_2}{} \qquad \overset{A_3 \quad A_4}{} \qquad \qquad \overset{A_2}{}$$

$$A_2 \to a \qquad A_7 \to c$$
$$\overset{A_3 \quad A_7}{}$$

Step 6. For every starting productions

$$A_i \to a \qquad\qquad S \to a$$
$$\overset{A_1 \; A_2 \; \cdots \; A_n}{} \qquad \overset{A_1 \; A_2 \; \cdots \; A_n}{}$$

Remarks. The productions obtained in Step 6 allow generation by the grammar G of all trees in its language by starting from a common nonterminal. These productions are introduced for convenience.

Step 7. The inferred tree grammar $G_t = (V, r, S, P)$ is formed by using the productions obtained in Steps 5 and 6 along with the nonterminals, terminals, and ranks present in these productions.

ISBN 0-201-02930-8/0-201-02931-6, pbk

6.4.3 Examples

In this section we discuss two simulation results using the inference technique developed in the previous section. The purpose behind the following experiments is only to illustrate basic characteristics of the algorithm and not to present an exhaustive evaluation of its capabilities.

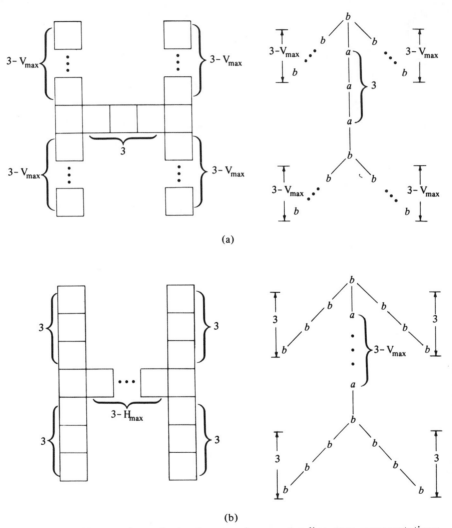

(a)

(b)

Figure 6.13. Two caslses of structures and corresponding tree representations. (From Gonzalez, Edwards, and Thomason [1976].)

ISBN 0-201-02930-8/0-201-02931-6, pbk

6.4.3.1 A simple experiment

The effects of varying the self-embedding and regularity depths can be illustrated by using the two classes of structures shown in Fig. 6.13. The first class, shown in Fig. 6.13(a), consists of structures that have three horizontal elements (denoted by a's) but may have a large number, V_{max}, of vertical elements, denoted by b's. The lengths of the four vertical substructures need not be the same. The class shown in Fig. 6.13(b), by contrast, may have a large number, H_{max}, of horizontal elements, but its vertical substructures can have only three elements. It is evident that the two classes share one common structure (three horizontal and three vertical elements), but the general trend is for the first class to have vertical substructures that are long compared to the horizontal substructures, whereas the opposite is true of the second class.

A set of structures of each class was generated with V_{max} and H_{max} varying between 3 and 20. Each set was then submitted to the inference algorithm in order to obtain a grammar for each category. A first experiment with the foregoing patterns consisted of specifying self-embedding and regularity of depth zero. These specifications resulted in the grammars

$$G_{t1} = G_{t2} = (V, r, P, S)$$

with

$$N = \{A_1, A_2, A_3, A_4, A_5, S\},$$

$$\Sigma = \{a, b\},$$

$$V = N \cup \Sigma,$$

$$r = \{r(a) = 1, r(b) = [1, 2, 3]\},$$

and productions

$$
\begin{array}{lllll}
S \to b & A_1 \to b & A_2 \to b & A_2 \to b & A_4 \to b \\
\quad \diagup \;\big|\; \diagdown & \quad \diagup \big| \diagdown & \quad \big| & \quad \big| & \\
A_2 \;\; A_3 \;\; A_2 & A_2 \; A_3 \; A_2 & A_2 & A_4 & \\[2mm]
A_3 \to a & A_3 \to a & A_5 \to b & & \\
\quad \big| & \quad \big| & \quad \diagup \diagdown & & \\
A_3 & A_5 & A_2 \quad A_2 & &
\end{array}
$$

There are two productions that reflect regularity, but there are none associated with self-embedding. It is evident that the depth specifications were too weak to detect the basic difference between the two classes since the resulting grammars were identical.

In a second experiment, the following assignments were made: for class one, $D_R(a) = 1$ and $D_R(b) = 0$; for class two, $D_R(a) = 0$ and $D_R(b) = 1$. A self-embedding depth of $D_S = 0$ was again specified, which in this case is redundant since no self-embedding was detected in the first part of the experiment. Using these assignments and applying the inference algorithm to the foregoing patterns yielded the following productions for G_{t1}:

$$
\begin{array}{cccccc}
S \to b & A_1 \to b & A_2 \to b & A_2 \to b & & A_4 \to b \\
\diagup | \diagdown & \diagup | \diagdown & | & | & & \\
A_2\ A_3\ A_2 & A_2\ A_3\ A_2 & A_2 & A_4 & & \\
\end{array}
$$

$$
\begin{array}{cccc}
A_3 \to a & A_5 \to a & A_6 \to a & A_7 \to b \\
| & | & | & \diagup \diagdown \\
A_5 & A_6 & A_7 & A_2\quad A_2 \\
\end{array}
$$

Similarly, the productions for G_{t2} were

$$
\begin{array}{ccccc}
S \to b & A_1 \to b & A_2 \to b & A_4 \to b & A_5 \to b \\
\diagup | \diagdown & \diagup | \diagdown & | & | & \\
A_2\ A_3\ A_2 & A_2\ A_3\ A_2 & A_4 & A_5 & \\
\end{array}
$$

$$
\begin{array}{ccc}
A_3 \to a & A_3 \to a & A_6 \to b \\
| & | & \diagup \diagdown \\
A_3 & A_6 & A_2\quad A_2 \\
\end{array}
$$

The tree grammar having the first set of productions can generate structures that have three horizontal elements and vertical elements of unlimited length. The grammar having the second set of productions, on the other hand, can generate structures that have three elements in the vertical substructures and a horizontal substructure that can be of unlimited length. It is also noted that the two grammars can generate one common structure. This is as it should be since the sets used in the inference process also share one common sample.

6.4.3.2 Experiments with two-dimensional binary images

The results of the previous experiment illustrate the self-embedding and regularity characteristics of the inference approach. In the following discussion, we focus attention on the reduction capabilities of the procedure.

ISBN 0-201-02930-8/0-201-02931-6, pbk

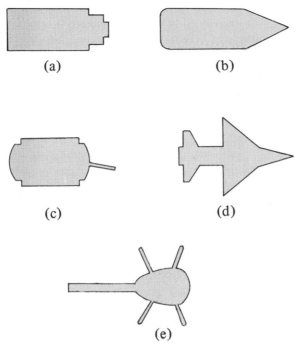

(a)   (b)

(c)   (d)

(e)

Figure 6.14. Two-dimensional test patterns. (From Gonzalez, Edwards, and Thomason [1976].)

Each of the patterns shown schematically in Fig. 6.14 was digitized and converted into a 128×128 binary matrix. A tree was extracted from each matrix using the following algorithm.

Tree-extraction algorithm. The procedure uses the following symbols:

$\$$:	root of a pattern tree
A:	pointer to the address of a node; sometimes informally referred to as the address of a node or pointer to a node
$\text{LINK}_j(A)$:	pointer to the jth descendant of the node whose address is A, where $j = 1$ denotes the left-most descendant node. For a node with n branches, $j = n$ denotes the right-most descendant node
λ:	empty tree
$\doteq$:	symbol indicating "points to"
LIST:	a list of addresses of points in the binary matrix with value 1

ISBN 0-201-02930-8/0-201-02931-6, pbk

1	2	3
4	×	6
7	8	9

Figure 6.15. Neighbors of point ×.

All points, except points on the border of the matrix, have eight neighbors, as shown in Fig. 6.15. A point × is said to be connected to all of its neighbors that have a value of 1 in the binary matrix.

Using this convention and the notation introduced earlier, the algorithm consists of the following steps:

   (i)   Scan the matrix in column order until the first point with value 1 is found. Label this point $ (the root). Let $LP = 0$, $L1 = 1$, LIST (1) = the address of $.
   (ii)   Let $LP = LP + 1$, $A =$ LIST(LP). If $A = \lambda$, go to Step (iv). Let $j = 0$, $m = 0$.
   (iii)   Let $m = m + 1$. If $m = 5$, go to Step (iii). If $m = 10$, go to Step (ii). If neighbor m of the point whose address is A has value zero or the address of this neighbor is already in LIST, go to Step (iii). Let $j = j + 1$, $\text{LINK}_j(A) =$ address of neighbor m. Label the point at this address with the value of m, a numeric label. Let $L1 = L1 + 1$, LIST($L1$) = address of neighbor m. Go to Step (iii).
   (iv)The algorithm terminates.

As an example, consider the 6×6 binary matrix shown in Fig. 6.16. To simplify the example, let the notation a_{ij}, where a_{ij} is the matrix location in the ith row and jth column, represent the address of that location. The first action is to find the root at a_{22}. This address is placed in the list. Now $ is checked for all possible connections. Neighbors 6, 8, and 9 have value 1 and are thus connected to $. The addresses of these neighbors are added to the list.

0	0	0	0	0	0
0	1	1	0	1	0
0	1	1	0	1	0
0	0	0	1	0	0
0	0	1	0	1	0
0	0	0	0	0	0

Figure 6.16. A simple binary image matrix.

ISBN 0-201-02930-8/0-201-02931-6, pbk

The tree is now

and the list contains a_{22}, a_{23}, a_{32}, and a_{33} in that order. This finishes the process for a_{22}. The next address in the list, a_{23}, is considered for possible connections. Neighbors 4, 7, and 8 of a_{23} have value 1, but they are already in the list. Therefore, no connections may be made. The same is true for the third address, a_{32}, so a_{33} is considered next. Neighbor 9 of a_{33} has value 1, so it is connected and added to the list. The tree is now

The list contains a_{22}, a_{23}, a_{32}, a_{33}, and a_{44}. The algorithm progresses down the list, making all possible connections. When the list is exhausted, the algorithm terminates. The final tree is

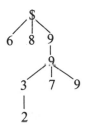

A tree was extracted from each of the patterns shown in Fig. 6.14 by using the algorithm just discussed, and the values $D_S = D_R = 0$ were used for all nodes in order to obtain maximum reduction of nonterminals, as compared to what would have been obtained for nonzero values of these variables. The results of the inference algorithm are summarized in Table 6.3. The second column gives the number of nonterminals, and the third column gives the number of expansive productions used in the original tree representations. These two numbers are always the same since there is one production associated with each nonterminal in the original tree representation. The next two columns give the number of nonterminals and productions determined by the inference technique. (The number of terminals does not change in the inference process.) Finally, the last two columns show the percentage reduction in nonterminals and productions.

ISBN 0-201-02930-8/0-201-02931-6, pbk

Table 6.3. Summary of Results with Two-Dimensional Patterns

Pattern	No. of original non-terminals	No. of original productions	No. of final non-terminals	No. of final productions	Reduction in non-terminals (%)	Reduction in productions (%)
Truck	2296	2296	15	24	99.3	99.0
Boat	2084	2084	19	29	99.1	98.6
Tank	1978	1978	27	49	98.6	97.5
Jet	1055	1055	32	58	97.0	94.5
Helicopter	861	861	38	69	95.6	92.0

As expected, the more complex patterns required more nonterminals and productions for their description. It should be noted, however, that considerable reductions were effected in all cases.

6.5 INFERENCE OF STOCHASTIC GRAMMARS

In this section we focus attention on two approaches related to the problem of inferring stochastic grammars. The first approach deals with learning the production probabilities for a given set of grammars. The second method is a stochastic formulation of the technique discussed in Section 6.2.3 for inferring finite automata.

6.5.1 Learning the Production Probabilities

As indicated in Section 5.2, a stochastic grammar has a set D of probabilities that are associated with the productions of the grammar. Clearly, if we wish to utilize stochastic grammars, we must have at our disposal some mechanism for estimating these production probabilities.

Consider an M-class problem characterized by the stochastic grammars $G_{sk} = (N_k, \Sigma_k, P_k, D_k, S_k)$ for $k = 1, 2, \ldots, M$. It is assumed that N_k, Σ_k, P_k, and S_k are known and that G_{sk} are unambiguous context-free or regular grammars. With these assumptions in mind, it is desired to estimate the production probabilities of D_k, $k = 1, 2, \ldots, M$, from a set of sample terminal strings

$$X = \{x_1, x_2, \ldots, x_m\}$$

where each string belongs to the language generated by one or more of the given stochastic grammars.

ISBN 0-201-02930-8/0-201-02931-6, pbk

When all strings have been gathered, we count them and denote by $n(x_h)$ the number of times that string x_h occurs. Each string is also parsed using each grammar, and we let $N_{kij}(x_h)$ represent the number of times that a production $A_i \to \beta_j$ of grammar G_{sk} is used in the parsing of string x_h. Although we do not know the production probabilities of the grammars, the productions themselves are assumed to be known, so that a parse is possible.

The expected number of times n_{kij} that the production $A_i \to \beta_j$ of grammar G_{sk} is used in parsing a given string can be approximated by

$$n_{kij} = \sum_{x_h \text{ in } X} n(x_h)p(G_{sk}|x_h)N_{kij}(x_h)$$

where $p(G_{sk}|x_h)$ is the probability that a given string x_h was generated by grammar G_{sk}. This probability must be provided for each string during training.

The probability p_{kij} associated with the production $A_i \to \beta_j$ in grammar G_{sk} can now be approximated by means of the relation

$$\hat{p}_{kij} = \frac{n_{kij}}{\sum_r n_{kir}}$$

where $\hat{p}_{kij}$ represents an estimate of p_{kij}, and the summation in the denominator is carried out over all productions in G_{sk} of the form $A_i \to \beta_r$; that is, over all productions in G_{sk} that have the same left part nonterminal A_i.

It has been shown by Lee and Fu [1972] that the estimate $\hat{p}_{kij}$ approaches the true production probability p_{kij} as the number of strings in X approaches infinity, if the following conditions are satisfied:

1. X is representative of the languages $L(G_{sk})$, $k = 1, 2, \ldots, M$, in the sense that $X \to L$, where L is the union of the languages, that is, $L = \bigcup_{k=1}^{M} L(G_{sk})$.
2. The estimate of the probability of string x_h occurring in X, given by

$$\hat{p}(x_h) = \frac{n(x_h)}{\sum_{x_h \text{ in } L} n(x_h)}$$

approaches the true probability $p(x_h)$.
3. The probability $p(G_{sk}|x_h)$ can be specified for each string x_h during the learning process.

The probability $p(G_{sk}|x_h)$ that a given string x_h belongs to class ω_k can usually be provided without difficulty during the learning phase. If it is

ISBN 0-201-02930-8/0-201-02931-6, pbk

known with certainty that a given string belongs exclusively to class ω_k, then $p(G_{sk}|x_h) = 1$. Similarly, if it is known that x_h cannot belong to ω_k, then $p(G_{sk}|x_h) = 0$. Often, however, some strings may belong to more than one class. In this case, we can obtain a simple estimate of the probabilities $p(G_{sk}|x_h)$, $k = 1, 2, \ldots, M$, for these strings by noting the relative frequency with which they occur in each class. Of course, it is required that

$$\sum_{k=1}^{M} p(G_{sk}|x_h) = 1.$$

When it is not possible to observe the relative number of times that ambiguous strings occur in a particular class, usually a reasonable assumption is to let $p(G_{sk}|x_h) = 1/M$ for these strings.

Example: Let us illustrate the concepts developed in this section by means of a simple numerical example. Consider the stochastic grammars $G_{s1} = (N, \Sigma, P, D_1, S)$ and $G_{s2} = (N, \Sigma, P, D_2, S)$, where, for both grammars, $\Sigma = \{a, b\}$ and $N = \{S\}$. The productions and corresponding probabilities are as follows:

	D_1	D_2
$S \rightarrow aS$	p_{11}	p_{21}
$S \rightarrow a$	p_{12}	p_{22}
$S \rightarrow bS$	p_{13}	p_{23}
$S \rightarrow b$	p_{14}	p_{24}

It is desired to learn the probabilities of D_1 and D_2.

In order to conform with our previous notation, we may change the foregoing notation as follows:

	D_1	D_2
$A_1 \rightarrow \beta_1$	p_{111}	p_{211}
$A_1 \rightarrow \beta_2$	p_{112}	p_{212}
$A_1 \rightarrow \beta_3$	p_{113}	p_{213}
$A_1 \rightarrow \beta_4$	p_{114}	p_{214}

ISBN 0-201-02930-8/0-201-02931-6, pbk

where we have let $A_1 = S$, $\beta_1 = aS$, $\beta_2 = a$, $\beta_3 = bS$, and $\beta_4 = b$. The subscripts on the probabilities are interpreted as before; that is, the first subscript represents the class, the second stands for the subscript of the left-hand side of the production, and the third indicates the subscript of the right-hand side of the production. In this case, all left-hand sides are identical.

Suppose for illustrative purposes that class ω_1 consists solely of strings of a's, and class ω_2 of strings of b's; however, because of noise corruption, mixed strings may sometimes occur. Note that although G_{s1} and G_{s2} can both produce mixed strings, it is postulated in this example that G_{s1} is used only to produce strings of a's and G_{s2} is used only to produce strings of b's. Let us further assume that 100 pattern strings are gathered for the purposes of training, with the following results:

String	Number of Occurrences
a	30
aa	20
aabbb	5
bb	25
b	20

Denoting the first string type by x_1, the second by x_2, and so forth, we obtain

$$n(x_1) = 30, \quad n(x_2) = 20, \quad n(x_3) = 5,$$

$$n(x_4) = 25, \quad n(x_5) = 20.$$

In order to estimate the probabilities p_{kij}, we must first compute the quantities n_{kij}. From the relation given above, we have

$$n_{kij} = \sum_{x_h \text{ in } X} n(x_h) p(G_{sk}|x_h) N_{kij}(x_h)$$

where X consists of 30 strings x_1, 20 strings x_2, and so forth. Using this equation, we obtain for class ω_1

$$n_{111} = n(x_1) p(G_{s1}|x_1) N_{111}(x_1) + n(x_2) p(G_{s1}|x_2) N_{111}(x_2)$$

$$+ n(x_3) p(G_{s1}|x_3) N_{111}(x_3) + n(x_4) p(G_{s1}|x_4) N_{111}(x_4)$$

$$+ n(x_5) p(G_{s1}|x_5) N_{111}(x_5).$$

Let us analyze these terms in some detail. The quantity $n(x_1)$ is known, and $p(G_{s1}|x_1)$ is the probability that x_1 belongs to class ω_1. We may assume

ISBN 0-201-02930-8/0-201-02931-6, pbk

that this probability is 1 since x_1 consists only of a's. The term $N_{111}(x_1)$ is the number of times that $A_1 \rightarrow \beta_1$ is used in parsing x_1. It can be determined by inspection that this production is not used in parsing x_1, so we have that $N_{111}(x_1) = 0$. The second term is similarly computed. The third string contains both a's and b's and therefore can belong to either class. Assuming that it is equally likely to belong to ω_1 or ω_2, we may let $p(G_{s1}|x_3) = 0.5$. In general, these probabilities can be meaningfully specified by having some knowledge of the problem, as was previously discussed. In the fourth and fifth terms, we assume that strings x_4 and x_5 belong to ω_2 since they consist solely of b's. It is also noted that $N_{111}(x_4) = N_{111}(x_5) = 0$ since $A_1 \rightarrow \beta_1$ is not used in the parse of these strings. With these considerations in mind we obtain

$$n_{111} = (30)(1)(0) + (20)(1)(1) + (5)(0.5)(2) + (25)(0)(0) + (20)(0)(0)$$

$$= 25.$$

Using a simple top-down parsing scheme, we obtain the following values of $N_{1ij}(x_h)$:

x_h	$N_{111}(x_h)$	$N_{112}(x_h)$	$N_{113}(x_h)$	$N_{114}(x_h)$
x_1	0	1	0	0
x_2	1	1	0	0
x_3	2	0	2	1
x_4	0	0	1	1
x_5	0	0	0	1

With these values, computation of the remaining n_{kij} yields

$$n_{112} = (30)(1)(1) + (20)(1)(1) + (5)(0.5)(0) + (25)(0)(0) + (20)(0)(0)$$

$$= 50,$$

$$n_{113} = (30)(1)(0) + (20)(1)(0) + (5)(0.5)(2) + (25)(0)(1) + (20)(0)(0)$$

$$= 5,$$

$$n_{114} = (30)(1)(0) + (20)(1)(0) + (5)(0.5)(1) + (25)(0)(1) + (20)(0)(1)$$

$$= 2.5.$$

We may now compute all the probabilities of class ω_1, using the relation

$$\hat{p}_{1ij} = \frac{n_{1ij}}{\sum_r n_{1ir}}$$

ISBN 0-201-02930-8/0-201-02931-6, pbk

where the summation is taken over all productions of G_{s1} having the same left part nonterminal A_i. In this example all left-hand productions are identical. Therefore,

$$\hat{p}_{111} = \frac{n_{111}}{\sum_r n_{11r}} + \frac{n_{111}}{n_{111} + n_{112} + n_{113} + n_{114}}$$

$$= \frac{25.0}{82.5} = 0.303,$$

$$\hat{p}_{112} = \frac{n_{112}}{\sum_r n_{11r}} = \frac{50.0}{82.5} = 0.606,$$

$$\hat{p}_{113} = \frac{n_{113}}{\sum_r n_{11r}} = \frac{5.0}{82.5} = 0.061,$$

$$\hat{p}_{114} = \frac{n_{114}}{\sum_r n_{11r}} = \frac{2.5}{82.5} = 0.030.$$

As expected, the productions of class ω_1 related to the generation of strings of a's have a higher probability.

The computation of the production probabilites for class ω_2 is similar to the foregoing procedure. Since the two grammars have identical productions, it follows that $N_{2ij}(x_h) = N_{1ij}(x_h)$. Using the values previously tabulated for these quantities yields the following n_{2ij}'s:

$$n_{211} = n(x_1)p(G_{s2}|x_1)N_{211}(x_1) + n(x_2)p(G_{s2}|x_2)N_{211}(x_2)$$

$$+ n(x_3)p(G_{s2}|x_3)N_{211}(x_3) + n(x_4)p(G_{s2}|x_4)N_{211}(x_4)$$

$$+ n(x_5)p(G_{s2}|x_5)N_{211}(x_5).$$

In this case x_1 and x_2 clearly belong to class ω_1, and therefore we may assume that $p(G_{s2}|x_1) = p(G_{s2}|x_2) = 0$. Similarly, $p(G_{s2}|x_4) = p(G_{s2}|x_5) = 1$. Also, since we are assuming strictly a two-class problem, it follows that $p(G_{s2}|x_3) = 1 - p(G_{s1}|x_3) = 0.5$. Using these probabilities and the quantities previously tabulated, we obtain

$$n_{211} = (30)(0)(0) + (20)(0)(1) + (5)(0.5)(2) + (25)(1)(0) + (20)(1)(0)$$

$$= 5,$$

$$n_{212} = (30)(0)(1) + (20)(0)(1) + (5)(0.5)(0) + (25)(1)(0) + (20)(1)(0)$$

$$= 0,$$

ISBN 0-201-02930-8/0-201-02931-6, pbk

$$n_{213} = (30)(0)(0) + (20)(0)(0) + (5)(0.5)(2) + (25)(1)(1) + (20)(1)(0)$$

$$= 30,$$

$$n_{214} = (30)(0)(0) + (20)(0)(0) + (5)(0.5)(1) + (25)(1)(1) + (20)(1)(1)$$

$$= 47.5.$$

The production probabilities can now be computed using the relation

$$\hat{p}_{2ij} = \frac{n_{2ij}}{\sum_r n_{2ir}}$$

where, as before, the summation is taken over all productions of G_{s2} having the same left part nonterminal A_i—in this case, this is true for all productions. Using the above relation yields

$$\hat{p}_{211} = \frac{n_{211}}{\sum_r n_{2ir}} = \frac{n_{211}}{n_{211} + n_{212} + n_{213} + n_{214}}$$

$$= \frac{5}{82.5} = 0.061,$$

$$\hat{p}_{212} = \frac{n_{212}}{\sum_r n_{21r}} = \frac{0}{82.5} = 0,$$

$$\hat{p}_{213} = \frac{n_{213}}{\sum_r n_{21r}} = \frac{30.0}{82.5} = 0.364,$$

$$\hat{p}_{214} = \frac{n_{214}}{\sum_r n_{21r}} = \frac{47.5}{82.5} = 0.576.$$

Having computed all production probabilities from sample strings, we may now completely specify the stochastic grammars of this example as follows: $G_{s1} = (N, \Sigma, P, D_1, S)$ and $G_{s2} = (N, \Sigma, P, D_2, S)$ where, for both grammars, $\Sigma = \{a, b\}$ and $N = \{S\}$. The productions with their probability assignments are

	D_1	D_2
$S \rightarrow aS$	0.303	0.061
$S \rightarrow a$	0.606	0
$S \rightarrow bS$	0.061	0.364
$S \rightarrow b$	0.030	0.576

$\square$

ISBN 0-201-02930-8/0-201-02931-6, pbk

6.5.2   Inference of Stochastic Finite Automata

The inference method described in Section 6.2.3, which synthesizes a finite automaton by k-tail evaluation of the strings in a finite sample set R^+, may be extended to the inference of a stochastic finite automaton based on a finite sample set containing strings together with their probabilities of occurrence (Fu [1972], Huang and Fu [1972]). This inference approach is made more complex by the fact that probabilistic state transitions must be developed in a way that maintains the string probabilities given in the sample set; for this reason, we shall restrict our attention to the case in which the parameter k is made equal to the length of the longest string in the sample.

It is assumed that we are given a finite sample set R_s^+ of strings and their probabilities. The elements of R_s^+ are of the form $(s_i, p(s_i))$ where s_i is a sentence in Σ^* and $p(s_i)$ is a number in the interval $(0, 1]$. If R_s^+ has n elements, we assume that

$$\sum_{i=1}^{n} p(s_i) = 1.$$

As a generalization of the concepts discussed in Section 6.2.3, consider a positive integer k and a string z in Σ^* such that $[zw, p(zw)]$ is in R_s^+ for some w in Σ^*. We define the k-tail of z as

$$h(z, R_s^+, k) = \{[w, p(zw)] | [zw, p(zw)] \text{ in } R_s^+, 0 < p(zw) \leqslant 1, |w| \leqslant k\}.$$

The stochastic finite automaton accepting the strings in R_s^+ with appropriate probabilities is denoted as $\mathcal{C}_{sf}(R_s^+, k) = (Q, \Sigma, \delta, q_0, F, D)$, where k must be set equal to the maximum length of any sentence in R_s^+. The finite sets in $\mathcal{C}_{sf}(R_s^+, k)$ are as follows:

$$Q = \{q | q = h(z, R_s^+, k) \text{ for } [zw, p(zw)] \text{ in } R_s^+, z \text{ in } \Sigma^*, w \text{ in } \Sigma^*\} \cup \{q_r\},$$

Σ is a finite input alphabet, $q_0 = h(\lambda, R_s^+, k)$, and $F = \{q | q \text{ in } Q, \lambda \text{ in } q\}$. The state q_r is used as a rejecting state for normalization of probabilities (a method also used in the construction of a stochastic machine from a probabilistic regular grammar in Section 5.4.1). All final states in F are merged into one single state for acceptance of strings.

For convenience in reference, we identify and order the states in Q as q_0, $q_1, \ldots, q_{n-1}, q_n$, where q_0 is the starting state, q_{n-1} is the final state, and $q_n = q_r$ is the rejection state.

ISBN 0-201-02930-8/0-201-02931-6, pbk

The remaining problem in the inference is the assignment of state transitions and their probabilities (i.e., the specification of δ and D) so as to preserve the string probabilities given in R_s^+. Let $p(q_j|a, q_i)$ be the probability that the machine will enter state q_j, given current input symbol a and current state q_i. For each symbol a in Σ, the mapping δ and the probability assignment D must meet the following requirements:

   (i)   For $i, j = 0, 1, \ldots, n - 2$, we have $p(q_j|a, q_i) \neq 0$ if, for some z in Σ^*, $h(z, R_s^+, k) = q_i$ and $h(za, R_s^+, k) = q_j$.
   (ii) For $i = 0, 1, \ldots, n - 2$, we have $p(q_{n-1}|a, q_i) \neq 0$ if, for some z in Σ^*, $h(z, R_s^+, k) = q_i$ and λ is in $h(za, R_s^+, k)$.
   (iii) $p(q_j|a, q_{n-1}) = 0$ for $j = 0, 1, \ldots, n - 1$; and $p(q_n|a, q_{n-1}) = 1$.
   (iv) $p(q_j|a, q_n) = 0$ for $j = 0, 1, \ldots, n - 1$; and $p(q_n|a, q_n) = 1$.

These probabilities must also satisfy the following two conditions to make $\mathcal{Q}_{sf}(R_s^+, k)$ a proper machine:

   (v) $\displaystyle\sum_{j=0}^{n-1} p(q_j|a, q_i) = 1$ for $i = 0, 1, \ldots, n - 2$;

   (vi) $\displaystyle\sum_{j=0}^{n} p(q_j|a, q_i) = 1$ for $i = 0, 1, \ldots, n$.

Furthermore, the transition probabilities have to satisfy a set of equations that reflect the fact that the probability of acceptance of sample string s_i by $\mathcal{Q}_{sf}(R_s^+, k)$ must be the value $p(s_i)$ found in R_s^+; that is,

   (vii) $\displaystyle p(s_i) = \sum_{l=1}^{m_i} p_l(s_i)$

where there are m_i distinct paths from starting state q_0 through the states in Q leading to the final state q_{n-1} and $p_l(s_i)$ is the product of the probabilities encountered along the lth path.

When all of the foregoing conditions are met, R_s^+ will be equal to $L[\mathcal{Q}_{sf}(R_s^+, k)]$, the language recognized by $\mathcal{Q}_{sf}(R_s^+, k)$ in its stochastic operation.

Example: Suppose we are given the sample set

$$R_s^+ = \{(a, 2/5), (ab, 2/5), (abb, 1/5)\}$$

and are required to construct a stochastic finite automaton $\mathcal{Q}_{sf}(R_s^+, 3) = (Q, \Sigma, \delta, q_0, F, D)$ such that $R_s^+ = L[\mathcal{Q}_{sf}(R_s^+, 3)]$. For this machine, $\Sigma = \{a, b\}$, $q_0 = h(\lambda, R_s^+, 3) = R_s^+$, and the entire state set Q is determined to

ISBN 0-201-02930-8/0-201-02931-6, pbk

be $\{q_0, q_1, q_2, q_3, q_4\}$, where

$$q_1 = h(a, R_s^+, 3) = \{(\lambda, 2/5), (bb, 2/5), (bb, 1/5)\},$$

$$q_2 = h(ab, R_s^+, 3) = \{(\lambda, 2/5), (b, 1/5)\},$$

$$q_3 = h(abb, R_s^+, 3) = \{(\lambda, 1/5)\},$$

with q_3 the final state. $q_4 = q_r$ in this case can be q_ϕ.

The state transition probabilities must be determined so as to satisfy conditions (i)–(vii). By condition (i), for example, it is seen that $p(q_1|a, q_0)$ has to be computed because $q_0 = h(\lambda, R_s^+, 3)$ and $q_1 = h(\lambda a, R_s^+, 3)$; but $p(q_2|a, q_0) = 0$ because $q_2 = h(ab, R_s^+, 3)$ and the characterizing string ab does not end in terminal a.

Proceeding systematically from conditions (i) through condition (vi) establishes that $p(q_4|a, q_i) = 1$ for $i = 1, 2, 3, 4$ and $p(q_4|b, q_j) = 1$ for j being 0, 3, or 4. Also, normalization requires that

$$p(q_1|a, q_0) + p(q_3|a, q_0) + p(q_4|a, q_0) = 1,$$

$$p(q_1|a, q_0) + p(q_3|a, q_0) = 1,$$

$$p(q_2|b, q_1) + p(q_3|b, q_1) + p(q_4|b, q_1) = 1,$$

$$p(q_2|b, q_1) + p(q_3|b, q_1) = 1,$$

$$p(q_3|b, q_2) + p(q_4|b, q_2) = 1,$$

$$p(q_3|b, q_2) = 1.$$

All other transition probabilities are 0. From the preceding equations, we find that

$$p(q_4|a, q_0) = p(q_4|b, q_0) = p(q_4|b, q_2) = 0.$$

The remaining probabilities must be determined by condition (vii). Since R_s^+ has element $(a, 2/5)$, we must have $p(q_3|a, q_0) = 2/5$, from which

$$p(q_1|a, q_0) = 1 - p(q_3|a, q_0) = 3/5.$$

Since R_s^+ has element $(ab, 2/5)$, we must have

$$p(q_1|a, q_0)p(q_3|b, q_1) = (3/5)p(q_3|b, q_1)$$

$$= 2/5,$$

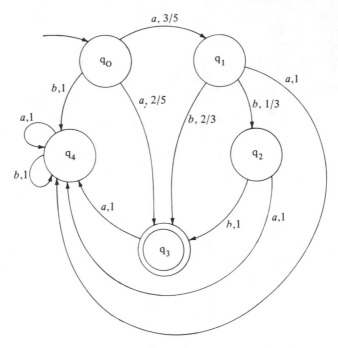

Figure 6.17. Inferred stochastic automaton $\mathcal{Q}_{sf}(R_s^+, 3)$.

which yields $p(q_3|b, q_1) = 2/3$, and

$$p(q_2|b, q_1) = 1 - 2/3 = 1/3.$$

This completes the computation of δ and D for the machine $\mathcal{Q}_{sf}(R_s^+, 3)$. The element $(abb, 1/5)$ of R_s^+ was not used in the final step, but it is easily verified that $p(abb) = 1/5$ for the automaton.

The state transition diagram of $\mathcal{Q}_{sf}(R_s^+, 3)$ is shown in Fig. 6.17. Only those transitions with nonzero probability of occurring are indicated. As indicated in Section 5.4.1, a stochastic grammar can be obtained directly directly from the inferred automaton.   □

6.6 CONCLUDING REMARKS

The material in this chapter exemplifies the principal ideas underlying the problem of obtaining a pattern grammar from a given set of samples. This is a central problem in the design of syntactic pattern recognition systems because of its implications in terms of autonomous learning from patterns of known classification.

ISBN 0-201-02930-8/0-201-02931-6, pbk

The algorithms discussed in this chapter are representative of available grammatical inference techniques. Our development has progressed from relatively simple algorithms for the inference of regular grammars to more complex procedures for handling context-free and expansive tree grammars. In addition to their simplicity, the advantage of the procedures involving regular grammars is that the results can always be minimized. This is in contrast to general context-free and tree grammars where a minimum cannot be guaranteed.[‡] The principal disadvantage of regular grammars is that they offer the least power for expressing structural relationships in a given pattern class.

The stochastic inference procedures discussed in Section 6.5 can be used in conjunction with the techniques presented in Sections 6.2 and 6.3. Thus, a nonstochastic grammar (or finite automaton) can be inferred first and then probabilities can be learned for the productions or transition mappings by using the available sample sentences.

As is true in earlier chapters, our emphasis on regular, context-free, and tree grammars reflects the fact that the majority of results in syntactic pattern recognition are based on these three types of grammars.

REFERENCES

The algorithm presented in Section 6.2.1 is based on a report by Chomsky and Miller [1957]. Although the practical value of this procedure is limited, it is of interest from a historical point of view. The algorithm presented in Section 6.2.2 was adapted from a report by Feldman [1967]. The material in Section 6.2.3 is based on an algorithm developed by Biermann and Feldman [1970, 1972a].

The algorithm in Section 6.3.1 is from a paper by Solomonoff [1959]. This material, which is an extension of the algorithm developed by Chomsky and Miller for regular grammars, is also of limited practical use, but is interesting from a historical point of view. The material in Section 6.3.2 is based on an algorithm developed by Crespi-Reghizzi ([1970, 1971], Crespi-Reghizzi et al. [1973]). The procedure given in Section 6.3.3 is due to Gips (see Feldman et al. [1969]).

The algorithm developed in Section 6.4 is based on a paper by Gonzalez, Edwards, and Thomason [1976]. The papers by Gonzalez and Thomason [1974a, b] and Bhargava and Fu [1974] are also of interest. For additional details on Section 6.5.1 see Lee and Fu [1971, 1972a, b], and Tou and

---

[‡]An algorithm developed by Barrero and Gonzalez [1976] can be used to minimize deterministic tree grammars and automata. This algorithm, which is beyond the scope of our present discussion, can also be used to minimize parenthesized context-free grammars by using the correspondence noted in Section 3.3.1.

ISBN 0-201-02930-8/0-201-02931-6, pbk

Gonzalez [1974]. The stochastic automaton procedure in Section 6.5.2 was adapted by Fu [1972] from Gip's approach (Section 6.3.3).

Some other references related to the material in this chapter are Solomonoff [1964], Gold [1967], Feldman [1969], Pao [1969], Horning [1969, 1971], Klein and Kuppin [1970], Evans [1971], Biermann and Feldman [1972b], Feldman [1972], Patel [1972], C. M. Cook [1974], Fu [1974], Fu and Booth [1975], and Barrero and Gonzalez [1976, 1977].

ISBN 0-201-02930-8/0-201-02931-6, pbk

BIBLIOGRAPHY

Aho, A. V., and Peterson, T. G. [1972]. "A Minimum Distance Error-Correcting Parser for Context-Free Languages," *SIAM J. Comput.*, vol. 1, pp. 305–312.

Aho, A. V., and Ullman, J. D. [1972]. *The Theory of Parsing, Translation, and Compiling*, vol. 1, Prentice-Hall, Englewood Cliffs, New Jersey.

Ali, F., and Pavlidis, T. [1977]. "Syntactic Recognition of Handwritten Numerals," *IEEE Trans. Sys., Man, Cyb.*, vol. SMC-7, pp. 537–541.

Anderson, R. H. [1968]. "Syntax-Directed Recognition of Hand-Printed Two-Dimensional Mathematics," Ph.D. dissertation, Harvard University, Cambridge, Massachusetts.

Barrero, A., and Gonzalez, R. C. [1976]. "Minimization of Deterministic Tree Grammars and Automata," *Proc. IEEE Conf. Dec. Contr.*, pp. 404–407.

Barrero, A., and Gonzalez, R. C. [1977]. "A Tree Traversal Algorithm for the Inference of Tree Grammars," *Proc. IEEE Comput. Soc. Conf. on Pattern Recognition and Image Processing*, pp. 129–133.

Bhargava, B. K., and Fu, K. S. [1974]. "Transformations and Inference of Tree Grammars for Syntactic Pattern Recognition," *Proc. Int. Conf. Sys., Man, and Cyb.*, Dallas, Texas, Oct. 2–4.

Birkhoff, G., and Bartee, T. C. [1970]. *Modern Applied Algebra*, McGraw-Hill, New York.

Biermann, A. W., and Feldman, J. A. [1970]. "On the Synthesis of Finite-State Acceptors," Artificial Intelligence Memo. 114, Computer Science Dept., Stanford University, Stanford, California. (Available from the Clearing House for Federal Scientific and Technical Information, Springfield, Virginia 22151.)

Biermann, A. W., and Feldman, J. A. [1972a]. "On the Synthesis of Finite-State Machines from Samples of Their Behavior," *IEEE Trans. Comput.*, vol. C-21, no. 6, pp. 592–597.

Biermann, A. W., and Feldman, J. A. [1972b]. "A Survey of Results in Grammatical Inference," in *Frontiers of Pattern Recognition* (S. Watanabe, ed.), Academic Press, New York.

Booth, T. L. [1968]. *Sequential Machines and Automata Theory*, Wiley, New York.

Booth, T. L. [1969]. "Probabilistic Representation of Formal Languages," *Convention Record, 10th Ann. IEEE Symp. on Switching and Automata Theory*.

Booth, T. L., and Thompson, R. A. [1973]. "Applying Probability Measures to Abstract Languages," *IEEE Trans. Comput.*, vol. C-22, pp. 442–450.

Brainerd, W. S. [1967]. "Tree Generating Systems and Tree Automata," Ph.D. dissertation, Purdue University, West Lafayette, Indiana.

Brainerd, W. S. [1968]. "The Minimization of Tree Automata," *Inform. Contr.*, vol. 13, pp. 484–491.

Brainerd, W. S. [1969]. "Tree-Generating Regular Systems," *Inform. Contr.*, vol. 14, pp. 217–231.

Brayer, J. M., Swain, P. H., and Fu, K. S. [1977]. "Modeling of Earth Resources Satellite Data," in *Syntactic Pattern Recognition, Applications* (K. S. Fu, ed.), Springer-Verlag, New York.

Button, B. K. [1977]. "A Compile-Time Error Diagnostic System for a Table-Driven, Interactive Compiler," M. S. thesis, Computer Science Dept., University of Tennessee, Knoxville.

Chang, S. K. [1971]. "Picture-Processing Grammar and Its Applications," *Inform. Sci.*, vol. 3, pp. 121–148.

Chomsky, N. [1956]. "Three Models for the Description of Language," *Proc. Group. Inform. Th.*, vol. 2, no. 3, pp. 113–124.

Chomsky, N. [1957]. *Syntactic Structures*, Mouton and Co., The Hague, The Netherlands.

Chomsky, N. [1959a]. "On Certain Formal Properties of Grammars," *Inform. Contr.*, vol. 2, pp. 137–167.

Chomsky, N. [1959b]. "A Note on Phrase Structure Grammars," *Inform. Contr.*, vol. 2, pp. 393–395.

Chomsky, N. [1965]. *Aspects of the Theory of Syntax*, M.I.T. Press, Cambridge, Massachusetts.

Chomsky, N., and Miller, G. A. [1957]. "Pattern Conception," Rep. No. AFCRC-TN-57-57. (ASTIA Document No. AD 110076).

Chomsky, N., and Miller, G. A. [1958]. "Finite State Languages," *Inform. Contr.*, vol. 1, pp. 91–112.

Clowes, M. B. [1969]. "Transformational Grammars and the Organization of Pictures," in *Automatic Interpretation and Classification of Images* (A. Grasselli, ed.), Academic Press, New York.

Cocke, J., and Schwartz, J. T. [1970]. *Programming Languages and Their Compilers*, Courant Institute of Mathematical Sciences, New York University, New York.

Conway, M. E. [1963]. "Design of a Separable Transition Diagram Compiler," *Comm. ACM*, vol. 6, pp. 396–409.

Cook, C. M. [1974]. "Grammatical Inference by Heuristic Search," Tech. Rep. No. 287, Computer Science Center, University of Maryland, College Park.

Cook, C. R. [1974]. "First Order Graph Grammars," *SIAM J. Comput.*, vol. 3, no. 1, pp. 90–99.

Cramer, H. [1961]. *Mathematical Methods of Statistics*, Princeton University Press, Princeton, New Jersey.

Crespi-Reghizzi, S. [1970]. "The Mechanical Acquisition of Precedence Grammars," Ph.D. dissertation, School of Engineering and Applied Science, University of California, Los Angeles.

Crespi-Reghizzi, S. [1971]. "An Effective Model for Grammar Inference," *Proc. IFIP Congr. 1971*, North-Holland Publ. Co., Amsterdam, pp. 524–529.

ISBN 0-201-02930-8/0-201-02931-6, pbk

Crespi-Reghizzi, S., Melkanoff, M. A., and Lichten, L. [1973]. "The Use of Grammatical Inference for Designing Programming Languages," *Comm. ACM*, vol. 16, no. 2, pp. 83–90.

Davis, M. [1968]. *The Undecidable: Basic Papers in Undecidable Propositions, Unsolvable Problems, and Computable Functions*, Raven Press, New York.

Doner, J. E. [1970]. "Tree Acceptors and Some of Their Applications," *J. Comput. Sys. Sci.*, vol. 4, pp. 406–451.

Duda, R., and Hart, P. [1973]. *Pattern Classification and Scene Analysis*, Wiley, New York.

Eden, M. [1961]. "On the Formalization of Handwriting," in "Structure of Language and Its Mathematical Aspects," *Proc. 12th Symp. Applied Mathematics*, American Mathematical Society, Providence, Rhode Island, pp. 83–88.

Eden, M. [1968]. "Handwriting Generation and Recognition," in *Recognizing Patterns* (P. A. Kolers and M. Eden, eds.), M.I.T. Press, Cambridge, Massachusetts.

Evans, G. T. [1971]. "Grammatical Inference Techniques in Pattern Analysis," in *Software Engineering* (J. T. Tou, ed.), Academic Press, New York.

Feder, J. [1968]. "Languages of Encoded Line Patterns," *Inform. Contr.*, vol. 13, pp. 230–244.

Feder, J. [1971]. "Plex Languages," *Inform. Sci.* vol. 3, pp. 225–241.

Feldman, J. A. [1967]. "First Thoughts on Grammatical Inference," Artificial Intelligence Memo. 55, Computer Science Dept., Stanford University, Stanford, California. (Available from the Clearing House for Federal Scientific and Technical Information, Springfield, Virginia 22151.)

Feldman, J. A. [1969]. "Some Decidability Results on Grammatical Inference and Complexity," Artificial Intelligence Memo. No. 93, Computer Science Dept., Stanford University, Stanford, California.

Feldman, J. A., Gips, J., Horning, J. J., and Reder, S. [1969]. "Grammatical Complexity and Inference," Tech. Rep. CS-125, Computer Science Dept., Stanford Univ., Stanford, California.

Feldman, J. A. [1972]. "Some Decidability Results on Grammatical Inference," *Inform. Contr.*, vol. 20, pp. 244–262.

Feller, W. [1968]. *An Introduction to Probability Theory and Its Applications*, vol. 1, 3rd edition, Wiley, New York.

Fisher, R. A. [1936]. "The Use of Multiple Measurements in Taxonomic Problems," *Ann. Eugenics*, vol. 8, pp. 179–188.

Floyd, R. W. [1961]. "A Descriptive Language for Symbol Manipulation," *J. ACM.*, vol. 8, pp. 579–584.

Floyd, R. W. [1963]. "Syntactic Analysis and Operator Precedence," *J. ACM.*, vol. 10, pp. 316–333.

Fu, K. S. [1970]. "Stochastic Automata as Models of Learning Systems," in *Adaptive, Learning, and Pattern Recognition Systems* (J. M. Mendel and K. S. Fu, eds.), Academic Press, New York.

Fu, K. S. [1971]. "Stochastic Automata, Stochastic Languages, and Pattern Recognition," *J. Cyb.*, vol. 1, pp. 31–49.

ISBN 0-201-02930-8/0-201-02931-6, pbk

Fu, K. S. [1972]. "On Syntactic Pattern Recognition and Stochastic Languages," in *Frontiers of Pattern Recognition* (S. Watanabe, ed.), Academic Press, New York.

Fu, K. S. [1974]. *Syntactic Methods in Pattern Recognition*, Academic Press, New York.

Fu, K. S. (ed.) [1977]. *Syntactic Pattern Recognition, Applications*, Springer-Verlag, New York.

Fu, K. S., and Bahargava, B. K. [1973]. "Tree Systems for Syntactic Pattern Recognition," *IEEE Trans. Comput.*, vol. C-22, no. 12, pp. 1087–1099.

Fu, K. S., and Booth, T. L. [1975]. "Grammatical Inference: Introduction and Survey—Part I," *IEEE Trans. Sys., Man, Cyb.*, vol. SMC-5, no. 1, pp. 95–111. Part II appeared in the same volume, no. 4, pp. 409–423.

Fu, K. S., and Huang, T. [1972]. "Stochastic Grammars and Languages," *Int. J. Comput. Inform. Sci.*, vol. 1, pp. 135–170.

Fu, K. S., and Swain, P. H. [1970]. "On Syntactic Pattern Recognition," in *Software Engineering*, vol. 2 (J. T. Tou, ed.), Academic Press, New York.

Fung, L. W., and Fu, K. S. [1974]. "Stochastic Syntactic Recognition of Noisy Patterns," in *Proc. 2nd Joint Int. Conf. Pattern Recognition*, Copenhagen, Denmark.

Fung, L. W., and Fu, K. S. [1975]. "Stochastic Syntactic Decoding for Pattern Classification," *IEEE Trans. Comput.*, vol. C-24, pp. 662–667.

Gips, J. [1975]. *Shape Grammars and Their Uses, Artificial Perception, Shape Generation and Computer Aesthetics*, Birkhäuser-Verlag, Basel and Stuttgart.

Gold, E. M. [1967]. "Language Indentification in the Limit," *Inform. Contr.*, vol. 10, pp. 447–474.

Gonzalez, R. C. [1972]. "Syntactic Pattern Recognition—Introduction and Survey," *Proc. Nat. Elec. Conf.*, vol. 27, no. 1, pp. 27–32.

Gonzalez, R. C., and Howington, L. C. [1977]. "Machine Recognition of Abnormal Behavior in Nuclear Reactors," *IEEE Trans. Sys., Man, Cyb.*, vol. SMC-7, no. 10, pp. 717–728.

Gonzalez, R. C., and Thomason, M. G. [1974a]. "Tree Grammars and Their Application to Pattern Recognition," Tech. Rep. TR-EE/CS-74-10, Electrical Engineering Dept., University of Tennessee, Knoxville.

Gonzalez, R. C., and Thomason, M. G. [1974b]. "Inference of Tree Grammars for Syntactic Pattern Recognition," Tech. Rep. TR-EE/CS-74-20, Electrical Engineering Dept., University of Tennessee, Knoxville.

Gonzalez, R. C., and Thomason, M. G. [1974c]. "On the Inference of Tree Grammars for Syntactic Pattern Recognition," *Proc. Int. Conf. Sys., Man, and Cyb.*, Dallas, Texas, Oct. 2–4.

Gonzalez, R. C., and Wintz, P. A. [1977]. *Digital Image Processing*, Addison-Wesley, Reading, Massachusetts.

Gonzalez, R. C., Edwards, J. J., and Thomason, M. G. [1976]. "An Algorithm for the Inference of Tree Grammars," *Int. J. Comput. Inform. Sci.*, vol. 5, no. 2, pp. 145–164.

ISBN 0-201-02930-8/0-201-02931-6, pbk

Gorn, S. [1967]. "Explicit Definitions and Linguistic Dominoes," in *Systems and Computer Science* (J. F. Hart and S. Takasu, eds.), University of Toronto Press, Toronto, Canada.

Grenander, U. [1970]. "A Unified Approach to Pattern Analysis," in *Advances in Computers*, vol. 10 (F. L. Alt and M. Rubinoff, eds.), Academic Press, New York.

Harary, F. [1969]. *Graph Theory*, Addison-Wesley, Reading, Massachusetts.

Harris, T. E. [1963]. *The Theory of Branching Processes*, Springer-Verlag, New York.

Hopcroft, J. E., and Ullman, J. [1966]. "Error Correction for Formal Languages," Tech. Rep. No. 52, Princeton University, Princeton, New Jersey.

Hopcroft, J. E., and Ullman, J. D. [1969]. *Formal Languages and Their Relation to Automata*, Addison-Wesley, Reading, Massachusetts.

Horning, J. J. [1969]. "A Study of Grammatical Inference," Tech. Rep. CS-139, Computer Science Dept., Stanford University, Stanford, California.

Horning, J. J. [1971]. "A Procedure for Grammatical Inference," *Proc. IFIP Congr. 1971*, North-Holland Publ. Co., Amsterdam, pp. 519–523.

Huang, T., and Fu, K. S. [1972]. "Stochastic Syntactic Analysis and Syntactic Pattern Recognition," Tech. Rep. TR-EE-72-5, School of Electrical Engineering, Purdue University, West Lafayette, Indiana.

Kain, R. Y. [1972]. *Automata Theory: Machines and Languages*, McGraw-Hill, New York.

Kasami, T. [1965]. "An Efficient Recognition and Syntax Analysis Algorithm for Context-Free Languages," Air Force Cambridge Research Laboratory Rep. No. AFCRL-65-758.

Kasami, T., and Torii, K. [1969]. "A Syntax Analysis Procedure for Unambiguous Context-Free Grammars," *J. ACM*, vol. 16, pp. 423–431.

Kemeny, J. G., and Snell, J. C. [1960]. *Finite Markov Chains*, Van Nostrand, Princeton, New Jersey.

Kirsch, R. [1964]. "Computer Interpretation of English Text and Picture Patterns," *IEEE Trans. Elec. Comput.*, vol. EC-13, pp. 363–376.

Kirsch, R. A. [1971]. "Computer Determination of the Constituent Structure of Biological Images," *Comput. and Biomed. Res.*, vol. 4, pp. 315–328.

Klein, S., and Kuppin, M. A. [1970]. "An Interactive Heuristic Program for Learning Transformational Grammars," *Computer Studies in the Humanities and Verbal Behavior*, vol. 3, pp. 144–162.

Knuth, D. E. [1973]. *The Art of Computer Programming*, vol. 1, 2nd ed. Addison-Wesley, Reading, Massachusetts.

Kolers, P. A. [1970]. "The Role of Shape and Geometry in Picture Recognition," in *Picture Processing and Psychopictorics* (B. S. Lipkin and A. Rosenfeld, eds.), Academic Press, New York.

Ledley, R. S. [1964]. "High-Speed Automatic Analysis of Biomedical Pictures," *Science*, vol. 146, no. 3461, pp. 216–223.

Ledley, R. S., *et al.* [1965]. "FIDAC: Film Input to Digital Automatic Computer and Associated Syntax-Directed Pattern-Recognition Programming System," in *Optical and Electro-Optical Information Processing* (J. T. Tippet,

ISBN 0-201-02930-8/0-201-02931-6, pbk

D. Beckowitz, L. Clapp, C. Koester, and A. Vanderburgh, Jr. eds.), pp. 591–613, M.I.T. Press, Cambridge, Massachusetts.

Lee, E. T. [1975]. "Shape-Oriented Chromosome Classification," *IEEE Trans. Sys., Man, Cyb.*, vol SMC-5, pp. 629–632.

Lee, E. T., and Zadeh, L. A. [1969]. "Note on Fuzzy Languages," *Inform. Sci.*, vol. 1, pp. 421–434.

Lee, H. C., and Fu, K. S. [1971]. "A Stochastic Syntax Analysis Procedure and Its Application to Pattern Classification," *Proc. Two-Dimensional Digital Signal Processing Conf.*, University of Missouri, Columbia, Missouri.

Lee, H. C., and Fu, K. S. [1972a]. "A Stochastic Syntax Analysis Procedure and Its Application to Pattern Classification," *IEEE Trans. Comput.*, vol. C-21, pp. 660–666.

Lee, H. C., and Fu, K. S. [1972b]. "A Syntactic Pattern Recognition System with Learning Capability," in *Information Systems*—COINS-72 (J. T. Tou, ed.), Plenum Press, New York.

Leinius, R. P. [1970]. "Error Detection and Recovery for Syntax Directed Compiler Systems," Ph.D. thesis, University of Wisconsin, Madison.

Lewis, P. M., II, Rosenkrantz, D. J., and Stearns, R. E. [1976]. *Compiler Design Theory*, Addison-Wesley, Reading, Massachusetts.

Lomet, D. B. [1973]. "A Formalization of Transition Diagram Systems," *J. ACM*, vol. 20, pp. 235–257.

Lyons, G. [1974]. "Syntax-Directed Least-Errors Analysis for Context-Free Languages," *Comm. ACM*, vol. 16, pp. 3–13.

Maryanski, F. J., and Thomason, M. G. [1977]. "Properties of Stochastic Syntax-Directed Translation," to appear in *Int. J. Comput. Inform. Sci.*

Milgram, D. L. [1972]. "Web Automata," Tech. Rep. 182, Computer Science Center, University of Maryland, College Park.

Milgram, D. L., and Rosenfeld, A. [1970]. "Array Automata and Array Grammars," Tech. Rep. 70-141, Computer Science Center, University of Maryland, College Park.

Milgram, D. L., and Rosenfeld, A. [1971]. "Array Automata and Array Grammars," *Proc. IFIP Cong. 1971*, North-Holland Publ. Co., Amsterdam, pp. 166–173.

Miller, W. F., and Shaw, A. C. [1968]. "Linguistic Methods in Picture Processing—A Survey," *Proc. Fall Joint Comput. Conf.*

Minsky, M. L. [1961]. "Steps Toward Artificial Intelligence," *Proc. IRE*, vol. 49, no. 1, pp. 8–30.

Moayer, B., and Fu, K. S. [1974]. "Syntactic Pattern Recognition of Fingerprints," Tech. Rep. TR-EE-74-36, School of Electrical Engineering, Purdue University, West Lafayette, Indiana.

Moayer, B., and Fu, K. S. [1975]. "A Syntactic Approach to Fingerprint Pattern Recognition," *J. Pattern Recognition*, vol. 7, pp. 1–23.

Moayer, B., and Fu, K. S. [1976a]. "An Application of Stochastic Languages to Fingerprint Pattern Recognition," *J. Pattern Recognition*, vol. 8, pp. 173–179.

Moayer, B., and Fu, K. S. [1976b]. "A Tree System Approach to Fingerprint Pattern Recognition," *IEEE Trans. Comput.*, vol. C-25, pp. 262–274.

ISBN 0-201-02930-8/0-201-02931-6, pbk

Montanary, U. G. [1970]. "Separable Graphs, Planar Graphs, and Web Grammars," *Inform. Contr.*, vol. 16, pp. 243–267.

Moore, J. L. [1977]. "An Interactive FORTRAN Compiler for the TICK System," M.S. thesis, Computer Science Dept. University of Tennessee, Knoxville.

Mylopoulos, J. [1972]. "On the Application of Formal Language and Automata Theory to Pattern Recognition," *J. Pattern Recognition*, vol. 4, pp. 37–51.

Narasimhan, R. [1962]. "A Linguistic Approach to Pattern Recognition," Rep. 21, Digital Computer Laboratory, University of Illinois, Urbana.

Narasimhan, R. [1966]. "Syntax-Directed Interpretation of Classes of Pictures," *Comm. ACM*, vol. 9, pp. 166–173.

Narasimhan, R. [1969]. "On the Description, Generation, and Recognition of Classes of Pictures," in *Automatic Interpretation and Classification of Images* (A. Grasselli, ed.), Academic Press, New York.

Pao, T. W. [1969]. "A Solution of the Syntactical Induction-Inference Problem for a Non-Trivial Subset of Context-Free Languages," Tech. Rep. 69–16, Moore School of Electrical Engineering, University of Pennsylvania, Philadelphia.

Parzen, E. [1962]. *Stochastic Processes*, Holden-Day, San Francisco, California.

Patel, A. R. [1972]. "Grammatical Inference for Probabilistic Finite State Languages," Ph.D. dissertation, Dept. of Electrical Engineering, University of Connecticut, Storrs.

Pavlidis, T. [1972]. "Linear and Context-Free Graph Grammars," *J. ACM*, vol. 19, no. 1, pp. 11–22.

Pfaltz, J. L. [1970]. "Web Grammars and Picture Description," Tech. Rep. 70-138, Computer Science Center, University of Maryland, College Park.

Pfaltz, J. L. [1972]. "Web Grammars and Picture Description," *Comp. Graphics and Image Processing*, vol. 1.

Pfaltz, J. L., and Rosenfeld, A. [1969]. "Web Grammars," *Proc. 1st Int. Joint Conf. Artificial Intelligence*, Washington, D. C., pp. 609–619.

Pratt, F. [1942]. *Secret and Urgent*, Blue Ribbon Books, Garden City, New York.

Rabin, M. D., and Scott, D. [1959]. "Finite Automata and Their Decision Problems", *IBM J. Res. Dev.*, vol. 3, pp. 114–125.

Rosenfeld, A., and Milgram, D. L. [1972]. "Web Automata and Web Grammars," in *Machine Intelligence-7* (B. Meltzer and D. Michie, eds.), Wiley, New York.

Rosenkrantz, D. J. [1967]. "Matrix Equations and Normal Forms for Context-Free Grammars," *J. ACM*, vol. 14, no. 3, pp. 501–507.

Rounds, W. C. [1969]. "Context-Free Grammars on Trees," *Conf. Rec. ACM Symp. Theory of Computing*, New York, pp. 143–148.

Shaw, A. C. [1969]. "A Formal Picture Description Scheme as a Basis for Picture Processing Systems," *Inform. Contr.*, vol. 14, pp. 9–52.

Shaw, A. C. [1970]. "Parsing of Graph-Representable Pictures," *J. ACM*, vol. 17, pp. 453–481.

Solomonoff, R. [1959]. "A New Method for Discovering the Grammars of Phrase Structure Languages," *Proc. Int. Conf. Inform. Processing*, UNESCO Publ. House, Paris, France, pp. 285–290.

Solomonoff, R. [1964]. "A Formal Theory of Inductive Inference," *Inform. Contr.*, vol. 7, pp. 1–22 and 224–254.

ISBN 0-201-02930-8/0-201-02931-6, pbk

Stiny, G. [1975]. *Pictorial and Formal Aspects of Shape and Shape Grammars*, Birkhäuser-Verlag, Basel and Stuttgart.

Stone, H. S. [1973]. *Discrete Mathematical Structures*, SRA, Inc., Chicago, Illinois.

Swain, P. H., and Fu, K. S. [1972]. "Stochastic Programmed Grammars for Syntactic Pattern Recognition," *J. Pattern Recognition*, vol. 4, pp. 83–100.

Thatcher, J. W. [1973]. "Tree Automata: An Informal Survey," in *Currents in the Theory of Computing* (A. V. Aho, ed.), Prentice-Hall, Englewood Cliffs, New Jersey.

Thatcher, J. W., and Wright, J. B. [1965]. "Generalized Finite Automata," *Amer. Math. Soc. Abstr.*, vol. 12.

Thatcher, J. W., and Wright, J. B. [1969]. "Generalized Finite Automata with an Application to a Decision Problem of Second Order Logic," *J. Math. Sys. Theory*, vol. 2, pp. 57–81.

Thomason, M. G. [1973]. "Finite Fuzzy Automata, Regular Fuzzy Languages, and Pattern Recognition," *J. Pattern Recognition*, vol. 5, pp. 383–390.

Thomason, M. G. [1974]. "Errors in Regular Languages," *IEEE Trans. Comput.*, vol. C-23, pp. 597–602.

Thomason, M. G. [1975]. "Stochastic Syntax-Directed Translation Schemata for Correction of Errors in Context-Free Languages," *IEEE Trans. Comput.*, vol. C-24, pp. 1211–1216.

Thomason, M. G., and Gonzalez, R. C. [1975]. "Syntactic Recognition of Imperfectly Specified Patterns," *IEEE Trans. Comput.*, vol. C-24, pp. 93–95.

Thomason, M. G., and Marinos, P. N. [1974]. "Deterministic Acceptors of Regular Fuzzy Languages," *IEEE Trans. Sys., Man, Cyb.*, vol. SMC-4, pp. 228–230.

Thompson, R. A. [1974]. "Determination of Probabilistic Grammars for Functionally Specified Probability-Measure Languages," *IEEE Trans. Comput.*, vol. C-23, pp. 603–614.

Thompson, R. A. [1976]. "Language Correction Using Probabilistic Grammars," *IEEE Trans. Comput.*, vol. C-25, pp. 275–286.

Tou, J. T. [1968]. "Information Theoretic Approach to Pattern Recognition," *IEEE Int. Convention Rec.*

Tou, J. T., and Gonzalez, R. C. [1972]. "Automatic Recognition of Handwritten Characters by Topological Feature Extraction and the Multilevel Categorization," *IEEE Trans. Comput.*, vol. C-21, no. 7, pp. 776–785.

Tou, J. T., and Gonzalez, R. C. [1974]. *Pattern Recognition Principles*, Addison-Wesley, Reading, Massachusetts.

Uhr, L. [1972]. "Flexible Linguistic Pattern Recognition," *J. Pattern Recognition*, vol. 3, pp. 363–383.

Velasco, F. R. D., and Souza, C. R. [1977]. "An Application of Formal Linguistics to Scene Recognition," *Int. J. Comput. Inform. Sci.*, vol. 6, no. 4, pp. 289–306.

Wagner, R. A., and Fischer, M. J. [1974]. "The String-to-String Correction Problem," *J. ACM*, vol. 21, pp. 168–173.

Wilcox, T. R., Davis, A. M., and Tindall, M. H. [1976]. "The Design and Implementation of a Table Driven, Interactive, Diagnostic Programming System," *Comm. ACM*, vol. 19, pp. 609–617.

Younger, D. H. [1967]. "Recognition and Parsing of Context-Free Languages in Time n^3," *Inform. Contr.*, vol. 10, pp. 189–208.

Zadeh, L. A. [1965]. "Fuzzy Sets," *Inform. Contr.*, vol. 8, pp. 338–353.

ISBN 0-201-02930-8/0-201-02931-6, pbk

INDEX